Publication 505
Agdex 640

ONTARIO WEEDS

Descriptions, Illustrations
and
Keys to their Identification

J.F. Alex, Professor
Ontario Agricultural College
University of Guelph
Guelph, Ontario

Consumer Information Centre
Ontario Ministry of Agriculture and Food
Main Floor, 801 Bay Street
Toronto, Ontario
M7A 2B2

CONTENTS

INTRODUCTION

What is a Weed?

Weeds are ordinary plants which have some undesirable features. They may grow where people do not want them. They may disfigure lawns (Dandelion) and gardens (Redroot pigweed), interfere with crop production (Field bindweed), reduce crop yield (Wild mustard), reduce crop quality (Wild garlic), lower feed palatability (Wormseed mustard), reduce visibility along roadsides (Nodding thistle), poison livestock (Water-hemlock), or cause prolonged human discomfort by contact (Poison-ivy) or by inhalation of their pollen (Common ragweed). On the other hand, many plants which are undesirable in one situation may have a valuable function in another: Quack grass is an excellent soil binder; Blueweed is a favorite bee pasture; many annuals rapidly cover bare soil and reduce erosion; some have valuable medicinal properties; and some are nutritious as well as edible.

Why Identify Weeds?

Being able to recognize weeds and to know their names are important to many people for physical comfort as well as for economic benefit or aesthetic value. If you can recognize Poison-ivy, you can avoid contact with it. If you need information on how to control a weed, the first step is to learn its name. After you know its name, you can inquire about or read up on its usual growth habits and recommendations for its control. Familiarity with these features is often essential in order to work out the best method of controlling the weed in your particular situation. This book is intended for use by all people who are involved with weeds.

About this Book

There are over 500 species of plants in Ontario that have been considered weedy in one way or another. This revision of *Ontario Weeds* includes some 45 new problem weeds that were not described in previous editions. It now contains the descriptions of some 315 of the most prevalent, widespread or important weeds in the province. Of these, 282 are illustrated by either black and white line drawings or colour photographs or both, showing general features and emphasizing certain distinctive characteristics. Word descriptions supplement the illustrations, often with letters and arrows focusing attention on important characteristics in the drawings. In an attempt to avoid technical terms for the benefit of the general public, the descriptions are in common everyday language. The period of flowering, distribution in Ontario, usual places of occurrence, and some of the main distinguishing characteristics are also given for each weed.

A **glossary** that defines or illustrates the terms used in referring to or describing the different parts of the weed plant is also included.

Some of the black and white illustrations are reprinted with modification from earlier editions of OMAF Publication 505. The rest were selected from drawings by B. Carrick, B. Dodge, G. Eden, B. Gordon, G. Spicer, Z. Zichmanis and the author. Colour plates were selected from photographs by D. Hamilton, Department of Environmental Biology, and the author.

The author wishes to express deep appreciation to Jennifer Sumner for her invaluable assistance in the writing and editing of this extensive revision of *Ontario Weeds.* He also wishes to express grateful appreciation to Dr. R. C. Jancey for assistance in developing the Identification Key, to R.D. McLaren for numerous suggestions, and to many other individuals who contributed in various ways.

Names of Weeds

Almost every weed has several names by which it is known in various parts of the country. Confusion exists because the same name can mean a different plant to different people. The Expert Committee on Weeds (part of the Canadian Agricultural Services Coordinating Committee) has attempted to minimize this confusion by selecting the most appropriate English and French names for Canada-wide usage for each weed. These names, together with the botanical name for each weed, are listed in Agriculture Canada Publication 1397 (revised in 1980), *Common and botanical names of weeds in Canada/Noms populaires et scientifiques des plantes nuisibles du Canada.*

The English name used for each weed in this book is the one selected for it by the Expert Committee on Weeds. It is given in bold-face print at first mention, thereafter in ordinary print. This is followed by its botanical name in italics and the author of the botanical name. Then, in square brackets are the 5-letter Bayer Code, the French name selected by the Expert Committee on Weeds, other English and French names, and other botanical names.

An Index of all the weed names is provided at the end of the book. It lists the selected English name, selected French name, other English and French names, and other botanical names for every weed included and gives page references. Also provided is a separate index of the Bayer Code designations for each weed.

WEED CONTROL

Weed control is a matter of management of the plant populations so that we can have the kinds of plants we want in any given area. For example,

Ox-eye daisy can be an attractive addition to a flower border but it is an aggressive, unpalatable intruder in lawns and pastures. Orchard grass and brome are productive and nutritious in hay and pasture fields but are coarse and unsightly in lawns and flower borders.

Successful weed control depends on effective integration of a variety of factors. These include the life habits and stage of growth of the weed, the crop or other vegetation with which it is growing, the moisture, nutrient and other soil factors and the mechanical or other methods of control that can be used in the area.

The life habits of plants may be classified as follows:

Annuals Weeds which germinate, bloom, produce seeds, and die in one growing season. Examples: Common ragweed, Wild mustard.

Winter Annuals Weeds which germinate and produce a leafy rosette in the fall and then bloom, seed, and die the following summer. Examples: Shepherd's-purse, Stinkweed.

Biennials Weeds which germinate and produce a leafy rosette during their first growing season, and then flower, complete their life cycle and die during the next. Examples: Wild carrot, Burdock.

Perennials (Herbaceous) Weeds which live a number of years, developing each year from underground stems, roots, or crowns, and usually flowering each year but dying back to the ground each winter. Examples: Perennial sow-thistle, Quack grass.

Perennials (Woody) Weedy trees, shrubs and woody vines which live for many years, producing new growth each year from their aboveground stems, branches and twigs, and in some cases from underground stems, or roots, or crowns. Examples: European buckthorn, Climbing nightshade.

Some weeds may exhibit two or more life habits. Examples: Stinkweed may be either annual or winter annual; Wild carrot is usually biennial but some plants are annual and others are short-lived perennials.

Control measures for annual, winter annual, and biennial weeds are largely designed to destroy the weed plants before they offer too much competition to the crop, or before they go to seed. Tillage, spraying or mowing are the main methods used. Eradication is usually difficult because seeds of many weeds may lie buried for years in the soil without germinating. Also, control is made difficult because the germination of many weed seeds coincides with the germination and early seedling growth of the crops in which they are troublesome.

Perennial weeds are even more difficult to eradicate because it is not only necessary to prevent their spread by seeds, but also their underground stem and root systems must be destroyed.

Brief discussions of several different methods of controlling weeds are given in the Ontario Ministry of Agriculture and Food (OMAF) Publication 529, *Weed Control in Lawns and Gardens,* under the following headings: (1) pulling by hand; (2) cutting or mowing; (3) hoeing; (4) cultivation; (5) fire; (6) the use of mulches; (7) competition (crowding, smothering, etc.); (8) crop rotation; (9) biological; (10) management practices for weed control; and (11) the use of herbicides (chemical weed killers). Publication 529 also provides information on the control of specific weeds in lawns and gardens, as well as illustrations and brief descriptions of each.

For control of weeds in field crops, pastures, rights-of-way and other non-crop areas see OMAF Publication 75, *Guide to Weed Control.*

Correct identification of weeds is essential for satisfactory control. The science of weed control is continually demonstrating that even closely related weeds may differ widely in response to particular methods of control. This need for precision in identification of weeds was the prime reason for expanding this edition of *Ontario Weeds* to include more weeds with more detailed descriptions, revised illustrations and more colour plates.

NOXIOUS WEEDS — THE WEED CONTROL ACT

In Ontario, a number of weeds are classed as noxious under the Weed Control Act. This Act states that "Every person in possession of land shall destroy all noxious weeds thereon."

Weeds are classed as noxious for several reasons. Some are noxious because they reduce crop yield and either are very difficult to control (Leafy spurge, Tuberous vetchling), or difficult to control and have seeds that blow on the wind (Canada thistle, Sow-thistle); some because of the health hazards they cause (Poison-ivy causes a severe rash; pollen from the Ragweeds causes hay fever); and others because they increase crop diseases (Common barberry is the alternate host for organisms which cause stem rust in oats, barley, rye and spring wheat; European buckthorn is the alternate host for organisms causing leaf rust and crown rust of oats). Copies of the Weed Control Act currently in force may be obtained from the Plant Industry Branch, Ontario Ministry of Agriculture and Food, 3rd Floor, Guelph Agriculture Centre, P.O. Box 1030, Guelph, Ontario N1H 6N1.

ASSISTANCE

If the identity of a weed cannot be determined using this book with its Identification Key, descriptions and pictures, the weed should be taken or sent to your local Agricultural Office or Crop Advisory Specialist. They can help to identify it and may also be able to assist you in choosing the most satisfactory method of control. But, in order to help identify your weed, you should provide the specialist with a reasonably intact plant. **Accurate identification often requires examination of all parts of a plant — its stems** with branches, leaves, flowers, seedpods, and some of the underground root system. Try to include as many of these parts as possible in the specimen that you submit. County and District offices are listed in OMAF Publication 75, *Guide to Weed Control.*

IDENTIFYING THE WEEDS

There are several ways to use this book to help identify weeds. Some people will flip through the pages looking for an illustration that resembles the plant whose name they want to know. Those who depend on colour will concentrate on the photographs. Others who are more comfortable with line drawings will look at both kinds of illustrations. However, the pictures should be only the beginning. Users of this book should develop the habit of also reading the text that accompanies each illustration. In addition to describing the variability in height, leaf size, flower colour, etc., that is normal for each weed, it also tells where the weed is likely to occur, and it emphasizes some of the main distinguishing characteristics of that weed.

Rather than flipping pages in anticipation of finding a picture resembling the weed at hand, a more direct approach is to "take it through the Identification Key."

An **Identification Key** is a step-wise elimination process for identifying plants. At each step there is a pair of contrasting or opposite statements about plants. The characteristics of the plant you wish to identify should agree with one statement but not with the other. The affirmative statement will lead you to the next step — another pair of choices. At each step you gradually eliminate plants which have characteristics which are different from the one you wish to identify. Eventually you reach a step at which the agreeing statement is followed by the name or names of one or more weeds. Finally, you check the description and illustration of one of the named weeds and discover it is the plant you were trying to identify.

The comprehensive **Identification Key** that begins on page 7 will enable the user to identify any weed that is described in this book. A few weed species, which possess certain very characteristic features, may be quickly identified using the Short Cut Keys. Instructions on how to use each key are included.

How to Use the Illustrations and Descriptions

The illustrations and descriptions should be used as a team. The words tell about the plant while the drawings and photographs show what the plant looks like. In this book the two are tied together with many cross-references. In the descriptions, most cross-references are *small letters between brackets* and they refer to lettered arrows in the *Figures.* When you come to each bracketed small letter, for example (a), while reading a description, find the arrow with that letter, for example a→, in the drawing and pay special attention to it. The arrows point to important characteristics which help to distinguish that plant from all others. *Capital letters* refer to individual drawings where there are two or more in one Figure. *Plates* are the colour photographs that begin on page 277.

The descriptions of weeds are written in non-technical language as far as possible. However, some terms could not be avoided. Most readers will know that a stem has *nodes* or joints and the leaves are attached to it only at these nodes; the *calyx* is the ring of *sepals* (usually but not always green in colour) making up the outer or lower part of a flower; the *corolla* is the ring of *petals* (usually a bright colour) next to the sepals; the *stamens* are next to the petals and have *anthers* which produce *pollen*; and the *pistil* or *pistils* are in the centre of the flower, each having a slender tip (*style*) with a sticky part (*stigma*) which receives the pollen and a larger lower part (*ovary*) which, after fertilization, develops into a seedpod. Where other terms have been used, a brief definition is usually included in brackets right after them. You will find further assistance with the definition of terms in the **Glossary** on page 16.

How to Use the Identification Key

The first step is to read the first pair of contrasting statements. They are numbered "1a" and "1b." Then look closely at the plant you wish to identify. Its characteristics should agree with one statement but not with the other. At the end of the affirmative statement are two numbers with letters. Go down the Key to the pair of statements having those numbers and letters. For example, if your plant has a reddish-green stem and green leaves, it agrees with Statement 1b. Because Statement 1b is followed by the numbers and letters "3a or 3b," you move down the Key to the pair of statements numbered "3a" and "3b." This is the beginning of the second step and you repeat the same process as in the first step. Read both statements; re-examine your plant (again the characteristics of your plant should match only one of the two statements); choose the matching statement; note the two indicator numbers with letters and move on to the next step. Continue this process until finally an agreeing statement is followed not by numbers and letters, but by the name or names of one or more weeds and page numbers. Turn to those pages for descriptions and illustrations of the named weeds.

The Key has been designed to assist you in identifying plants in various stages of growth. Many weeds can be keyed successfully while still in the rosette stage (if they have one), and some in the pre-flowering stage as well as in full flower. The Key will usually work in spite of some simple mistakes often made by non-botanists (for example, some plants with compound leaves can also be keyed as if each leaflet were a separate leaf).

Problems in Keying

The reader should not be discouraged if the Key apparently leads to an incorrect plant or group of plants. There are so many choices to be made, and so many opportunities for error or misinterpretation. A simple error at any step can put you on the wrong track.

If none of the descriptions and illustrations match your plant, you have two options. One option is to start again at the beginning of the Key (at la or lb). Go through the Key as before but carefully rethink each choice in case an error was made. The other option is to work backwards through the Key. To help you do this, the number and letter of the previous statement is given in brackets at the beginning of each new statement. However, if you still cannot reach a description which matches it, your plant may not be included among the 300 described or mentioned in this book. Assistance must then be sought elsewhere. For example, your plant may be a native plant that is not usually considered to be a weed so it may be included in one or more books on wildflowers of the region.

Short Cuts

Some groups of weeds have certain obvious characteristics which are seldom found in other plants. The presence of these characteristics is strong indication of what the weed may be. With a little practice you can become accustomed to looking for these features, several of which are in the following list.

If your plant has:	Look at the plants illustrated in:
Whole plant	
• No green colour	Plates 1, 99
	Figures 1, 139
Stems	
• Green stems without any leaves	Figure 1
• Square stems	Figures 50, 122, 145-152, 171, 181, 182
• Triangular stems; plant grass-like	Figures 25-27
• Stems with sharp spines or thorns	Figures 43, 65, 97, 104, 115, 157, 173, 207-211
• Stems prickly due to harsh hair or spiny sepal tips	Figures 18, 141, 148, 150
• Vine-like or twining stems	Figures 36, 113, 136-139, 154, Plates 31, 97, 98, 99
Stems and Leaves	
• Tendrils (slender curling or twisting structures)	Figures 101-103, 174, 175, Plates 66, 67
• Very fleshy stems and leaves	Figures 49, 91

Leaves

• Leaves with ocrea (membranous sheath) surrounding stem just above each node where leaf joins stem	Figures 30-37
• Leaves with base of leafstalk flattened and partly or wholly circling the stem	Figures 28, 63, 64, 124-131
• Leaf tips and edges with sharp spines	Figures 43, 207-211, 219
• Leaf surfaces with sharp prickles or spines	Figures 157, 173, 210, 222
• Leaves with a single row of stiff prickles only along underside of midrib of leaves; plant not prickly elsewhere	Figure 222

Flowers

• Flowers with 4 petals arranged in a cross	Figures 68-90
• Flowers in flower heads (see page 208)	Figures 177-228
• Flowers with stamens in a central column (Figure 116C)	Figures 116-119

Fruits

• Spiny or clinging burs	Figures 21E, 21F, 23, 95, 158, 173, 182, 185, 206

Some weeds can be identified by entering the Key at some distance past the beginning. You can save time by not going through all the earlier steps which bring you to that point anyway. However, if the shortcut fails, go back to the beginning and start at "1a" or "1b."

If your plant has:	Enter the Key at:
• Leaves alternate (single or 1 per node)	72a or 72b
• Leaves opposite (in pairs, or 2 per node)	44a or 44b, 51a or 51b
• Some leaves whorled (3 or more per node)	8a or 8b, 38a or 38b
• Leaves in rosettes (spreading like spokes of a wheel at ground surface)	6a or 6b
• White or yellowish milky juice	9a, 17a, 32a, 39a, 52a, 73a
• Underground parts with very small nut-like tubers, or fleshy potato-like tubers, or fleshy Dahlia-like or cigar-shaped tubers	127a or 127b

IDENTIFICATION KEY

1a. Plant apparently without green colour; stems and/or leaves orange, yellow, brown or gray...2a or 2b

1b. Plant with at least some green colour; stems and/or leaves green, or grayish-green, or reddish-green. **CAUTION! If leaves or leaflets in groups of 3's, suspect Poison-ivy (see page 136); or, if a shrub with more or less opposite leaflets and growing in a wet area, suspect Poison sumac (see page 138)**...3a or 3b

2a. (1a) Stems thread-like, twining around other normal green plants; flowers white...Dodder p. 168

2b. (1a) Stems as thick as lead pencils or thicker, not twining; without true flowers but with spore-producing cone at top of stem...Field horsetail p. 19

3a. (1b) Plants apparently without leaves, consisting only of rather firm, green stems, usually with whorls of thinner green branches (3 or more per node, like spokes of a wheel) from some of the nodes (joints) of stem; never spiny...Field horsetail p. 19

3b. (1b) Plants producing more or less normal leaves, or its leaves with flat or thin portions, or with finely divided portions; may or may not be spiny...4a or 4b

4a. (3b) Underground parts without tuberous thickenings; vertical fleshy carrot-like taproot may or may not be present; **or these features unknown due to lack of adequate material**...5a or 5b

4b. (3b) Underground parts with various fleshy, or tuberous thickenings such as small nut-like tubers (Figure 26), or larger fleshy potato-like tubers, or fleshy Dahlia-like or cigar-shaped tubers (Figure 128), or just thick, fleshy, brittle roots (Figure 151); vertical fleshy, carrot-like taproot usually not present...127a or 127b

5a. (4a) Leaves only in a rosette or produced singly from below the ground surface, either lying flat on the ground and spreading out like spokes of a wheel, or in more or less erect tufts; stem absent, or if one or more stems present, these do not have any leaves but produce only flowers and seeds...6a or 6b

5b. (4a) Leaves and their petioles (leafstalks) attached to distinct stems; the stems may be erect, or inclined, or prostrate or vines; rosette leaves may also be present in addition to the stem leaves...37a or 37b

6a. (5a) Leaves grass-like or very narrow for their lengths, never divided or compound; their length usually 8 or more times greater than their width; the main veins parallel, or the veins not obvious...7a or 7b

6b. (5a) Leaves not grass-like but variously shaped; their length usually much less than 8 times greater than their width; the main veins branching or net-veined...12a or 12b

7a. (6a) Leaves, stem and other parts of the plant with a strong onion- or garlic-like odour and taste; leaves and stems very soft and smooth but without milky juice...Wild garlic p. 49

7b. (6a) Leaves, stem and other parts of the plant not smelling or tasting like onion or garlic, may or may not have milky juice...8a or 8b

8a. (7b) Leaves coarsely ribbed or somewhat folded lengthwise; the main veins nearly parallel and very prominent; flowering or seed-producing stem always bare of leaves except at the very base...Narrow-leaved plantain p. 200

8b. (7b) Leaves not coarsely ribbed lengthwise; flowering stem if present on older plants may have leaves similar to those of the rosette...9a or 9b

9a. (8b) Leaves, stem and other parts with milky, white, sticky juice...Goat's-beards pp. 255-256

9b. (8b) Leaves, stem, and other parts without milky juice...10a or 10b

10a. (9b) Leaves needle-like, round in cross-section, tipped with a sharp point...Russian thistle p. 64

10b. (9b) Leaves grass-like, flat or folded lengthwise, not spiny-tipped but may have sharp edges...11a or 11b

11a. (10b) Leaves, often somewhat yellowish-green, 3-ranked (point out from base or stem in 3 directions); stem usually pithy inside, triangular in cross-section (Figure 25); thin underground rhizomes (root-like stems) producing small thickenings (nuts or nutlets about 0.5 - 1 cm, 1/5 - 2/5 in. in diameter) that are the reproductive tubers...Yellow nut sedge p. 47

11b. (10b) Leaves, usually green or slightly bluish-green, 2-ranked (point out from base or stem in 2 directions); stems usually hollow, round or flattened in cross-section; rhizomes, if present, not producing nutlets or tubers...Grass Family pp. 21-45

12a. (6b) Flowering or seed-producing stem present but essentially bare without either normal or scale-like leaves; this bare stem in addition to the strictly rosette leaves...13a or 13b

12b. (6b) Flowering or seed-producing stem not present, no stem visible, leaves only in a rosette or rising singly or in groups from ground surface...15a or 15b

13a. (12a) Leaf blades much longer than wide; their margins smooth or irregularly lobed and toothed...Compare: Narrow-leaved plantain p. 200, Hawkweeds pp. 245-246, Dandelion p. 252

13b. (12a) Leaf blades about as wide as long...14a or 14b

14a. (13b) Leaf blades with several main veins, all coming from the tip of the leafstalk; flower buds, flowers and seedpods greenish, in slender elongate spikes... Broad-leaved plantain p. 199

14b. (13b) Leaf blades with only 1 main vein or midrib, flowers white to pink to reddish, or yellow, in flower heads...Compare: English daisy p. 231, Colt's-foot p. 225

15a. (12b) Leaves with very stiff hairs or definite sharp prickles or spines on edges and/or on upper or lower surfaces...16a or 16b

15b. (12b) Leaves without stiff hairs or sharp prickles or spines...18a or 18b

16a. (15a) Leaf edges smooth, without teeth; surface of leaf blade with harsh, stiff hairs ...Blueweed p. 170

16b. (15a) Leaf edges variously toothed or shallowly or deeply lobed...17a or 17b

17a. (16b) Leaves with white milky juice...Compare: Sow-thistles pp. 247-249, Prickly lettuce p. 250

17b. (16b) Leaves without milky juice...Compare: Buffalobur p. 187, Teasel p. 203, Canada thistle p. 239, Bull thistle p. 240, Scotch thistle p. 241, Globe thistle p. 241, Milk thistle p. 241, Spotted knapweed p. 243

18a. (15b) Leaves densely white-woolly (like a felt insole) on 1 or both surfaces...19a or 19b

18b. (15b) Leaves hairless or with some hair but not densely white-woolly on 1 or both surfaces...21a or 21b

19a. (18a) Margins of leaves usually without lobes or teeth, or with very shallow teeth... Compare: Common mullein p. 189, Burdocks p. 236, Colt's-foot p. 225

19b. (18a) Margins of leaves more or less deeply lobed, toothed or divided...20a or 20b

20a. (19b) Leaves almost fern-like with very deep and fine lobes or divisions...Compare: Absinth p. 221, Yarrow p. 218

20b. (19b) Leaves usually lobed or divided but not fern-like...Compare: Silvery cinquefoil p. 116, Silverweed p. 116, Absinth p. 221, Mugwort p. 221

21a. (18b) Leaves divided into numerous, very fine segments, almost fern-like...22a or 22b

21b. (18b) Leaves either not divided or divided into lobes of various widths but not into very fine segments...27a or 27b

22a. (21a) Odour of crushed leaves distinctive, either pleasant or otherwise, especially when fresh...23a or 23b

22b. (21a) Odour of crushed leaves not particularly distinctive when fresh, or odour not recognizable because leaves are dry or cold or otherwise...Compare: Eastern bracken p. 20, Buttercups pp. 82-84, Stinking wall-rocket p. 91, Narrow-

leaved wall-rocket p. 91, Flixweed p. 96, Tansy mustards p. 96, Wild carrot p. 149, Yarrow p. 218, Tansy p. 220, Biennial wormwood p. 223, Absinth p. 221, Mugwort p. 221, Pineappleweed p. 217, Stinking mayweed p. 217, Chamomile p. 218, Common ragweed p. 213

23a. (22a) Odour of leaves sour, offensive...Compare: Stinking wall-rocket p. 91, Narrow-leaved wall-rocket p. 91, Stinking mayweed p. 217

23b. (22a) Odour of leaves distinctive, but not sour or offensive...24a or 24b

24a. (23b) Odour of crushed leaves sweet and pineapple-like...Pineappleweed p. 217

24b. (23b) Odour of crushed leaves not sweet and pineapple-like...25a or 25b

25a. (24b) Odour of crushed leaves not pungent, suggestive of carrot...Compare: Wild carrot p. 149, Biennial wormwood p. 223

25b. (24b) Odour of crushed leaves rather pungent ...26a or 26b

26a. (25b) Odour of crushed leaves pungent and suggestive of mustard...Compare: Wall-rockets p. 91, Flixweed p. 96, Tansy mustards p. 96

26b. (25b) Odour of crushed leaves pungent and suggestive of sage...Compare: Yarrow p. 218, Tansy p. 220

27a. (21b) Margins of leaves smooth, usually not toothed, wavy, or divided...28a or 28b

27b. (21b) Margins of leaves irregular, or toothed, or wavy, or lobed, or completely divided into compound leaves...29a or 29b

28a. (27a) Leaf surface hairy; the longer hairs rather firm and with enlarged or bulb-like bases (as viewed through a hand lens) ...Blueweed p. 170

28b. (27a) Leaf surface with soft hair or without hair ...Compare: Docks pp. 50-52, White cockle p. 77, Night-flowering catchfly p. 78, Biennial campion p. 79, Wormseed mustard p. 98, Tall wormseed mustard p. 99, Shepherd's-purse p. 109, Evening-primroses p. 148, Hound's-tongue p. 172, Plantains pp. 199-200, Hawkweeds pp. 245-246

29a. (27b) Length of whole leaf (including all segments or parts of a lobed or compound leaf) usually much more than 2 times the width of the whole leaf (as in Figures 30, 224)...30a or 30b

29b. (27b) Length of whole leaf usually about equal to its width or rarely more than 2 times its width (as in Figures 63, 92, 102)...35a or 35b

30a. (29a) Leaves with wavy margins or very shallow teeth...31a or 31b

30b. (29a) Leaves lobed or divided, with small or large, shallow or deep lobes...32a or 32b

31a. (30a) Leaves generally larger, often 15 cm (6 in.) or longer, and often numerous in a large rosette...Compare: Curled dock p. 50, Evening-primroses p. 148, Hound's-tongue p. 172, Moth mullein p. 190, Teasel p. 203,

Elecampane p. 233, Tall blue lettuce p. 250, Canada lettuce p. 250, Chicory p. 252, Black-eyed Susan p. 209, Knapweeds pp. 243-245, Dandelion p. 252

31b. (30a) Leaves generally smaller, seldom more than 15 cm (6 in.) long, few or many in small to medium-sized rosettes...Compare: Tall wormseed mustard p. 99, Stinkweed p. 105, Shepherd's-purse p. 109, Hoary alyssum p. 104, False flaxes p. 110, Black-eyed Susan p. 209, English daisy p. 231, Knapweeds pp. 243-245, Prickly lettuce p. 250, Dandelion p. 252

32a. (30b) White or yellowish milky juice present in leaves, stems or other parts... Compare: Greater celandine p. 86, Hawkweeds pp. 245-246, Sow-thistles pp. 247-249, Lettuces p. 250, Chicory p. 252, Dandelion p. 252, Fall hawkbit p. 254

32b. (30b) White or yellowish milky juice not present in any part of plant... 33a or 33b

33a. (32b) Leaves palmately lobed (clefts or spaces between lobes or leaflets all pointing towards or starting very close to petiole or leafstalk, as in Figures 92, 128G, 150)... Compare: Cinquefoils pp. 114-116, Goutweed p. 150, Cow-parsnip p. 156, Water-hemlocks pp. 155, 158, Angelica p. 155, Poison hemlock p. 151, Motherwort p. 179, Tall coneflower p. 209

33b. (32b) Leaves pinnately lobed (clefts or spaces between lobes or leaflets pointing towards midrib of leaf, as in Figures 74, 96, 127)...34a or 34b

34a. (33b) Leaves generally larger, often 15 cm (6 in.) or longer...Compare: Wall-rockets p. 91, Tumble mustard p. 93, Hedge mustard p. 94, Tall hedge mustard p. 94, Yellow avens p. 117, Caraway p. 149, Water-parsnip p. 152, Wild parsnip p. 159, Tall beggarticks p. 212

34b. (33b) Leaves generally smaller, seldom more than 15 cm (6 in.) long... Compare: Dog mustard p. 90, Yellow rocket p. 102, Flixweed p. 96, Pepper-grasses pp. 106-108, Shepherd's-purse p. 109, Small burnet p. 118, Field violet p. 146, Ox-eye daisy p. 219, Spotted knapweed p. 243, (also check for small plants of all plants listed in 34a)

35a. (29b) Leaves lobed or divided...36a or 36b

35b. (29b) Leaves not lobed or divided...Compare: Broad-leaved dock p. 52, Mallows pp. 140-141, Speedwells pp. 193-198, Broad-leaved plantain p. 199, Fleabanes pp. 228-230, English daisy p. 231

36a. (35a) Leaves palmately lobed or divided (clefts or spaces between lobes or leaflets all pointing towards or starting very close to petiole or leafstalk, as in Figures 63, 93, 117...Compare: Eastern bracken p. 20, Buttercups pp. 82-84, Cinquefoils pp. 114-116, Low hop clover p. 120, Black medick p. 121, White clover p. 123, Mallows pp. 140-141, Flower-of-an-hour p. 144, Goutweed p. 150, Henbit p. 178, Motherwort p. 179, Corn speedwell p. 195, Ragweeds pp. 213-215, Absinth p. 221, Fleabanes pp. 228-230

36b. (35a) Leaves pinnately lobed or divided (clefts or spaces pointing towards midrib, as in Figures 73, 102, 192)...Compare: Greater celandine p. 86, Mustard Family pp. 88-111 (especially Wild mustard, Black mustard, Wild radish, Dog mustard, Wall rockets, Yellow rocket, Tumble mustard, Hedge mustard, Tall hedge mustard, Flixweed, Tansy mustards, Shepherd's-purse), Yellow avens p. 117, Small burnet p. 118, Bird's-foot trefoil p. 123, Vetches pp. 124-125, St. John's-wort p. 145, Flower-of-an-hour p. 144, Field violet p. 146, Goutweed p. 150, Water-parsnip p. 152, Water-hemlocks pp. 152-155, Wild parsnip p. 159, Tall beggarticks p. 212, Common ragweed p. 213, Tansy p. 220, Biennial wormwood p. 223, Tansy ragwort p. 224, Fleabanes pp. 228-230, Sow-thistles pp. 247-249

37a. (5b) Leaves that are attached to stems (not the rosette leaves) arranged in whorls (arranged in groups of 3 or more leaves at each node, like spokes of a wheel, Figures 50, 135, 171); occasionally with only 2 or just 1 leaf per node in the upper part of the plant near the flowers...38a or 38b

37b. (5b) Leaves that are attached to stems (not the rosette leaves) arranged either alternate (arranged singly, only 1 per node as in Figures 11, 33, 69) or opposite (arranged in pairs, 2 per node as in Figures 53, 61, 150) but never in whorls...43a or 43b

38a. (37a) Leaves much lobed, divided or compound; only 1 whorl of 3 fern-like leaves at tip of a bare stem...Eastern bracken p. 20

38b. (37a) Leaves not lobed, or divided or compound; few to many whorls of leaves on each stem...39a or 39b

39a. (38b) Milky juice present in stems and leaves ...40a or 40b

39b. (38b) Milky juice not present in stems or leaves...41a or 41b

40a. (39a) Leaves whorled (3 or more per node) only near top of stem, but just opposite (2 per node) or alternate (1 per node) in lower portion of stem...Compare: Spurges pp. 129-135, Milkweeds pp. 162-164

40b. (39a) Leaves whorled at every node... Whorled milkweed p. 164

41a. (39b) Stems erect with few branches; leaves 3-20 cm (1½ - 8 in.) long and more than 1 cm wide, flowers purple...Compare: Purple loosestrife p. 147, Spotted Joe-Pye weed p. 235

9

41b. (39b) Stems prostrate, or weak or, if erect, then with very narrow, slender leaves... 42a or 42b

42a. (41b) Stems square or somewhat 4-angled, prickly, hairy or smooth; leaves in whorls of 4, 6, or 8 per node, narrow, linear to narrowly oblong...Compare: Carpetweed p. 71, Smooth bedstraw p. 201, Cleavers p. 202

42b. (41b) Stems round, smooth or slightly sticky-hairy, or slightly angled with alternate green and pink parallel lines; leaves in whorls of up to 16 per node, narrowly linear or long-pointed...Compare: Russian thistle p. 64, Carpetweed p. 71, Corn spurry p. 72, Black medick p. 121, Wood-sorrels p. 122

43a. (37b) Leaves all or mostly opposite (2 per node) throughout the plant (as in Figures 132, 163)...44a or 44b

43b. (37b) Leaves alternate (1 per node) throughout the plant, sometimes so close together that they appear to be opposite (2 per node, as in Figures 85, 111, 161)... 72a or 72b

44a. (43a) Stems woody at the base or throughout, perennial, vines, shrubs or small trees... 45a or 45b

44b. (43a) Stems not woody; herbaceous annuals or biennials, or perennials with stems which may be firm or hard but die back to the ground each winter...50a or 50b

45a. (44a) **CAUTION** Leaves compound with 3 leaflets on each long stalk (see Figure 113), usually low-growing (20-90 cm, 8-36 in. high), occasionally a vine climbing 3 m (10 ft.) or higher on tree trunks, etc. ...Poison-ivy p. 136

45b. (44a) Leaves not compound, or compound with 5 or more leaflets, low- or tall-growing... 46a or 46b

46a. (45b) Leaves and stems with milky juice... Compare: Spreading dogbane p. 160, Indian hemp p. 160, Dog strangling vine p. 165

46b. (45b) Leaves and stems without milky juice ...47a or 47b

47a. (46b) Stems and branches very prickly with numerous, short, triangular-based prickles, these prickles usually in pairs... Prickly-ash p. 127

47b. (46b) Stems and branches without prickles but tips of branches may end in thorns... 48a or 48b

48a. (47b) Leaves narrow, linear-oblong, with transparent dots (Plate 83B); flowers bright yellow in terminal, branched bunches; seed in small, dry seedpods; plant usually less than 50 cm (2 ft.) high...St. John's-wort p. 145

48b. (47b) Leaves or leaflets ovate to broadly elliptic without translucent dots...49a or 49b

49a. (48b) **CAUTION** Leaves compound with 7 to 13 leaflets; margins of leaflets smooth or irregularly wavy but not with regular teeth; leaflets with one main vein and usually 6 or more relatively straight branch veins on each side; flowers and berries white in long-stalked clusters... Poison sumac p. 138

49b. (48b) Leaves simple; their margins smooth or slightly toothed but not wavy; leaves with one main vein and either with 2 or 3 branch veins on each side that curve towards the tip of the leaf, or with more than 3 branch veins that do not curve; flowers greenish-yellow in many small clusters along the branches; seed in juicy blue-black berries...Buckthorns p. 139

50a. (44b) Stems square, or nearly so, in cross-section...51a or 51b

50b. (44b) Stems more or less round in cross-section...52a or 52b

51a. (50a) Leaves opposite throughout; flowers produced singly in leaf axils (hence 2 at a node, Figure 150) or few to many in clusters in leaf axils; plants usually with a "minty" or similarly aromatic odour... Mint Family pp. 173-181

51b. (50a) Lower and middle stem leaves opposite or whorled; upper leaves in inflorescence alternate; plant without a "minty" odour ...Purple loosestrife p. 147

52a. (50b) Plants with milky juice...53a or 53b

52b. (50b) Plants without milky juice...55a or 55b

53a. (52a) Leaves small, rarely more than 2.5 cm (1 in.) long; flowers or general inflorescence green, yellowish-green or somewhat reddish-green...Spurges pp. 129-135

53b. (52a) Leaves larger, usually more than 3 cm (1-1/5 in.) long; flowers white, pink, purplish or maroon...54a or 54b

54a. (53b) Flowers small, bell-shaped, white or pinkish, in branching clusters... Dogbane Family pp. 160-161

54b. (53b) Flowers not bell-shaped; the 5 petals bent backwards along the flower stalk; flowers; purplish-green, whitish-green or maroon to deep purple, in umbel-like clusters...Milkweed Family pp. 162-165

55a. (52b) Flowers in umbels (all flower stalks within a cluster joined to the tip of a stem or branch)...Carrot or Parsley Family pp. 149-159

55b. (52b) Flowers not in umbels...56a or 56b

56a. (55b) Leaves finely dissected, almost lacy... Common ragweed p. 213

56b. (55b) Leaves not finely dissected...57a or 57b

57a. (56b) Leaves and stems prickly; flowers in dense, spiny, egg-shaped clusters... Teasel p. 203

57b. (56b) Leaves and stems not prickly but may have hooked bristles around the seed clusters; flowers not in dense egg-shaped clusters...58a or 58b

58a. (57b) Leaves large, usually 7.5 cm (3 in.) wide or wider, oval to rounded in outline, shallowly and irregularly toothed or deeply 3- to 5-lobed...59a or 59b

58b. (57b) Leaves or leaflets usually less than 7.5 cm (3 in.) wide...60a or 60b

59a. (58a) Most leaves opposite and deeply 3- to 5-lobed, bases of leaves flat or more or less rounded or pointed; all main branching veins well inside leaf blade; seeds angular with a few short erect spines around upper end...Giant ragweed p. 215

59b. (58a) Most leaves alternate (except a few may be opposite near the bottom of the main stem) and only shallowly 3- to 5-lobed, or just coarsely toothed; bases of leaves somewhat angular heart-shaped, usually with edges of lowermost main branching veins exposed in a broad V or M [as in Figure 185 (a), (b)]; flowers and seeds in burs covered with hooked bristles...Cocklebur p. 216

60a. (58b) Flowers or seeds in small, loose to very dense, greenish to yellowish or bright red clusters, the clusters somewhat granular in appearance...61a or 61b

60b. (58b) Flowers or seeds not in small, greenish, grandular-appearing clusters; variously coloured...64a or 64b

61a. (60a) Leaf surfaces harsh (like sandpaper) in texture...Giant ragweed p. 215

61b. (60a) Leaf surfaces smooth...62a or 62b

62a. (61b) Flower or seed clusters very dense and almost spherical, in axils of leaves, at first small and greenish, enlarging and turning juicy and bright red at maturity...Strawberry-blite p. 62

62b. (61b) Flower or seed clusters usually rather loose, on branches from leaf axils as well as near the ends of the main stems...63a or 63b

63a. (62b) Most leaves opposite; each seed enclosed between 2 flat bracts...Atriplexes p. 63

63b. (62b) Only lowermost 2 or 4 leaves opposite, the rest alternate; each seed in a thin, rounded hull without wings...Compare: Lamb's-quarters p. 60, Jerusalem-oak, p. 60, Goosefoots pp. 61-62

64a. (60b) Flowers in "flower heads" (each head composed of several to many individual, tightly packed florets, and may be daisy-like, dandelion-like, ragweed-like, etc. see page 208), bright yellow, yellow-green, yellow and white, white or dusty pink... 65a or 65b

64b. (60b) Flowers arranged individually (single flowers with not more than 5 petals and either on long or short stalks or in leaf axils) or flowers grouped in loose or tight clusters along stems and branches but not in flower heads, variously coloured including yellow...68a or 68b

65a. (64a) Flower heads white or dusty pink, usually several to many in umbel-like clusters at ends of stems and branches...66a or 66b

65b. (64a) Flower heads yellow, yellow-green or yellow and white...67a or 67b

66a. (65a) Flower heads pink; stem leaves usually in whorls of 3 or more...Spotted Joe-Pye weed p. 235

66b. (65a) Flower heads white, stem leaves always opposite in pairs...Compare: White snakeroot p. 234, Boneset p. 235

67a. (65b) Flower heads small, less than 1 cm (2/5 in.) across, with yellowish-green centres and usually with 5, tiny, white ray florets [as in Figures 177 A,B,C,E, 181(b)]; seeds very small, smooth, not barbed...Galinsogas p. 211

67b. (65b) Flower heads larger, more than 2 cm (4/5 in.) across, yellowish-green, with or without bright yellow ray florets [as in Figures 177 A,B,C,E, 182(a)]; seeds more than 3 mm (1/2 in.) long, smooth or with 2 or 4 barbed awns...Compare: Beggar-ticks p. 212, Jerusalem artichoke p. 210

68a. (64b) Flowers bright yellow or orange-yellow ...St. John's-wort p. 145

68b. (64b) Flowers white, pink, mauve, blue or purple...69a or 69b

69a. (68b) Plants mostly with a minty or mint-like odour; flowers with petals united forming a tubular corolla with 2 lips at the end, the upper lip 2-lobed, the lower lip 3-lobed (as in Plate 105C)...Mint Family pp. 173-181

69b. (68b) Plants without a mint-like odour; flowers with petals separate, or if united not forming a 2-lipped tube...70a or 70b

70a. (69b) Flowers purple or red-purple in small dense clusters in axils of small, mostly alternate leaves, forming many-flowered spikes at tops of tall stems...Purple loosestrife p. 147

70b. (69b) Flowers mostly white, pink, mauve or blue; if purple then borne singly on long stalks from normal, opposite upper leaves... 71a or 71b

71a. (70b) Leaves without teeth, opposite (2 per node) on stems and in the inflorescence; flowers with 5 or 10 petals or petal lobes, and stamens as many as or usually twice as many as the petals...Pink Family pp. 72-81

71b. (70b) Leaves with shallow teeth or almost without teeth, opposite on stems below the inflorescence but alternate (1 per node) in the inflorescence; flowers with 4 petal lobes and only 2 stamens...Speedwells pp. 193-198

72a. (43b) Leaves alternate and straight- or parallel-veined or apparently so, very narrow (their length 5 or more times their width), the long leaves may be grass-like...73a or 73b

72b. (43b) Leaves alternate and net-veined (with 1 or more main veins and branches from them), either narrow or broad...80a or 80b

73a. (72a) Plants with white milky juice...74a or 74b
73b. (72a) Plants without milky juice...76a or 76b
74a. (73a) Leaves prominently hairy...Hawk-weeds pp. 245-246
74b. (73a) Leaves smooth, usually without any hairs or only sparsely hairy...75a or 75b
75a. (74b) Leaves usually longer than 10 cm (4 in.); plant somewhat grass-like before flowering; flowers in large yellow or purple flower heads (see page 208); seeds in a large, spherical, fluffy ball...Goat's-beards, Salsify pp. 255-256
75b. (74b) Leaves usually less than 7.5 cm (3 in.) long; plant not grass-like; flowers in branching clusters or in axils of leaves, green, yellowish-green or reddish-green; seeds in tiny 3-seeded pods...Spurge Family pp. 128-135
76a. (73b) Plants not grass-like, with erect firm stems and numerous narrow, short leaves; flowers yellow and orange or bluish-white, snapdragon-like, in spikes, or single from leaf axils...Toadflaxes p. 191
76b. (73b) Plants grass-like or somewhat so; flowers greenish or apparently not produced, or white to pink in a dense ball at the top of the stem...77a or 77b
77a. (76b) Plant with a strong odour of onion or garlic; texture soft and fleshy; flowers white, bluish, or greenish, in a dense ball at tip of stem...Wild garlic p. 49
77b. (76b) Plant without odour of onion; texture firm, not fleshy; flowers greenish or apparently not produced...78a or 78b
78a. (77b) Leaves spiny-tipped, grass-like in seedling stages only...Russian thistle p. 64
78b. (77b) Leaves not spiny-tipped, all stages grass-like...79a or 79b
79a. (78b) Stems mostly hollow, round or somewhat flattened in cross-section; leaves 2-ranked (from 2 sides of stem)...Grass Family pp. 21-45
79b. (78b) Stems solid, triangular; leaves 3-ranked (from 3 sides of stem)...Sedges pp. 46-48
80a. (72b) Plants woody throughout, or at least at the base, low to tall shrubs, or low trees; may also be vines or vine-like...81a or 81b
80b. (72b) Plants not woody; stems herbaceous (soft or firm, more or less green); above-ground parts dying at the end of each growing season but roots may be perennial; some may be vine-like...89a or 89b
81a. (80a) **CAUTION** Leaves in 3's (actually, leaf is compound with 3 leaflets, the terminal leaflet is stalked)...82a or 82b
81b. (80a) Leaves not in 3's, either simple or, if compound, not with 3 leaflets...85a or 85b
82a. (81a) Plant more or less spiny, with prickles on stem, leaf petiole and often on undersides of leaves...Compare: Raspberries and Blackberries
82b. (81a) Plant not spiny...83a or 83b

83a. (82b) Stems soft, and very slender; flowers purplish to whitish and pea-like...Hog-peanut p. 137
83b. (82b) Stems firm, hard; flowers not pea-like ...84a or 84b
84a. (83b) Most leaves compound with 5 to 7 leaflets; usually only a few with 3 leaflets; fruit blue berries or winged keys...Compare: Virginia creeper p. 137, Manitoba maple p. 137
84b. (83b) Most leaves compound with 3 leaflets; flowers small, greenish-white, in branching clusters below the leaves; berries yellowish-green or grayish and hanging on all winter...Poison-ivy p. 136
85a. (81b) Stems without thorns; leaf petiole usually with 1 or 2 tiny glands (bumps) just below the blade; flowers in elongated white clusters; berries blue-black or red, juicy, each with a single round stone; bruised twigs and leaves with odour of almond... Chokecherry p. 139
85b. (81b) Stems usually with thorns, either along the sides or at tips of branches, or in crotches between branches; leaf petioles without glands; flowers white, pink, yellow or greenish-yellow; bruised twigs not smelling of almonds...86a or 86b
86a. (85b) Stems with pairs of short, stout, narrowly triangular spines [as in Figure 104(a)] at each node; leaves compound with 5 to 11 leaflets; flowers opening early in spring, before plants leaf out...Prickly-ash p. 127
86b. (85b) Stems with 1 to 3 slender spines [as in Figure 65(a)] at each node, or long stout thorns [as in Figures 97(a), 115(a)] or without spines or thorns; leaves not compound; flowers opening with or after the leaves...87a or 87b
87a. (86b) Flowers bright yellow, in drooping racemes; sepals 6; petals 6; stems with usually 3 slender spines at each node; fruit red and berry-like with 1 to 3 seeds ...Common barberry p. 85
87b. (86b) Flowers white, pinkish or greenish-yellow, sepals and petals in 4's or 5's; stems without 3 spines at each node; thorns may be present or absent...88a or 88b
88a. (87b) Sepals 4 or 5; petals 4 or 5; flowers greenish and in stalkless axillary clusters along the stems and branches; fruit black, juicy, bitter, with 2-4 hard seeds; twigs may end in a thorn; no thorns along sides of twigs...Buckthorns p. 139
88b. (87b) Sepals 5; petals 5; flowers showy, white or pinkish in stalked clusters usually towards ends of branches; fruit red or purplish, rather apple-like and with hard seeds; stems and twigs usually with long stout thorns along sides but not at tip ...Hawthorn p. 119
89a. (80b) Plant with 3-branched tendrils (as in Figure 174B) opposite each leaf; a high-

climbing herbaceous vine with broad, lobed leaves, and long clusters of greenish-white flowers...Melon Family pp. 204-206

89b. (80b) Plant without tendrils, or with tendrils at ends of compound leaves which are not 5-lobed...90a or 90b

90a. (89b) Flowers in "flower heads" (each head composed of several to many individual, tightly packed florets, and may be daisy-like, dandelion-like, ragweed-like, etc., see page 208)...Composite Family pp. 208-256

90b. (89b) Flowers borne singly, or in spikes or clusters but not in "flower heads"...91a or 91b

91a. (90b) True petals absent; sepals usually green and bract-like, but in some species sepals may be petal-like and white, yellowish or pinkish; individual flowers small and inconspicuous, usually less than 3 mm (1/8 in.) across...92a or 92b

91b. (90b) True petals present, either white or variously coloured; flowers large or small, usually showy; both sepals and petals present...98a or 98b

92a. (91a) Plants with a distinct ocrea [membranous sheath, Figure 33(b)] at each node (joint) of the stem and branches...Buckwheat or Smartweed Family pp. 50-59

92b. (91a) Plants without an ocrea at each node ...93a or 93b

93a. (92b) Plants with white milky juice; flowers in axils of leaves or in open, umbel-like inflorescences; bracts under or around the "flowers" often petal-like and yellowish-green or rosy-green...Spurge Family pp. 128-135

93b. (92b) Plants without white milky juice; flowers in small, dense clusters or in loose or dense spikes or racemes...94a or 94b

94a. (93b) Flowers or flower clusters only at tip of main stem or at tips of main stem and branches; seedpods appearing very different from the tiny flowers...95a or 95b

94b. (93b) Flowers or flower clusters often in axils of leaves as well as at tips of stems and branches; seedpods or seed-bearing clusters appearing not much different from the flowers or flower clusters except somewhat larger...96a or 96b

95a. (94a) Flowers whitish to pinkish; each flower producing a ring-shaped juicy berry with about 6 one-seeded sections; at least the berries and upper part of plant with reddish juice...Pokeweed p. 69

95b. (94a) Flowers white, yellow or greenish; each flower producing a non-fleshy seedpod that may be as wide as long or much longer than wide; plants with clear, watery juice...Mustard Family pp. 88-111

96a. (94b) Flowers or seeds in small, loose to very dense greenish to bright red clusters; the clusters somewhat granular in appear-

ance; sepals of each tiny flower small, greenish and leaf-like in texture; some plants with mealy or scurfy surface... Goosefoot Family pp. 60-64

96b. (94b) Flowers and seeds not in granular clusters, either single in axils of spiny bracts on elongating stems, or many and intermixed with many small, slender, pointed bracts in loose to dense spikes; sepals of each tiny flower bract-like, papery, brownish or greenish but not leaf-like; plants not mealy...97a or 97b

97a. (96b) Leaves slender, needle-like or wedge-shaped, sharp-pointed; flowers produced singly in axils of very sharp, short bracts along all branches...Russian thistle p. 64

97b. (96b) Leaves more or less oval, flat; flowers produced in loose to dense, short to long or thick inflorescences...Amaranth Family pp. 65-68

98a. (91b) Sepals 2, sometimes dropping off before the flowers open...99a or 99b

98b. (91b) Sepals 4 or more and remaining during the life of the flower, or absent, or not distinguishable; if present, they may be either separate or united and, if united they may form a cup-shaped or tubular calyx with 4 or more teeth or lobes at the end...101a or 101b

99a. (98a) Flowers mauve with purplish tips, leaves finely divided, often bluish-green... Fumitory p. 87

99b. (98a) Flowers yellow; leaves simple, or deeply lobed or divided and the lobes or divisions more than 6 mm (1/4 in.) wide... 100a or 100b

100a. (99b) Petals 4, large and yellow; flowers in few-flowered umbels at ends of stems and branches; seedpods long and linear; plant erect; juice yellow-orange, sticky ...Greater celandine p. 86

100b. (99b) Petals 5, small and yellow; flowers in axils of leaves; seedpods nearly spherical; plants fleshy and prostrate; juice clear, watery...Purslane p. 70

101a. (98b) Flowers mauve with purplish tips, slender; each with one rounded spur on one side at the base; leaves finely divided... Fumitory p. 87

101b. (98b) Flowers and leaves not as described in 101a...102a or 102b

102a.(101b) Leaves and stems with a sticky yellow juice; leaves deeply lobed with 5 to 9 lobes; each lobe wider than 6 mm (1/4 in.) ...Greater celandine p. 86

102b.(101b) Leaves and above ground stems with clear watery juice...103a or 103b

103a.(102b) Stems fleshy, succulent, reddish, more or less prostrate; leaves thick, succulent, green or reddish-green; flowers with 5 yellow petals, in axils of leaves throughout the plant...Purslane p. 70

103b.(102b) Stems not succulent or only weakly so, more or less erect; leaves usually not succulent but if succulent then short, very thick and nearly round in cross-section ...104a or 104b

104a.(103b) Sepals 4 and petals 4, flowers always regular (all petals or corolla lobes within one flower have the same size and shape, and all sepals have the same size and shape such that the flower appears uniform from all sides) ...105a or 105b

104b.(103b) Sepals usually 5 or more; petals variable in number, flowers regular or irregular (size or shape of 1 or more petals or corolla lobes different from the others in the same flower, or shape of 1 or more sepals or calyx lobes different from the others in the same flower, flower not appearing uniform from all sides)... 106a or 106b

105a.(104a) Flowers in bare (leafless) racemes, not in axils of smaller upper leaves (except in Dog and Garlic mustards); stamens 2, 4 or 6, if 4 or 6, then 2 are shorter than the others; sepals, petals and stamens attached below ovary; seedpod developing from inside of flower...Mustard Family pp. 88-111

105b.(104a) Flowers in axils of smaller upper leaves and forming a spike; stamens 8 of equal size and length; sepals, petals and stamens on top of ovary; seedpod developing below flower...Evening-primroses p. 148

106a.(104b) Flower with a distinct spur that is usually the same colour as the corolla and protrudes downward from between two of the sepals...107a or 107b

106b.(104b) Flower without a spur...108a or 108b

107a.(106a) Flowers large, yellow and orange or yellow and white, 2 cm (4/5 in.) long or longer including the spur...Toadflaxes p. 191

107b.(106a) Flowers small, white, bluish-white or yellow, usually less than 1 cm (2/5 in.) long including spur...Compare: Field violet p. 146, Dwarf snapdragon p. 192

108a.(106b) Flowers irregular...109a or 109b

108b.(106b) Flowers regular...114a or 114b

109a.(108a) Flowers in umbels (all flower stalks within a cluster joined to the tip of a stem or branch); stems often hollow; base of each leafstalk expanded and surrounding the stem...Carrot or Parsley Family pp. 149-159

109b.(108a) Flowers not in umbels, or if in umbels, the base of the leafstalks slender and not surrounding the stem...110a or 110b

110a.(109b) Flowers resembling those of pea or bean, lower 2 petals (the keel) often appearing fused at the tips; leaves compound, with stipules...Legume or Bean Family pp. 120-121, 123-126

110b.(109b) Flowers not pea-like or bean-like; leaves simple, may be lobed...111a or 111b

111a.(110b) Flowers pansy-like, yellow or yellowish-white, each on a long slender stalk from among the leaves...Field violet p. 146

111b.(110b) Flowers not pansy-like, white, yellowish, or blue...112a or 112b

112a.(111b) Flowers blue, tubular, with slender lobes and long protruding stamens; plant covered with stiff hairs which have thickened bases, not woolly...Blue-weed p. 170

112b.(111b) Flowers white, yellow or greenish-yellow ...113a or 113b

113a.(112b) Flowers white or yellowish, each with 5 rounded petals, in long, slender racemes or thick spikes; leaves smooth or white woolly, not lobed...Mulleins pp. 189-190

113b.(112b) Flowers yellow or greenish-yellow in racemes; petals small, each with 3 tiny finger-like lobes at the end; middle and upper leaves pinnately lobed and not woolly...Yellow mignonette p. 112

114a.(108b) Flowers in umbels (all flower stalks within a cluster joined to the tip of a stem or branch); leaves variously compound, bases of leafstalks broad-based and surrounding stem; plants usually aromatic; flowers white or yellow...Compare: Buttercup Family pp. 82-84, Carrot or Parsley Family pp. 149-159

114b.(108b) Flowers not in umbels, or if in umbels, then leafstalks with slender bases that do not surround the stem...115a or 115b

115a.(114b) Leaves small, very fleshy, almost round in cross-section, very numerous and overlapping; seedpods small and separate... Mossy stonecrop p. 113

115b.(114b) Leaves not both fleshy and round in cross-section...116a or 116b

116a.(115b) Flowers with 8 or more stamens...117a or 117b

116b.(115b) Flowers usually with not more than 5 stamens...121a or 121b

117a.(116a) Flowers yellow, each petal small and with 3 tiny finger-like lobes at the end; middle and upper leaves with narrow pinnate lobes...Yellow mignonette p. 112

117b.(116a) Flowers white, pink, red, blue or yellow, but if yellow the petals without finger-like lobes and the middle and upper leaves without narrow pinnate lobes...118a or 118b

118a.(117b) Flowers pink to red or purple, or blue; fruit 10-25 mm (2/5-1 in.) long and 3 mm (1/8 in.) in diameter with usually 5 seeds in a ring around the base...Geranium Family p. 142

118b.(117b) Flowers yellow or white, if flowers pink, red or blue then fruit not long and narrow, and seeds usually at least 10 or more per flower...119a or 119b

119a.(118b) Stamens many but united by their filaments into an erect column or tube in the center of the flower [as in Figures 116B, C(e)]; seeds either many in a capsule or seedpod with several sections (as in Figure 118B) or about 15-20 in a ring (as in Figure 117D, E)...Mallow Family pp. 140-141, 143-144

119b.(118b) Stamens many and separate (their filaments not united into a central column)...120a or 120b

120a.(119b) Stipules [as in Figures 92(c), 94(b)] present at the base of each leafstalk; base of leafstalk not expanded and not surrounding stem; sepals, petals and stamens attached to an hypanthium (distinct rim or shallow cup) surrounding pistils...Rose Family pp. 114-119

120b.(119b) Stipules not present at base of each leafstalk; base of leafstalk expanded and surrounding the stem; sepals, petals and stamens attached directly to the receptacle around or below the pistils...Buttercups pp. 82-84

121a.(116b) Plants trailing or twining...122a or 122b

121b.(116b) Plants erect or spreading...123a or 123b

122a.(121a) Flowers large, trumpet- or funnel-shaped, white or pinkish, about 2.5 cm (1 in.) in diameter or larger; leaves spade-shaped...Morning-glory Family pp. 166-168

122b.(121a) Flowers small, star-shaped, blue, purple, or rarely white, less than 12 mm (1/2 in.) in diameter; leaves either ovate without lobes, or mitten-shaped with 1 or 2 (or more) small lobes at base of the blade; plant with unpleasant odour when bruised...Climbing nightshade p. 183

123a.(121b) Stem and leaves densely white-woolly; stem stiffly erect, tall, thick; flowers dense in long, thick, club-shaped spikes...Common mullein p. 189

123b.(121b) Stems and leaves not densely white-woolly...124a or 124b

124a.(123b) Seeds produced in clusters of 4 small, hard nutlets which separate but do not open up; plants rough-hairy or soft-hairy, stems round...Borage Family pp. 169-172

124b.(123b) Seeds produced in fleshy berries or dry pods which open and release the seeds; plants hairless or if hairy, not rough-hairy...125a or 125b

125a.(124b) Seeds produced in small fleshy berries or large spiny pods; leaves simple or compound; plants usually with unpleasant odour when bruised...Nightshade or Potato Family pp. 182-188

125b.(124b) Seeds produced in small, dry, non-spiny pods; leaves simple; plants usually without disagreeable odour...126a or 126b

126a.(125b) Flowers blue or mauve, bell-shaped, at least 1.5 cm (3/5 in.) long...Creeping bellflower p. 207

126b.(125b) Flowers yellow, disk-shaped or almost flat, arranged in long, slender racemes; petals 5, nearly equal...Moth mullein p. 190

127a. (4b) Plants with underground bulbs, tubers or nutlets, and their leaves long, slender, and grass-like...128a or 128b

127b. (4b) Plants also with underground bulbs, tubers or nutlets, but their leaves not grass-like, their length seldom more than 2 times their width...129a or 129b

128a.(127a) Leaves hollow, round or flattened or V-shaped in cross-section, thick but easily compressed; plant with strong onion or garlic odour...Wild garlic p. 49

128b.(127a) Leaves not hollow, flat or V-shaped, thin and somewhat firm; plant without onion odour...Yellow nut sedge p. 47

129a.(127b) Plant with tendrils...130a or 130b

129b.(127b) Plant without tendrils...131a or 131b

130a.(129a) Leaves broad-ovate or somewhat heart-shaped, softly to harshly hairy; flowers bright yellow...Goldencreeper p. 204

130b.(129a) Leaves (actually leaflets) narrowly elliptic; flowers pinkish to red-purple...Tuberous vetchling p. 126

131a.(129b) Stems more or less square; all leaves opposite; flowers mauve to light purple; corolla irregular and not bell-shaped; fleshy roots irregularly thickened, white, usually very brittle...Compare: Marsh hedge-nettle p. 180, Germander p. 173

131b.(129b) Stems mostly round; leaves alternate or opposite, but if lower leaves opposite, the upper leaves near the flower heads are usually alternate; flowers white, yellow or, if blue, then bell-shaped; fleshy underground parts smooth or irregular, usually firm and not easily broken...132a or 132b

132a.(131b) Leaves simple, heart-shaped, elliptic, or lance-shaped; flowers blue or yellow....133a or 133b

132b.(131b) Leaves compound (made up of several leaflets), flowers white...134a or 134b

133a.(132a) Leaves at the ground surface heart-shaped; leaves on the stem lance-shaped, pointed, not rough to the touch; flowers blue, bell-shaped...Creeping bellflower p. 207

133b.(132a) Leaves ovate or elliptic, harsh or rough to the touch, never in a rosette at the ground surface, opposite (2 per node) on the lower part of the stem, alternate (1 per node) nearer the yellow flower heads...Jerusalem artichoke p. 210

134a.(132b) Tuberous roots Dahlia-like or cigar-shaped, surrounding base of plant...Compare: Water-hemlocks pp. 155, 158, Angelica p. 155

134b.(132b) Tuberous roots not Dahlia-like, usually just a thickening (sometimes cigar-shaped) on a whitish horizontal root at some distance from the aboveground shoot...Goutweed p. 150

GLOSSARY

Achene a dry, 1-seeded fruit with a firm close-fitting outer coat that does not open by any regular dehiscence (the process of splitting open at maturity). All fruits ("seeds") of the Smartweed and Composite Families are achenes [Figures 32B(d), 182C, 183E(d)].

Acuminate a description of the shape of a leaf tip whose sides are somewhat concave and appear "stretched out" to a protracted point [Figures 37(j), 77].

Alternate placed singly at different heights on the stem or axis (Figures 25A, 41, 78); any arrangement of leaves or other parts that are not strictly opposite or whorled.

Annual a plant which completes its life cycle in one growing season. Compare with winter annual, biennial, perennial.

Anther the enlarged outer portion of the stamen that produces pollen.

Auricle an appendage near the lower part of a leaf blade or petal; it may be pointed [Figures 11(g), 85B(b)] or rounded and shaped like the lobe of a human ear [Figure 220B(a)].

Awn a bristle-like part or appendage, usually needle-shaped [Figure 10(h)].

Axil the upper angle formed by the junction of a leaf or branch with the stem.

Basal Offset a short side shoot arising at the base of a stem or from a root crown.

Biennial a plant which germinates in the spring, producing a rosette of leaves and remaining vegetative during the first summer; overwinters as a rosette; bolts (sends up a flowering stalk) during the second summer; sets seed; and dies at the end of the second growing season. Compare with annual, winter annual, perennial.

Blade the expanded part of a leaf or petal.

Bloom in this book, it is used only in the sense of "a fine, powdery coating on leaves, stems, etc." Also see "glaucous." (When referring to a flower, the word "blossom" is used.)

Blossom a flower.

Bract a leaf that is much reduced; particularly the small or scale-like leaves immediately below each flower in a flower cluster [Figures 123B (b), 147B(b)], or associated with the inflorescence [Figures 124B(d), 128(p)].

Calyx the sepals of a flower; the outermost series of flower parts; it is usually, but not always, green and leaf-like in texture.

Ciliate fringed with fine hairs along the edge or margin [Figure 21B(d)].

Clasping partly or wholly surrounding the stem [Figures 85B(b), 220B(a), 221B(c)].

Cleft divided to or almost to the midrib, as a palmately cleft leaf [Figures 63A(b), 184B] or pinnately cleft leaf (Figures 70, 225).

Collar the junction between leaf blade and leaf sheath in grass and sedge leaves (Figures 3, 25).

Compound made up of two or more similar parts, united into one whole. A compound leaf is divided into several separate leaflets. A compound umbel is made up of several simple umbels.

Corolla the petals of a flower; an inner series of flower parts, usually between sepals and stamens; it is usually white or coloured, and usually not leaf-like in texture.

Cotyledon a seed leaf. These tiny leaves are present in the embryo in the seed. In most broad-leaved dicotyledonous plants, they emerge when the seed germinates. They are the first green leaves of these seedlings and are always an opposite pair.

Crown the part of the stem at the surface of the ground. Also, specialized appendages on the corolla in a flower as the hoods and horns in Milkweed [Figure 134A(b)], or the "trumpet" in the cultivated daffodil.

Culm the stem of grasses and bamboos, usually hollow except at the swollen nodes (Figure 3).

Cyathium a specialized cup-like structure that encloses one or more tiny flowers in the Spurge Family (Figure 112B).

Cyme an inflorescence in which virtually every stem and branch ends in a flower, and does not have a well-defined central axis (Figures 53, 57C, 59, 61). The central or uppermost flower usually blossoms first.

Dentate with sharp teeth that are perpendicular to the margin; the two sides of each tooth being of about equal length and having the same slope (Figure 109).

Diploid with 2n (2 complete sets of) chromosomes per cell; one complete set having come from each parent.

Disk floret a tubula flower in the central part of the flower head of many members of the Composite Family (Figure 177D), as distinguished from a ray floret (Figure 177E).

Divided separated to very near the base (Figure 63).

Entire with a continuous margin, not in any way toothed or otherwise indented or divided (Figures 59, 132).

Filament the stalk of the stamen.

Floret a small flower, especially the individual flowers in a flower head of the Composite Family (Figure 177); or the flower plus its two enclosing bracts, the lemma and palea, in the Grass Family [Figure 11D(m)].

Frond the leaf blade of a fern, whether single or much divided (Figure 2).

Fruit a mature ovary with or without associated parts. In the botanical sense, it is not restricted to something sweet and juicy but includes all kinds of berries [Figures 115(f), 154(e)], dry seedpods [Figures 69C, 112B(g), 118(c), 164B (d)], spiny burs [Figures 23C, 158(e)], and single-seeded achenes [Figures 32B(d), 63C(e), 64(c), 183E(d,e)].

Glaucous covered with a powdery whitish substance or bloom that is easily rubbed off.

Haustoria the absorbing organs (often root-like) of parasitic plants (Figure 139).

Hypanthium the floral cup or tube in a flower to which are attached the sepals, petals and stamens.

Inflorescence the flowering portion of a plant.

Internode the part of a stem or rhizome between any two nodes [Figures 11A(b), 25A, 37A(f)].

Involucre one or more whorls of small leaves or bracts immediately underneath a flower, flower cluster or umbel, or surrounding a flower head [Figures 119(a), 177].

Lanceolate lance-shaped; much longer than broad, and narrowed or pointed toward the tip (Figure 56).

Leaf Axil the upper angle between the stalk or blade of a leaf and the stem.

Leaf Sheath the basal portion of a leaf that surrounds the stem, especially in grasses and sedges; the portion of a leaf between the stem node and leaf collar (Figures 3, 25A).

Leaflet one part of a compound leaf [Figures 98(a,b), 102B(a), 113A(c)].

Ligule a flat membrane or band of hair arising from the inner surface of the leaf sheath at its junction with the leaf blade [Figures 3, 22B(b)].

Midrib the main or central rib or large vein of a leaf or leaf-like part; appears to be a continuation of the petiole.

Node the "joint" of a stem or rhizome; that portion of a stem to which the leaf is attached [Figures 3, 11A(a), 25, 33A(a), 33B(a), 128A(j)], and at which axillary buds and branches are produced.

Ocrea a membranous or somewhat leaf-like tube surrounding the stem above each node in the Buckwheat or Smartweed Family [Figures 31B (c), 33A(b), 33B(b)].

Opposite placed two at a node; on opposing sides of a stem, immediately across from each other (Figures 57, 150).

Ovary the lower part of the pistil; it contains the ovules that later become the seeds.

Ovule the tiny structure inside an ovary that develops into a seed after fertilization.

Palmate the arrangement of leaflets, or of lobes, divisions, ribs or veins in a leaf or petal in which all of these units arise from almost the same point, as fingers from the palm of a hand (Figures 117, 184).

Panicle a type of inflorescence that usually has a central axis and many branches that are themselves more or less rebranched (Figures 10C, 18C).

Pappus the specialized calyx of members of the Composite Family; may consist of hairs, plumes, bristles or scales [Figures 226B, 227E(g)].

Parted cut or cleft, but not quite to the midrib or base (Figure 70).

Pedicel stalk of a single flower or of one flower in a cluster.

Peduncle the stalk of a cluster of flowers, or of a flower head (Figure 177).

Perennial a plant that lives through three or more growing seasons. Compare with annual, winter annual, biennial.

Perianth a collective term for the calyx (sepals) plus corolla (petals).

Petiole stalk of one leaf.

Pinnate the arrangement of leaflets, or of lobes, divisions or veins in a leaf or petal in which these units are arranged on each side of an elongated, central axis (Figures 102, 178, 192).

Pistil the female part of a flower, consisting of stigma, style and ovary; it contains the ovules and develops into the fruit which contains the seeds.

Pistillate having one or more pistils but no stamens; female.

Raceme an inflorescence composed of several to many flowers, and later fruits or seedpods, each with a distinct pedicel, arranged along a central axis which continues to elongate throughout the flowering period (Figures 82B, 85). The lower flower blossoms first.

Rachilla the central axis of a spikelet, particularly in the grasses and sedges; the axis to which the florets are attached (Figure 11D).

Rachis the central axis of either a pinnate leaf or of an inflorescence [Figures 11C(k), 95, 96, 102B].

Radical Leaf a leaf that arises from an underground stem (rhizome) and whose petiole emerges directly from the soil surface (Figure 176A).

Ray one of several branches of an umbel or similar inflorescence [Figures 110(a), 128].

Ray Floret the outer florets in the flower head of some members of the Composite Family, as distinguished from a disk floret (Figure 177).

Rhizome an underground stem, usually horizontal [Figures 11A, 37A, 125A(a)].

Rosette a circular cluster, with the parts spreading outward like spokes of a wheel (Figures 70, 82, 207A).

Sepal one of the separate parts of a calyx; usually the outermost part of a flower, and usually (but not always) green.

Septum a membranous partition.

Serrate with sharp teeth that point forward along the margin; one side of each tooth being longer than the other (Figures 92, 145, 182B).

Sessile without a stalk; said of a leaf in which the leaf blade has no petiole but is attached directly to the stem (Figures 59, 85), or of a flower that has virtually no pedicel but appears to be attached directly to the stem (Figures 159, 169).

Silicle the relatively short fruit of certain members of the Mustard Family, usually not more than twice as long as wide (Figures 85, 89).

Silique the relatively long fruit of certain members of the Mustard Family, usually at least four times longer than wide [Figures 69C, 73B(c), 78A (c)].

Sinus a distinct space between two lobes, as on a leaf blade [Figures 70(b), 208A(b)].

Spathe a large bract enclosing an inflorescence, at least when young; may be papery in texture and white or brownish [Figure 28B(b)] or more leaf-like and green, white or highly coloured, as in the woodland wild flower, Jack-in-the-pulpit.

Spike an inflorescence with sessile flowers, and later fruits, arranged along a central axis. The lower flowers blossom first [Figures 11C, 39B(b), 169].

Spikelet the basic unit of a grass or sedge inflorescence (Figures 11D, 24E). It contains the flower(s) and seed(s) that are enclosed by the "chaff" (by the lemma, palea and glumes).

Stalk the "stem" or supporting structure of any organ, as the petiole of a leaf, the peduncle of an inflorescence, the pedicel of a flower, or the filament of a stamen.

Stamen the male or pollen-bearing part of a flower, consisting of an anther and a filament.

Staminate having stamens but not pistils; male.

Stigma the part of the pistil that receives the pollen; usually the uppermost or outermost part of a pistil.

Stipe the stalk of a pistil, between the bottom of the pistil and the top of the receptacle (found inside the flower); not to be confused with the pedicel that occurs below the receptacle to which the petals and sepals are usually attached.

Stipulate having stipules.

Stipule an appendage at the junction of the leaf petiole and stem [(Figures 95(d), 121(b)]; usually occur in pairs, one on each side of the petiole, and may be attached to the petiole or to the node of the stem.

Stolon a horizontal stem at or slightly below the surface of the ground, and gives rise to a new plant at its tip [Figure 216(a)].

Style the more or less elongated part of the pistil between the ovary and the stigma.

Succulent juicy or fleshy, often brittle.

Taproot the primary root; usually larger than the branch roots; and usually present in most annual and biennial plants.

Tendril the slender, twining or clasping structure at the ends of some compound leaves [Figure 102(b)] or coming directly from the stem [Figure 174(a)].

Tetraploid with 4n (4 complete sets of) chromosomes per cell.

Tiller a new or additional shoot arising from the base of the original stem; very common in grasses (Figure 13A); equivalent to a sucker from the base of a tree.

Tuber a thickened, short underground stem or root serving as a storage organ containing reserve food (Figure 128A). The common potato that we eat is a tuber.

Umbel a spherical, rounded or flat-topped inflorescence with the pedicels of the individual flowers, or the peduncles of the umbellets, arising from approximately the same point (Figures 124-131).

Umbellet a secondary umbel [Figures 127B(h), 128B (n)] within a compound umbel [Figures 127B (g), 128B(m)].

Unisexual of one sex; having only stamens or only one or more pistils in each flower (Figures 57C, 183D, 183E).

Whorl three or more leaves or flowers at one node; with the parts encircling the stem and pointing outward like the spokes of a wheel (Figure 51).

Winter Annual a plant that germinates in the fall; usually overwinters in the rosette stage; flowers and sets seed the following spring; and dies in the summer.

HORSETAIL FAMILY (Equisetaceae)

Field horsetail, *Equisetum arvense* L., (Figure 1, Plates 1, 2) [EQUAR, prèle des champs, Horse-pipes, Joint-grass, Mare's-tail, queue-de-renard, prèle commune] Perennial. Never has flowers or seeds but reproduces by spores and by horizontal underground stems **(rhizomes)**. These are dark brown or blackish, spread out for long distances and are often 1 m (3-1/3 ft) below the ground surface. They send up numerous **aboveground shoots** but of two different types at different times of the year. In early spring, the shoots are ashy-gray to light brown, unbranched, hollow, jointed stems (B, Plate 1); each node (joint) surrounded by a toothed (b) sheath (a); and the tip of stem ending in a brownish, spore-producing cone (c). After the cones have shed their spores (early May) these whitish to light brown stems wither and die down. At the same time, the second type of shoot emerges from the ground. These are green, slender, erect, hollow stems (A, Plate 2), leafless but with whorls of 6 to 8 branches at nearly every node; each branch may branch again with whorls of smaller branches; stems and branches surrounded by a small, toothed sheath (d) at each node but never end in a spore-producing cone. Both kinds of stems are easily pulled apart at the nodes and can be fitted back together like sections of a stove pipe.

Field horsetail occurs in all parts of Ontario in depressional areas with poorly drained soils, as well as in sandy or gravelly soils with good drainage such as railroad embankments and roadsides. An intense competitor, it can severely suppress crops and other plants. In addition, it contains a substance which destroys vitamin B in animals. **It is especially poisonous to young horses. Hay containing this weed may be more poisonous than fresh plants in the field.**

It is distinguished by its ashy-gray, unbranched, leafless shoots tipped with brownish, spore-producing cones in early spring, and later, from late spring or early summer onwards, by its whorls of 6 to 8 green, leafless branches and complete absence of flowers.

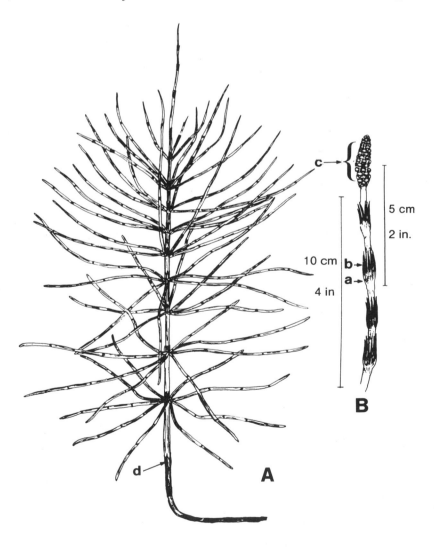

Figure 1. **Field horsetail** A. Vegetative shoot (green). B. Spore-producing reproductive shoot (whitish to light brown).

FERN FAMILY (Polypodiaceae)

Eastern bracken, *Pteridium aquilinum* (L.) Kuhn var. *latiusculum* (Desf.) Underw., (Figure 2, Plates 3, 4) [PTEAL, fougère d'aigle, Bracken, Bracken fern, Brake, Fiddlehead, Pasture-brake, grande fougère, fougère à l'aigle] Perennial. Never has flowers or seeds but reproduces by spores and by shallow or deep, widely spreading, dark brown **underground stems.** Young **leaves** (crosiers) are curled like a fiddlehead as they emerge from the ground. After straightening out, the leaf is compound with 3 main divisions from the tip (a) of the leafstalk (b) and all 3 redivided into numerous smaller divisions. The whole compound leaf may be 30 - 140 cm (1 - 4½ ft) long and 30 - 100 cm (1 - 3-1/3 ft) broad and has a triangular appearance. The leaf usually bends at the tip of the erect leafstalk, so that the 3 major divisions of the leaf are held more or less parallel to the ground surface. After midsummer, brown **spores** are produced in dense bands on the undersides of many of the leaf segments (B), but may be partly hidden at first by the inrolled leaf margins (c).

Eastern bracken occurs throughout central, eastern, northern and northwestern Ontario in many soil types ranging from moist to dry situations, but usually near or under open woods. **Leaves of Eastern bracken are poisonous to livestock both when fresh and dry in hay.** Its poisonous properties are complex, including an interference with vitamin B (like Field horsetail page 19). Recent evidence has indicated that leaves of Eastern bracken will produce certain types of cancer in cattle and in laboratory animals. **The practice by some people of eating young crosiers of this fern in early spring as a "wild asparagus" should be strongly discouraged.**

It is distinguished by its bare, erect leafstalk at the tip of which the 3-parted compound leaf is held more or less parallel to the ground surface.

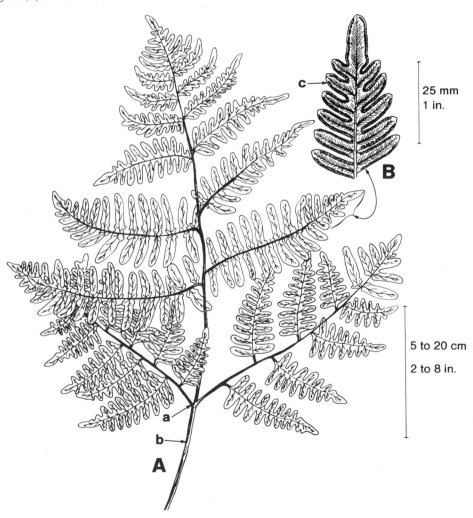

Figure 2. **Eastern bracken** A. Leaf (frond). B. Underside of portion of leaf showing spore-producing area along margins.

GRASS FAMILY (Gramineae)

Many kinds of grasses grow in places where, for one reason or another, they are not wanted. Space permits inclusion of only the more important weedy kinds in Ontario. Identification of a grass is usually easy with a good specimen. A good specimen includes all the parts: root, stem, leaves and inflorescence (the seed-producing "head"). But farmers and others often have to identify grasses in very young stages, long before the head emerges. Fortunately, this is also possible as most grasses have distinctive "leaf-base" characteristics, just as individual people have distinctive fingerprints. Leaf-base features can be seen with the naked eye or with an inexpensive hand magnifying glass. The chief stem and leaf-base characteristics of a typical grass are illustrated in Figure 3 and Plate 15.

The general public tends to confuse grasses and sedges but they can be readily distinguished by comparing the features illustrated in Figure 3 for a typical grass with those in Figure 25 A and B for a typical sedge. In grasses the **stem** is usually round but may also be somewhat flattened, whereas in sedges it is usually triangular in cross-section. In grasses the leaf sheath is usually split for at least part of its length, and there is almost always a membranous or hairy ligule, whereas in sedges the leaf sheath is closed except for a small V-shaped notch and there is no ligule.

The grass leaf has two major parts: the **leaf blade** which sticks out at an angle from the stem, and the **leaf sheath** which is more or less tightly wrapped around the stem and is the connecting part between the leaf blade and the **node** or joint of the stem (culm). Leaf-base characteristics are at the junction of leaf blade and leaf sheath. The **ligule** is right next to the stem where the leaf blade joins the sheath. It sticks upwards from the inside of the sheath, and may be a very thin, soft, erect membrane of white tissue, or a dense row of short, fine hair like an eyelash. It is most easily seen when one grasps the leaf blade close to the stem and gently pulls both the blade and sheath away from the stem. Nearly all grasses have a ligule of some kind. One or 2 **auricles** may also be present on some grasses. Auricles are small soft claws or points of tissue which stick out (Plate 15) from the uppermost margins of the leaf sheath and clasp the stem on the side opposite the leaf blade.

In the following pages, the illustrations and descriptions of weedy grasses include characteristics which are useful for identifying both young and old plants.

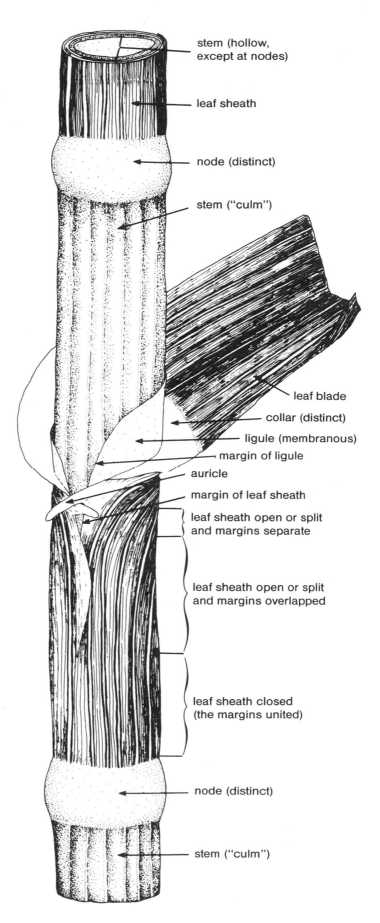

stem (hollow, except at nodes)

leaf sheath

node (distinct)

stem ("culm")

leaf blade

collar (distinct)

ligule (membranous)

margin of ligule

auricle

margin of leaf sheath

leaf sheath open or split and margins separate

leaf sheath open or split and margins overlapped

leaf sheath closed (the margins united)

node (distinct)

stem ("culm")

Figure 3.   Stem and leaf-base characteristics of a typical grass.

Smooth brome, *Bromus inermis* Leyss., (Figure 4) [BROIN, brome inerme, Brome grass, brome] Perennial spreading by seed and by dark-coloured underground stems (**rhizomes**). These have nodes or joints (a) and internodes (b), and blunt tips (c). They produce roots and branches from the nodes. Some branches turn upwards to emerge as leafy stems. Others remain underground producing still more branches. Each internode (b) is covered by a large brown to blackish, dry, scaly sheath giving the whole rhizome a dark colour. **Stems** erect, 20 - 100 cm (8 - 40 in.) tall, leafy. **Leaves** 10 - 40 cm (4 - 16 in.) long, pointed, flat, 5 - 12 mm (1/5 - ½ in.) wide, and usually marked with a light green or wrinkled "tatoo" resembling the letter W near the middle of the blade; **leaf sheath** closed (d) (margins united) except for a small V-shaped notch (e) at the top; **ligule** (f) a membrane 1 - 2 mm (1/25 - 1/12 in.) long; **auricles** absent or very short (g) and rounded. **Inflorescence** or "seed head" is a branched panicle, 10 - 20 cm (4 - 8 in.) long, the stiff branches spreading when pollinating but afterwards more erect and tighter. Each **spikelet** (h) 2 - 2.5 cm (4/5 - 1 in.) long, without awns (hence the name "smooth"), or with awns (j) not over 2 mm (1/12 in.) long, and 5 to 9 flowered (having 5 to 9 fertile **florets** which become the individual "seeds"). Flowers from June to September.

Smooth brome is widely cultivated as an excellent hay and pasture grass, and as a soil binder along roadsides, eroded banks, etc., throughout Ontario. But it often persists after cultivation and may infest succeeding crops, gardens and lawns. Old stands may become sod-bound, producing many short, leafy stems but few or no seed heads.

It is distinguished by the letter W on some leaf blades, its closed leaf sheath (d), the absence of distinct auricles (compare (g) in Figures 4B and C with (g) in Figure 11B), its blunt-tipped rhizomes (c) with dark brown scaly sheaths as long as or longer than each internode (b) (compare with Quack grass, Figure 11A), and its branched, erect panicle with fairly large smooth spikelets.

Figure 4. **Smooth brome** A. Plant. B. Leaf-base of a lower leaf. C. Leaf-base of an upper leaf. D. Panicle.

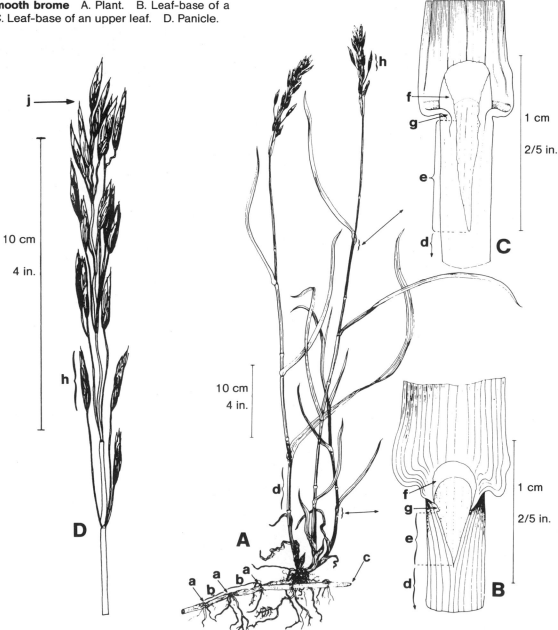

Chess, *Bromus secalinus* L., (Figure 5) [BROSE, brome des seigles, Cheat, brome sécalin] Annual or winter annual, reproducing only by seed. **Stems** 30 - 90 cm (1 - 3 ft) tall, single or 3 to 4 stems from 1 root crown; **roots** fibrous. Stems smooth but finely hairy on the nodes (a) hairiness visible with magnification; **leaves** 3 - 9 mm (⅛ - ⅜ in.) wide, either smooth or softly hairy (b) on either or both surfaces; **leaf sheaths** smooth or lower ones hairy; leaf sheaths of lower leaves closed (margins united) nearly to the top (c); upper leaf sheaths split with margins (d) overlapping or separate; **ligule** (e) membranous, 1 -2 mm (1/25 - 1/12 in.) long. No **auricles. Inflorescence** a panicle with rather stiff, nearly erect branches; **spikelets** (f) have a firm, plump appearance 1 - 3 cm (2/5 - 1-1/5 in.) long, 6 - 10 mm (¼ - 2/5 in.) wide, hairless and awnless or with short awns (g) usually less than 2 mm (1/12 in.) long, each spikelet having 5 to 15 **florets** ("seeds") (h). Flowers from June to August.

Chess occurs in fields and waste places throughout the agricultural areas of Ontario but is more common in the southern and eastern counties.

It is distinguished by its annual habit, its firm, plump spikelets, its smooth stems with finely hairy nodes, and the combination of lower leaf sheaths closed and upper ones split with overlapping margins.

Figure 5.   **Chess**   A. Plant.   B. Leaf-base of a lower leaf.
C. Leaf-base of an upper leaf.   D. Panicle.

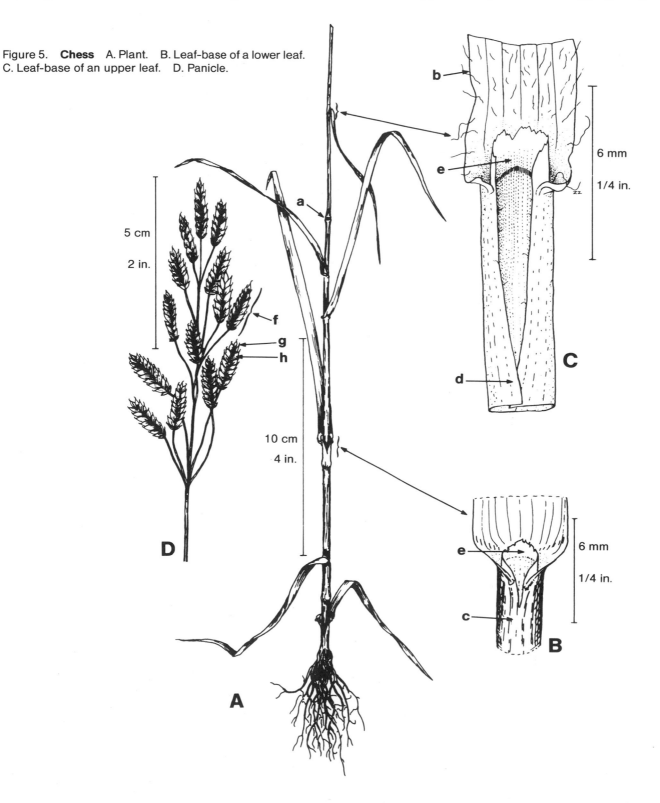

Upright brome, *Bromus racemosus* L., (Figure 6) [BRORA, brome dressé, brome en grappe] Annual, reproducing only by seed. **Stems** erect, 30 - 100 cm (12 - 40 in.) tall; **leaves** hairy; lower **leaf sheaths** velvety with short, downward-pointing hair; upper leaf sheaths and bare stems above the leaves rough with extremely short, downward-pointing hair (a); leaf sheaths closed (margins united), lower ones with a small V-shaped notch (b), upper with a notch as long as 1 - 5 cm (2/5 - 2 in.) (B) and may have overlapping margins; **ligule** (c) membranous, 0.3 - 1.5 mm (1/75 - 1/16 in.) long; no **auricles.** Branches of **panicle** short and stiffly erect (hence the name "upright"); **spikelets** (d) 12-22 mm (½ - ⅞ in.) long not including the awns (e) which add another 5 - 8 mm (1/5 - 1/3 in.) to their length, 4 - 7 mm (1/6 - ¼ in.) wide; 4 to 10 **florets** ("seeds") (f) per spikelet. Flowers from June to July.

Upright brome occurs in grainfields and waste places, mainly in south central and southwestern Ontario.

It is distinguished from Chess by its rough stems, its hairy leaves and its prominently awned spikelets, and from Downy brome by its thicker spikelets with much shorter awns.

Figure 6. **Upright brome** A. Plant. B. Leaf-base of an upper leaf. C. Panicle.

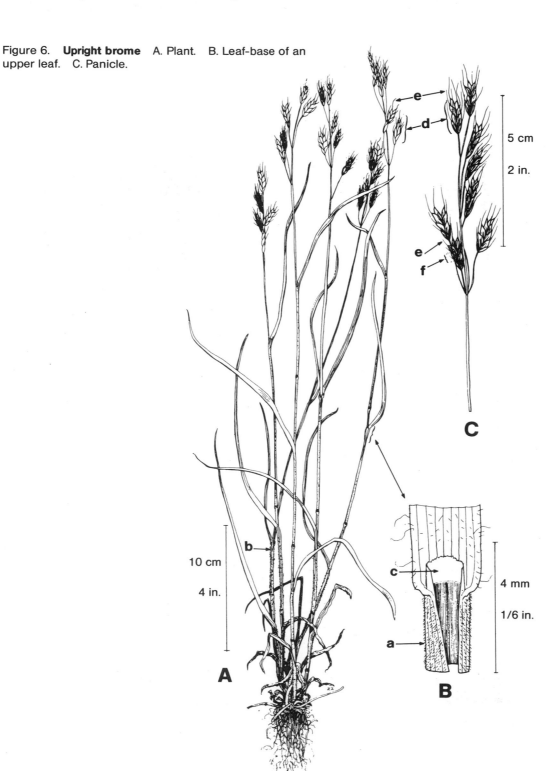

24

Downy brome, *Bromus tectorum* L., (Figure 7) [BROTE, brome des toits, Cheat, Cheat grass, Cheat grass brome, Downy chess, Slender chess] Annual or winter annual, reproducing only by seed. **Stems** 20 - 60 cm (8 - 24 in.) tall and slender, but may be only 5 cm (2 in.) in dry gravelly situations; stems, **leaves** and leaf sheaths densely and softly hairy; leaf sheaths of lower leaves closed (margins united) nearly to the top (as in Figure 5B), middle and upper leaf sheaths progressively more split with margins separate (a) or overlapping; **ligule** (b) membranous, 3 mm (⅛ in.) long, its margin frequently lacerated or irregularly torn; no **auricles**; **panicle** 7 - 20 cm (3 - 8 in.) long with many soft, slender, drooping to partly erect branches; **spikelets** (C), including awns (e) 2 - 4 cm (4/5 - 1-3/5 in.) long, and having 2 to 7 **florets** ("seeds") (d). Young plants are bright green but stems, leaves and inflorescence often turn pinkish to purplish-brown with age. On mature and dry plants, the awns become quite stiff and spreading, and the hairy leaves rather harsh. Flowers from May to July.

Downy brome occurs throughout southern Ontario, especially on sandy or gravelly soils, in poor pastures, roadsides, embankments, beaches and waste places.

It is distinguished from Smooth brome, Chess and Upright brome by its hairy texture and its thin, long-awned spikelets.

Figure 7. **Downy brome** A. Plant. B. Leaf-base. C. Spikelet with 2 developed florets.

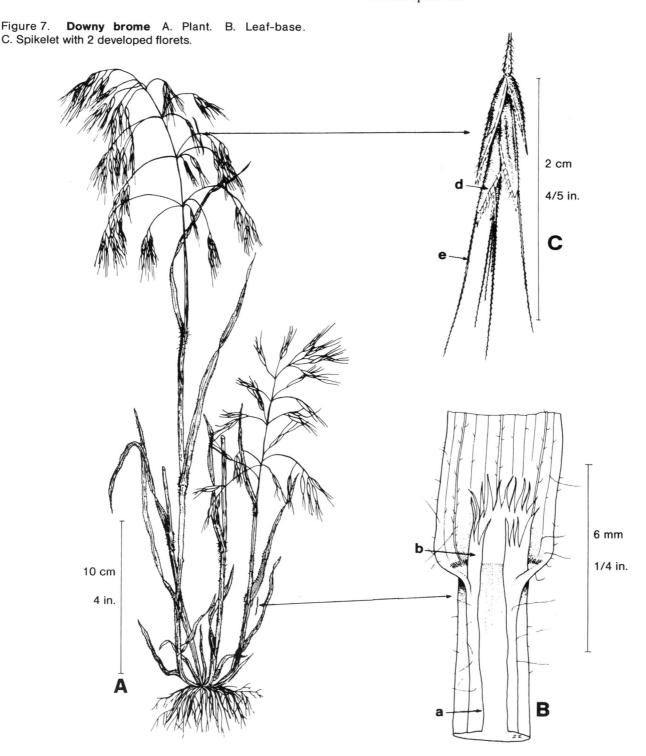

Stink grass, *Eragrostis cilianensis* (All.) Lutati, (Figure 8) [ERAME, éragrostide, fétide, Love grass, Stinking love grass, éragrostide à forte odeur, *E. megastachya* (Koel.) Link] Annual, reproducing only by seed. **Stems** 10 - 50 cm (4 - 20 in.) long, tufted, outer stems of a bunch often lying on the ground and rooting at the nodes (a) but with upturned tips; **leaves** hairless, flat, 3 - 10 mm (⅛ - ⅜ in.) wide; **leaf sheaths** split, the margins overlapping, not hairy except for a tuft of short (1 - 3 mm, 1/25 - 1/8 in.) hair (b) on either side at the junction of blade and sheath; **ligule** a band of hairs about .5 mm (1/50 in.) high; no **auricles** but the tufts of hairs (b) on each side of the collar might be mistaken for auricles; tiny **glands** (c) present on leaf margins, sheaths, and in a ring (d) encircling the stem just below each node (e). **Inflorescence**, dark gray-green to light brownish, branching but either dense and compact (f) or open and spreading (g), both kinds often on the same plant; **spikelets** (h) small, oblong, 5 - 15 mm (1/5 - 3/5 in.) long, 3 mm (⅛ in.) wide but

having 10 to 40 florets; each **floret** about 2.5 mm (1/10 in.) containing a single, tiny, yellowish to reddish-orange, egg-shaped kernel ("seed") about 0.7 mm (1/30 in.) long. Fresh plants have a distinct odour which many people find disagreeable. Flowers from August to September.

Stink grass occurs in coarse sandy or gravelly soils in edges of fields, waste areas, right-of-way throughout southern Ontario, being most common in central and southwestern areas. Introduced from Europe.

It is distinguished by its tufted habit, its gray-green to light brownish inflorescences that may be both compact and loose on the same plant, and its small, compact, many-floreted spikelets that readily shed their tiny yellowish to orange kernels at maturity.

Tufted love grass, *Eragrostis pectinacea* (Michx.) Nees, (not illustrated) [ERAPE, éragrostide pectinée, éragrostis pectiné] Has a similar growth form but is smaller, with finer **leaves** and **stems**, a more open branching **panicle** with smaller **spikelets**, and lacks the glands which are so characteristic of Stink grass. Its leaf-base characteristics (ligule, no auricles, and tufts of hairs on each side of the collar) are almost identical to those of Stink grass (B), differing only by the absence of glands (c) on the margins of its leaves. This native plant is found throughout southern Ontario in coarse soils along beaches, rights-of-way, and disturbed areas, and occasionally between patio stones and bricks of walkways.

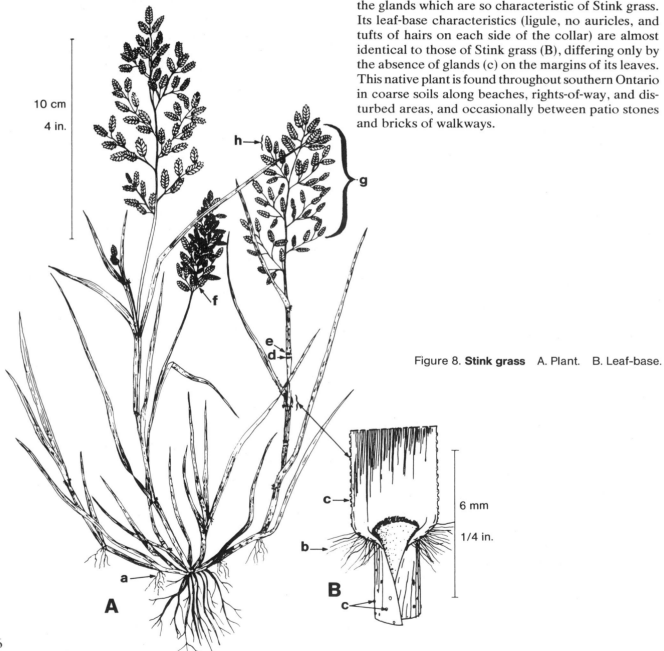

Figure 8. **Stink grass**   A. Plant.   B. Leaf-base.

26

Common reed, *Phragmites australis* (Cav.) Trin. ex Streud., (Figure 9), [PHRCO, phragmite commun, jonc à balais, roseau commun, *P. communis* Trin.] Perennial, reproducing by rhizomes and rarely by seed. **Stems** smooth, erect, thick (to 10 mm, 2/5 in. in diameter), almost woody, sometimes purplish, up to 4 m (13 ft) high, arising from long, firm, extensively creeping rhizomes; **leaf sheaths** smooth and hairless with apparently smooth, often purple margins that may overlap or be separate, the margins ciliate with very fine hairs seen only with magnification; collar (junction between leaf sheath and leaf blade) (a) yellowish-green with wrinkled edges, and forming prominent (almost 1 mm, 1/25 in. high) auricle-like shoulders (b) where its edges join the margins of the

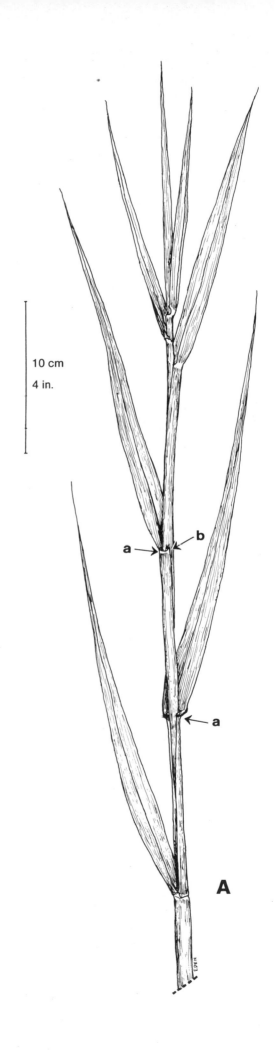

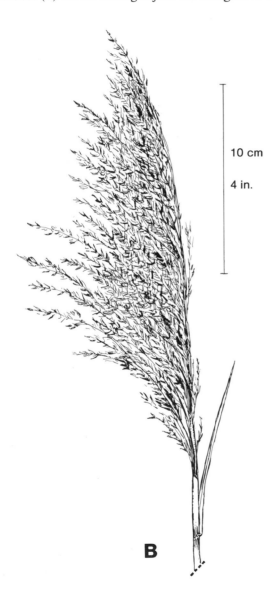

10 cm
4 in.

Figure 9. **Common reed** A. Upper portion of stem with leaves, before flowering. B. "Flag-like" or "plume-like" inflorescence. (Cont'd.)

sheath; **ligule** complex, a very short (0.2 mm, 1/100 in.) yellowish or purplish membrane (c) topped by a dense band of very short white hairs (d) about 0.5 mm (1/50 in.) long together with a single line of very long, relatively firm hairs (e) about 5 - 15 mm (1/5 - 3/5 in.) long (C,D); most of these long hairs soon falling off leaving only a band of short hairs on ligules of older leaves (E); and the tuft of medium length, straight or kinky hairs (f) arising from the margin of the collar each side of the leaf blade; **leaf blades** flat and smooth, 5 - 60 cm (2 - 24 in.) long and 0.3 - 6 cm (⅛ - 2½ in.) wide, very tapered at the tips; **inflorescence** at first purplish, becoming tawny and nearly dark brown at maturity, 12 - 40 cm (4½ - 16 in.) long with ascending branches and forming a thick, densely branched, silky panicle; **spikelets** 10 - 17 mm (2/5 - ¾ in.) long, each with 3 - 7 seeds; hairs of the rachilla long and white, their abundance giving the whole inflorescence its silky appearance. Flowers from August to September.

Common reed occurs both as a native plant distributed widely throughout temperate North America and as a very closely related variety introduced from Europe. It is found in fresh to alkaline marshes, lakeshores, pond margins, ditches, roadsides and fields throughout most of Ontario. The rhizomes are easily spread from place to place by farm and road machinery, and once established, the plant spreads rapidly by these rhizomes.

It is distinguished by its great height, its stiffly erect, unbranched stems, its large, soft panicles that are purplish when first headed-out but become feathery and turn brownish with age, and by the very dense patches that it forms wherever it grows.

Common reed is occasionally confused with **Johnson grass** (page 45), or with the ornamental grass **Eulalia**, *Miscanthus sinensis* Anderss., (Plate 5) [MISSI], both of which are tall perennials with spreading rhizomes. It is distinguished from them by its purplish to brownish, feathery-hairy **inflorescence** [tan coloured but not feathery in Johnson grass (Figure 24D), or feathery-hairy but white to silvery in Eulalia (Plate 5)]; by its very fine, almost hair-like **seeds** (longer, plump and hard in Johnson grass [Figure 24F (g)], or thin with a membranous covering and usually enclosed in silky-hairy chaff in Eulalia); and by its **complex leaf-base** with tufts of hairs (f) on each side of the collar and the very long ligule hairs (e) that soon fall off leaving only a band of very short hairs (d) on an even shorter membranous base (c) [ligule only membranous and 2 - 5 mm (1/12 - 1/5 in.) long in Johnson grass, or, in Eulalia, although it has a similar band of short hairs (about 2 mm, 1/12 in. long) on a very short membrane, it does not have the very long hairs that are present in ligules of young leaves of Common reed].

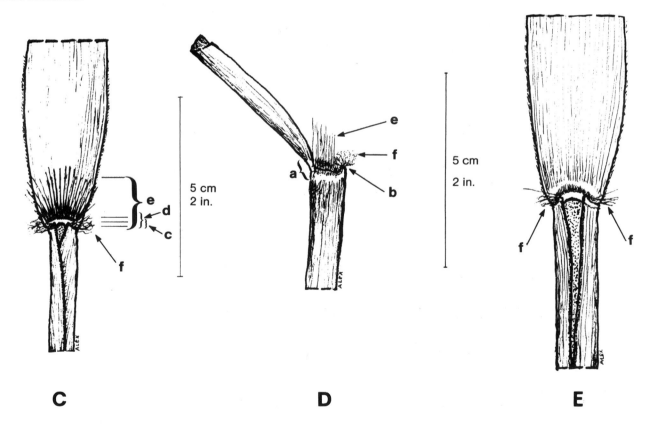

C   D   E

Figure 9. **Common reed** (Cont'd.) C. Leaf-base of young leaf; front view. D. Leaf-base of young leaf with leaf blade pulled back to show long hairs on ligule; side view. E. Leaf-base of older leaf showing long hairs gone from ligule; front view.

Wild oats, *Avena fatua* L., (Figure 10, Plate 6) [AVEFA, folle avoine, Black oats, avoine folle, avoine sauvage] Annual, reproducing only by seed. Very similar to cultivated oats. **Stems** 60 - 120 cm (2 - 4 ft) high, with distinct dark-coloured nodes; **leaves** flat, 10 - 60 cm (4 - 24 in.) long, often 15 mm (3/5 in.) wide or wider, tapered to a long thin point, and with a prominent, light-coloured midrib; **leaf sheath** without hair or slightly hairy, split, with margins transparent (a) and overlapping in the lower 2/3 of each leaf sheath; **ligule** (b) membranous 2 - 5 mm (1/12 - 1/5 in.) long; occasionally with a few prominent hairs (c) on the margins of the **collar**; no **auricles**; **inflorescence** a large panicle with slender branches; **spikelets** (d) with 2 large papery glumes (e) and usually 2 to 4 **florets** ("seeds") (f, D); florets varying from dull white through yellow or gray to brown or nearly black, usually hairy but sometimes nearly smooth, with a sharp-pointed sucker mouth (g) at the lower end and a long (3 - 4 cm, 1¼ - 1-5/8 in.), bent, twisted awn (h). Flowers from June to August.

Figure 10. **Wild oats** A. Base of plant. B. Leaf-base. (Cont'd.)

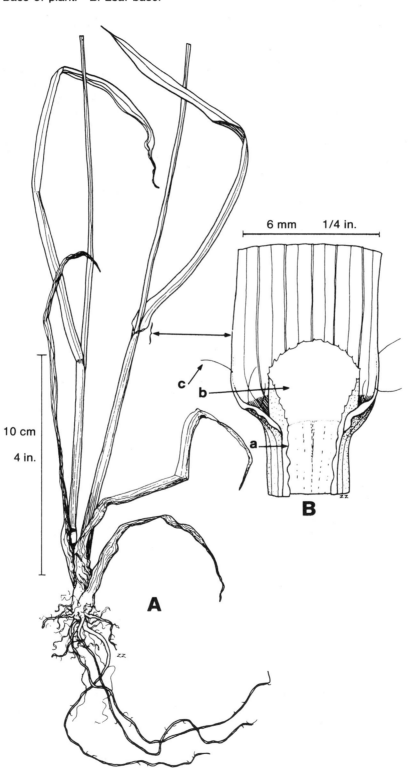

29

Wild oats occurs in cultivated land on all soil textures throughout Ontario and seems to be increasing. This is one of the most serious weeds in Canada in terms of its competition with annual grain crops.

It is distinguished from tame or cultivated oats by its frequently taller growth, its somewhat yellowish-green inflorescence when compared to the light bluish-green of cultivated oats, and its hairy, dark-coloured, sharp-pointed "seed" having a long, twisted, black awn whereas the seed of cultivated oats is hairless, always a tawny white, lacks a sharp point, and is either without an awn or with a very short straight awn. The seeds of Wild oats shatter very readily when ripe but their germination is delayed, often for several years, in the ground. Cultivated oats normally does not shatter after ripening and its seeds are able to germinate as soon as mature. Some plants of oats have characteristics which are intermediate between the wild and cultivated kinds. These have been called "False wild oats" and "Dormoats" and may be hybrids between the two types.

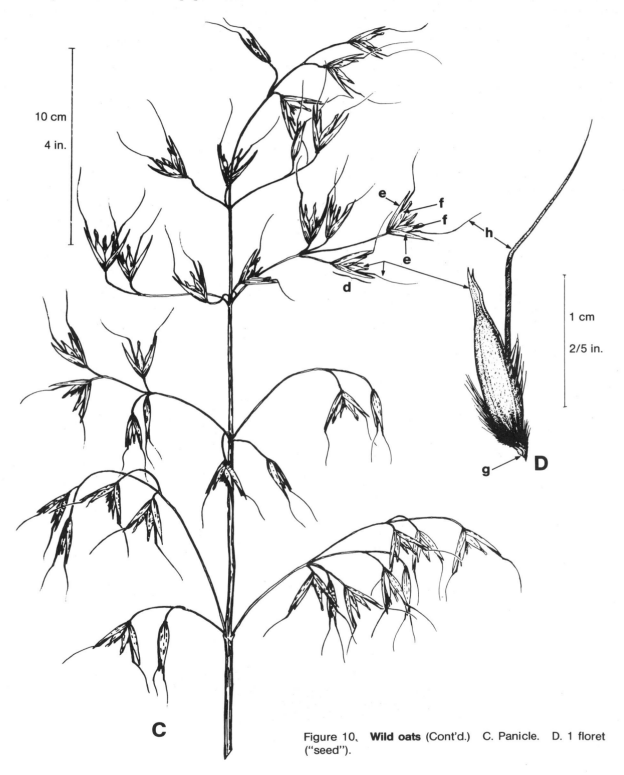

10 cm
4 in.

1 cm
2/5 in.

C

Figure 10. **Wild oats** (Cont'd.) C. Panicle. D. 1 floret ("seed").

Quack grass, *Agropyron repens* (L.) Beauv., (Figure 11, Plate 7) [AGGRE, chiendent, Couch grass, Quitch grass, Scutch grass, Twitch, Twitch grass, chiendent rampant, agropyron rampant, *Elytrigia repens* (L.) Nevski, *Elymus repens* (L.) Gould] Perennial, spreading by seed and by light-coloured underground stems (rhizomes). **Rhizomes** have nodes or joints (a) and internodes (b), and hard, white, very sharp-pointed tips (c). They produce roots and branches from the nodes. Some branches turn upwards to emerge as leafy stems. Others continue growing and branching horizontally and expand the patch. Each internode is partly covered by a short, light brown, dry, scaly sheath (d). **Stems** erect, 30 - 120 cm (1 - 4 ft) tall, either not flowering during the whole growing season (A) or producing a slender, unbranched **inflorescence** called a spike (C); stem nodes (joints) (e) distinct and often purplish. **Leaves** flat, nearly smooth; lower **leaf sheaths** hairy, upper ones often smooth, sheaths split with margins overlapping (f);

auricles (g) present and clasping the stem like little hooks (Plate 7B). **Spike** (seed head) with 1 (rarely 2) unstalked spikelet (h, D) at each node or joint (j); **spikelets** alternating from one side of the rachis (central stalk of the spike) (k) to the other, and with their flat or broad side towards the rachis; each spikelet made up of 3 to 7 **florets** ("seeds") (m) side by side between 2 outer glumes (empty chaff) (n), and either with short awns (bristles) (p) or awnless (as in D). Flowers from June to September.

Quack grass occurs in cultivated fields, pastureland, waste places, rights-of-way, lawns and gardens in almost any soil texture throughout Ontario. This is the most troublesome perennial weedy grass in Ontario and throughout Canada.

It is distinguished from Smooth brome by its slender, unbranched seed head (spike) (C), the presence of auricles (g), its split sheath (f), and its sharp-pointed (c) light-coloured rhizomes with short scaly sheaths (d).

Figure 11. **Quack grass** A. Non-flowering plant. B. Leaf-base. C. Spike. D. 1 Spikelet.

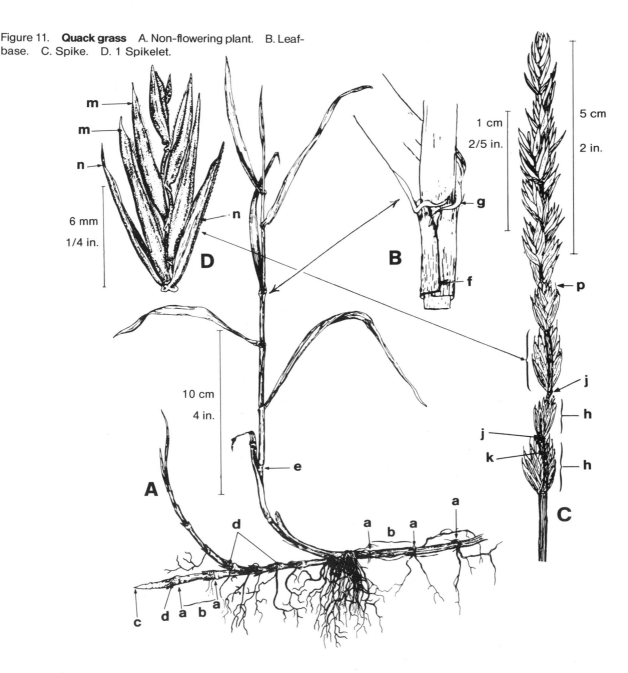

Canada wild rye, *Elymus canadensis* L., (not illustrated, see lettered arrows in Figures 11C and 11D for similar structures) [ELYCA, elyme du Canada, seigle sauvage]. Has **stems** and **heads** about the same size and height as Quack grass but it grows as a bunch grass (does not spread by rhizomes) and its spike has usually 2 or 3 **spikelets** (clusters of "seeds") (Figure 11D) at each node (j) instead of only 1. **Perennial rye grass,** *Lolium perenne* L., [LOLPE, ivraie vivace, Perennial ray grass, ray-grass anglais] and **Persian darnel,** *Lolium persicum* Bois and Hoh., [LOLPS, ivraie de Perse] (both not illustrated, see lettered arrows in Figures 11C and 11D for similar structures), also have spike **inflorescences** but they have only 1 spikelet (h) at each node (j) and these single spikelets are arranged edgewise to the rachis (k), have only 1 outer glume (empty chaff) (n), and give the whole spike a very flat appearance. Persian darnel is annual while Perennial rye grass is a short-lived perennial, and both are usually shorter than Quack grass.

Foxtail barley, *Hordeum jubatum* L., (Figure 12, Plate 8) [HORJU, orgequeue d'écureuil, Foxtail, Skunk grass, Skunktail, Squirreltail, Wild barley, orge agréable, queue-d'écureuil, orge sauvage] Annual, biennial or usually a short-lived perennial, reproducing only by seed. **Stems** 20 - 60 cm (8 in. - 2 ft) high, erect or spreading as a bunch grass from a mass of fibrous **roots**; stems smooth or slightly rough below; **leaves** bluish-green to grayish-green, 1.5 - 4 mm (1/16 - 1/6 in.) wide, prominently ribbed and rough on the back; **leaf sheath** split (a) with overlapping margins; **ligule** (b) very short, less than 1 mm (1/25 in.) long; **auricles** (c) usually absent but occasionally 1 or 2 present; **inflorescence** (seed head) a dense, unbranched, barley-like spike, 5 - 12 cm (2 - 5 in.) long, with finely barbed, long, green or purplish awns (d), erect or nodding slightly to one side; turning yellowish or straw-coloured when mature and breaking apart into separate seed-bearing units; each unit having a very sharp point and 7 long, spreading awns. These may be blown by the wind or carried in animal fur, clothing, etc. Flowers from June to October.

When animals walk through or graze in areas containing mature Foxtail barley or eat hay contaminated with the ripe heads of this weed the sharp-pointed, bristly segments may get into their hair, mouth, nose or eyes. Because these bristles have tiny, forward-pointing barbs, they will only slide in one direction. Motion of the animal's body forces these sharp-pointed segments deeper into the skin causing skin sores, irritation of back of mouth and nasal passages, and sometimes blindness.

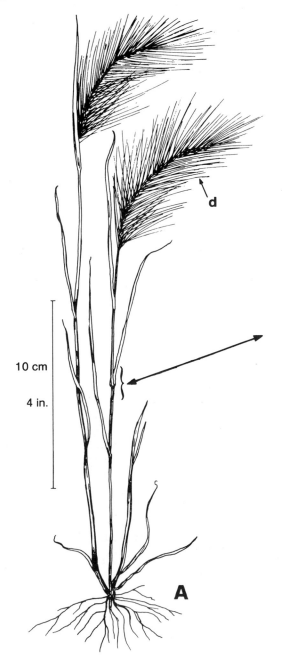

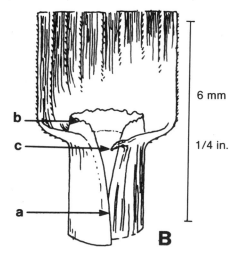

Foxtail barley is a native grass throughout Canada, chiefly in moist or saline depressions, but it also occurs in cultivated fields, roadsides, waste areas and lawns.

Before heading out, it is distinguished by its bluish to grayish-green colour, its split sheath (a) and its short ligule (b) and by the presence of a very short auricle on some plants. After heading out, the dense 1-sided "foxtail" inflorescence with its long, green or purplish awns is unmistakable.

Figure 12. **Foxtail barley** A. Plant. B. Leaf-base.

Silky bent grass, *Agrostis spica-venti* L., (Figure 13, Plate 9) [APESV, agrostide jouet-du-vent, Loose silky bent grass, Wind grass, *Apera spica-venti* (L.) Beauv.] Winter annual or annual, reproducing only by seed. **Stems** erect to a height of 150 cm (60 in.), unbranched, but usually with several tillers from the base; **leaf sheaths** smooth with separate, membranous margins (a); **ligule** (b) membranous 2 - 14 mm (1/12 - 1/2 in.), short and pointed in very young plants but lengthening with age, becoming rather firm and the tip somewhat torn or toothed, its margins continuous with the membranous margins of the sheath; no **auricles**; **leaf blades** long (up to 30 cm, 12 in.), flat, 0.5 - 6 mm (1/50 - 1/4 in.) wide, gradually tapering towards the tip; stem nodes (c) distinctly darker than stem or leaf sheaths; **panicle** at first narrow and dense (d), becoming open and loosely branched (C), up to 35 cm (14 in.) long and 25 cm (10 in.) wide, with numerous fine branches each ending in a single **spikelet** (e) 1.5 - 3.2 mm (1/16 - 1/8 in.) long; the whole inflorescence conspicuously reddish at maturity; each spikelet containing a single floret ("**seed**") with a slender awn (f) 4 - 9 mm (1/6 - 3/8 in.) long; seed without its awn is about 1.6 mm (1/15 in.) long. Flowers from June to August.

Originally introduced from Europe, Silky bent grass is a common weed in fields of winter wheat and fall rye on sandy soils in the "tobacco belt" of southwestern Ontario. It also occurs in ditches and other non-cultivated areas.

It is distinguished from other common annual grasses by its winter annual habit, its slender stems and leaves with long, 1-several-pointed, membranous ligules, its loose, open, reddish, mature inflorescence, and the short, straight awn on each seed.

Interrupted silky bent grass, *Agrostis interrupta* L., (not illustrated) [APEIN, *Apera interrupta* (L.) Beauv.], is a closely related species that is distinguished from Silky bent grass by its usually much shorter stature (about 15 - 75 cm, 6 - 30 in. high), its short, compact inflorescence with its very short, lateral branches usually not much larger than the unexpanded inflorescence of Silky bent grass, (d) in Figure 13B, its spikelets with longer awns (usually 8 - 12 mm, 1/3 - 1/2 in. long) and the absence or near-absence of reddish colour in the inflorescence at maturity. It is an occasional weed in commercial turf farms in Ontario where it rarely gets more than 15 cm (6 in.) high. It also may be found in winter wheat and other fall-sown crops.

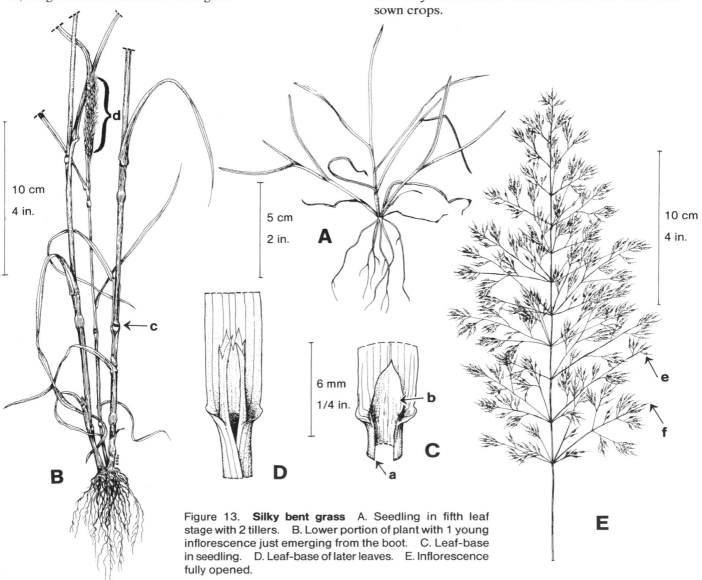

Figure 13. **Silky bent grass** A. Seedling in fifth leaf stage with 2 tillers. B. Lower portion of plant with 1 young inflorescence just emerging from the boot. C. Leaf-base in seedling. D. Leaf-base of later leaves. E. Inflorescence fully opened.

33

Wire-stemmed muhly, *Muhlenbergia frondosa* (Poir.) Fern., (Figure 14) [MUHFR, muhlenbergie feuillée] Perennial, reproducing by seed and by rhizomes. **Rhizomes** usually in a tangled mass at or just below the soil surface and consisting of many short, scaly, much branched, beige to pink or purplish, brittle segments (a); **stems** slender, wiry, up to 100 cm (40 in.) long, varying from upright to nearly prostrate, usually much branched and bushy in aspect, smooth; exposed stem internodes yellowish-green above each node and grading upward (b) to pinkish-purple below the next node (c); **leaf sheaths** (d) green, smooth, shorter than the stem internodes, with separate margins (e) that open and expose the internodes of the stem; **ligule** (f) membranous, its outer margin ragged, 0.5 mm (1/50 in.) long; no **auricles**; **leaf blades** rather thin, 2.5 - 15 cm (1 - 6 in.) long and 2 - 8 mm (1/12 - 1/3 in.) wide, tapering to a long, thin point; **inflores-**

cence of small, soft, somewhat silky **panicles** (g), these at first green, then becoming greenish-purple to purple at maturity, very numerous, being produced at the ends of stems and from most leaf axils, each with clusters of crowded spikelets; **spikelets** (h) soft, hairy, 2 - 3.3 mm (1/12 - ⅛ in.) long, each spikelet with 1 floret and an awn (i) 4-12 mm (1/10 - ½ in.) long or awnless. Flowers from July to September.

Wire-stemmed muhly is a native plant found in southern and eastern Ontario in moist, rich soil in woods, thickets, shores, banks and flood plains, from which it has spread into cultivated fields, roadsides and waste places.

It is distinguished by its tangled mass of beige-purple, scaly rhizomes, its slender somewhat purplish stems and its numerous compact inflorescences from upper leaf axils as well as ends of stems.

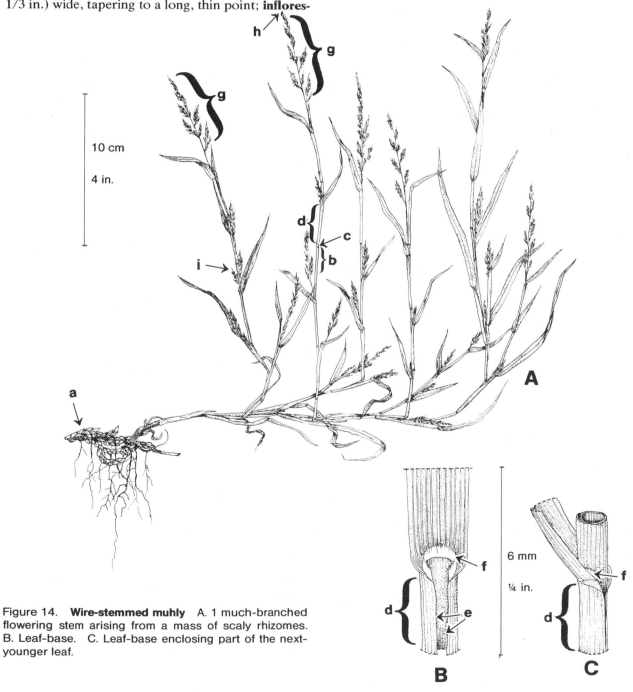

Figure 14. **Wire-stemmed muhly** A. 1 much-branched flowering stem arising from a mass of scaly rhizomes. B. Leaf-base. C. Leaf-base enclosing part of the next-younger leaf.

Rice cut grass, *Leersia oryzoides* (L.) Sw., (Figure 15) [LEROR, léersie faux-riz, Cut grass, Saw grass, léersie à fleurs de riz, léersie à feuilles de riz] Perennial, reproducing only by seed. **Stems** 1 to several from a small, hard crown with a small cluster of slightly thickened or spongy **roots** (a), especially when growing in wet soil. **Stems** 90 - 150 cm (3 - 5 ft) long, weak, at first upright but later bending or falling over, light green to straw-coloured, smooth except for a narrow band of hair encircling each node (b); **leaves** few, widely spaced on the longer stems; **leaf blades** 5 - 25 cm (2 - 10 in.) long, 6 - 15 mm (¼ - 3/5 in.) wide, tapering gradually to a long, thin point, bright green with a lighter green midrib; larger veins and margins of leaf blades usually with a mixture of short hair (about 1 mm, 1/25 in. long) and much shorter, extremely sharp, backward-pointing barbs (c); **leaf sheath** split and usually not overlapping (B, d); **ligule** (e) mem-

branous, short, flat-topped; no **auricles**; **inflorescence** a much-branched panicle (f), pale yellowish-green, with stalkless spikelets (g, C) along each branch; each **spikelet** having no glumes but consisting only of a single **floret** or "seed." Flowers from August to September.

Rice cut grass occurs only in southern Ontario. A native plant of swampy shores and streambanks, this plant is spreading along irrigation channels and drainage ditches which become clogged by its tangled stems; it is also spreading along moist roadside ditches and to farms, meadows and stock watering ponds.

It is distinguished by its bright green leaves with extremely sharp, backward-pointing barbs (c) which can cut or tear the skin of farm animals and humans alike (hence the common name "cut grass") and its pale yellowish-green, much-branched inflorescence, with single-seeded spikelets.

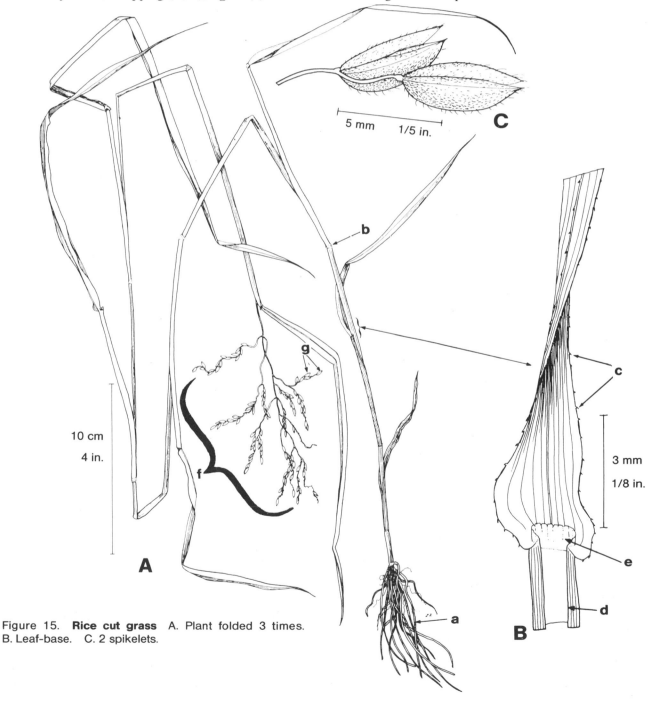

Figure 15. **Rice cut grass** A. Plant folded 3 times. B. Leaf-base. C. 2 spikelets.

35

Large crab grass, *Digitaria sanguinalis* (L.) Scop., (Figure 16, A-D, Plate 10) [DIGSA, digitaire sanguine, Finger grass, Hairy crab grass, digitaire pourpre, panic sanguin] Annual, reproducing only by seed. **Stems** 5 - 120 cm (2 in. - 4 ft) long, erect, spreading, or lying on the ground and rooting at nodes (a) in contact with the soil; **leaves** numerous near the base of the plant and scattered along the stems, 4 - 20 cm (1½ - 8 in.) long, 5 - 10 mm (1/5 - 2/5 in.) wide and gradually tapered towards the pointed tip; **leaf blades** and **leaf sheaths** sparsely to densely soft-hairy; the hair (b) standing more or less straight out; leaf sheaths split, the margins (c) hairless and overlapping; **ligule** (d) membranous, 0.5 - 2 mm (1/50 - 1/12 in.) long; no **auricles; inflorescence** finger-like, with several thin, slender, spikes (e) in a whorl at the top of the stem (A), or more usually with 2 or 3 sets of branches from the upper 2 - 4 cm (4/5 - 1½ in.) of stem (Plate 10); each spike ("finger") flattened and with the single-seeded spikelets (f) closely arranged along only one side (C, D); **seeds** purplish-green and ridged lengthwise. Flowers from July to September.

Smooth crab grass, *Digitaria ischaemum* (Schreb.) Muhl., (Figure 16 E, Plate 11) [DIGIS, digitaire astringente, Finger grass, Small crab grass, digitaire glabre] Very similar to Large crab grass but is usually shorter, has smooth, hairless **leaf blades**, and upper **leaf sheaths** usually smooth and hairless, but the lower ones may be somewhat hairy; **ligule** (g) also membranous but usually a bit longer (2 - 3 mm, 1/12 - ⅛ in.), and there is a tuft of long hair on either side of the leaf-base (h) of the lower leaves; no **auricles; inflorescence** almost identical to that of Large crab grass (A) but usually with only a single whorl of spikes at the end of the stem (as illustrated in A). Flowers from August to September.

Both kinds of crab grass are common in southern Ontario but they also occur sporadically in northern and northwestern Ontario. Both occur in row crops and other fields, waste places, gardens and lawns.

Before heading out, they are distinguished by their tapered leaf blades, their split sheaths with hairless margins (c), their membranous ligules (d, g) with no auricles, their more or less hairy lower leaf sheaths (b), and their either hairy or smooth blades. After heading out, the slender finger-like spikes are distinctive.

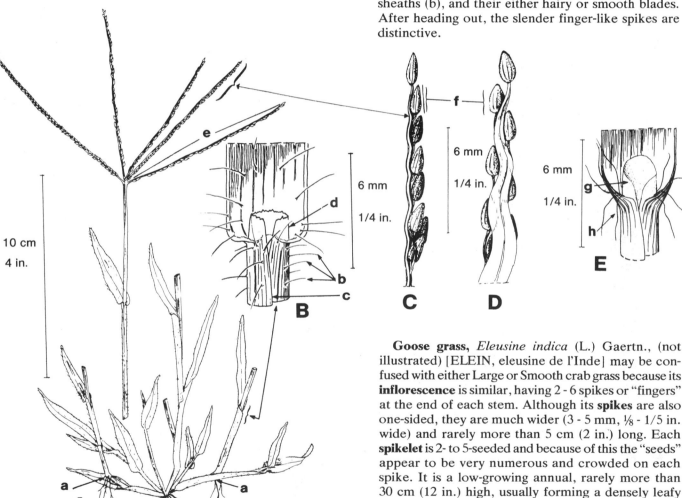

Figure 16. **Large crab grass** A. Plant. B. Leaf base. C. Side view. D. Back view of a portion of spike with several spikelets. **Smooth crab grass** E. Leaf-base of lower leaf.

Goose grass, *Eleusine indica* (L.) Gaertn., (not illustrated) [ELEIN, eleusine de l'Inde] may be confused with either Large or Smooth crab grass because its **inflorescence** is similar, having 2 - 6 spikes or "fingers" at the end of each stem. Although its **spikes** are also one-sided, they are much wider (3 - 5 mm, ⅛ - 1/5 in. wide) and rarely more than 5 cm (2 in.) long. Each **spikelet** is 2- to 5-seeded and because of this the "seeds" appear to be very numerous and crowded on each spike. It is a low-growing annual, rarely more than 30 cm (12 in.) high, usually forming a densely leafy clump or tuft with few to many flowering **stems**, a very short, membranous **ligule** 0.5 mm (1/50 in.) long, no **auricles**, and a split sheath with membranous margins that are somewhat hairy just below the collar. Flowers from July to November.

Goose grass is an occasional weed in row crops, gardens, lawns and waste places in the Hamilton area and in southwestern Ontario.

Proso millet, *Panicum miliaceum* L., (Figure 17, Plate 12) [PANMI, panic millet, Proso, Wild proso millet, Millet, Broom-corn millet] Annual, reproducing only by seed. **Stems** stout, up to 1 m (40 in.) or more high, smooth or somewhat hairy (a) for several cm below each node (b), especially where not enclosed within the leaf sheath; **leaf sheaths** (c) densely hairy, the hairs somewhat harsh and standing more or less perpendicular to the surface; leaf sheaths split, their margins membranous, overlapping just above each node but becoming separate upwards nearer the leaf blade; **leaves** smooth to sparsely hairy, elongate, to 30 cm (12 in.) or longer, and 5 - 25 mm (1/5 - 1 in.) wide, widest just above the rounded base and tapering towards the tip; **ligule** (d) a band of hairs 2 - 5 mm (1/12 - 1/5 in.) long, the bases of the hairs united and more or less membranous; no **auricles**; **panicle** either dense and arching or nodding to one side (D) (usually associated with cream-, orange- or reddish-seeded forms) or erect and loose or open (E) (usually associated with black-seeded forms), 8 - 30 cm (3-1/5 - - 12 in.) long; **spikelets** (e) ovoid, 4 - 5.5 mm (1/6 -

¼ in.) long and ½ to 2/3 as wide; **seeds** 3 - 3.5 mm (1/9 - 1/7 in.) long by about 1.6 - 2.0 mm (1/15 - 1/12 in.) wide, hard and usually shiny, varying in colour from white through shades of yellow, orange and brown to black, the darker coloured seeds with 5 parallel beige veins. Flowers from July to September.

Proso millet was introduced from Europe. Some forms are cultivated for bird seed and some of these along with other wild forms are major weeds of grain-fields in parts of southern Ontario.

It is distinguished from the very similar Witch grass by its much larger seeds that may vary in colour from white through cream, orange, reddish or brownish-green to black, and by the arching or nodding panicle in some forms (the erect, open-panicled forms usually being larger, coarser and having fewer seeds than Witch grass); and it is distinguished from Fall panicum by its hairy leaf sheaths and its larger spikelets. Seedlings of Proso millet can be distinguished from those of Witch grass only by the size, shape and colour of the mother seed (f) clinging to the primary root.

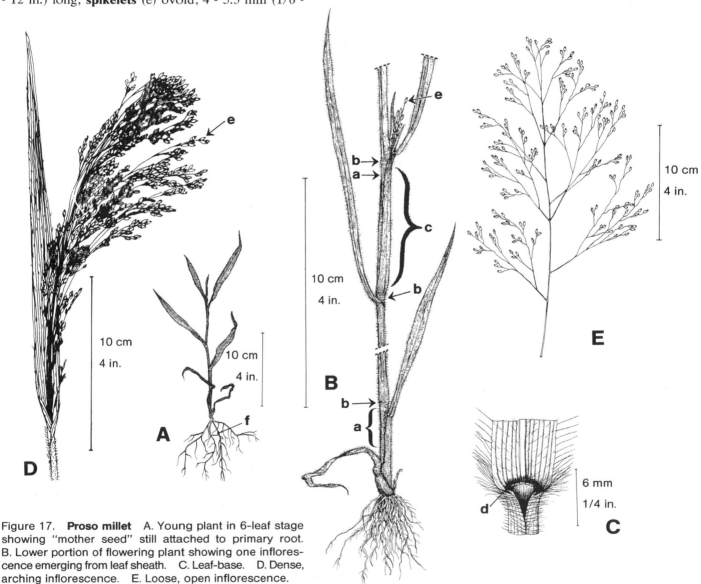

Figure 17. **Proso millet** A. Young plant in 6-leaf stage showing "mother seed" still attached to primary root. B. Lower portion of flowering plant showing one inflorescence emerging from leaf sheath. C. Leaf-base. D. Dense, arching inflorescence. E. Loose, open inflorescence.

Witch grass, *Panicum capillare* L., (Figure 18, Plate 13) [PANCA, panic capillaire, Capillary, Common witch grass, Hair grass, Old witch grass, Panic grass, Tickle grass, Tumble grass, mousseline] Annual, reproducing only by seed. **Stems** 5 - 120 cm (2 in. - 4 ft) high, erect, or spreading; **leaf blades** and **leaf sheaths** densely hairy, the hair 2 - 3 mm (1/12 - ⅛ in.) long and becoming harsh and prickly as the plant matures; leaf sheath split (B), its margins (a) either separate or overlapping; **ligule** (b) a dense fringe of hair 1 -2 mm (1/25 - 1/12 in.) long; no **auricles**; **inflorescence** (C) a large, loose, open, fluffy panicle with numerous, very fine branches and tiny **spikelets** (d) at the ends of those branches; the much-branched panicle often wider than long and, on small- to medium-sized plants, often making up ½ to 2/3 the total height of the plant; mature spikelets 0.7 - 0.8 mm wide by 2.0 - 2.3 mm long (1/35 by 1/12 - 1/10 in.); **florets**

("seeds") 0.6 - 0.7 mm wide and 1.3 - 1.4 mm long (about 1/40 by 1/16 in.), shiny gray-brown with 5 parallel beige veins. At maturity, the stem breaks easily below the inflorescence and the whole panicle is rolled and tumbled by the wind, dropping seed with every bounce. Flowers from July to September.

Witch grass is very common in fields, waste areas, roadsides, backyards, gardens and occasionally in lawns throughout southern Ontario and sporadically in northern and northwestern Ontario.

It is distinguished from Fall panicum by its densely hairy leaves and leaf sheaths, its very fine, bushy panicle and its smaller seeds; and from Proso millet by its much smaller seeds that are only gray-brown in colour. Seedlings of Witch grass can be distinguished from those of Proso millet only by the size, shape and colour of the mother seed clinging to the primary root.

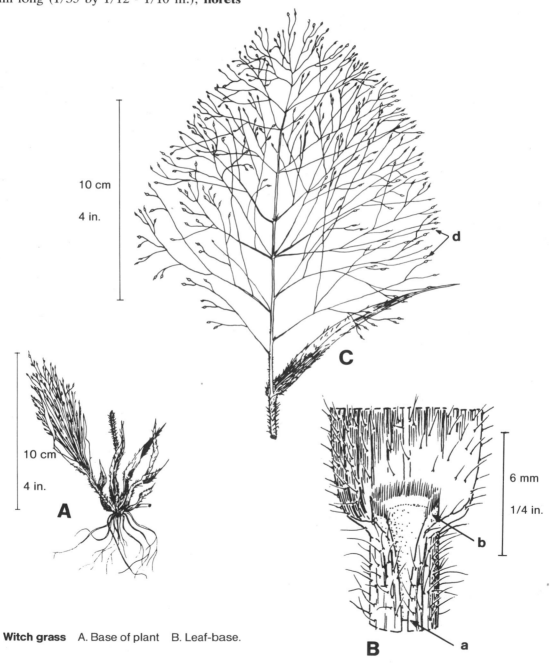

Figure 18.   **Witch grass**   A. Base of plant   B. Leaf-base. C. Panicle.

Fall panicum, *Panicum dichotomiflorum* (L.) Michx. var. *geniculatum* (Wood.) Fern. (Figure 19, Plate 14) [PANDI, panic d'automne géniculé, Smooth panicum, Smooth witch grass, Spreading panic grass, Wire grass] Annual, reproducing only by seed. **Stems** 1 to many from a coarse fibrous **root** system, 10 - 180 cm (4 in. - 6 ft) long, erect or spreading or lying nearly prostrate on the ground; often rooting from nodes in contact with the soil, usually bending in a zigzag manner at each node or joint (a); lower **leaf blades** and **leaf sheaths** of very young plants finely hairy (b), blades and leaf sheaths produced higher up the stem usually completely hairless; nodes (a) of stem enlarged and prominent; leaf sheath somewhat inflated (c) or loosely fitting around the stem just above each node; leaf sheaths split (B), their margins (d) very thin, membranous, white or colourless, and separate or overlapping each other; **ligule** (e) a fringe of hair 1.5 - 3 mm (1/16 - ⅛ in.) long; no **auricles; inflorescence** of several much-branched panicles; terminal panicle (C) at the end of each stem large and bushy, 15 - 50 cm (6 - 20 in.) long and almost as wide, the branches thin but quite stiff; panicles on lower branches (f) small, compact, and often remaining partially enclosed (g) by the leaf sheath from which they emerge; **spikelets**

(h) borne singly at the ends of the tiny branches, about 2.5 - 2.7 mm (1/10 in.) long by 1.0 - 1.1 mm (1/25 in.) wide, each containing a single **floret** ("seed") about 1.8 - 2.0 mm (1/14 - 1/12 in.) long by 0.9 - 1.0 mm (1/25 in.) wide, gray-brown with 5 parallel beige veins. Flowers from August to September.

Fall panicum is a native plant in eastern North America but has become a weed of significance in cultivated land only since about 1968. It now infests many thousands of acres of prime corn land in the 6 southwestern counties of Ontario and is present in many more farms in all the counties south and west of a line from Hamilton to Grand Bend. Outside this region it is known to occur only occasionally in cultivated land in central Ontario, in streamside locations along Bear Creek southeast of Ottawa, and in several waste areas in Ottawa city and along the St. Lawrence River.

It is distinguished from Witch grass by its coarser panicle, the zigzag appearance of its longer stems, and the absence of hair on the leaf sheaths and leaf blades in the upper part of the plant; and from Proso millet by its hairless upper leaf sheaths and blades and its smaller spikelets and "seeds" that are only gray-brown in colour.

Figure 19. **Fall panicum** A. Plant. B. Leaf-base. C. Panicle. D. 2 spikelets.

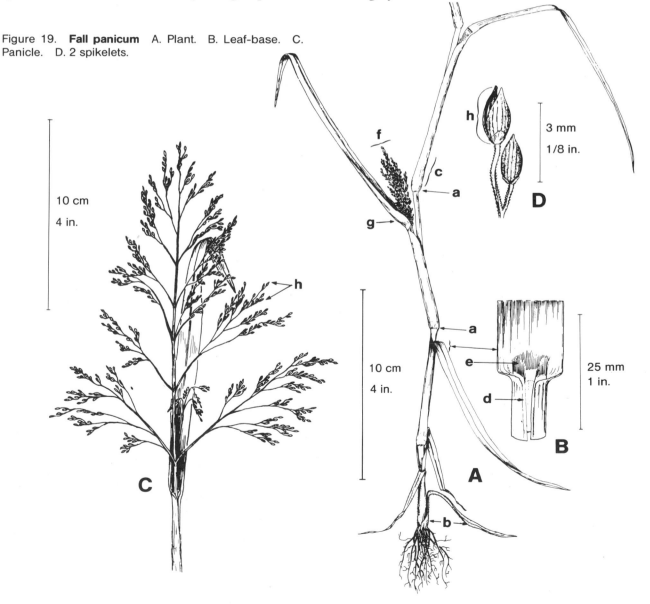

Barnyard grass, *Echinochloa crusgalli* (L.) Beauv., (Figure 20, Plate 15) [ECHCG, échinochloa pied-de-coq, Summer grass, Water grass, pied-de-coq] Annual, reproducing only by seed. **Stems** erect, spreading or lying horizontally on the ground and bending upwards but rooting from nodes (a) in contact with the soil; stems 5 -150 cm (2 in. - 5 ft) long, coarse, smooth, usually round in cross-section but occasionally much flattened; **leaves** 5 - 50 cm (2 - 20 in.) long, 6 - 22 mm (¼ - ¾ in.) broad, deep green or somewhat purplish, hairless or with 1 to 3 solitary hairs (b) near the base of the blade (c); **leaf sheaths** split with overlapping margins (d); **ligule** absent (e); no **auricles**; **inflorescence** 5 - 25 cm (2 - 10 in.) long having a central stem with several spreading, nearly erect, thick branches with rather dense clusters of spikelets; their

colour varies from green to yellowish-green to dark purplish-green to almost black; each **spikelet** is covered with short, stiff hair and may either be awned or awnless; and contain a single fertile **floret** ("seed" or "grain"); awns straight or twisted (f), varying from 1 - 40 mm (1/25 - 1-3/5 in.) long; "seeds" about 3 mm (⅛ in.) long, hard, shiny, pale yellow, and rounded on one surface but flattened on the other. Flowers from July to August.

Barnyard grass is a very widespread and troublesome weed throughout southern Ontario and occurs sporadically in the north and northwest as well. It occurs in cultivated fields, waste places, along roadsides, in gardens and occasionally in lawns, usually being more abundant in moist soil and becoming conspicuous in late summer and fall.

It is distinguished from all other weedy grasses in Canada by the complete absence of a ligule (e, and see Figure 3) at the junction of leaf blade and leaf sheath, and its rather coarse, chunky inflorescence.

A strain of Barnyard grass, that was cultivated under the name "Billion dollar grass," can occasionally be found in southwestern Ontario and is recognized by its erect stature and its dark purple, almost black inflorescence.

Green foxtail, *Setaria viridis* (L.) Beauv., (Figure 21 A - C, Plate 16) [SETVI, sétaire verte, Bottle brush, Bottle grass, Bristle grass, Foxtail millet, Millet, Pigeon grass, Wild millet, mil sauvage] Annual, reproducing only by seed. **Stems** erect or spreading, 10 - 100 cm (4 - 40 in.) tall or occasionally taller, usually round in cross-section but occasionally much flattened; **leaves** and **leaf sheaths** of very young plants often densely hairy but with upward-pointing hair; upper leaf blades and leaf sheaths mostly without hair; margins (a) and both surfaces (b) of leaf blades rough with very fine forward-pointing barbs; leaf sheath split with overlapping margins (c), both margins being fringed with a band of short hair (d); **ligule** (e) a fringe of hair 1.5 - 2 mm

Figure 20. **Barnyard grass**   A. Plant.   B. Leaf-base.   C. Panicle.

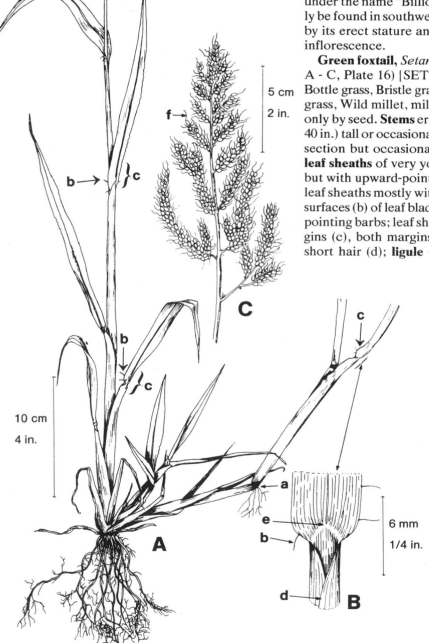

(1/16 - 1/12 in.) long; no **auricles**; **inflorescence** a very dense spike 1 - 15 cm (2/5 - 6 in.) long and 0.6 - 2.0 cm (¼ - 4/5 in.) wide, usually straight and erect or rarely somewhat curved, the larger ones sometimes with short branches up to 1 cm (2/5 in.) long, and covered with short green to slightly purplish bristles which give the inflorescence a bottle-brush appearance; the bristles have microscopic forward-pointing barbs that allow the seed head to be dragged downwards but not pushed upwards over the skin or a rough surface. **Spikelets** about 2 mm (1/12 in.) long by 1 mm (1/25 in.) wide; each contains a single fertile **floret** ("seed" or "grain"), that is rounded on one surface but flattened on the other, finely cross-ridged (seen only with magnification), and dull yellowish-green with brownish spots. Flowers from July to August.

Green foxtail is very common and widespread throughout all agricultural regions of Ontario. It grows well in all soil textures and occurs in cultivated lands, waste places, roadsides, gardens and occasionally lawns.

It is distinguished from Yellow foxtail by its green or purple bristles, the absence of long, kinky hair on the upper surface of the leaf blade near the stem (see Figure 22), the presence of a fringe of hair (d) on both margins (c) of the leaf sheath, and its somewhat smaller grains or seeds. It is distinguished from Bristly foxtail by its denser, more continuous spike whose bristles do not cling when sliding the fingers upwards on it. It is distinguished from Giant foxtail by its usually shorter stature, its shorter, thinner and usually erect inflorescence (rarely curved or nodding) and the absence of a covering of short hair on leaf surfaces in the middle and upper parts of the plant.

Figure 21. **Green foxtail** A. Plant with stem folded twice. B. Leaf-base. C. Spike. **Bristly foxtail.** D. Leaf-base. E. Spike. F. Cluster of 3 spikelets and 6 bristles with backward-pointing barbs. (Cont'd.)

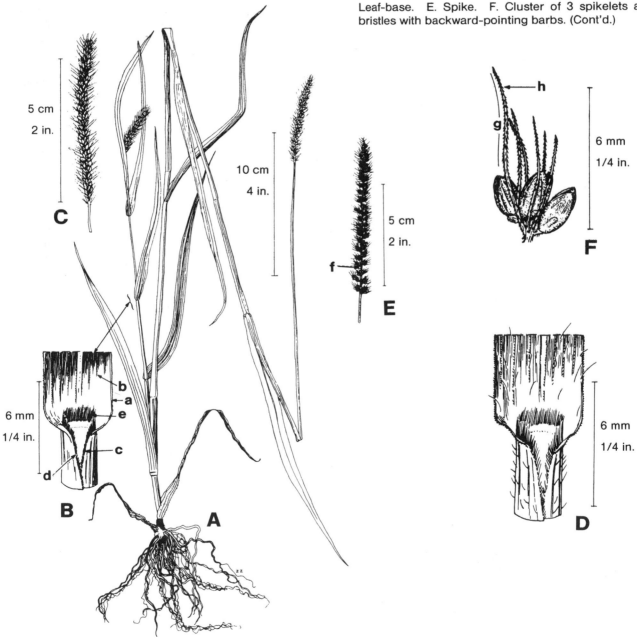

Giant foxtail, *Setaria faberii* Herrm., (Figure 21G, H, Plate 17) [SETFA, sétaire géante, sétaire de Faber] Annual, reproducing only by seed. Similar to Green foxtail (Figure 21 A-C), but generally larger. **Stems** up to 2 m (6.5 ft) high, smooth; **leaf sheaths** mostly smooth, except hairy along the margins; **leaf blades** 30 - 55 cm (12 - 21.5 in.) long, 3 - 17 mm (1/8 - 2/3 in.) wide, usually finely hairy throughout the entire upper surface (G, H) of all leaves and occasionally also on the undersurface (seen by rolling the leaf over a finger and viewing it against the light); **ligule** a dense band of hairs, about 1.0 mm (1/25 in.) long; no **auricles**; **inflorescence** dense, spike-like, erect or the larger ones usually somewhat curved or nodding, 4.5 - 17 cm (1-4/5 - 6-7/10 in.) long and 1.5 - 3 cm (3/5 - 1-1/5 in.) thick, surrounded by light yellowish-green awn-like bristles which give the inflorescence a bottle-brush appearance; **spikelets** 1.5 - 3 mm (1/16 - 1/8 in.) long; grains (**"seeds"**) light green and abundantly cross-wrinkled. Flowers from late July to October.

Giant foxtail is native to China and was recently introduced from the USA where it is a very common weed; it is becoming abundant in fields and waste places in southern and eastern Ontario.

It is distinguished from Green foxtail by its usually larger, nodding inflorescence, its distinctly cross-wrinkled grains and usually hairy upper surface of leaves, and from Yellow foxtail by its larger, greenish-yellow rather than orange-yellow inflorescence, and by the upper surfaces of its leaf blades being finely short-hairy throughout their length rather than bearing a few long, kinky hairs near the stem. The technical character that distinguishes Giant foxtail from Green foxtail is that its second or upper glume covers only about ¾ of the fertile floret, whereas in Green foxtail it covers nearly the entire floret.

Bristly foxtail, *Setaria verticillata* (L.) Beauv., (Figure 21 D-F, Plate 18) [SETVE, sétaire verticillée, Bristle grass, Catch grass, Garden grass] Annual, reproducing only by seed. Stems, leaves and general habit of growth very similar to those of Green foxtail. The spike (E) is "interrupted," the clusters of **spikelets** being somewhat separated from one another along the central stalk (f). The greenish bristles (g) are covered with tiny, sharp, backward-pointing barbs (h) and these cause the whole spike to cling to the skin, hair, other spikes and, indeed, any rough surface (hence the name "bristly"). When the stems are whipped around by the wind and the spikes touch each other, they cling together in a tangled mass. Its "seeds" are about the same size, shape and colour as those of Green foxtail.

Bristly foxtail is less abundant than Green foxtail, occurring in scattered localities throughout the southern part of Ontario but apparently not reported in the north or northwest. Although it is usually found in wastelands and gardens, its occurrence in cultivated fields is on the increase, especially in the southwestern part of the province.

It is distinguished by it somewhat "interrupted" spike and by the backward-pointing barbs (h) on the bristles (g) which cause the heads to stick together or cling to skin, clothes or fur.

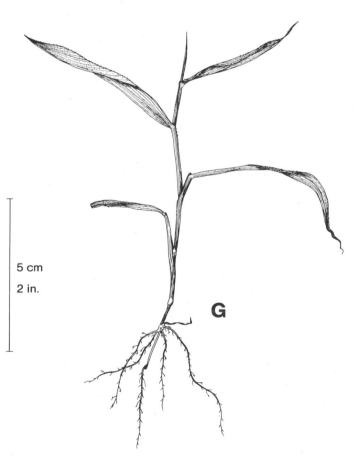

6 mm
¼ in.

H

5 cm
2 in.

G

Figure 21. (Cont'd.) **Giant foxtail** G. Young plant showing finely hairy leaf surfaces.   H. Leaf-base showing dense covering of very short hairs on upper surface of leaf-base, hairy ligule with longer hairs at margins of collar, and short hairs along edge of leaf sheath.

Yellow foxtail, *Setaria glauca* (L.) Beauv., (Figure 22) [SETLU, sétaire glauque, Bottle brush, Bottle grass, Bristle grass, Millet, Pigeon grass, Wild millet, sétaire jaune, foin sauvage, mil sauvage, *Setaria lutescens* (Weigel) Hubb.] Annual, reproducing only by seed. In general appearance similar to Green foxtail but is characterized by having a few, prominent, silky, kinky hairs (a) 3 - 10 mm, ⅛ - 2/5 in. long) on the upper surface of the **leaf blade** just near the stem; **ligule** (b) a fringe of hair; no **auricles**; **leaf sheaths** split, their margins (c) smooth, green or slightly membranous and transparent; **stems** normally round, but occasionally distinctly flattened; **inflorescence** a spike (C) 2 - 10 cm (4/5 - 4 in.) long, covered with numerous, yellow to orange bristles (d) with forward-pointing barbs. **Spikelets** ("seeds" or "grains") slightly larger than Green foxtail, more prominently cross-ridged, and yellowish or straw-coloured. Flowers from July to August.

Yellow foxtail occurs throughout the agricultural regions of Ontario, having essentially the same distribution as Green foxtail but often being less abundant.

It is distinguished from the other foxtails and, indeed, from all other grasses in Ontario by the prominent silky, kinky hairs on the upper surfaces of the leaf blades just near the stem.

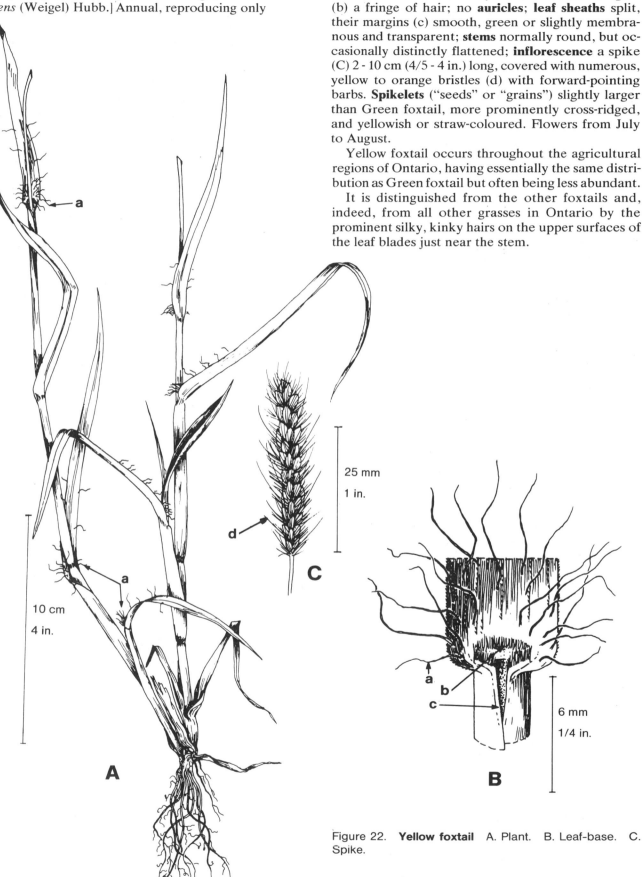

Figure 22. **Yellow foxtail** A. Plant. B. Leaf-base. C. Spike.

43

Long-spined sandbur, *Cenchrus longispinus* (Hack.) Fern., (Figure 23, Plate 19) [CCHPA, cenchrus épineux, Bur grass] Annual, reproducing only by seed. **Stems** mostly 10 - 60 cm (4 - 24 in.) long, erect or spreading or lying on the ground; **leaves** flat or margins inrolled (a), usually constricted and partially twisted (b) at the junction with the leaf sheaths, 2 - 12 cm (1 - 5 in.) long, mostly hairless but rough in one direction; **leaf sheaths** split with overlapping margins (c) these margins on young plants membranous and without hair, but on upper leaf sheaths of older stems membranous and usually also with few to many hairs (d) 1 - 2 mm (1/25 - 1/12 in.) long; **ligule** a fringe of hair (e) mostly less than 1 mm (1/25 in.) long; there is also a tuft of short and long (2 - 3 mm, 1/12 - 1/8 in.) hair on each side (f) of the **collar** at the junction between blade and sheath; no **auricles; inflorescence** a group of spiny burs at the end of each stem; each bur (C) 4 - 6 mm (1/6 - 1/4 in.) long, containing 1 or 2 "seeds," and covered with extremely sharp spines (g) 2 - 6 mm (1/12 - 1/4 in.) long with backward-pointing barbs (h) which anchor into skin, etc., the whole bur breaking off when mature. Flowers from August to September.

Long-spined sandbur is a native grass in areas of sandy soil throughout southern Ontario. Though normally found along sandy beaches, sand dunes, riverbanks and roadsides, it is becoming a problem in tobacco fields, other row crops and occasionally in lawns and gardens on sandy soils.

Once the burs have emerged, Long-spined sandbur cannot be confused with any other grass in Ontario. Younger plants can be distinguished from most other grasses by the split sheath with membranous margins (c), and usually some hair on the margin, together with the hairy ligule (e) and the tufts of long hair (f) on either side at the junction between blade and sheath.

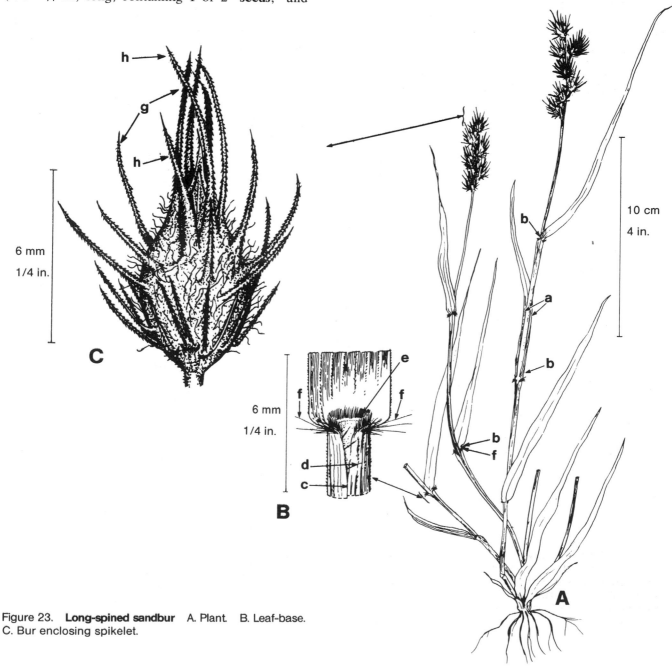

Figure 23. **Long-spined sandbur** A. Plant. B. Leaf-base. C. Bur enclosing spikelet.

Johnson grass, *Sorghum halepense* (L.) Pers., Figure 24, Plate 20) [SORHA, sorgho d'Alep, sorgho de Johnson] Perennial reproducing by seed and by large, coarse underground stems (rhizomes). **Stems** 50 - 270 cm (2 - 9 ft.) tall, 5 - 20 mm (1/5 - 4/5 in.) in diameter, smooth and stiff or wiry; **leaves** 20 - 60 cm (8 - 24 in.) long, 1 - 2 cm (2/5 - 4/5 in.) wide, bright green, and smooth; **leaf sheaths** split with smooth overlapping margins (a); **ligule** (b) membranous, 2 - 5 mm (1/12 - 1/5 in.) long; no **auricles**; **collar** (junction between leaf blade and leaf sheath) often with purplish blotches on its sides; **rhizomes** thick and fleshy, at first white to pinkish, but turning chestnut brown over winter, as much as 1 cm (2/5 in.) in diameter and up to 1 m (40 in.) long, with many nodes (c) and internodes, frequently rooting from the nodes, and the internodes partially covered with brown scale-like sheaths (d); **inflorescence** up to 50 cm (2 ft.) long, with whorls of upright branches; at first compact (D), later spreading and open; **spikelets** arranged in pairs at each node along the thin branches, 1 member of the pair is sterile (non-seed bearing) (e), rather dull in texture and has a short stalk (f); the second member (g) of each pair is fertile (contains the grain or "seed"), rather plump, about 5 mm (1/5 in.) long by 2.5 mm

(1/10 in.) wide, does not have a stalk, and may have a twisted awn (h) 1 - 1.5 cm (2/5 - 3/5 in.) long. Flowers from July to September.

Johnson grass is presently known to occur in 13 counties in southern and southwestern Ontario.

Young plants of Johnson grass might be mistaken for very thin plants of corn, Sudan grass, or an annual grain sorghum. They can be distinguished from corn by the size and shape of the mother seed (j) attached to the primary root of the seedling, or if growing as a shoot from an overwintered rhizome, by the presence of the thick, hard, brownish rhizome. Older plants can be distinguished by their large, open, non-silky inflorescences with plump seeds, and in autumn by the presence of coarse, whitish, rope-like, branching rhizomes (horizontal underground stems) about 1 cm (2/5 in.) in diameter in late autumn. Most rhizomes are killed by Ontario winters, but 2 or 3 stands are apparently hardy enough that their rhizomes are not killed, and these plants are acting as true perennials. Also compare with Common reed (page 27, Figure 9).

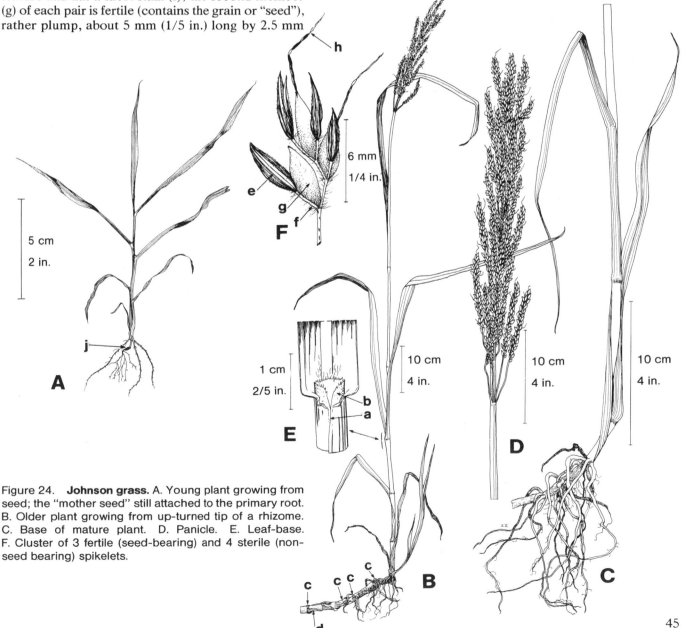

Figure 24. **Johnson grass.** A. Young plant growing from seed; the "mother seed" still attached to the primary root. B. Older plant growing from up-turned tip of a rhizome. C. Base of mature plant. D. Panicle. E. Leaf-base. F. Cluster of 3 fertile (seed-bearing) and 4 sterile (non-seed bearing) spikelets.

SEDGE FAMILY (Cyperaceae)

Plants that belong to the Sedge Family are very similar to those of the Grass Family. However, there are a number of characteristic features that help to separate them, although exceptions do occur. In the Sedge Family, the stem is usually triangular in cross-section (Figure 25) rather than round or somewhat flattened as in the grasses (Figure 3). Sedge stems are also solid or filled with pith rather than hollow, and have indistinct nodes rather than the distinct nodes or joints that are often marked by differences in thickness, colour or texture in the grasses. While the leaf sheaths of grasses are usually split with their margins separate or overlapping, in the sedges the leaf sheaths are closed for almost their entire length. In sedges, the leaves are 3-ranked; that is, they protrude from the stem in line with each of the three angles of the triangular stem (B). In grasses, the leaves are 2-ranked, being produced alternately from opposite sides of the stem.

The technical differences between the Grass and the Sedge Families are found in their inflorescences and flowers, but are beyond the scope of this book.

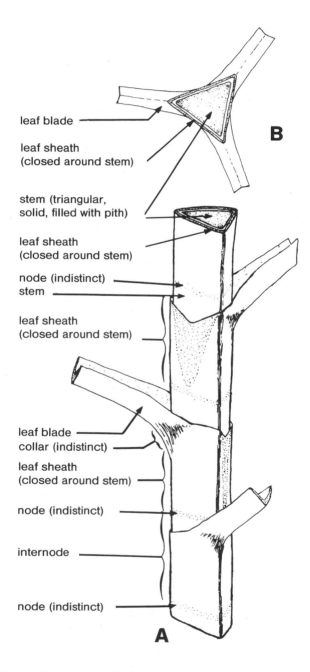

leaf blade

leaf sheath
(closed around stem)

stem (triangular,
solid, filled with pith)

leaf sheath
(closed around stem)

node (indistinct)
stem

leaf sheath
(closed around stem)

leaf blade
collar (indistinct)

leaf sheath
(closed around stem)

node (indistinct)

internode

node (indistinct)

B

A

Figure 25.   Stem and leaf-base characteristics of a typical sedge.   A. Side view of triangular stem with 3-ranked arrangement of leaves.   B. Top view of "A."

Yellow nut sedge, *Cyperus esculentus* L., (Figure 26, Plate 21) [CYPES, souchet comestible, Chufa, Earth almond, Ground almond, Northern nut-grass, Nut-grass, Rushnut, Yellow nut-grass, amande de terre, souchet rampant]Perennial, reproducing by seed and by underground stems (rhizomes) and tubers. The underground system is a mixture of long, thin, wiry rhizomes 5 - 20 cm (2 - 8 in.) long or longer, and a mass of fine fibrous **roots. Rhizomes** are light brown to whitish, have nodes (a) and internodes (b) with short, dark brown, dry scale-like sheaths; **tubers** (c) produced at the tips of some rhizomes, dark brown, somewhat spindled-shaped, 5 - 20 mm (1/5 - 4/5 in.) long and usually narrower, edible with a taste somewhat suggestive of almonds; **stems** 10 - 90 cm (4 in. - 3 ft) high, distinctly triangular in cross-section (Figure 25 A, B) and usually less than 1 cm (2/5 in.) thick; **leaves** numerous at the base of the plant and sparse up the stem except for a cluster of usually 3 to 5 at the base of the inflorescence; leaf arrangement alternate and 3-ranked, that is, the leaves pointing outwards in 3 direc-

tions from the stem (Figure 25 A, B); **leaf sheath** closed forming a 3-sided cylinder around the stem; **leaf blades** grass-like, long (often longer than the stem) and narrow, 3 - 10 mm (⅛ - 2/5 in.) wide, flat or somewhat folded, light green to yellowish-green; no **ligule** and no **auricles**; **inflorescence** an umbrella-like cluster of yellowish to brownish branches at the tip of the stem; **spikelets** (containing the seeds) very small and closely arranged along slender secondary branches (d). Flowers from July to August.

Yellow nut sedge is native on moist, sandy soils throughout much of North America. It is common in Southern Ontario, frequently infesting moist areas of cultivated fields, pastures, roadsides, gardens and lawns.

It is easily distinguished from all grasses (see Figure 3 and accompanying description page 21) by its triangular stem together with slender, tuber-bearing (c) rhizomes. Several other species of nut sedge also occur in Ontario but this is the most troublesome one and the most likely to occur in cultivated land.

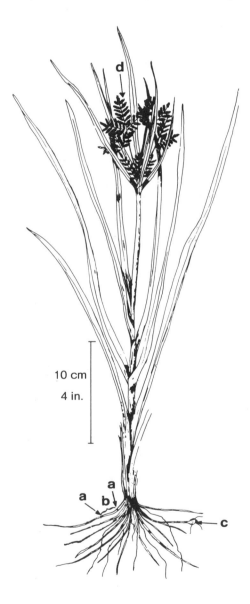

10 cm
4 in.

Figure 26. **Yellow nut sedge**

Spiked sedge, *Carex spicata* Huds., (Figure 27) [CAXSP, carex à épi]Perennial, reproducing only by seed. Plants grass-like, forming clumps that may range from 2 - 3 cm (1 in.) to 30 cm (1 ft) or more across, with a dense mass of fibrous roots. **Stems** erect or spreading, short (5 - 20 cm, 2 - 8 in.) and slender in regularly mowed lawns, or up to 90 cm (3 ft) or longer where not mowed, triangular in cross-section; **leaves** 3-ranked (Figure 25B), usually flat, mostly basal or from the lowermost quarter of the stem, 1 - 3 mm (1/25 - ⅛ in.) wide and up to 45 cm (18 in.) long, green or yellowish-green; **inflorescence** (a) a short (1 - 2 cm, 2/5 - 4/5 in.), loose or dense cylindrical spike, made up of 25 to 40 greenish spikelets, each **spikelet** (b) pear-shaped and containing one **seed**.

Spiked sedge is native to southern Ontario in both moist and dry situations. It is a pest of lawns if its seed has been introduced as a contaminant in topsoil. Numerous clumps may form mats so dense that they virtually exclude the original lawn grasses.

It is distinguished by the more or less circular yellow-green patches that it forms in mowed lawns, and by its long, thin, sprawling leaves and stems with short, cylindrical inflorescences where not regularly mowed.

10 cm

4 in.

Figure 27. **Spiked sedge** Representative of a plant growing in a lawn.

LILY FAMILY (Liliaceae)

Wild garlic, *Allium vineale* L., (Figure 28, Plate 22) [ALLVI, ail des vignes, Field garlic, Scallions, Wild onion]Perennial, reproducing by seed and by 3 kinds of bulbs. Young plants very grass-like in appearance with erect, slender, rounded or flattened, smooth-textured leaves; flowering **stems** erect, mostly unbranched, 30 - 100 cm (12 - 40 in.) high, round, solid or sometimes hollow; stem **leaves** with a tubular sheath (a) and long slender blades; the blades channeled or flattened near the base, thicker and nearly round towards the tip; **flowers** in a head-like cluster (umbels) at the tip of the stem, each cluster at first surrounded by a papery bract (b) or spathe; each flower (c) with 6 small petals, greenish to white, pink or purplish-red, 6 stamens and 1 pistil, but usually most or all flowers replaced by small bulblets (D); **bulblets** about 3 - 5 mm (1/8 - 1/5 in.) long and closely resembling but much smaller than the bulbs normally produced in the base of the plant. Base of plant usually producing 2 kinds of **bulbs**, a soft-shelled bulb that is teardrop-shaped, usually 8 - 17 mm (1/3 - 2/3 in.) long and white, and hard-shelled bulbs (C) which are light brownish, about the same size but distinctly flattened on 1 side and with a thick, hard shell. The whole plant has a very strong garlic odour. The flower or bulbet heads are produced during July and August and when growing in fields of wheat, oats or barley, may be harvested with the grain. They shatter readily into individual bulblets that cannot easily be separated from the cereal grain because of their size and shape.

Wild garlic occurs only in the Niagara peninsula of southern Ontario, growing in fields, vineyards, roadsides and edges of woods.

It is distinguished by its slender, erect stems and leaves, its soft, smooth texture, its cluster of little bulblets (D) instead of flowers at the tips of stems, its hard-shelled bulbs produced around the mother bulb in the ground, and the strong garlic odour in all parts of the plant.

Other kinds of Wild onion also grow in Ontario but their aerial bulblets, if produced at all, are two to three times larger than those of Wild garlic, and hard-shelled bulbs are rarely produced in the bases of these plants.

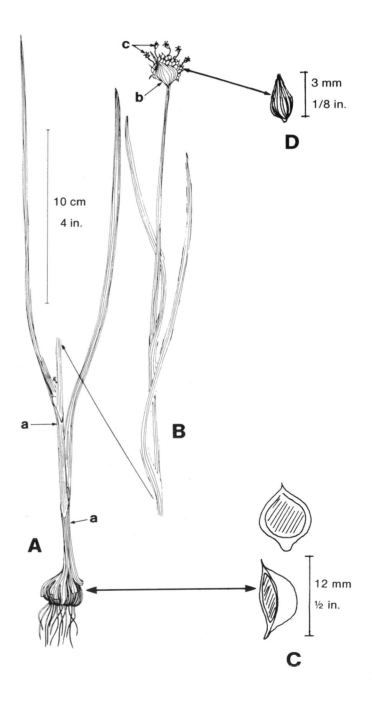

Figure 28. **Wild garlic** A. Base of plant. B. Top of plant. C. Hard-shelled bulbs. D. Aerial bulblet.

BUCKWHEAT or SMARTWEED FAMILY (Polygonaceae)

Sheep sorrel, *Rumex acetosella* L., (Figure 29, Plate 23) [RUMAA, petite oseille, Field sorrel, Red sorrel, petite osielle des brebis, surette] Perennial, reproducing by seed and by spreading horizontal **roots** (a). These produce whitish buds (b) which grow into leafy aboveground shoots and result in very dense patches. The plant may also grow as an annual: germinating from seed, flowering, producing a new crop of seed and dying, all in one growing season. **Stems** 10 - 60 cm (4 - 24 in.) high, slender, tough and wiry; **leaves** alternate (1 per node), variable in size and shape; lower leaves long-stalked, usually spade-shaped with a pair of slender lobes near the base of the blade, but occasionally very slender and without any lobes; middle leaves short-stalked and nearly always with a lateral lobe (c) on each side; upper leaves stalkless and usually without lobes; leaf **ocrea** (d) (a thin membranous sheath arising with the leafstalk; also see Figure 27 B,C,D and E) at each node (e) of the stem, colourless or faintly greenish-yellow, quite ragged (f) on older stems; **flowers** small, clustered in whorls in a branching inflorescence; plants unisexual so all flowers on one plant are either female (seed-producing) or male (pollen-producing); female flowers greenish, male flowers yellowish, the whole plant often with a reddish-green to brownish cast; **seeds** (tiny fruits) about 1.5 mm (1/16 in.) long, triangular or 3-sided in cross-section, smooth, shiny, and reddish-brown to golden-brown. Flowers from May to July.

Sheep sorrel occurs throughout Ontario but is more common in the southern parts of the province in pastures, meadows, waste areas and roadsides, rarely persisting in cultivated fields. It is common in sandy and gravelly soils, especially in areas which are so low in fertility that they do not adequately support other kinds of plants.

It is distinguished by its usually low stature, its spade-shaped leaf blades that usually have 1 or 2 slender lobes near the base of the blade, its membranous ocrea (d) surrounding the stem just above each leaf, its inflorescence of two types — one producing seed and the other producing only pollen — and its frequently reddish or brownish colour.

Curled dock, *Rumex crispus* L., (Figure 30, Plate 24) [RUMCR, patience crépue, Curly dock, Narrow-leaved dock, Sour dock, Yellow dock, patience, rumex crépu] Perennial, spreading only by seed. **Stems** erect, 1 m (40 in.) or taller, from a thick, yellowish, deeply penetrating, simple or branching **taproot**, **leaf** shape variable: cotyledons (first 2 seed leaves) very narrow (A, a), dull green and mealy-surfaced; first true leaves (B) roundish in outline; rosette leaves long, 10 - 30 cm (4 - 12 in.) or longer, narrow, with rounded or tapered bases, very wavy-margined, curled or "crisped," sour-tasting; stem leaves alternate (1 per node), similar but smaller upwards, base of each leafstalk flattened, expanded and somewhat encircling the stem at the node (b), and with a prominent ocrea (membranous sheath) (c) up to 5 cm (2 in.) long which becomes brown and papery with age; the lower stem leaves (d) dying as the plant matures; **flowers** small, greenish, clustered in whorls around the branches of the terminal **inflorescence** (E), becoming at maturity a thick branched mass of light brown to dark brown "fruits"; each **fruit** with 3 tiny sepals (e) and 3 large, wing-like, smooth-margined, papery sepals or "valves" (f), with 1 prominent, egg-shaped, corky bump (tubercle or "grain") (g) on the back of each of the 3 large sepals, and enclosing a small, shiny, reddish-brown fruit ("**seed**") which is triangular in cross-section, pointed at both ends and about 2 mm (1/12 in.) long. Flowers from June to July.

Figure 29. **Sheep sorrel** A. Horizontal root with 4 aboveground shoots. B. Stem with inflorescence.

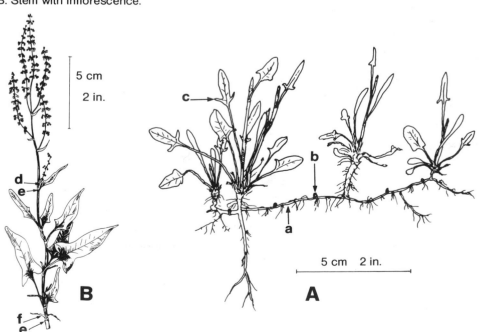

50

Curled dock is a common weed of moist situations such as meadows, low pastures, riversides, roadsides (Plate 24), depressions in cultivated fields, and occasionally on sandy uplands throughout Ontario.

It is distinguished from similar plants by its long, narrow leaves with curled and wavy margins, the base of the leaf blades being rounded or narrowed towards the leafstalks, and the 3 wing-like sepals (valves) (f) of the fruit with relatively smooth margins (no teeth) and each one bearing an enlarged corky tubercle (g).

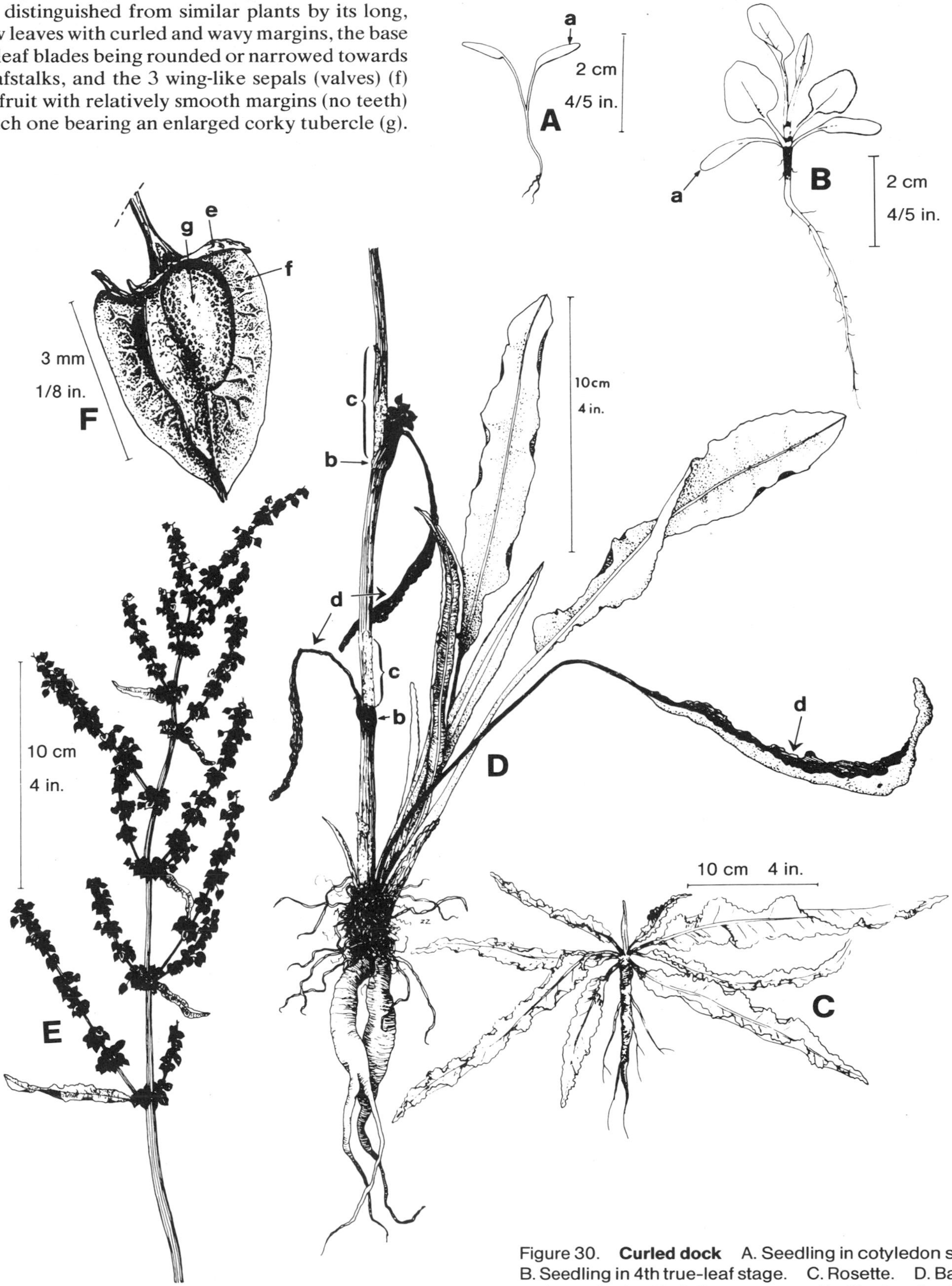

Figure 30. **Curled dock** A. Seedling in cotyledon stage. B. Seedling in 4th true-leaf stage. C. Rosette. D. Base of mature plant. E. Inflorescence. F. Single, 3-winged "fruit."

51

Broad-leaved dock, *Rumex obtusifolius* L., (Figure 31) [RUMOB, patience à feuilles obtuses, Bitter dock, Blunt-leaved dock, Red-veined dock, rumex à feuilles obtuses, rumex sanguin] Perennial, reproducing only by seed. Very similar to Curled dock but cotyledons (seed leaves) (a) 1/3 as wide as long; first few true **leaves** (b) either round in outline or with heart-shaped bases; rosette and stem leaves broad with rounded or more usually heart-shaped bases; their margins flat or somewhat wavy up and down but never strongly curled or wavy-margined; veins green or somewhat reddish, prominent and somewhat white-hairy on the undersurface; **ocrea** (membranous sheath) (c) surrounding stem above each node (d), up to 5 cm (2 in.) long, becoming brown and papery with age; **inflorescence** similar to but thicker than Curled dock; the 3 wing-like inner sepals (e) of each "**fruit**" with several irregular teeth (f) along the margins, but only 1 of the 3 sepals bearing a prominent egg-shaped corky enlargement (tubercle) (g) on its back. Flowers from June to July.

Broad-leaved dock occurs in moist situations throughout southern Ontario but is seen only scarcely in the north and northwest. It occurs along streams, meadows, wet roadside ditches, moist waste areas, and in depressional areas in cultivated land.

It is distinguished from similar plants by its broad leaves with heart-shaped bases and the prominently toothed margins (f) of the 3 wing-like sepals (valves) (e) of the fruit, only 1 of which usually develops an enlarged, egg-shaped corky or fleshy tubercle (g) on its outer surface.

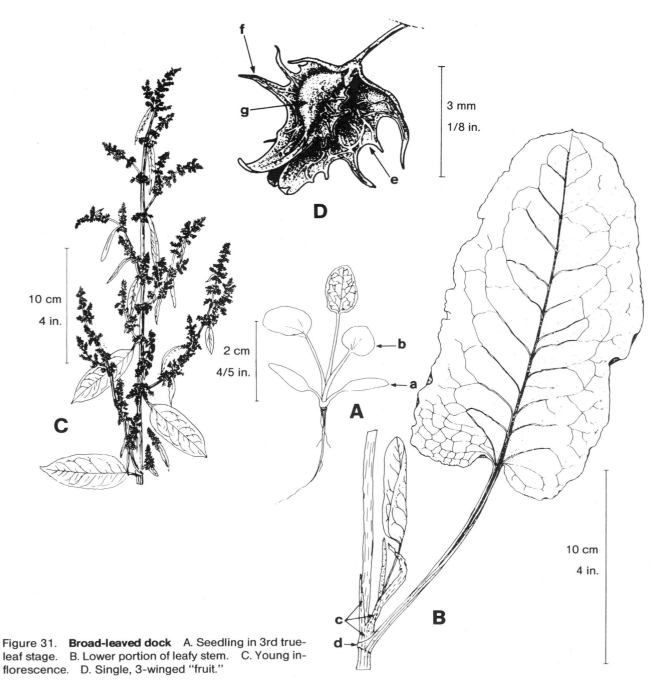

Figure 31. **Broad-leaved dock** A. Seedling in 3rd true-leaf stage. B. Lower portion of leafy stem. C. Young inflorescence. D. Single, 3-winged "fruit."

Prostrate knotweed, *Polygonum aviculare* L., (Figure 32, Plate 25) [POLAV, renouée des oiseaux, Doorweed, Knot-grass, Mat-grass, Road-spread, traînasse, renouée aviculaire] Annual, reproducing only by seed. Stems prostrate or semi-erect from a thin, tough, wiry, deeply penetrating **taproot**; stems slender, tough and wiry; growth habit variable: in open sunny situations **stems** fully prostrate, to 1 m (40 in.) or longer, or main stems prostrate with short, upturned branches, but in partly shaded situations, such as a grain crop, stems are nearly erect to 30 or 40 cm (12 - 16 in.) high; stem nodes (joints) (a) distinct, thickened, and surrounded by a thin, papery **ocrea** (membranous sheath) (b) that usually has a torn or jagged margin; **leaves** alternate (1 per node), up to 5 cm (2 in.) long but usually much shorter, their width about 1/3 - 1/5 of their length, usually broadest near or past the middle, and narrower towards both ends; **flowers** small and inconspicuous, 2 mm (1/12 in.) or less long, without petals but with 5 tiny greenish, pinkish or purplish sepals (c), produced in axils of leaves and partially enclosed in the ocrea; mature "**seed**" (d) more or less enclosed by the drying sepals, slightly rough, dull brown, triangular in cross-section and about 2 mm (1/12 in.) long. Flowers from June to September.

Prostrate knotweed occurs throughout Ontario in areas of moderately heavy foot- or wheel-traffic where the soils may be low in fertility and so heavily compacted that other plants are unable to survive. It is one of the most common weeds along roadsides, edges of or cracks in sidewalks and pavement, and heavy-traffic areas in lawns. It also occurs in gardens and cultivated fields where it tends to have a more erect habit of growth.

It is distinguished by its thin, wiry stems with small leaves, the ragged ocrea surrounding the stem above every leaf, and its tiny greenish to pinkish or purplish flowers in axils of leaves.

Prostrate knotweed, an introduction from Eurasia, is similar to several, closely related, native species of knotweed. One of the more common of these is **Striate knotweed,** *Polygonum achoreum* Blake, (not illustrated) [POLAH, renouée coriace, Erect knotweed] This plant sometimes occurs in similar situations, especially roadsides, and is distinguished from Prostrate knotweed by its coarser, more erect **stems**, broader and more rounded **leaves**, and by its triangular **seeds** being smooth and olive-coloured. All knotweeds have wiry stems with swollen nodes, membranous ocrea (b), and tiny flowers arising inside the ocrea in leaf axils.

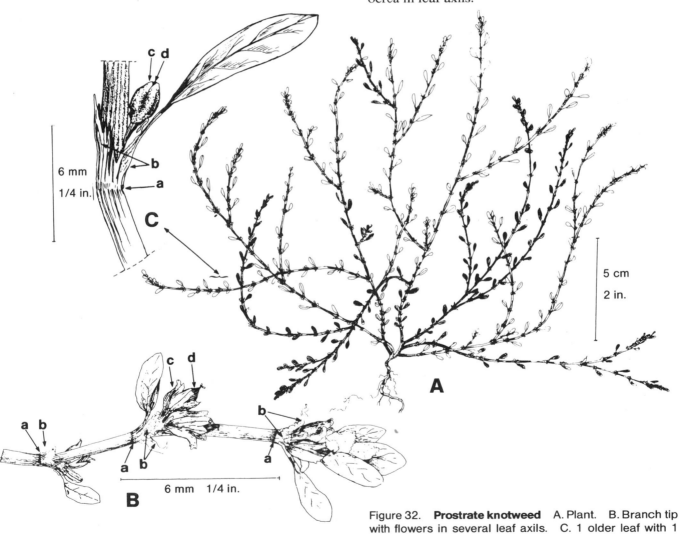

Figure 32. **Prostrate knotweed** A. Plant. B. Branch tip with flowers in several leaf axils. C. 1 older leaf with 1 "seed" in its axil, the "seed" still enclosed in its sepals.

Lady's-thumb, *Polygonum persicaria* L (Figure 33 A, B, Plate 26) [POLPE, renouée persicaire, Red shank, Smartweed, persicaire pied rouge, persicaire] Annual, reproducing only by seed. **Stems** erect from a **taproot**, 20 - 100 cm (8 - 40 in.) high, green or reddish, smooth except for slightly swollen at the distinct nodes (a); each node with a hairy ocrea (cylindrical membranous sheath surrounding the stem) (b, B); **leaves** alternate (1 per node), narrowly elliptic, 2 - 15 cm (4/5 - 6 in.) long, greenish above and slightly paler below, usually with a reddish to brownish or purplish blotch (c) near the middle; undersurface of leaf often slightly rough with tiny bumps, but never glandular or hairy, **ocrea** (b, B) arising with the leafstalk at each node (a), membranous and somewhat papery, its surface covered with short, upward slanting hair (d) and its upper margin ciliate with a fringe of short, erect hair (e) about 1 - 2 mm (1/25 - 1/12 in.) long; **flowers** small, densely crowded into narrow cylindrical spikes (1 - 4.5 cm, 2/5 - 2 in.) long at ends of stems and branches; each flower with 5 pinkish sepals 2 - 4 mm (1/12 - 1/6 in.) long, sometimes nearly white; fruits ("**seeds**") more or less enclosed by the sepals when mature, shiny, smooth, black, broadly ovate in outline, about 2 mm (1/12 in.) long; of 2 kinds, either rounded-triangular or flattened or somewhat lens-shaped in cross-section; the seed often slightly thickened near the middle. Seedling with cotyledons (seed leaves) about 8 - 12 mm (1/3 - ½ in.) long by 2 - 3 mm (1/12 - 1/8 in.) wide, tapered towards both ends, reddish on the undersurface; stem below the cotyledons often reddish to brownish-green; cotyledons soon withering (f) on developing stems. Flowers from June to September.

Lady's-thumb is an introduced weed which occurs in cultivated land on nearly all soil textures throughout Ontario as well as along roadsides and waste places. The seed is a frequent contaminant in small grains.

It is distinguished from other members of the Smartweed Family by the following combination of characteristics: undersurface of leaves without matted white hair or yellowish glands, ocrea (b, B) with hair (d) on the surface and a fringe of longer hair (e) on the margin, and the stem lacking glands on the upper portion near the spikes of flowers. **The reddish or purplish blotch (c) usually present on the upper surface of the leaves cannot be relied upon as a distinguishing feature of Lady's-thumb. Occasionally it is absent from this species and frequently can be found on leaves of other species as well.**

Pale smartweed, *Polygonum lapathifolium* L., (Figure 33C, Plate 27) [POLLA, persicaire pâle, Pale persicaria, White smartweed, persicaire à feuilles de patience, persicaire élevée] Closely resembling Lady's-thumb but more variable in height, occasionally exceeding 2 m (6½ ft) in swampy areas, usually only 45 - 90 cm (1½ - 3 ft) in cultivated fields, or nearly prostrate in open areas; **stems** somewhat swollen at or just above the nodes (g, C), particularly on large plants; **leaves** about the same size and shape as in Lady's-thumb but the **undersurface** of the first 5 to 7 true leaves above the cotyledons (seed leaves) with a short, dense, felt-like mat of whitish hair, then abruptly changing with the next leaf (6th to 8th leaf above coty-

ledons); that leaf and all others above it lacking the whitish hair, but instead having numerous, extremely tiny, yellowish to amber glands (h), slightly imbedded in the undersurface of the leaf; these glands visible as glints of reflected light when the leaf is rolled backwards over the finger or their presence indicated by a yellowish smudge if a fresh leaf is rubbed against white paper or cloth; **ocrea** smooth and papery in texture, lacks surface hair, and is either without a fringe on the margin or has such a short fringe of hair (j) it cannot be seen by the naked eye; lower **stems** smooth and hairless but upper stems and branches near and in the inflorescence somewhat rough or gummy due to tiny, yellowish to amber, unstalked glands mostly less than 0.2 mm (1/100 in.) high, resembling but much shorter than (n) in Figure 33E; **flowering spikes** whitish, or rarely pinkish, long and slender, 7 - 10 cm (3 - 4 in.) long and often drooping, those on side branches usually shorter and rarely drooping; lateral spikes usually with at least 1 cm (2/5 in.) of bare stem below the lowest flower (as k in Figure 33A); sepals of flowers longer than the seed, their tips folded together into a "beak" above the fruit ("**seed**"); "seed" shiny, black, roundish in outline but flattened in cross-section, the flattened sides slightly hollowed or dented in the middle, usually less than 2 mm (1/12 in.) in diameter. Flowers from June to August.

Pale smartweed is a common native plant around streams, lakes and wet depressions throughout Ontario, often persisting as a weed in those locations whenever they come under cultivation. It also occurs on moderately well-drained upland soils and is a frequent weed in cultivated fields, pastures, roadsides and gardens.

It is distinguished from Lady's-thumb by the matted white-hairy undersides of its lowermost 5 to 7 leaves, the tiny, yellow to amber glands (h) on the undersides of its upper leaves, the lack of hair on its ocrea (j), its upper stems glandular-roughened, and its "seeds" never rounded-triangular but always flattened and with the sides slightly depressed.

Green smartweed, *Polygonum scabrum* Moench., (Plate 28) [POLSC, renouée scabre, Pale persicaria, Pale smartweed (due to misidentification), renouée grêle rosée] Introduced from Europe but almost identical to the smaller plants of Pale smartweed with ocrea and undersurface of upper leaves as in Figure 33C; distinguished from Pale smartweed by having its **flowers** in shorter and plumper pale green to greenish-white spikes (1 - 5 cm long by 0.8 - 1.5 cm wide; 2/5 - 2 in. by 1/3 - 2/3 in.), its lateral spikes unstalked (no bare stem) in the axils of leaves or on stalks mostly less than 1 cm (2/5 in.) long, its sepals only as long as or slightly shorter than the "seed," and its flattened "**seed**" usually 2 mm (1/12 in.) in diameter or larger.

Green smartweed occurs in fields, pastures and gardens throughout Ontario but is far less common than Pale smartweed.

Pennsylvania smartweed, *Polygonum pensylvanicum* L., (Figure 33D, E, Plate 29) [POLPY, renouée de Pennsylvanie, Pinkweed, persicaire glanduleuse] Native to North America and very similar to Pale smartweed in general shape and habit of growth; distinguished from Pale smartweed by the absence of matted whitish hair on the undersurface of lower **leaves**

although a few, scattered, short, straight hairs (m) may be present; by the absence of, or only occasional presence of tiny, yellowish, unstalked **glands** on the undersurfaces of upper leaves; by the presence of orange to red or purplish, distinctly stalked glands (glandular hairs) (n) on the uper stems below and in the flower spikes; by the deep pink to reddish colour of the **flowering spikes**; and by the larger "**seeds**" that are round-ovate, flattened, slightly hollowed on one side but not the other, and about 3 mm (⅛ in.) long by 2.5 mm (1/10 in.) wide; their larger size giving the spikes a coarser texture than in Pale smartweed

(compare Plates 27 and 29). Flowers from July to September.

Pennsylvania smartweed is native to moist soils in much of southern Ontario. It occurs as a weed in meadows, hay fields, depressional areas in cultivated land, and in roadside ditches.

It is distinguished from Lady's-thumb by the complete absence of hair from the surface of the ocrea (D, E), the complete absence of a fringe of hair from the margin of the ocrea (p), the presence of stalked glands (n) on the upper stems, and by its coarser spikes and larger seeds.

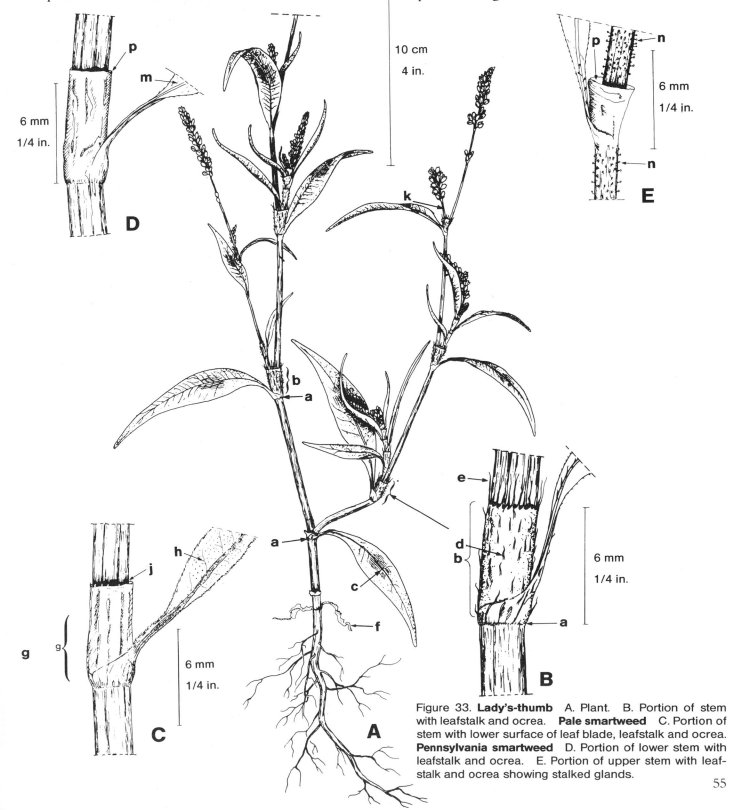

Figure 33. **Lady's-thumb** A. Plant. B. Portion of stem with leafstalk and ocrea. **Pale smartweed** C. Portion of stem with lower surface of leaf blade, leafstalk and ocrea. **Pennsylvania smartweed** D. Portion of lower stem with leafstalk and ocrea. E. Portion of upper stem with leaf-stalk and ocrea showing stalked glands.

55

Water smartweed, *Polygonum amphibium* L., (Figure 34) [POLAM, renouée amphibie, renouée aquatique, *P. natans* (Michx.) Eat] Perennial reproducing by seed and by rhizomes. Occurs in two forms depending on wet or dry habitat, both forms arising from slender, tough, forking rhizomes, or surface stolons. Rhizomes, and stolons when present, are coarse, wiry, often strongly intertwined, much-branched and root abundantly from the nodes [as illustrated at (b) and (c) in Figure 35]. **Terrestrial or dry habitat forms** with stems erect to nearly prostrate, smooth or more or less hairy; leaves alternate, lanceolate to oblong, up to 20 cm (8 in.) long; ocrea (a) membranous or slightly leaf-like in texture, its outer margin smooth or torn and either with or without a distinct horizontal, leaf-like flange (b). **Aquatic forms** rooting in shallow water with floating, hairless stems, elliptic leaves and ocreae without horizontal, leaf-like flanges. **Inflorescence** of both forms a compact, ovoid- or conic-cylindric, spike-like raceme (c), 1 - 4 cm (2/5 - 1¼ in.) long and 1 - 1.7 cm (2/5 - 2/3 in.) wide, usually blunt; flowers light to deep pink, without true petals, the coloured sepals 2 - 5 mm (1/12 - 1/5 in.) long.

Both terrestrial and aquatic forms have a thick, lens-shaped, pale brown to nearly black **achene**, 2.5 mm (1/10 in.) long and wide. Flowers from June to September.

Water smartweed is a native plant in shallow water and along the margins of lakes, ponds, rivers, creeks and roadside ditches, and persists in depressional areas in cultivated fields throughout Ontario.

Both terrestrial and aquatic forms of Water smartweed are distinguished from the closely related Swamp smartweed by their short, thick, more or less cylindric inflorescences, the occasional presence of pubescence and a leaf-like flange on the ocrea of the terrestrial form, and from most other Smartweeds by having thick, tough, forking rhizomes.

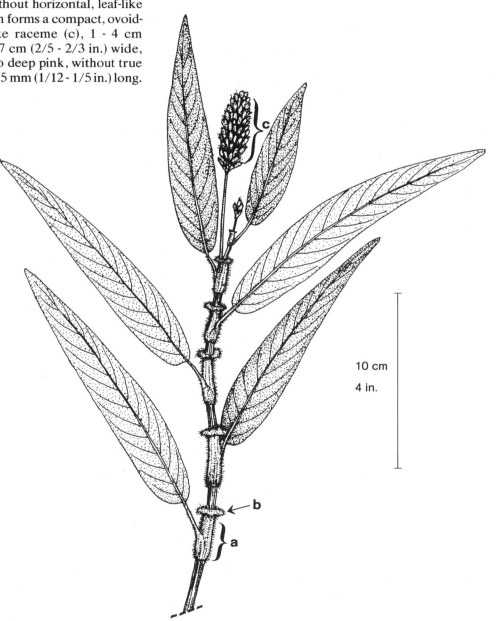

Figure 34. **Water smartweed** Top of flowering plant.

Swamp smartweed, *Polygonum coccineum* Muhl., (Figure 35, Plate 30) [POLCC, renouée écarlate, persicaire des marais] Perennial, reproducing by seed and by rhizomes (a) that root (b) abundantly from the nodes (c). Like Water smartweed, Swamp smartweed also occurs in two forms: terrestrial and aquatic. The two smartweeds are very similar and nearly impossible to distinguish from each other before flowering, except that Swamp smartweed never has a leaf-like flange at the top of its **ocrea** (d). The **inflorescence** is also a spike-like raceme (e) but is usually longer and narrower than that of Water smartweed, the terminal raceme being 2 - 18 cm (4/5 - 7 in.) long and 7 - 15 mm (¼ - 3/5 in.) wide, and less compact than that of Water

smartweed; flowers are scarlet to pink or rarely white. Both the terrestrial and aquatic forms have lens-shaped, dark brown to black **achenes**, 2.5 - 3 mm (1/10 - ⅛ in.) long and wide. Flowers from July to September.

Like Water smartweed, Swamp smartweed is also a native plant and occurs in similar habitats throughout Ontario.

It is distinguished from the terrestrial form of Water smartweed by never having a leaf-like flange on its ocrea and from both terrestrial and aquatic forms of Water smartweed by its longer, thinner inflorescence. It is usually coarser than Water smartweed.

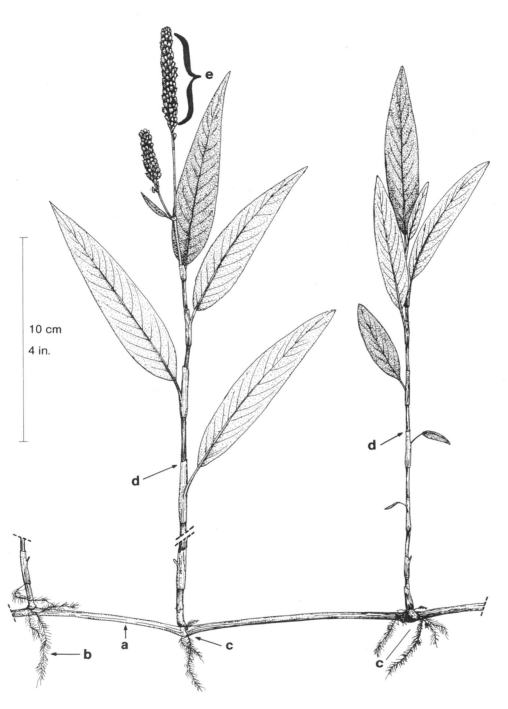

Figure 35. **Swamp smartweed** Underground rhizome with 1 flowering shoot and 1 vegetative shoot.

57

Wild buckwheat, *Polygonum convolvulus* L., (Figure 36, Plate 31) [POLCO, renouée liseron, Black bindweed, Climbing bindweed, Corn bindweed, faux liseron, sarrasin sauvage] Annual, reproducing only by seed. **Stems** 5 cm (2 in.) to more than 2 m (6½ ft) long, slender, prostrate or twining vine-like over other plants or any available support, with a short **ocrea** (membranous sheath) (a) at each node (joint); **leaves** alternate (1 per node), arrowhead-shaped with pointed basal lobes (b) and elongated slender tips (c); **flowers** (d) small, 5 mm (1/5 in.) across, with 5 greenish to whitish sepals (no petals), in small clusters at tips of short branches or from axils of leaves (C); **"seeds"** dull black, 3 mm (⅛ in.) long, pointed at both ends but sharply triangular in cross-section and often partly or wholly enclosed by the dry sepals even after shat-tering from the plant. Flowers from July to August.

Wild buckwheat is a common weed in cultivated fields and gardens throughout all of Ontario and its "seeds" frequently contaminate small grains.

It is distinguished from all other weedy members of the Smartweed Family by its twining stems, its arrowhead-shaped leaves, and its seedling usually having longer cotyledons (e) (7 - 33 mm, ¼ - 1¼ in. long). It is distinguished from Field bindweed (Figure 137) by its annual root system with thin, downward-tapering taproot (f), the presence of an ocrea (a) around the stem at each node (joint), its very small, short-stalked greenish flowers (d), borne in the axils of leaves (C) or in clusters along short branches, and its dark, sharply triangular seeds.

Figure 36. **Wild buckwheat** A. Base of plant. B. Portion of stem twining around another stalk. C. Section of stem with leafstalk, ocrea and 2 flowers.

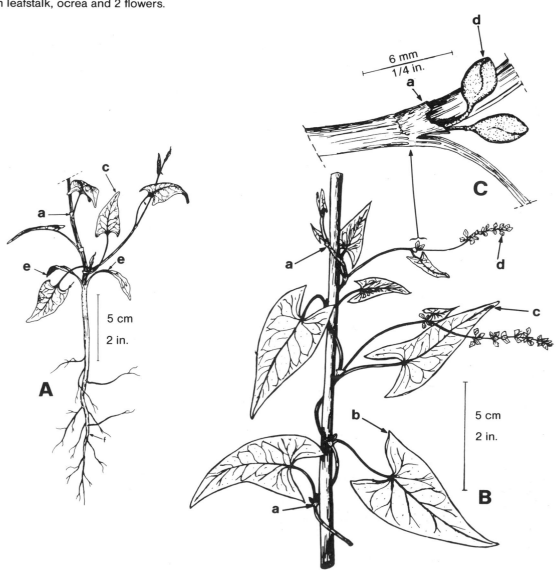

Japanese knotweed, *Polygonum cuspidatum* Sieb. & Zucc., (Figure 37, Plate 32) [POLCU, renouée japonaise, Mexican bamboo, bambou, *Polygonum sieboldii* de Vriese] Perennial, reproducing by widely spreading underground rhizomes and only rarely by seed. **Stems** erect, 75 cm - 3 m (2½ - 10 ft) high, branched or unbranched, round, smooth, often mottled reddish-purple, hollow (a) except at the nodes (b), dying back to the ground each winter, arising in early spring and throughout the growing season from widely spreading, shallow or deeply penetrating, thick, vigorous, whitish underground **rhizomes**, the younger rhizomes (c) whitish except for dark brown, papery sheaths (d), with distinct nodes (e) and internodes (f), the older ones (g) thick, brownish, firm and often somewhat woody; **leaves** alternate (1 per node), long-stalked, broadly ovate, 7.5 - 15 cm (3 - 6 in.) long, 5 - 12.5 cm (2 - 5 in.) wide, square-cut (h) or slightly angled at the base, abruptly pointed at the tip (j) with the tip often stretched out; **ocrea** (membranous sheath) (k) surrounding stem at and immediately above every node, colourless or light greenish and turning brownish, hairless, often somewhat inflated, but soon disintegrating (m); **flowers** (n) individually small but numerous and forming showy, greenish-white branching panicles (p) from the axils of upper leaves; flowers unisexual, the sexes on separate plants; **seeds** (C) only rarely produced, these hanging from the branches, triangular, about 7 mm (¼ in.) long, shiny, enclosed in a papery, 3-winged (r), teardrop-shaped, dry calyx. Flowers from July to September.

Japanese knotweed occurs in southern Ontario in gardens, around old buildings or former building sites, waste places and roadsides, having been introduced as a bushy, hardy perennial for use as a screen or foundation planting.

It is distinguished by its very vigorous growth beginning in early spring and continuing to late autumn, its thick, widely spreading, whitish (c) or brownish (g) rhizomes, its erect stems, often mottled, hollow (a) except at the nodes (b), its broad leaves with abruptly narrowed tip (j) and a prominent ocrea (k, m) around the stem at the base of each leafstalk, and its showy bunches (p) of small greenish-white flowers. Two or more similar but smaller and usually less vigorous relatives of Japanese knotweed, presently grown as foundation or ground cover, may occasionally also escape from cultivation.

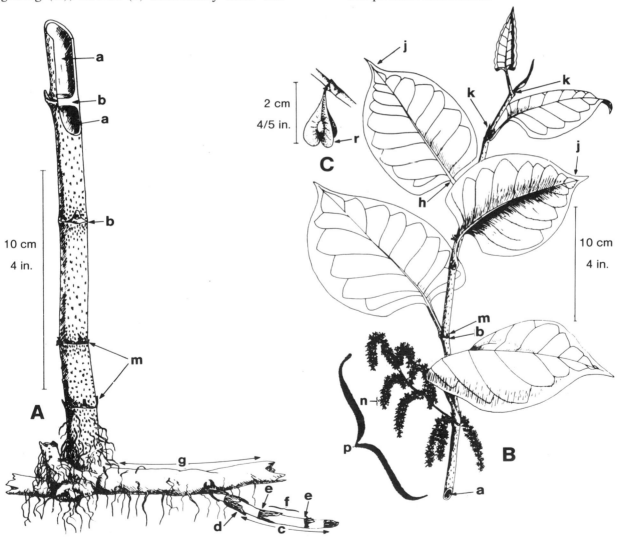

Figure 37. **Japanese knotweed**   A. Hollow stem from branching rhizome.   B. Top of flowering stem.   C. Winged "seed."

GOOSEFOOT FAMILY (Chenopodiaceae)

Jerusalem-oak, *Chenopodium botrys* L., (Figure 38) |CHEBO, chénopode botrys, Feather geranium, herbe à printemps|Annual, reproducing only by seed. **Stems** erect, finely branched, up to 60 cm (2 ft) high; the whole plant, stems, leaves and flowers covered with very short-stalked glandular hairs (a) giving it a sticky texture; **cotyledons** (seed leaves) very small, 5 mm (1/5 in.) or shorter and ¼ as wide, soon shriveling (b); first 3 or 4 true **leaves** with nearly smooth margins (c) or only shallowly lobed (d); all other leaves deeply and irregularly lobed (e); individual **flowers** extremely small, about 1 mm (1/25 in.) across, but crowded into small clusters on short branches from the axils of smaller upper leaves; flowers lacking petals but with yellowish-green to greenish sepals; whole plant with a characteristic though not unpleasant odour. Flowers from June to September.

Jerusalem-oak is an introduced plant which occurs throughout southern Ontario in coarse-textured soils, often along sandy shores of lakes and streams and occasionally in gardens, roadsides and waste places.

It is distinguished from other members of the Goosefoot Family by its sticky texture, its distinct odour, its irregularly lobed leaves and its fine-textured inflorescence.

Lamb's-quarters, *Chenopodium album* L., (Figure 39, Plate 33) |CHEAL, chénopode blanc, Fat-hen, Pigweed, White goosefoot, White pigweed, chou gras, poulette grasse, ansérine blanche|Annual, reproducing only by seed. Very variable in appearance: **stems** 20 - 200 cm (8 in. - 6½ ft) high, branched or unbranched, smooth, green or with reddish or purplish lengthwise stripes and ridges; first 2 or 4 true **leaves** (a) apparently opposite (2 per node), but all later leaves and branches distinctly alternate (1 per node) (b); leaves stalked, the blades 3 - 10 cm (1 - 4 in.) long, lance-shaped or more often broadly triangular with irregular, usually shallow teeth; leaves green or grayish due to a covering of a white mealiness or powderiness, sometimes with reddish undersurface on young plants; **flowers** very small, greenish, densely grouped together into small, thick, granular clusters (c) along the main stem and upper branches, having 5 green sepals but no petals; **seeds** small, rounded in outline, somewhat flattened, 1 - 1.5 mm (1/25 - 1/16 in.) in diameter, enclosed in a very thin, membranous, smooth, whitish covering (pericarp) which is readily fractured and lost when dry. Flowers from June to August.

Lamb's-quarters is very widespread throughout Canada, occurring in cultivated fields, pastures, wasteland, roadsides, gardens and almost anywhere the soil is disturbed.

It is distinguished from the Atriplexes by having only the first 2 or 4 leaves arranged in opposite pairs, and from most other weeds by its broadly triangular leaves with irregular, shallow teeth, its smooth, occasionally mealy or scurfy leaves and stem, and its inflorescence of small, greenish flowers in granular clusters.

5 cm
2 in.

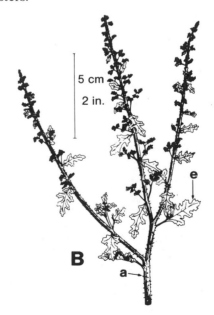

5 cm
2 in.

Figure 38. **Jerusalem-oak** A. Base of young plant. B. Top of flowering plant.

Maple-leaved goosefoot, *Chenopodium giganto-spermum* Aellen, (not illustrated) [CHEHQ, chéno-pode hybride, ansérine à feuilles d'érable, *C. hybri-dum* L.] Resembling Lamb's-quarters but distinguished by its softer and thinner, bright green to yellowish-green **leaves** having 2 or 3 broad, deep, rather sharp-pointed lobes on each side, thus resembling maple leaves in general outline, and by its **inflorescence** being much larger and open, with the individual, small flowers usually well separated from each other.

Maple-leaved goosefoot occurs throughout south-ern Ontario in gardens, waste areas, roadsides, and occasionally along the edges of fields.

Net-seeded lamb's-quarters, *Chenopodium ber-landieri* Moq. var. *zschackei* (Murr.) Murr., (not illus-trated) [CHEBS, chénopode de Berlandier] Closely resembling Lamb's-quarters but its **leaves** are usually narrower and thicker; after flowering, 1 or 2 **seeds** (fruits) usually stick out from each granular cluster on stalks 1 - 3 mm (1/25 - 1/8 in.) long; all seeds and seed covering (pericarp) have honeycombed markings over their surfaces which can be seen only under magnification; and the plant has a rather unpleasant odour.

Lamb's-quarters and the goosefoots are distinguish-ed from the related atriplexes (Figure 42) by having all leaves alternate except sometimes the first 2 or rarely 4 which appear to be opposite, whereas the first 6 or 8 leaves in most of the atriplexes are distinctly opposite and so are the branches which grow from their axils.

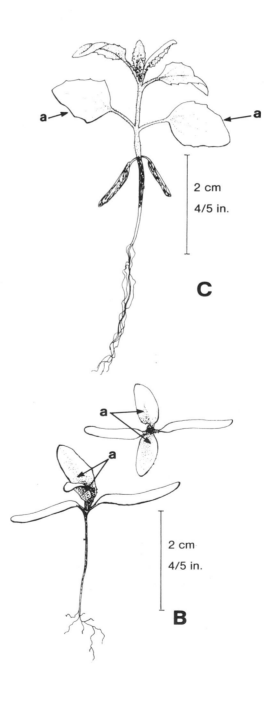

Figure 39. **Lamb's-quarters** A. Young flowering plant. B. Seedling in 2nd true-leaf stage, top and side views. C. Seedling in 6th true-leaf stage.

61

Oak-leaved goosefoot, *Chenopodium glaucum* L., (Figure 40, Plate 34) [CHEGL, chénopode glauque, Saline goosefoot, ansérine glauque, *C. salinum* Standl.] Annual, reproducing only by seed. Similar to Lamb's-quarters in general appearance but much shorter, rarely exceeding 40 cm (16 in.) in height and often prostrate or nearly so; **leaves** alternate (1 per node), generally smaller, up to 4 cm (1-½ in.) long, white on the undersurface, green or sometimes slightly reddish on the upper surface, shallowly and more or less uniformly round-toothed around the margins; granular clusters of tiny greenish **flowers** (later fruits) smaller and forming short, irregular spikes in the axils of the upper leaves; **seeds** dark brown. Flowers from July to September.

Oak-leaved goosefoot occurs throughout Ontario along roadsides and rights-of-way, in pastures, waste places, edges of fields and gardens in situations ranging from dry to moist soils and from very coarse gravels to fine-textured clays, and is often the main weed in depressional areas with saline soils.

Strawberry-blite, *Chenopodium capitatum* (L.), Aschers, (Figure 41) [CHECA, chénopode capité, Blited goosefoot, Red goosefoot, Strawberry-spinach, chénopode en têtes] Annual or occasionally winter annual, reproducing only by seed. **Stems** erect, single or branching, 20 - 60 cm (8 - 24 in.) high, smooth or ridged lengthwise, light green to yellowish-green, sometimes reddish; young plants either developing into a rosette of numerous, long-stalked leaves or immediately producing an elongated stem with only a few leaves; lower **leaves** long-stalked; blade somewhat triangular, with large irregular teeth (a) or lobes; **flowers** tiny, greenish, lacking petals and densely crowded into fleshy masses (b) in the axils of leaves in the upper part of the plant, each dense cluster of flowers at first green but turning red with maturity and forming the "strawberry;" **seeds** dull black, flattened, rounded in outline, 1.5 mm (1/16 in.) wide. Flowers from July to August.

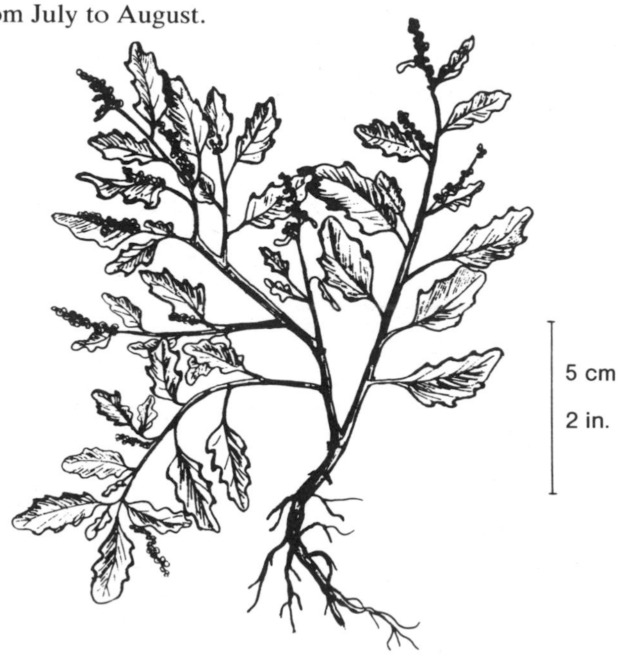

Strawberry-blite is native throughout Ontario, occurring in edges of woods, wasteland, roadsides and gardens, but only rarely in cultivated fields.

Young plants of Strawberry-blite can be confused with those of Maple-leaved goosefoot, but the leaves of Strawberry-blite usually have more and finer teeth (a) and frequently have a reddish cast, whereas those of Maple-leaved goosefoot are yellowish-green to bright green. Older plants are characterized by the bright red, fleshy, seed-containing clusters (b), the "strawberries," in axils of the leaves.

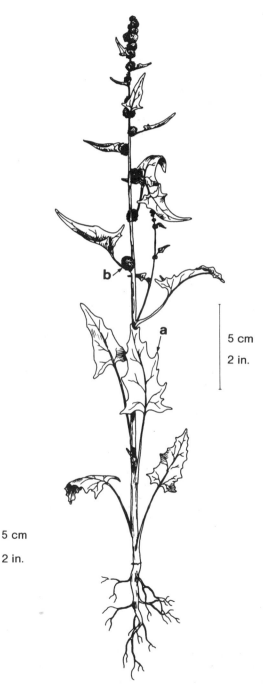

Figure 41. **Strawberry-blite**

5 cm
2 in.

Figure 40. **Oak-leaved goosefoot**

Spreading atriplex, *Atriplex patula* L., (Figure 42 A-B) [ATXPA, arroche étalée, Orache, Spreading orache, arroche des champs] Annual, reproducing only by seed. Plants variable; **stems** prostrate or nearly erect; at least the first 6 leaves opposite (2 per node), but usually alternate (1 per node) towards the ends of stems and branches; branching pattern therefore opposite near the base and alternate farther from the base; **leaves** linear to narrowly lance-shaped (a) and without teeth or lobes, or somewhat broader and with 1 or 2 lateral lobes (b) and sometimes with a few teeth along the margins above the lobes, green, somewhat fleshy, mostly 1 - 5 cm (2/5 - 2 in.) long; **flowers** very small and unisexual; male flowers with only stamens and sepals (no pistil or petals); female flowers with only a single pistil (without stamens, petals or sepals) and enclosed between 2 green, triangular to broadly diamond-shaped **bracts** (c) about 1 - 4 mm (1/25 - 1/6 in.) long and wide, and 2 to 5 of these usually clustered together in the axils of smaller leaves (B) along nearly all the stems and branches; both sexes on one plant. Flowers from July to September.

Spreading atriplex is a native plant in both saline and non-saline moist soils throughout Ontario but frequently occurs as a weed in gardens, waste areas, and row crops in the southern part of the province.

It is distinguished from Halbred-leaved atriplex by usually being prostrate, and by its narrower leaves (a) without lobes or teeth and its wider leaves having a pair of lobes (b) near the base that point outwards and upwards. It is distinguished from Lamb's-quarters by its several pairs of opposite leaves and branches, and its triangular to diamond-shaped bracts (c, B) enclosing each flower.

Halbred-leaved atriplex, *Atriplex hastata* L., (Figure 42C) [ATXHA, arroche hastée, Atriplex, Orache, Spreading orache, arroche à feuilles en hallebarde, *Atriplex patula* L. var. *hastata* (L.) Gray] Very similar to Spreading atriplex but usually more erect, often 1 m (40 in.) or taller; **stems** round or ridged lengthwise and usually with lengthwise stripes of alternate dark green and yellowish-green lines; **leaves** long-stalked, the blades more or less triangular in outline, their bases nearly flat or broadly tapering, usually with 2 lateral lobes (d) that point outwards (halbred-shaped), green to dark green and somewhat fleshy; the pair of **bracts** enclosing each tiny female flower triangular, flat-based, about 4 mm long and 2.5 mm wide (1/6 in. x 1/10 in.).

The distribution and occurrence of Halbred-leaved atriplex are similar to that of Spreading atriplex.

Both kinds are often mistaken for Lamb's-quarters or one of the other goosefoots. The atriplexes are readily distinguished by having more than just 1 or 2 pairs of opposite leaves and branches on the lower part of the stem, and by the coarser appearance of their clusters of flowers because each tiny female (seed-producing) flower is enclosed between 2 triangular or diamond-shaped bracts.

Garden atriplex, *Atriplex hortensis* L., (not illustrated) [ATXHO, arroche des jardins, Hungarian spinach, arroche-épinard] Similar to Halbred-leaved atriplex but larger, with erect **stems,** up to 2 m (6½ ft) high and usually erect branches; **leaves** variable from narrow and lance-shaped, to ovate or very broad triangular, these as much as 20 cm (8 in.) long and 10 - 15 cm (4 - 6 in.) wide, greenish above and whitish below, becoming bronzy-green both above and below towards maturity; **flowers** very small but enclosed in a pair of round **bracts** which enlarge as the seed forms and may be 12 mm (½ in.) or more in diameter at maturity.

Garden atriplex occurs in scattered localities throughout Ontario, usually persisting around old gardens and in waste areas.

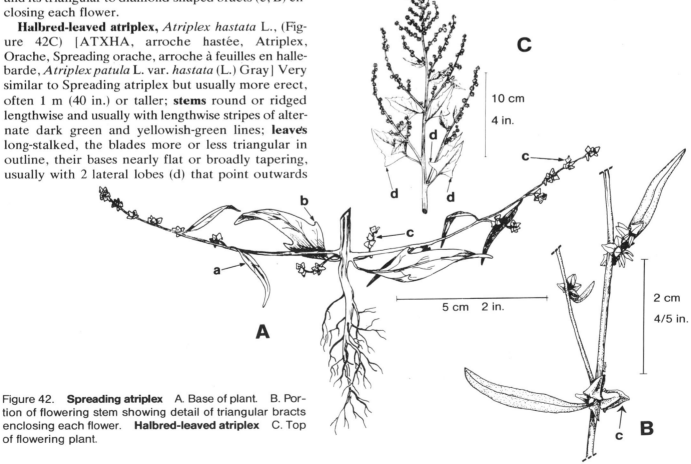

Figure 42. **Spreading atriplex** A. Base of plant. B. Portion of flowering stem showing detail of triangular bracts enclosing each flower. **Halbred-leaved atriplex** C. Top of flowering plant.

63

Russian thistle, *Salsola pestifer* A. Nels., (Figure 43, Plate 35) [SASKR, soude roulante, Saltwort, Tumbleweed, chardon de Russie, herbe roulante de Russie, *Salsosa iberica* Sennen & Pau. *S. Kali* L. var. *tenuifolia* Tausch, *S. tragus* L. subsp. *iberica* Sennen & Pau] Annual, reproducing only by seed. A very bushy, much-branched, spiny plant 5 - 120 cm (2 in. - 4 ft) high, its diameter often exceeding its height; **stems** green, usually striped with red lines, and rough with short, firm hair; **cotyledons** (seed leaves) (a) very narrow and grass-like, gradually lengthening and reaching 3 - 5 cm (1 - 2 in.) long; first true **leaves** (b) apparently opposite (2 per node), as long as or longer than the cotyledons, needle-like, round or slightly flattened in cross-section, softly sharp-pointed; later leaves gradually shorter but mostly alternate (1 per node); young plants often with crowded erect leaves and resembling a grass; older plants with firm, short, bract-like leaves (c), usually only 6 mm (¼ in.) long, with a broad base tapering to a slender point and ending in a hard, sharp spine; **flowers** (d) small, lacking petals but with 5 pinkish to greenish-white, membranous-winged **sepals**, stalkless in the axil of each cluster of 3 spine-tipped bract-like leaves (D). At maturity, the brittle stem breaks at the top of the root and the whole plant is rolled and tumbled by the wind, dropping seeds with each bounce and turn. **Seeds** cone- or top-shaped, the broader end flattened or hollowed and with a small point in the centre, about 2 mm (1/12 in.) across and the same long; the coiled embryo being visible through the nearly transparent seed coat. Flowers from July to August.

Russian thistle occurs throughout Ontario, usually in coarse soils along roadsides, railroads, waste areas, and occasionally in pastures and fields on sandy soils.

It is distinguished from most other plants by its spininess and nearly spherical shape and from other so-called "tumbleweeds" by the long, thin, needle-like leaves (a, b) of the young plant, and by the short, bract-like leaves (c) and extremely spiny nature of the older plant.

Wingless Russian thistle, *Salsosa collina* Pall. (not illustrated) [SASCO, soude des collines, Spineless Russian thistle] is very similar to Russian thistle. It differs mainly by its **stems** usually lacking the characteristic red colouration, its **leaves** being flatter and gradually narrowing to their tips which are spineless or only weakly spiny, and its **sepals** being without membranous wings. It is still rare in Canada, occurring only near Ottawa and in southern Saskatchewan.

Figure 43. **Russian thistle** A. Seedling. B. Base of young plant. C. Mature plant. D. Portion of branch with 3 flowers.

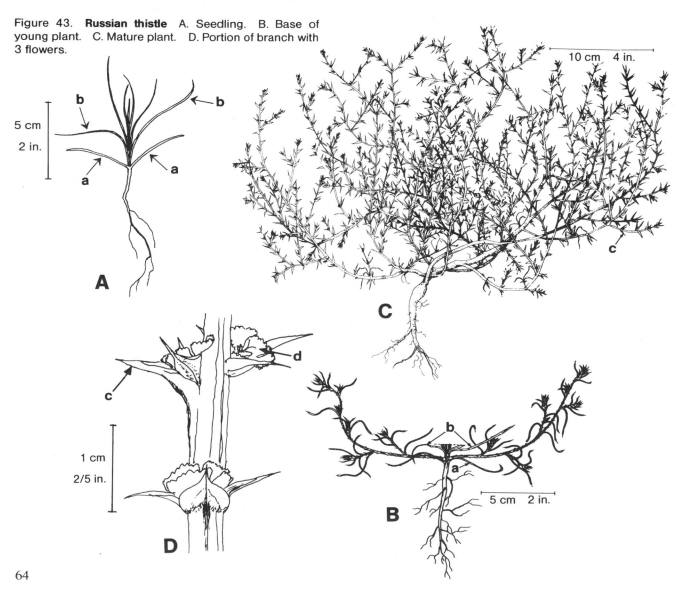

AMARANTH FAMILY (Amaranthaceae)

Prostrate pigweed, *Amaranthus blitoides* S. Wats., (Figure 44) [AMABL, amarante fausse-blite, Prostrate amaranth, Spreading amaranth, Tumbleweed, amarante étalée, amarante basse, amarante charnue, *Amaranthus graecizans* L.] Annual, reproducing only by seed. **Stems** and leaves prostrate or with tips of some branches raised 2 - 5 cm (1 - 2 in.) above the ground surface, 10 - 120 cm (4 in. - 4 ft) long, much-branched and often forming thick, circular mats, usually not rooting from the nodes, green or purplish-red, somewhat fleshy; **leaves** alternate (1 per node), numerous along the branches, 1 - 5 cm (2/5 - 2 in.) long, the blade paddle-shaped, light green or sometimes a bit reddish, rounded or slightly indented at the end and usually ending in a short, very soft spine (a), not succulent; **flowers** very small (3 mm, ⅛ in. long), greenish, without petals; **sepals** narrow, bract-like; 2 or more flowers plus several narrow bracts (b) in clusters (c) on short lateral branches in the axils of small leaves (B); each flower unisexual, either female (seed-producing) with only a pistil (d) or male (pollen-producing) with only stamens (e); **seeds** black, disk-shaped, about 1.5 mm (1/16 in.) in diameter. Flowers from June to September.

Prostrate pigweed occurs throughout southern Ontario in waste areas, roadsides, gardens and in some row crops, usually on coarse or sandy soils.

It is distinguished from Tumble pigweed by its prostrate habit, its narrow bracts (b) about the same length as the sepals and its larger seed; from Redroot, Smooth and Green pigweed by its prostrate habit, its flowers in small clusters on very short branches (c) in the axils of leaves, the absence of large, terminal inflorescences and by its larger seeds; from Purslane by its thinner leaves with pointed tips (a), its clusters of narrow-bracted flowers (b) and its relatively non-succulent nature.

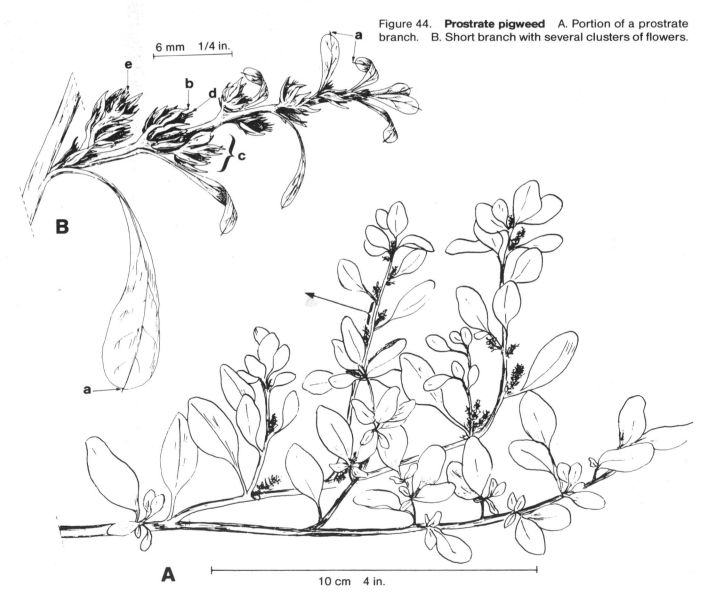

Figure 44. **Prostrate pigweed** A. Portion of a prostrate branch. B. Short branch with several clusters of flowers.

65

Tumble pigweed, *Amaranthus albus* L., (Figure 45, Plate 36) [AMAAL, amarante blanche, Amaranth, Tumbling amaranth, Tumbleweed, Tumbling pigweed, White pigweed, herbe roulante]Annual, reproducing only by seed. Very much like Prostrate pigweed but its main branches more or less erect, up to 1 m (3¼ ft) high, bushy-branched, yellowish-green to whitish in colour; young **leaves** up to 8 cm (3¼ in.) long, the blade rounded or paddle-shaped; **flowers** very similar to those of Prostrate pigweed, but the **bracts** (a) around the sepals firmer, sharper, and longer (about 6 mm, ¼ in.), being about twice as long as the flowers, these borne in small clusters on short branches in the axils of leaves (B) as with Prostrate

pigweed; **seed** round, flattened, less than 1 mm (1/25 in.) in diameter. Flowers from July to August.

Tumble pigweed occurs throughout Ontario, being more common in the southern portion in cultivated fields, wasteland, roadsides and gardens, usually on coarse or sandy soils.

It is distinguished from Prostrate pigweed by its erect, whitish stems, smaller seeds, and its spiny-tipped long-bracted (a) flower clusters; and from Redroot, Smooth and Green pigweed by its smaller leaves, its flowers in small clusters (B) in axils of leaves along the branches, and the absence of large, terminal inflorescences.

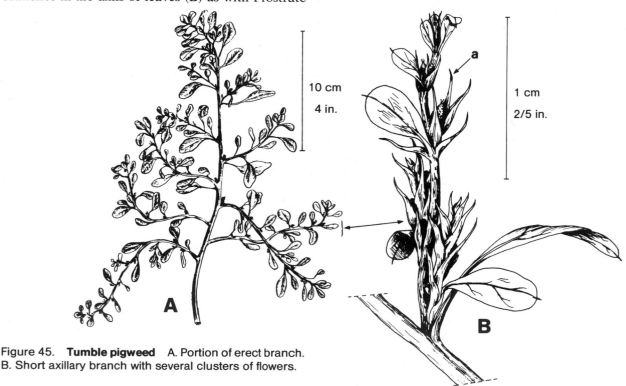

Figure 45. **Tumble pigweed** A. Portion of erect branch. B. Short axillary branch with several clusters of flowers.

Redroot pigweed, *Amaranthus retroflexus* L., (Figure 46, Plate 37) [AMARE, amarante à racine rouge, Green amaranth, Pigweed, Redroot, Rough pigweed, Tall pigweed, amarante réfléchie, amarante pied rouge]Annual, reproducing only by seed. **Stems** erect, 10 cm - 2 m (4 in. - 6½ ft) high, but usually 50 - 90 cm (20 - 36 in.), simple or branched, lower part thick and smooth, upper part usually rough with dense short hair, greenish to slightly reddish but usually red near the roots; **leaves** alternate (1 per node), long-stalked, ovate with a shallow notch at the tip on young plants but on older plants somewhat diamond-shaped, dull green above but lighter green and with prominent whitish veins below, and somewhat hairy; **inflorescence** a coarse, branching, bristly panicle made up of a short, thick terminal spike (a) and below it several to many short, lateral finger-like spikes (b), these pointing upward (B) if not crowded or outward if densely crowded, and smaller spikes in some lower leaf axils (c), each spike made up of many tiny flowers and spiny-tipped **bracts** (d) up to 8 mm (1/3 in.) long; each flower unisexual, having either 1 pistil or 5 sta-

mens but never both (similar to Prostrate pigweed, Figure 44 B, d and e); **seeds** black, shiny, round, flattened with a narrow, thin margin, and about 1 mm (1/25 in.) in diameter. Flowers from July to August.

Redroot pigweed is a common weed in cultivated fields, gardens, pastures, waste places, roadsides and other disturbed areas throughout Ontario.

It is distinguished from Tumble pigweed and Prostrate pigweed by its tall, erect habit of growth, its larger and broader leaves, and its flowers crowded into a thick, terminal panicle as well as in some of the lower leaf axils; from Smooth pigweed by its coarse, harsh inflorescence; and from Green pigweed by the somewhat dull green colour of its leaves, the dense covering of short hair on its upper stem, its thick, coarse, bristly terminal panicle with the uppermost central spike (a) extending only a short distance above the rest of the panicle, and by two features requiring magnification to see: the sepals of each flower are broader above the middle and rounded or somewhat flattened at their tips, and its male flowers usually have 5 stamens each.

Smooth pigweed, *Amaranthus hybridus* L., (not illustrated) [AMACH, amarante hybride, Green amaranth, Prince's-feather, Wild beet, amarante verte, *A. hypochondriacus* L.] Similar in general appearance to both Redroot pigweed and Green pigweed. It is distinguished from Redroot pigweed by being less hairy; its **inflorescence** much finer, the individual spikes being nearly always less than 1 cm (2/5 in.) thick, much less spiny because of their shorter bracts (3 - 4 mm, 1/8 - 1/6 in.), and having smaller flowers (2 mm, 1/12 in.), hence the name "smooth," both terminal and lateral spikes usually longer and pointing upward. It is distinguished from Green pigweed by its more slender and less spiny spikes.

Smooth pigweed occurs in gardens, fields and waste places in southern Ontario, especially in the southwestern counties.

Hybridization is known to occur among Redroot pigweed, Green pigweed and Smooth pigweed. Plants which seem to be intermediate or have a mixture of characteristics from any of these species could be hybrids between them.

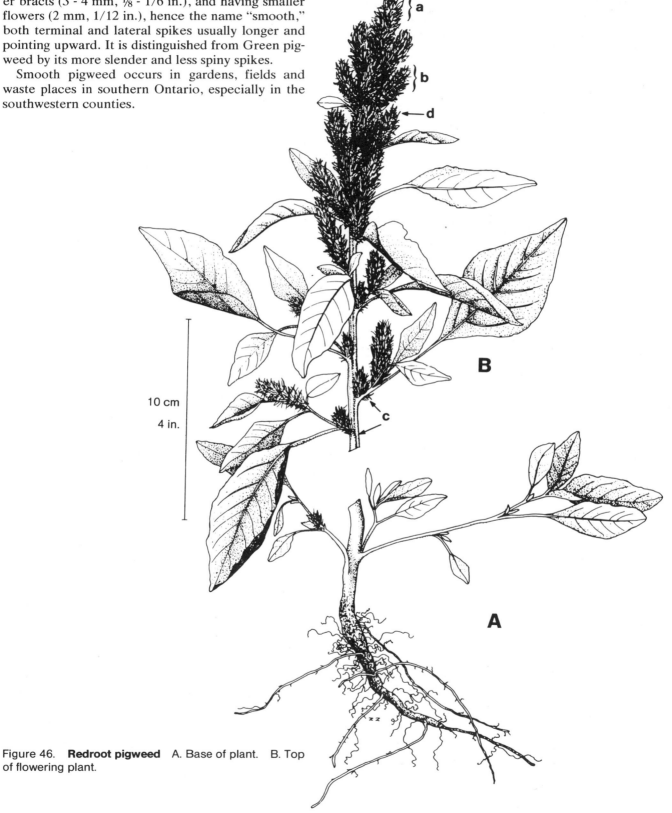

10 cm
4 in.

Figure 46. **Redroot pigweed** A. Base of plant.   B. Top of flowering plant.

Green pigweed, *Amaranthus powellii* S. Wats., (Figure 47, Plate 38) [AMAPO, amarante de Powell, Green amaranth, Powell's amaranth, Powell's pigweed] Very similar to both Redroot pigweed and Smooth pigweed in habit of growth, size and general appearance; young plants distinguished from Redroot pigweed by their somewhat shiny green or slightly reddish-green colour and somewhat less hairy stem and leaves. Compared to Redroot pigweed, older plants of Green pigweed have a brighter green, thinner, looser **inflorescence** in which the individual bristly, finger-like spikes (a) are usually longer (4 - 12 cm, 2 - 5 in.) and tend to point upwards. The terminal spike (b) is much longer (10-25 cm, 4-10 in.), narrower, about 1 - 1.5 cm (2/5 - 3/5 in.) thick, and either stands erect or frequently hangs over a bit. Flowers and flower bracts are about the same length as in Redroot pigweed, but male flowers usually have only 3 stamens, and the chaff-like **sepals** are broadest at or below the middle and taper towards the tip. Compared to Smooth pigweed, older plants have thicker, spinier spikes and slightly larger flowers. Flowers from July to September.

Green pigweed occurs throughout southern Ontario but is more abundant in the southwest, in some areas it is probably more important than Redroot pigweed.

Figure 47. **Green pigweed** A. Base of plant. B. Top of flowering plant.

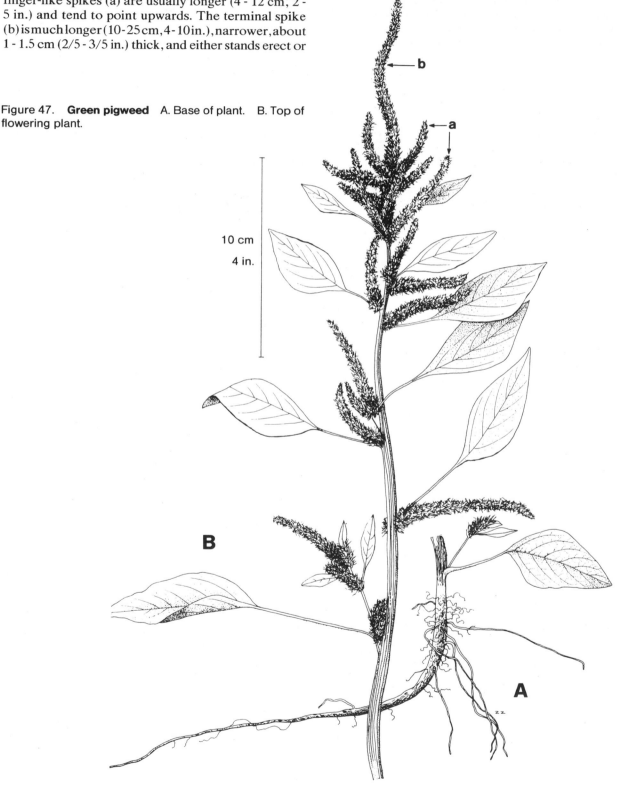

10 cm
4 in.

POKEWEED FAMILY (Phytolaccaceae)

Pokeweed, *Phytolacca americana* L., (Figure 48, Plate 39) [PHTAM, phytolaque d'Amérique, Inkweed, Pokeberry, phytolaque commun, raisin d'Amérique] Perennial, reproducing only by seed. **Stems** erect, usually 1 - 2 m (3 - 6½ ft) high but up to 3 m (10 ft) high, smooth and hairless, pinkish to bright red, dying down to the ground each year; these produced from a thick perennial **taproot**, as much as 10 - 15 cm (4 - 6 in.) in diameter and **very poisonous**; **leaves** alternate (1 per node), the lower quite large, up to 30 - 50 cm (12 - 20 in.) long and about 1/3 as wide, upper leaves shorter and smaller and with shorter leafstalks; all leaves usually dark green above, lighter green to pinkish-green below and with prominent pinkish veins; **flowers** greenish-white to pinkish in slender racemes at the ends of the main stem and branches. There are no petals, 5 petal-like sepals (a), 5 to 30 stamens but usually only 10, and a ring of 10 pistils in the centre; at maturity these form a flat, ring-shaped, juicy, purplish berry with 4 to 10 (usually about 6) sections (b), each with 1 large hard **seed**. The whole plant, but especially the ripe berries, has an intense purplish-red juice that was used for dyeing. Flowers from June to October.

Pokeweed is a native plant which occurs in meadows, edges of woods and waste areas in the southwestern part of southern Ontario; elsewhere in the province it may persist in old gardens after having been cultivated for the young leafy sprouts which are used as a green vegetable if properly cooked and re-cooked, with the cooking water discarded 3 times. **The plant is poisonous to livestock.**

The soft, smooth, fleshy texture of leaves and young stems and the absence of an ocrea at the base of each leaf distinguish Pokeweed from Lamb's-quarters, Pigweeds and the Docks, respectively, with which it might be confused. The flat, juicy, 4 - 10-seeded purplish berries arranged in a spike at the ends of smooth stems and branches distinguish it from wild blackberries and raspberries.

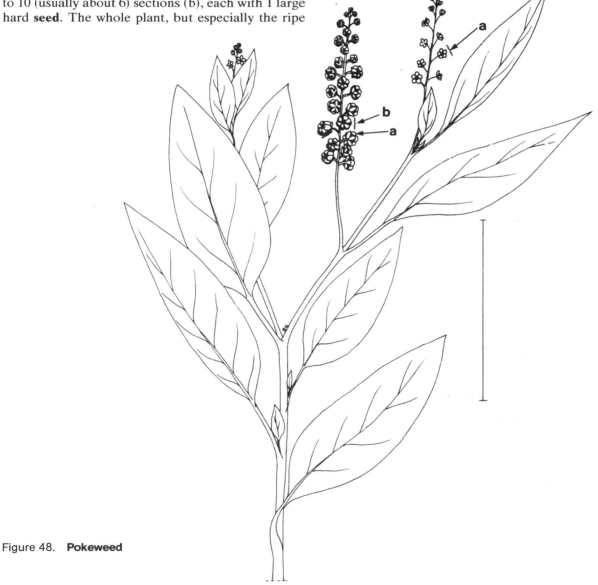

Figure 48. **Pokeweed**

PURSLANE FAMILY (Portulacaceae)

Purslane, *Portulaca oleracea* L., (Figure 49, Plate 40) [POROL, pourpier potager, Portulaca, Pursley, Pusley, Pussley, Wild portulaca, pourpier gras] Annual, reproducing only by seed. A low-growing or prostrate plant with succulent reddish stems, thick leaves and small flowers. Stems and leaves flat on the ground or slightly raised, 2 - 3 cm (1 in.) high; **stems** very fleshy or watery, smooth, reddish-green to purplish-red, repeatedly branched and often forming circular mats 30 - 60 cm (1 - 2 ft) in diameter or larger; **cotyledons** (seed leaves) of emerging seedlings 2 - 5 mm (1/12 - 1/5 in.) long, and half or less wide (a), thick, fleshy and reddish-green on a bright red stalk; **leaves** mostly alternate (1 per node) except the first few apparently opposite (2 per node), and those near the tips of branches crowded together; all leaves flat but thick and fleshy, deep green to reddish-green, broadest near the rounded or squared tip and narrowed towards the base, completely hairless; **flowers** (b) small, 5 - 10 mm (1/5 - 2/5 in.) across, in axils of stem leaves or near the tips of branches, opening only on bright sunny mornings with 5 small, pale yellow petals which soon fall off, 6 - 10 tiny yellowish stamens and 1 pistil; **seedpods** (c) nearly spherical, about 5 mm (1/5 in.) in diameter, opening by a slit that goes all the way around the seedpod just below the middle so the top part comes off as a lid; **seeds** numerous, flattened, rounded or somewhat kidney-shaped, about 0.6 mm

(1/40 in.) across, black and shiny. Flowers from July to September.

Purslane is one of the most common weeds in gardens throughout Ontario, occurring also in row crops, waste areas and edges of driveways but not surviving under heavy shade and thus rarely seen in grainfields, hay fields or pastures. The very fleshy nature of Purslane enables it to continue flowering and ripening seeds for several days after being hoed or uprooted. Though rarely producing roots from the stem, if even a small portion of the root of an uprooted plant touches the soil, it can grow a new root system and become re-established.

Purslane is distinguished from similar prostrate plants by its reddish, fleshy stem with watery juice, its fleshy, thick, greenish leaves without teeth, its small flowers with yellow petals and its small, inconspicuous, spherical seedpods which open with a circular lid, scattering many tiny black seeds. Prostrate pigweed has a tougher stem, thin leaves, and tiny greenish flowers in somewhat spiny clusters in axils of leaves. The prostrate annual spurges have thinner stems and leaves, and all plant parts contain a white milky juice that is never found in Purslane.

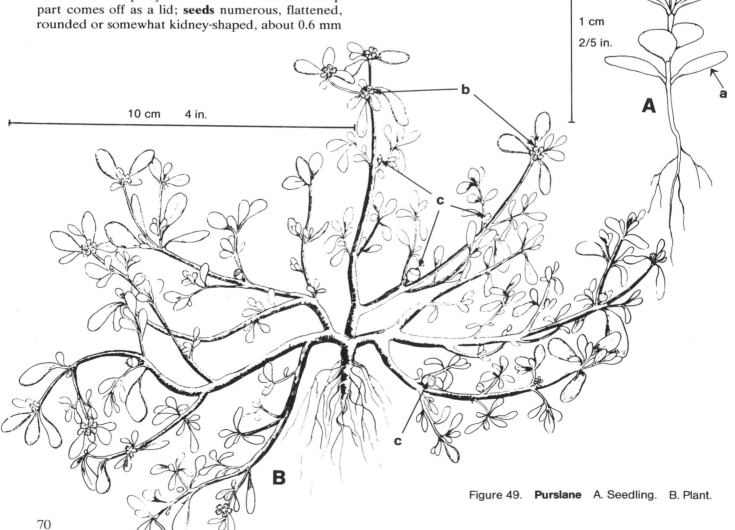

Figure 49. **Purslane** A. Seedling. B. Plant.

70

CARPETWEED FAMILY (Aizoaceae)

Carpetweed, *Mollugo verticillata* L., (Figure 50) [MOLVE, mollugine verticillée, Mollugo, mollugo verticillé] Annual, reproducing only by seed. This prostrate plant is occasionally confused with Purslane but is distinguished by its thinner, yellowish-green **stems**, its thin, flat **leaves** produced in whorls of 3 to 8 leaves (a) at each node (b), and its clusters of usually 2 to 5 small, pale green to whitish **flowers** (c) on short stalks (5 - 15 mm, 1/5 - 3/5 in.) from axils of those whorled leaves. The flowers usually have 3 stamens

and are followed by small, ovoid **seedpods** (d) (3 mm, 1/8 in. long) which split lengthwise and have very tiny **seeds**. Flowers from June to August.

Carpetweed occurs in moist sandy or coarse soils in gardens, row crops, waste places and along railways and roadsides throughout Ontario, chiefly in the southern part.

It is distinguished from the prostrate spurges, such as Hairy-fruited spurge, by its whorls of leaves and the complete absence of white, milky juice.

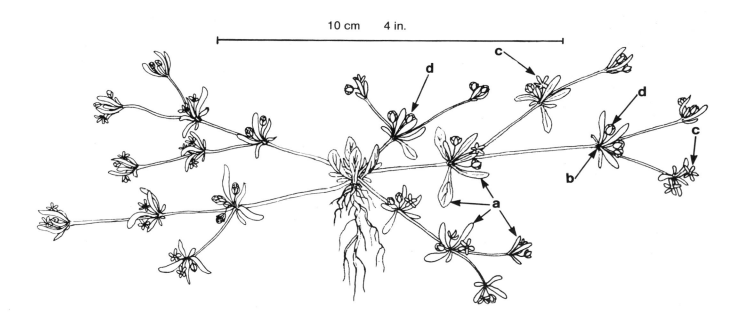

Figure 50. **Carpetweed**

PINK FAMILY (Caryophyllaceae)

Corn spurry, *Spergula arvensis* L., (Figure 51) [SPRAR, spargoute des champs, Spurrey, spargoute, herbe à Bolduc] Annual, reproducing only by seed. **Stems** single or much-branched, 10 - 50 cm (4 - 20 in.) high, bright green, finely hairy and sometimes slightly sticky; **leaves** 2 - 5 cm (4/5 - 2 in.) long, very narrow, flat or slightly rounded in cross-section, those on young plants (B) in a rosette-like cluster resembling grass, on older plants in whorls of 6 to 30 or more at each node (a); **flowers** small but often very numerous on short stalks (1 - 3 cm, 2/5 - 1¼ in.) in the upper part of the plant, with 5 green sepals and 5 white petals (b) about 3 mm (⅛ in.) long, usually 10 stamens, and 5 styles on the top of the small oval **seedpod**; mature seedpod (c) longer than the sepals and splitting into 5 divisions to release the numerous black, flat, round **seeds**, each of which has a narrow pale or white wing around its margin. Flowers from June to October.

Corn spurry is found in all parts of Ontario but is most common on light sandy soils.

It is distinguished from other plants in the Pink Family by its whorled leaves; from the bedstraws by its annual habit, its whorls of usually more than 8 narrow leaves on round stems, and its somewhat larger flowers with seedpods containing many small seeds; from the Prostrate spurges by the absence of white, milky juice; from Carpetweed by its erect stature and its flowers at the ends of the branches rather than in axils of leaves; and young plants are distinguished from those of Russian thistle by their whorled leaves, their blunt leaf tips, and the absence of reddish lines on the stem.

Figure 51. **Corn spurry** A. Plant. B. Seedling, side view. C. Seedling, top view.

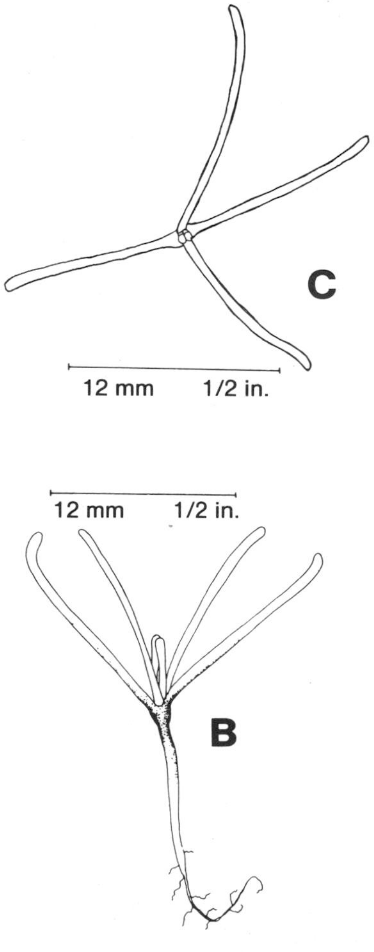

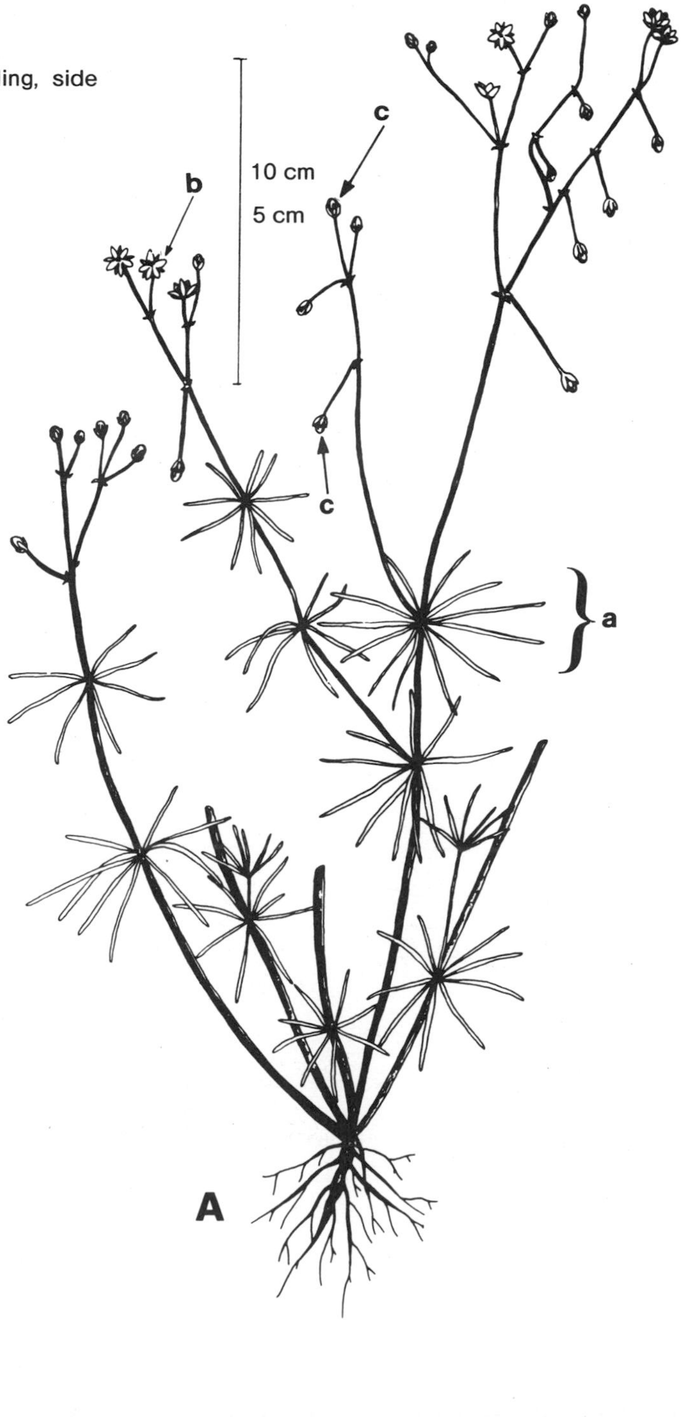

Chickweed, *Stellaria media* (L.) Vill., (Figure 52, Plate 41) [STEME, stellaire moyenne, Common chickweed, mouron des oiseaux] Annual or winter annual, reproducing by seed and by horizontally spreading leafy stems which root at the nodes (a). **Stems** prostrate, spreading or nearly erect, much-branched, 5 - 50 cm (2 - 20 in.) long, soft, delicate, bright green, with swollen nodes (b), smooth except for a single, narrow lengthwise line (about 1 mm, 1/25 in. wide) of fine white hair (c) on one side of each branch, this line of hair alternating from one side of the branch to the other on successive internodes; stems rooting from nodes which touch the ground, and the plant spreading by this means to form dense, matted patches; **leaves** opposite (2 per node), stalked near the base, stalkless near ends of branches, blades oval with pointed tips, smooth or slightly hairy; **flowers** small, white (d), produced at tips of stems and in angles between branches (B); petals white, shorter

than the 3 - 4 mm (⅛ - 1/6 in.) long green sepals (e); each of the 5 petals is 2-lobed so the flower may appear to have 10 tiny petals; **seedpod** somewhat egg-shaped, about as long as or slightly longer than the sepals, the tip splitting into 6 tiny teeth and releasing the reddish-brown somewhat spherical **seeds** which are about 1.2 mm (1/20 in.) in diameter. It may start blooming in early spring and produce flowers and seeds throughout the growing season.

Chickweed occurs throughout Ontario in a wide variety of habitats and soil textures. It is one of the most common weeds in lawns but is equally at home in gardens, cultivated fields, pastures, waste areas and even under deciduous forests.

It is distinguished from similar plants by its bright green colour, its ovate-pointed leaves, and the single lengthwise line of fine white hair (c) on one side of the stem but switching sides above and below each node.

Figure 52. **Chickweed** A. Plant. B. Section of stem with a single flower between the pair of branches and showing narrow lengthwise lines of hair on alternate sides of the stem. C. Seedling, top view. D. Seedling, side view. E. Young plant.

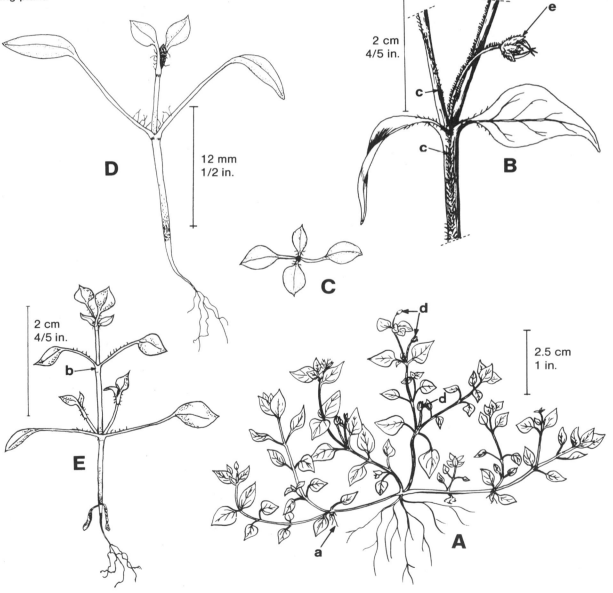

73

Grass-leaved stitchwort, *Stellaria graminea* L., (Figure 53) [STEGR, stellaire à feuilles de graminées, Common stitchwort, Narrow-leaved chickweed, mouron des champs] Perennial, reproducing by seed and spreading by horizontal stems which root at the nodes (a). **Stems** nearly horizontal, as much as 60 cm (24 in.) long with numerous leaning or partly erect branches, nearly square, the corners angled and sometimes rough-hairy; **leaves** opposite (2 per node), narrow, grass-like, up to 5 cm (2 in.) long but rarely over 5 mm (1/5 in.) wide, widest near the base and tapering towards the tip; **inflorescence** diffuse with long, thin flowering stalks and branches; leaves in the inflorescence (b) much smaller than those down the stem; petals (c) 5, white, about 6 mm (¼ in.) long, about as long as the green sepals; **seedpods** light brown, about as long as the sepals and opening with 6 fine teeth at the tip; **seeds** dark reddish-brown, rounded to nearly kidney-shaped and about 1 mm (1/25 in.) across. Flowers from June to October.

Grass-leaved stitchwort occurs sporadically throughout Ontario in pastures, meadows, roadsides and waste areas but only rarely in cultivated land, gardens or lawns.

It is distinguished from Chickweed by its square stem, its very narrow leaves, the absence of the lengthwise band of hair on the stem, and its distinct perennial habit; and from the bedstraws by having only two opposite leaves at each node, by its flowers having 5 petals surrounding the pistil, and its seedpod containing many small seeds. **Field chickweed,** *Cerastium arvense* L., (not illustrated) [CERAR, céraiste des champs, mouron des champs à oreille de souris] A native perennial resembling Grass-leaved stitchwort, but distinguished by having a more compact habit of growth with its narrow **leaves** much closer together, the frequent production of densely leafy, short branches near the base of the plant, round **stems**, and large white **flowers** with their petals 10 - 20 mm (2/5 - 4/5 in.) long, being 2 to 3 times the length of the sepals.

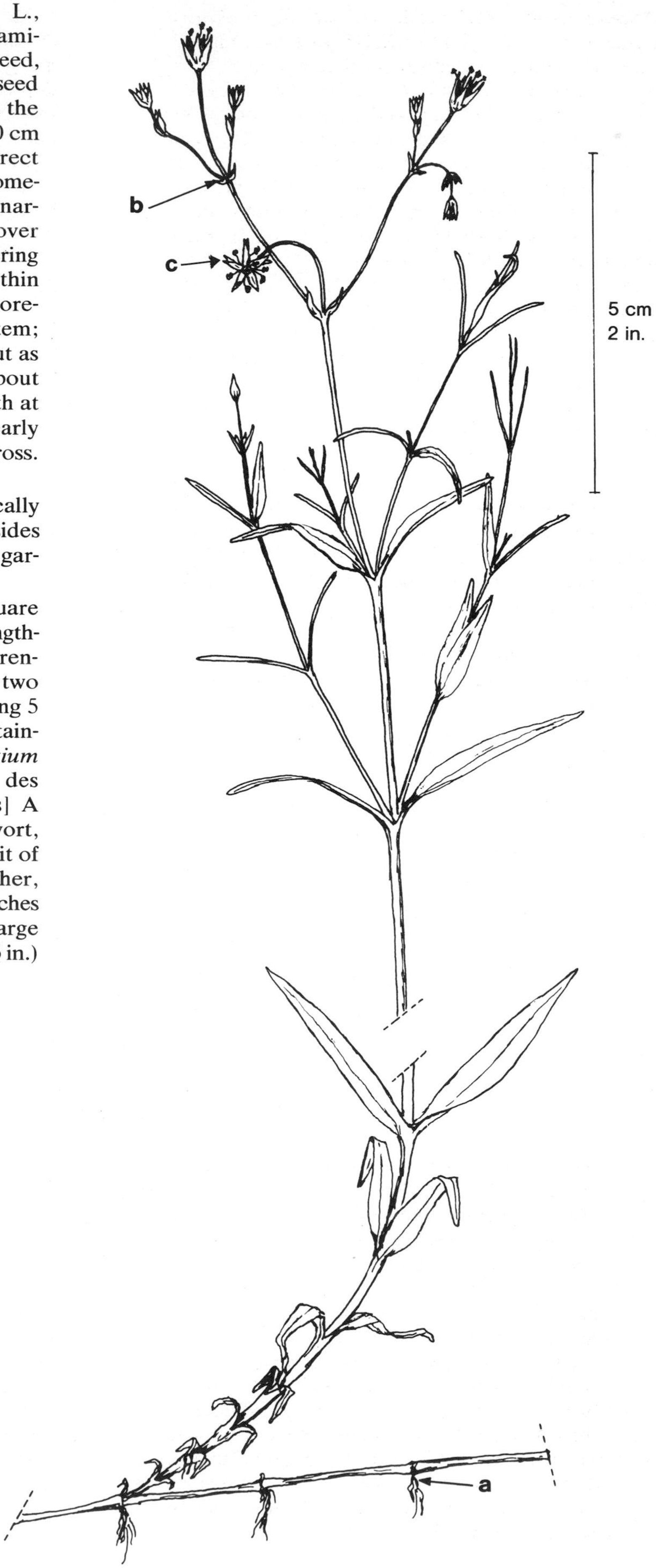

Figure 53. **Grass-leaved stitchwort**

Mouse-eared chickweed, *Cerastium fontanum* Baumg. ssp. *triviale* (Link) Jalas (Figure 54, Plate 42) [CERVU, céraiste vulgaire, céraiste commun, *Cerastium vulgatum* L.] Annual or more usually perennial, reproducing by seed and by horizontal stems which root at the nodes and form dense patches. **Stems** nearly prostrate, as much as 50 cm (2 ft) long, with short upright branches, or stems erect if growing amongst taller plants, densely but very finely hairy, soft, often slightly sticky to the touch, dark green, round in cross-section with swollen nodes; **leaves** opposite (2 per node), stalkless, ovate (1 - 2 cm, 2/5 - 4/5 in. long) with pointed tips and covered with hair (a) up to 2 mm (1/12 in.) long (hence the name "mouse-eared"); **flowers** white, in compact groups or spreading out with long branches and flower stalks up to 12 mm (½ in.) long, sepals 5, green, hairy, (about as long as the 5 white, deeply notched petals), 4 - 6 mm (1/6 - ¼ in.) long; **seedpod** (b) cylindrical and straight or slightly curved, 8 - 10 mm (1/3 - 2/5 in.) long, light or straw-coloured, opening at the end with 10 small teeth (c) and releasing many, tiny, reddish-brown, roundish to 4-sided **seeds** about 0.75 mm (1/30 in.) long. Flowering and seed-set continue from late spring until freeze-up in autumn.

Figure 54. **Mouse-eared chickweed** A. Plant. B. Section of stem with pair of leaves. C. Tip of branch with 2 seedpods.

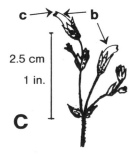

Mouse-eared chickweed is common throughout Ontario and occurs in almost any kind of habitat including gardens, lawns, fields, pastures, meadows, wet depressions, rock outcrops, dry sandy areas, and under moist woods. It is one of the most common and persistent weeds of lawns and occasionally is thick enough to be troublesome in gardens and fields.

It is distinguished from other chickweeds, Grass-leaved stitchwort and Thyme-leaved sandwort by its distinctly hairy stem and stalkless leaves covered with long hair (a) on both surfaces, and its cylindrical, light-coloured seedpods.

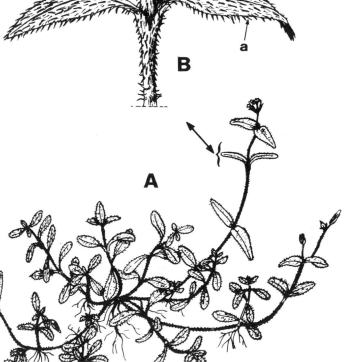

Thyme-leaved sandwort, *Arenaria serphyllifolia* L., (Figure 55, Plate 43) [ARISE, sabline à feuilles de serpolet, Sandwort, sabline à feuilles de thym] Annual or more frequently winter annual, reproducing only by seed. **Stems** erect, usually much-branched from near the base, 5 - 25 cm (2 - 10 in.) high, covered with very short inward-curved or nearly flat-lying hair which gives a somewhat rought texture and a bluish-green colour; **leaves** small, opposite (2 per node), stalkless, slightly rough-hairy, ovate with a pointed tip, 4 - 8 mm (1/6 - 1/3 in.) long and usually shorter than the length of stem between pairs; **flowers** very small, 2 - 3 mm (1/12 - ⅛ in.) long, greenish (the tiny white petals too small to show), on very slender stalks up to 10 mm (2/5 in.) long in branching inflorescences; **seedpod** ovoid, about 3 mm (⅛ in.) long, open-

ing at the tip and releasing many, extremely fine (0.5 mm, 1/50 in. in diameter) **seeds.** Flowers from late spring to late summer but is dry, shriveled, and virtually gone by fall at which time the tiny new seedlings are appearing.

Thyme-leaved sandwort occurs throughout Ontario in dry sandy soils. It is most common in fall rye and winter wheat where its winter annual habit is an advantage; but it also occurs in spring-sown crops, gardens, roadsides, orchards, sandy beaches and in rocky places.

It is distinguished by its bluish-green appearance, very small leaves, slightly rough stems and leaves, and tiny greenish flowers.

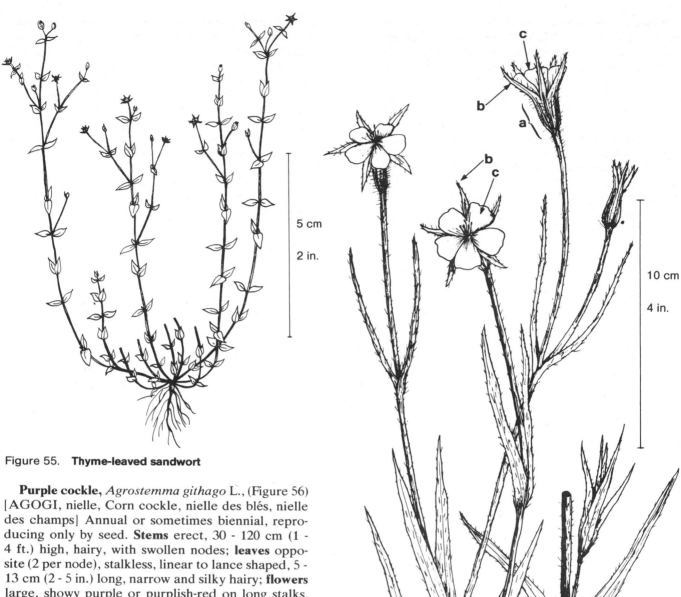

Figure 55. **Thyme-leaved sandwort**

Purple cockle, *Agrostemma githago* L., (Figure 56) [AGOGI, nielle, Corn cockle, nielle des blés, nielle des champs] Annual or sometimes biennial, reproducing only by seed. **Stems** erect, 30 - 120 cm (1 - 4 ft.) high, hairy, with swollen nodes; **leaves** opposite (2 per node), stalkless, linear to lance shaped, 5 - 13 cm (2 - 5 in.) long, narrow and silky hairy; **flowers** large, showy purple or purplish-red on long stalks, the 5 green sepals united for 1/3 to ½ their length forming a calyx tube (a) 12 - 18 mm (½ - ¾ in.) long; the calyx lobes (sepal tips) (b) 2 - 4 cm (4/5 - 1½ in.) long, narrow and projecting between and past the petals (c); petals 5, large, spreading, purple or purplish-red with black spots; as the **seedpod** expands inside the calyx tube, it emphasizes the 10 prominent, hairy green, lengthwise ribs on the calyx tube; the mature seedpod inside the calyx being smooth, hairless and orange-brown, and opening with 4 or usually 5 teeth at the top; **seeds** purplish-black, rounded-angular, about 3 mm (⅛ in.) across and densely covered with tiny, sharp bumps. Flowers from June to September.

Purple cockle was a very common weed in southern Ontario in the days of horse-drawn farm implements but, with the change in farming techniques, it has largely disappeared. However, it still occurs sporadically in cultivated fields, especially in fall-sown crops such as wheat and rye, in the central and western parts of southern Ontario. Though rare, it is important because **its seeds are poisonous to livestock and fowl** so it should be eliminated from feed grain.

Figure 56. **Purple cockle**

It is distinguished by its silky hairy stems with opposite, long, narrow leaves, large purple flowers and large purplish-black seeds.

White cockle, *Silene alba* (Mill.) E. H. L. Krause (Figure 57, Plate 44) [MELAL, lychnide blanche, compagnon blanc, Evening lychnis, White campion, oeillet de Dieu, floquet, *Lychnis alba* Mill.] Biennial or short-lived perennial, reproducing only by seed. Stems erect, 30 - 120 cm (1 - 4 ft.) high, round, swollen at nodes, hairy but not sticky, usually several from a coarse branching crown on a single, fleshy **taproot** (B). **Seedlings** pale yellowish-green; all **leaves** opposite (2 per node), the first few pairs usually appearing as a rosette, or on an elongating stem (as in A) when partly shaded by other plants, softly hairy on both surfaces with longer hair on the edges of the leafstalks; margins of leaf blades somewhat wavy (b) or wrinkled; middle and upper leaves stalkless, entire (without teeth), hairy, 2.5 - 10 cm (1 - 4½ in.) long, lance-shaped to elliptic but tapering to a point; **flowers** white, large and showy, unisexual, all flowers on 1 plant with 5 united sepals, 5 deeply lobed petals and either male, having 10 stamens but no pistil, or female, having 1 pistil with 5 slender styles (c) but no stamens; sepals 5, united along their edges to form a tubular calyx with 5 short lobes at the tip; calyx cylindrical in male flowers, usually purplish-green and distinctly 10-veined lengthwise; calyx of female flowers (d) narrowly ovoid at first

but becoming wide-ovoid to nearly spherical as the seedpod expands inside, green, with 5 very prominent lengthwise veins (e) lined up with the 5 pointed lobes (f) and usually 3 much fainter veins (g) between the pairs of prominent ones for a total of 20 veins; **seedpods** firm, 10 - 15 mm (2/5 - 3/5 in.) long, smooth and hairless but usually remaining surrounded by the calyx tube, opening by 10 short teeth (h) at the tip, releasing many small (1.2 mm, 1/20 in. across), kidney-shaped, grayish-orange, slightly rough **seeds.** Flowers and sets seed all summer.

White cockle is common in pastures, roadsides, waste areas, gardens and occasionally in cultivated fields throughout southern Ontario but is comparatively rare in the north and northwest.

It is distinguished from Purple cockle by its broader leaves and white or pinkish flowers with short calyx lobes; from Cow cockle, Bouncingbet and Bladder campion by its hairy leaves and stem; and from Night-flowering catchfly by its comparative lack of stickiness, biennial or short-lived perennial habit, unisexual flowers, seedpod with 5 styles (c), opening by 10 teeth (h), and the short lobes (f) and weakly branching veins (g) on the calyx tube.

Figure 57. **White cockle** A. Seedling with 3 pairs of true leaves.   B. Base of 2-year-old flowering plant.   C. Flowering stem of plant with female flowers.   D. Seedpod with 10 teeth.

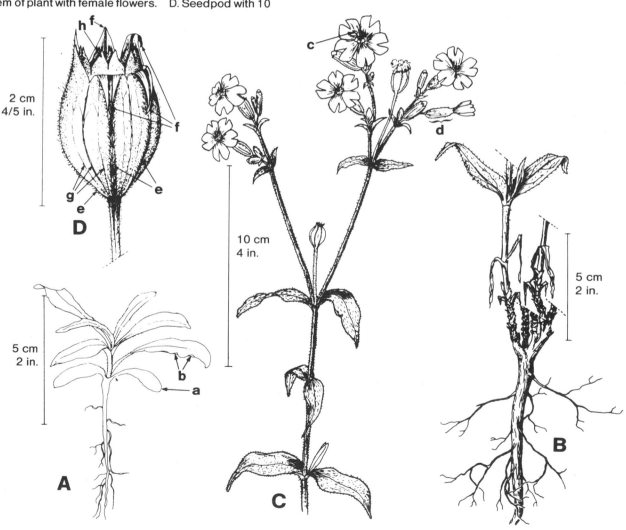

Night-flowering catchfly, *Silene noctiflora* L., (Figure 58, Plate 45) [MELNO, silène noctiflore, Sticky cockle, silène de nuit, attrape-mouche] Annual or sometimes winter annual, reproducing only by seed. Very similar in general appearance to White cockle; **seedlings** nearly identical (Figure 57A) but are somewhat sticky-hairy; **stems** of flowering plants 20 cm - 1 m (8 - 40 in.) high, erect, often much-branched near the top but always single (A) at the ground surface because they start from seed each year, often with remnants of the cotyledons (seed leaves) (a) still visible; and the root tapering downwards as a slender **taproot** with fine branches; **leaves** opposite (2 per node), tapering towards both ends, lower ones widest near the tip (A), middle and upper ones widest nearer the stem (B); upper leaves and stem branches densely sticky-hairy; **flowers** showy, usually opening in the evening but often open throughout the next day as well; sepals light green, united to form a calyx tube (b) with 5 promi-

nent veins (c) lined up with the 5 long-tapered teeth (d), and 5 less prominent but distinctly branched veins (e); petals white, creamy-white or pinkish, flaring outwards in a circle 1 - 3 cm (2/5 - 1¼ in.) in diameter, each petal deeply lobed (f); flowers bisexual, having 10 stamens and 1 pistil, although rarely some may be unisexual; pistil with 3 long styles, becoming an ovoid **seedpod** which usually opens with 6 teeth (g) and scatters many kidney-shaped, small (0.8 - 1 mm, 1/30 - 1/25 in.), grayish-orange, rough **seeds**. Flowers from June to August.

Night-flowering catchfly grows in much the same situations as White cockle but is more common in cultivated fields and is more widespread through northern Ontario.

It is distinguished by its dense covering of sticky hair on upper stems, leaves and calyx, its calyx with long-tapered teeth (d) and 10 distinctly branching lengthwise veins (c, e) clearly visible as the seedpod expands inside, its seedpod opening by usually 6 teeth (g), and its annual or winter annual habit.

Figure 58. **Night-flowering catchfly** A. Base of annual plant. B. Flowering stem. C. Seedpod with 6 teeth.

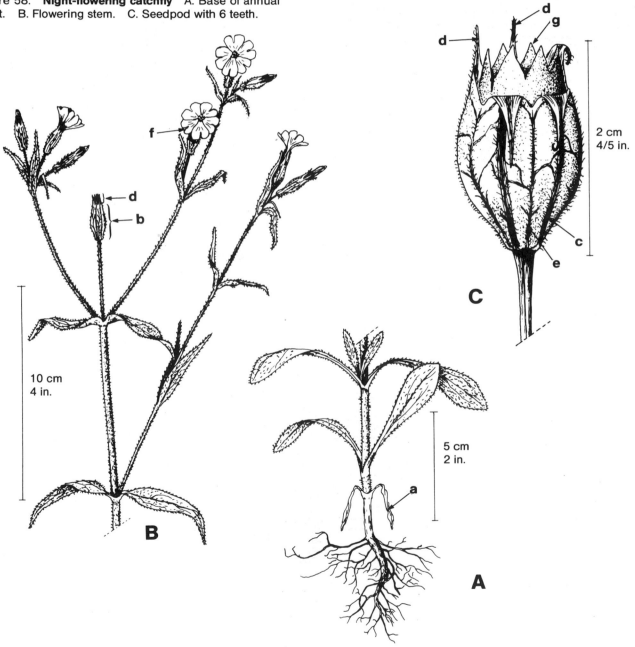

Bladder campion, *Silene vulgaris* (Moench) Garcke, (Figure 59, Plate 46) [SILVU, silène enflé, Cow bell, Rattleweed, Pétards, silène gonflé, *Silene cucubalus* Wibel, *Silene latifolia* (Mill.) Britten & Rendle] Perennial, reproducing by seed, by rooting of short underground branches which slant outwards from the crown, and from pieces of crown cut off by implements. Root system a coarse, whitish **taproot** with numerous, deeply penetrating and widely spreading wiry branches, very persistent (tolerant of cultivation); **stems** 30 - 60 cm (1 - 2 ft) high, erect or spreading, smooth, light green to whitish with a waxy bloom (fine powdery coating), usually swollen at the nodes; **leaves** opposite (2 per node), narrowly oval, tapered, deep green or whitish with a waxy bloom, the margins without teeth but occasionally wavy or curled and appearing toothed; **flowers** in branching clusters; sepals united and forming a bladder-like calyx (a), light green or pinkish with darker green or purplish veins and 5 very short teeth at the end; petals 5, deeply lobed, white to pinkish, about 1.5 cm (3/5 in.) across when open, soon curling up and shriveling after pollination; **seedpods** nearly spherical, about 6 mm (¼ in.) long, enclosed by the loose, papery, bladder-like calyx; **seeds** grayish, kidney-shaped, 1.5 mm (1/16 in.) across, rough with tiny warty bumps. Flowers from mid-June to September.

Bladder campion occurs throughout Ontario in medium to coarse soils in well-drained locations. It is common in pastures, waste places, roadsides, open woods, gardens, lawns and hedges, but is rather uncommon in regularly cultivated fields.

It is easily distinguished by its smooth, hairless, waxy texture throughout, and the smooth, papery, bladder-like calyx enclosing the small seedpod.

Biennial campion, *Silene csersei* Baumg., (not illustrated) [SILCS, silène de Cserei, silène bisannuel] Nearly identical to Bladder campion, the most important difference being that, instead of being a perennial, it is a biennial which forms a rosette of leaves the first year, then flowers, sets seed and dies in the second year. Biennial campion usually also has slightly larger and thicker **leaves**, smaller **calyx** and an egg-shaped **seedpod** which protrudes slightly from the calyx at maturity. It is not common in Ontario, occurring at only a few places along railway lines.

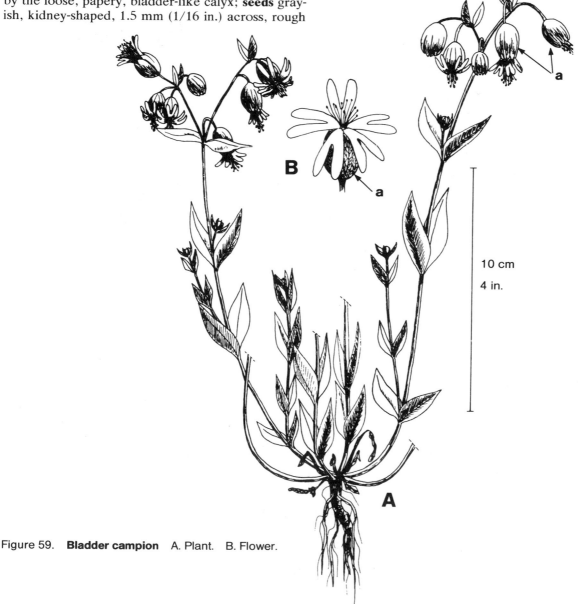

10 cm
4 in.

Figure 59. **Bladder campion** A. Plant. B. Flower.

Bouncingbet, *Saponaria officinalis* L., (Figure 60) [SAWOF, saponaire officinale, Bouncing Bet, Soapwort, savonière, herbe à savon] Perennial, reproducing by seed and by spreading underground stems, often forming dense patches. Underground parts very coarse and almost woody. **Stems** 30 - 120 cm (1 - 4 ft) high, smooth, very leafy; **leaves** opposite (2 per node), ovate or elliptic, rounded or tapered towards both ends, with 3 to 5 prominent lengthwise veins on the underside; **flower** bright, showy, white to pinkish, clustered in a thick short-branched inflorescence; sepals united in a tubular calyx with many (usually 20), fine, lengthwise veins and 5 very short teeth (a), petals 5 or many in "doubled flowers," usually fragrant; **seedpods** cylindrical, enclosed in the calyx; **seeds** dull black, roundish kidney-shaped, 1.5 mm (1/16 in.) across, and rough. Flowers from midsummer to late autumn.

Bouncingbet is common throughout southern Ontario occurring along roadsides, in waste places and old building sites, but only occasionally in fields and pastures. The leaves and seeds of Bouncingbet contain saponins (soap-like natural chemicals) which **can be poisonous to livestock.** Indeed, the leaves were used by early settlers as a poor but effective substitute for soap.

It is distinguished by growing in thick patches, its smooth stems with opposite leaves, its dense inflorescence, and smooth, cylindrical calyx tube with many veins.

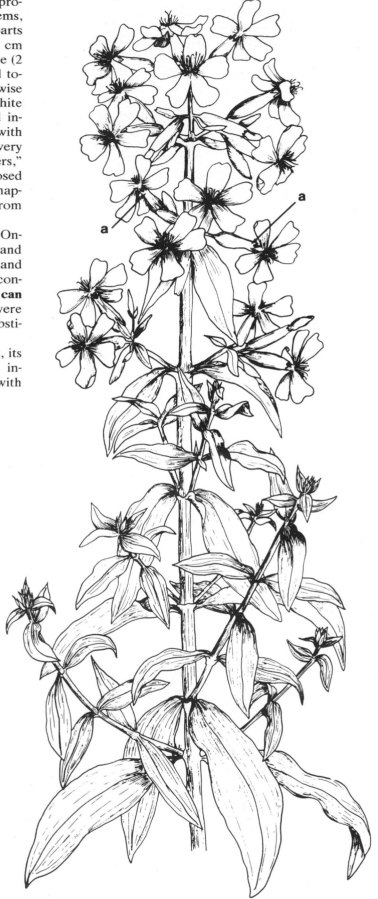

10 cm
4 in.

Figure 60. **Bouncingbet**

Cow cockle, *Saponaria vaccaria* L., (Figure 61) [VAAPY, saponaire des vaches, China cockle, Cowherb, vaccaire, *Vaccaria pyramidata* Med., *V. segetalis* (Neck.) Garcle, *V. vulgaris* Host]Annual, reproducing only by seed. **Stems** 10 - 60 cm (4 - 24 in.) high, erect, usually much-branched in the upper part, smooth with swollen nodes; **leaves** opposite (2 per node), 5 - 10 cm (2 - 4 in.) long, tapered to a pointed tip, rounded towards the stalkless base, sometimes somewhat clasping the stems, thick and a bit fleshy in texture, very smooth; **flowers** showy in a much-branched inflorescence; sepals united forming an angular calyx with 5 prominent ribs (a); petals 5, pink, spreading 10 - 20 mm (2/5 - 4/5 in.) in diameter; **seedpods** flask-shaped inside the sharply 5-angled calyx, opening with 4 to 6 teeth; **seeds** purplish-black, nearly spherical, 2 - 2.5 mm (1/12 - 1/10 in.) in diameter. Flowers from mid-July to September by which time the plant is mature, dull yellowish, very brittle, and it breaks and rolls with the wind, scattering its seed.

Cow cockle occurs at scattered locations throughout Ontario, most frequently along railroads and in waste areas near feed mills, but in recent years it has appeared more frequently in grainfields. Like Bouncingbet, Cow cockle seeds and foliage also contain saponins (soap-like chemicals) and are considered **potentially poisonous to livestock.**

It is distinguished from other members of the Pink Family by its annual habit, the bases of the leaves rounded or partly clasping the stem, the bright pink petals and the strongly 5-angled calyx (a).

Figure 61. **Cow cockle**

10 cm
4 in.

81

Celery-leaved buttercup, *Ranunculus sceleratus* L., (Figure 62) [RANSC, renoncule scélérate, Cursed crowfoot] Annual or short-lived perennial, reproducing only by seed. **Stems** erect, 5 - 60 cm (2 - 24 in.) high, stout, hollow, smooth, branched above, often somewhat succulent; basal and lower stem **leaves** succulent, long-stalked, somewhat kidney-shaped in outline and distinctly 3-lobed to nearly 3-parted (a), the segments again cleft or lobed or with rounded teeth; upper leaves much smaller, commonly either having 3 linear-oblong segments with entire or only slightly toothed divisions, or simple (b); **flowers** (B) numerous but borne singly on long stalks (c) at the ends of branches, the whole inflorescence being either rounded or elongated; sepals (d) 2 - 5 mm (1/12 - 1/5 in.) long, with soft hairs; petals (e) pale yellow, 1 - 5 mm (1/25 - 1/5 in.) long; stamens (f) many in a ring surrounding the many tiny pistils (g); **seeds** (achenes) (h) individually very small, 0.8 - 1.4 mm (1/30 - 1/20 in.) long, but very numerous in a short, cylindric cluster (C). Flowers from May to September.

Celery-leaved buttercup is found in southern and western Ontario in swamps, ditches, roadsides, pastures, fields, mudflats and the edges of ponds and lakes.

It is distinguished by its celery-like, 3-lobed lower leaves having long petioles and rounded teeth, its small, yellow flowers and its elongated cluster of seeds.

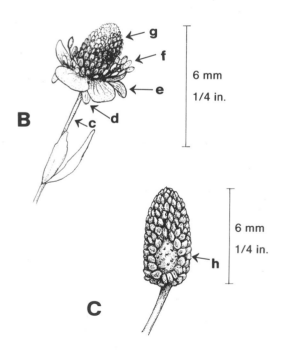

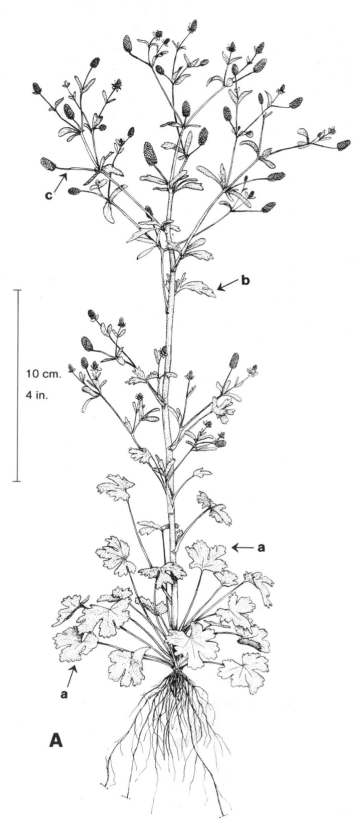

Figure 62. **Celery-leaved buttercup** A. Plant. B. One flower with many stamens and pistils. C. One seed head with many seeds.

Tall buttercup, *Ranunculus acris* L., (Figure 63, Plate 47 right) [RANAC, renoncule âcre, Field buttercup, Meadow buttercup, Tall crowfoot, Tall field buttercup, bouton-d'or] Perennial, reproducing only by seed. **Stems** 1 or several from a thick rootstalk with numerous, spreading, coarse, fibrous **roots**, erect, 30 - 100 cm (12 - 40 in.) high, branched in the upper part, hairy throughout; **leaves** basal and alternate (1 per node) on the stem, softly hairy, very deeply lobed and toothed; basal and lower leaves long-stalked (a), the blade deeply divided into 5 main lobes (b) palmately arranged (like fingers from the palm of the hand), each of the 5 lobes irregularly jagged or coarsely toothed (c); middle leaves with similar shape but nearly stalkless; upper leaves progressively smaller with fewer and smoother lobes; the base (d) of each leafstalk flattened and partly surrounding the stem at each node; **flowers** bright yellow, about 2 - 3 cm (4/5 - 1¼ in.) in diameter, grouped on long stalks in a much-branched inflorescence; sepals 5, green and small; petals 5; stamens numerous around the cluster of tiny pistils; after the petals fall, the cluster of seeds (e) is nearly spherical with each **seed** about 3 mm (⅛ in.) long, flattened, egg-shaped in outline with a short hooked

tip. Flowering and setting seed from late May throughout the summer and fall.

Tall buttercup is one of the most common weeds of pastures, meadows, and roadsides throughout Ontario. It can grow in a wide variety of habitats from low wet meadows, to rich woods, to the coarse soils of gravel pits and railroad cinders. There are many species of native and introduced buttercups, but only Tall buttercup is of wide importance as a weed. **The Buttercups have a bitter, acrid juice which causes severe pain and inflammation when grazed by livestock.** They are normally avoided, but when other feed becomes scarce they may be grazed with serious consequences.

It is distinguished by its erect habit, the lower and middle leaves being similar in appearance, and the leaf blades deeply lobed but not completely divided into sections with distinct stalks.

Figure 63. **Tall buttercup** A. Base of plant. B. Lower leaf. C. Flowering branch.

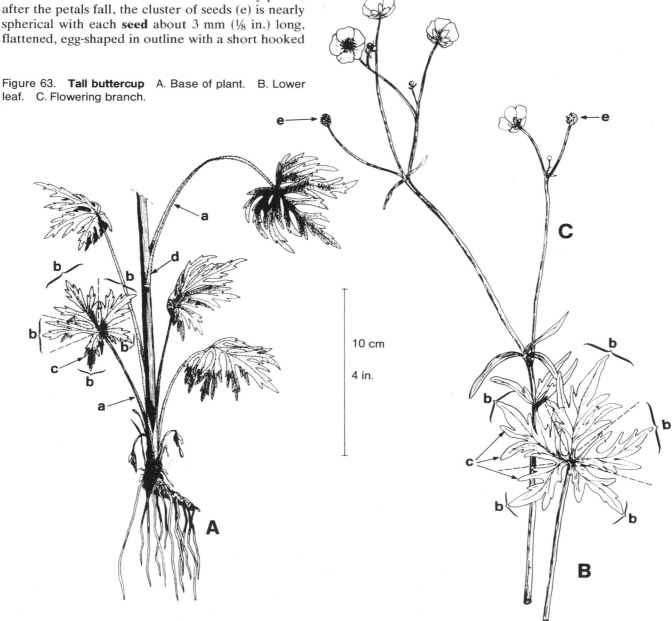

Creeping buttercup, *Ranunculus repens* L., (Figure 64, Plate 47 left) [RANRE, renoncule rampante, petite-douve] Perennial, reproducing by seed and by trailing horizontal stems which root at the nodes (a). **Stems** prostrate or sometimes nearly erect and 20 - 30 cm (8 - 12 in.) high, ranging from smooth to densely hairy; **leaves** alternate (1 per node), often clustered, mostly with long stalks; the blades 3-parted and the middle segment with a distinct short stalk (b); each segment again lobed and toothed; **flowers** and **seed heads** (c) similar to Tall buttercup. Flowers from April to July.

Creeping buttercup occurs in scattered localities throughout Ontario in habitats similar to those of Tall buttercup, but is much less common. It grows particularly well in moist or poorly drained situations and it is often a bad weed in well-watered lawns. Like Tall buttercup this species also has a bitter, acrid juice and **may be poisonous to livestock.**

It is distinguished from Tall buttercup by its prostrate stems which root at the nodes (a) and by the 3-parted leaf blade in which the central or terminal lobe has a distinct stalk (b).

Figure 64.   **Creeping buttercup**

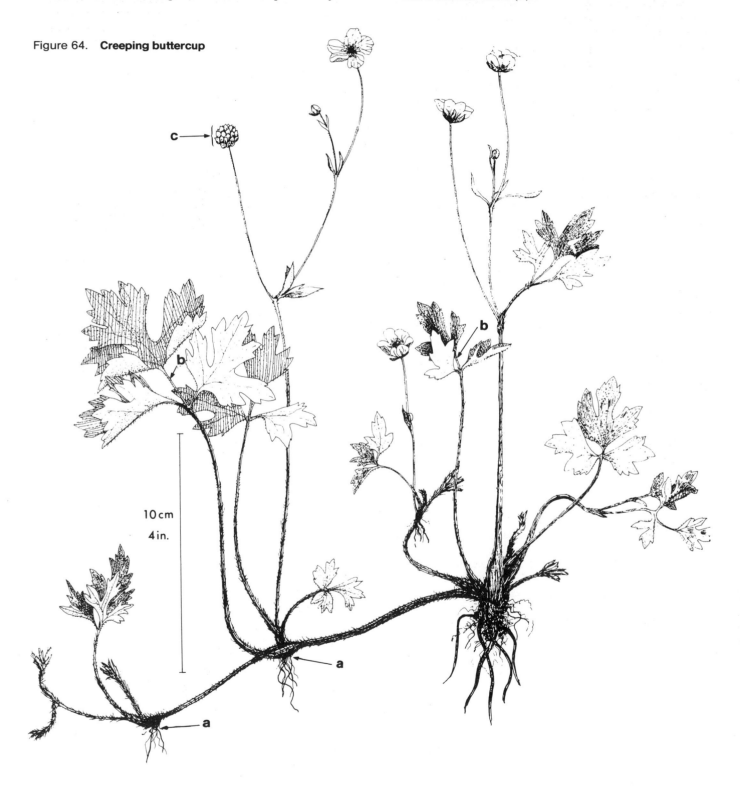

10 cm

4 in.

BARBERRY FAMILY (Berberidaceae)

Common barberry, *Berberis vulgaris* L., (Figure 65, Plate 48) [BEBVU, épine-vinette commune, épine-vinette, vinettier] Perennial, reproducing only by seed; bushy shrub 1 - 3 m (3 - 10 ft) high, **stems** erect; branches gray to yellowish-gray with short, sharp, slender, 3-branched **spines** (a) (occasionally single or unbranched) at nearly every node; **leaves** in clusters or short lateral spurs along the main branches, but distinctly alternate (1 per node) on young, rapidly elongating branches; leaf blades broadest above the middle, tapering towards the base, prominently net-veined and grayish-green on the undersurface, with numerous, prominent, sharp or spiny-tipped teeth (b); **flowers** bright yellow in elongated, drooping racemes from leaf axils from the ends of branches (Plate 48B), small, each with 6 yellow sepals, 6 yellow petals, 6 stamens and 1 pistil; **berries** bright red (Plate 48A), elliptical, about 1 cm (2/5 in.) long and containing 1 to 3 or rarely more seeds. Flowers in May and June; the yellow sepals and petals fall very soon afterwards, but the bright red berrries often hang on all winter.

Common barberry was introduced as an ornamental shrub, but now occurs wild along fence lines, road-sides, riverbanks, edges of woods and in wasteland throughout southern Ontario.

It is distinguished from other shrubs by its clusters of bristly toothed leaves, its 3-branched spines, its small yellow flowers in long drooping racemes, and its red berries. This plant is a very important pest because **its leaves become infested with the fungus which causes stem rust on oats, barley, rye and wheat**; the fungus overwinters in these leaves and spreads from them to cause early-season infections of stem rust on nearby grain crops. Eradication of this shrub is essential to help protect grain crops from the stem rust fungus.

For additional information, see Ontario Ministry of Agriculture and Food Factsheet, *Common Barberry and European Buckthorn; Alternate Hosts of Cereal Rust Diseases,* Agdex 110/632.

Japanese barberry, *Berberis thunbergii* DC., (not illustrated) [épine-vinette du Japon] A commonly planted ornamental that is normally not subject to the stem rust fungus. It differs from Common barberry by the absence of bristle-tipped teeth on the **leaves,** the **spines** on the stems usually single instead of 3-branched, and the **flowers** and **berries** borne singly or in very small clusters of only 2 or 3 from leaf axils. However, hybrids between these two species have occurred and many of these are host to the rust fungus just as is Common barberry.

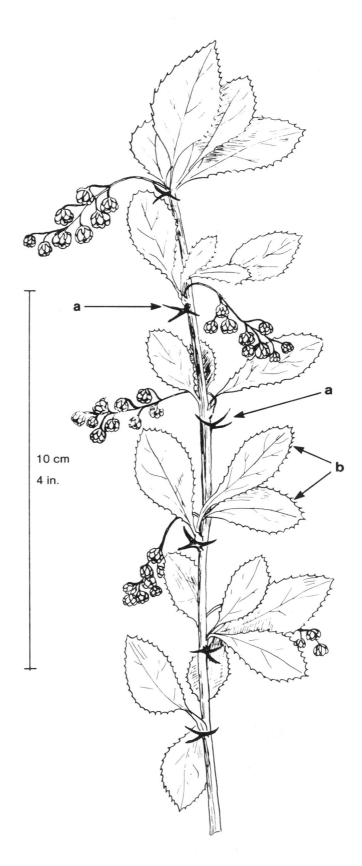

10 cm
4 in.

Figure 65. **Common barberry**

POPPY FAMILY (Papaveraceae)

Greater celandine, *Chelidonium majus* L., (Figure 66) [CHQMA, grande chélidoine, Celandine, Lesser celandine, grande-éclaire, chélidoine] Biennial or sometimes a short-lived perennial, reproducing only by seed. **Stems** up to 80 cm (32 in.) high containing an orange-coloured juice, hairy in the lower part but smooth towards the top, succulent, rather brittle; **leaves** of first-year plants basal, green or bluish-green, smooth, divided into usually 5 or 7 segments with rounded teeth or coarse lobes; stem leaves of second-year plants alternate (1 per node), similar but usually smaller; leaves with a thick, sticky orange-yellow juice; **flowers** bright yellow, usually in umbel-like clusters at the ends of short branches; sepals 2; petals 4, spreading about 2 cm (4/5 in.) across; stamens numerous and 1 slender pistil; **seedpods** 2.5 - 5 cm (1 - 2 in.) long and opening on 2 sides from the bottom upwards. Flowering may begin in late April and continue throughout the summer and fall.

Greater celandine occurs in scattered localities throughout southern Ontario, occasionally being a common weed in moist soils around farmyards, in waste areas, roadsides and edges of woods.

It is easily identified by its characteristic saffron-coloured juice, smooth divided leaves with coarsely lobed divisions, and yellow flowers with numerous stamens.

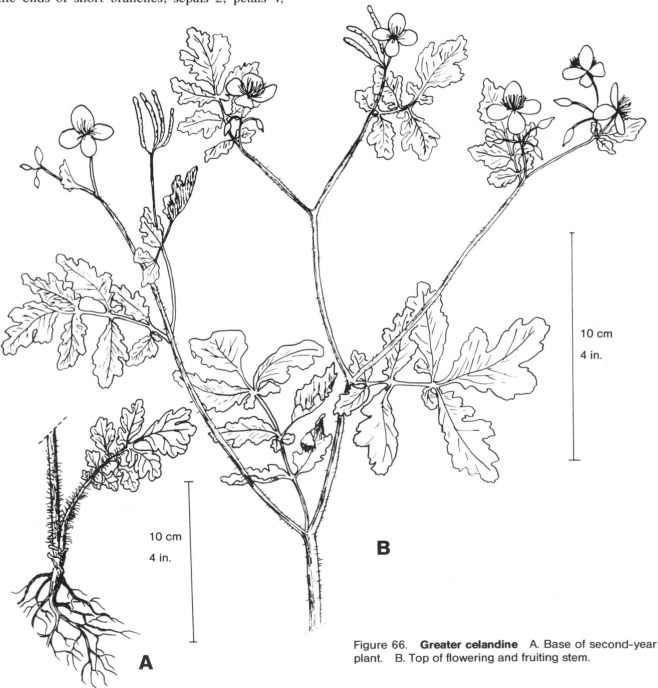

10 cm
4 in.

10 cm
4 in.

A

B

Figure 66. **Greater celandine** A. Base of second-year plant. B. Top of flowering and fruiting stem.

FUMITORY FAMILY (Fumariaceae)

Fumitory, *Fumaria officinalis* L., (Figure 67) [FUMOF, fumeterre officinale, fumeterre] Annual, reproducing only by seed. **Stem** 20 - 80 cm (8 - 32 in.) long, often much-branched, loosely spreading, hairless; **leaves** bluish-green, finely dissected, the ultimate segments (a) being flat and only 1 - 2 mm (1/25 - 1/12 in.) wide; **inflorescence** a compact raceme 1 - 7.5 cm (2/5 - 3¼ in.) long, with many small flowers; corollas (b) tubular, 3 - 8 mm (⅛ - 1/3 in.) long, flesh-coloured to purple and deep purple at the tip, each corolla with a single, rounded, basal spur (c); **fruit** (d) 1.5 - 2.5 mm (1/16 - 1/10 in.) long, broadly lens-shaped to nearly spherical, with a very small depression at the outer end, and containing only one **seed.** Flowers from May to August.

Fumitory was introduced from Europe and is occasionally found throughout Ontario in both cultivated and waste ground.

It is distinguished by its finely dissected bluish-green leaves, its flesh-coloured to purplish flowers, its nearly spherical seedpods each having only one seed and the whole plant being hairless and glaucous. When first pulled from the ground, the roots have a pungent, ammonia-like odour.

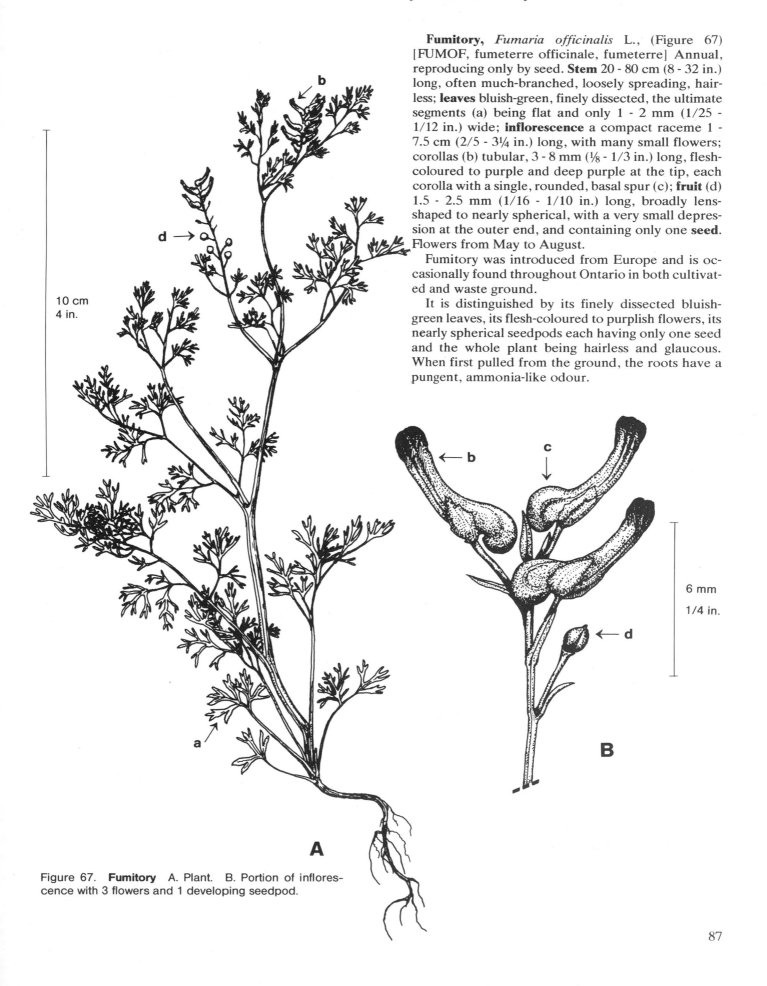

Figure 67. **Fumitory** A. Plant. B. Portion of inflorescence with 3 flowers and 1 developing seedpod.

MUSTARD FAMILY (Cruciferae)

Wild radish, *Raphanus raphanistrum* L., (Figure 68) [RAPRA, radis sauvage, jointed charlock, Jointed radish, Jointed wild radish, ravenelle] Annual, reproducing only by seed. **Stems** either smooth or with short, bristly hairs, arising from a stout **taproot** (a) to a height of 20 - 80 cm (8 - 32 in.); lower **leaves** obovate-oblong, 5 - 20 cm (2 - 8 in.), pinnately lobed into 5 to 15 oblong segments (b); segments nearer the stem very small, those further out progressively larger; the upper leaves (c) reduced; **petals** (d) usually white with violet veins, or occasionally yellow or purple-violet, 10 - 20 mm (2/5 - 4/5 in.) long; **seedpods** (siliques) nearly cylindric when fresh, but when dry becoming several-ribbed lengthwise and prominently constricted between the seeds such that the 1- to 10-seeded pods somewhat resemble beads on a string; the seed-bearing portion (e) 2 - 4 cm (4/5 - 1½ in.) long and 3 - 6 mm (⅛ - ¼ in.) thick, and tipped with a seedless beak (f) 1 - 3 cm (2/5 - 1¼ in.) long. Flowers from June to October.

Wild radish occurs in scattered localities in southern and eastern Ontario in fields, waste places and roadsides.

It is distinguished by its lower leaves being deeply parted, its usually white petals being conspicuously violet-veined, and its characteristic "string-of-beads" seedpods (e) with long, seedless beaks (f).

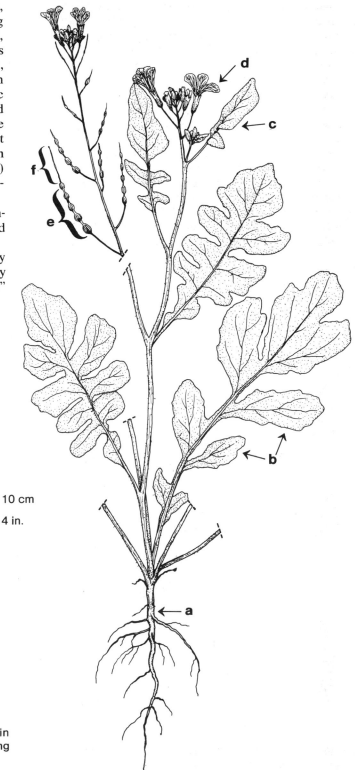

10 cm
4 in.

Figure 68. **Wild radish** Lower portion of a plant in flower, and a portion of the inflorescence with developing seedpods.

Wild mustard, *Sinapis arvensis* L., (Figure 69, Plate 49) [SINAR, moutarde des champs, Charlock, Common mustard, Field mustard, Herrick, Kale, Mustard, Yellow mustard, moutarde sauvage, séneve, *Brassica kaber* (DC.) L.C. Wheeler var. *pinnatifida* (Stokes) L.C. Wheeler] Annual, reproducing only by seed. **Stems** erect, 20 - 90 cm (8 - 36 in.) high, branching in the upper part, harshly hairy near the base but weakly hairy or smooth upwards, greenish or sometimes purplish; **seedling** with broad kidney-shaped cotyledons (a); stem **leaves** alternate (1 per node), somewhat hairy; lowermost leaves on young plants long-stalked and either without lobes (D) or with shallow to deep lobes (b) near the base of the blade; upper leaves stalkless and coarsely toothed but usually not lobed; **flowers** in small clusters which lengthen as the seedpods develop, bright lemon yellow, about 1.5 cm (3/5 in.) across with 4 small sepals, 4 larger petals arranged in the form of a cross (Family name "Cruciferae" means crucifix or cross), 4 long and 2 short stamens (total 6) and 1 slender pistil; flower stalks thin and short (3 - 5 mm, 1/8 - 1/5 in. long), becoming thicker but not longer as the seedpods develop, sometimes nearly as thick as the pod itself; **seedpods** (siliques) 3 - 5 cm (1¼ - 2 in.) long, sometimes bristly hairy but usually without hair, often with lengthwise ribs, erect and pressed to the stem or spreading out; each pod has a flattened terminal beak (c) with 1 or rarely 2 seeds in its base (d) and a main section (e) containing several seeds which are released when the 2 sides or valves split apart from the bottom end and fall away entirely; **seeds** spherical, 1.5 mm (1/16 in.) in diameter, black or purplish. Flowering may begin as early as late May and continue throughout the summer.

Wild mustard occurs throughout Ontario, being most frequent in cultivated fields and gardens, but occasionally appearing in fence lines, along roadsides and in waste areas.

It is distinguished from similar mustards by its somewhat kidney-shaped cotyledons (a) being broad with a deep, wide, rounded notch at the end, the hairy stem with lower leaves stalked and either lobed or unlobed but upper ones stalkless and merely toothed (b), its large flowers and its seedpod with a short thick stalk and a flat beak (c) that is about 1/3 the total length of the pod and usually contains an additional seed or two; and from Yellow rocket by being annual with hairy stems, its lemon-yellow flowers usually not appearing before late May and its seedpods on short, thick stalks and having a prominent, flat beak containing 1 or 2 seeds.

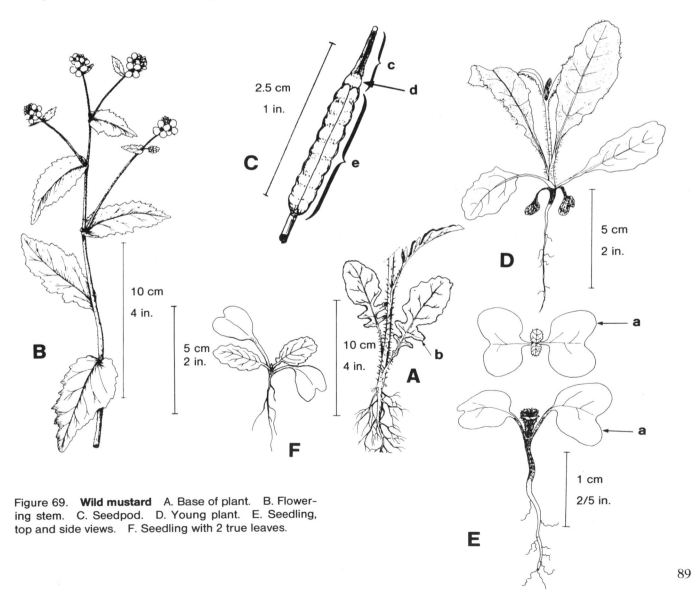

Figure 69. **Wild mustard** A. Base of plant. B. Flowering stem. C. Seedpod. D. Young plant. E. Seedling, top and side views. F. Seedling with 2 true leaves.

89

Indian mustard, *Brassica juncea* (L.) Czern., (not illustrated) [BRSJU, moutarde de l'Inde, moutarde joncée] Very similar to Wild mustard but has little or no hair, paler yellow **flowers, pods** with a slender stalk about 12 mm (½ in.) long and a slender beak which does not have a seed in its base, and brownish-red **seeds**.

Its distribution is much the same as that of Wild mustard although it is generally less common.

Black mustard, *Brassica nigra* (L.) Koch, (not illustrated) [BRSNI, moutarde noir, River mustard, moutarde] Resembling Wild mustard when young but grows much taller (up to 2.5 m, 8.5 ft); **leaves** generally broader, longer and darker green; lower leaves have coarser lobed divisions, upper leaves narrow and nearly without teeth; **flowers** in very long thin racemes in a widely branched inflorescence as much as 1 m (40 in.) across; **seedpods** erect and pressed closely to the stem, only 10 - 20 mm (2/5 - 4/5 in.) long with a seedless beak about 3 mm (⅛ in.) long.

It occurs in a few localities in southern Ontario, especially in fields and waste areas bordering river valleys, and along railways.

Bird rape, *Brassica campestris* L., (not illustrated) [BRSRA, moutarde des oiseaux, Field mustard, chourave, navette] Resembling small plants of Wild mustard but has a bluish-green colour, smooth, stalkless **leaves** with enlarged bases that clasp the stem (similar to the leaf-bases illustrated in Figure 69B); long flower stalks (often 2 cm, 4/5 in., or longer); and smooth plump **seedpods** 3 - 5 cm (1¼ - 2 in.) long with a thin, seedless beak 6 - 12 mm (¼ - ½ in.) long.

It occurs in a few grainfields and waste areas in southern Ontario where it is sometimes mistaken for plants of cultivated oil-seed rape with which it is closely allied.

Dog mustard, *Erucastrum gallicum* (Willd.) O. E. Schulz., (Figure 70, Plate 50) [ERWGA, moutarde des chiens, fausse roquette] Annual or winter annual, reproducing only by seed. **Stems** erect, 10 - 60 cm (4 - 24 in.) high, lower part with short, downward-pointing hairs; **leaves** alternate (1 per node), often in a dense rosette in late autumn and early spring, dark green to blackish-green, oblong in general outline, pinnately cut or divided into coarsely lobed segments (a), the bottoms of the spaces (b) between segments more or less rounded; **flowers** similar to Wild mustard but pale yellow, the lowermost several flowers and pods of each raceme in axils of small leaves (c); **seedpods** 2 - 5 cm (4/5 - 2 in.) long, with a narrow beak (d) about 3 mm (⅛ in.) long, on slender stalks, pointing outwards and upwards; **seeds** oval, reddish-brown, about 1.2 mm (1/20 in.). Flowers from late May to late fall.

Dog mustard occurs throughout Ontario but is more common in the south. It is frequently found around railway yards, waste places, orchards, gardens, roadsides and occasionally in grainfields.

It is distinguished from most other plants of the Mustard Family in Ontario by having several of its lowermost flowers and seedpods in the axils of small leaves (c). Only Garlic mustard also has this characteristic. Rosettes of young plants resemble Tumble mustard but

Dog mustard leaves are usually darker in colour, the segments (a) are broader and more coarsely lobed, and the tips of the lobes are usually rounded in Dog mustard but somewhat sharp-pointed in Tumble mustard.

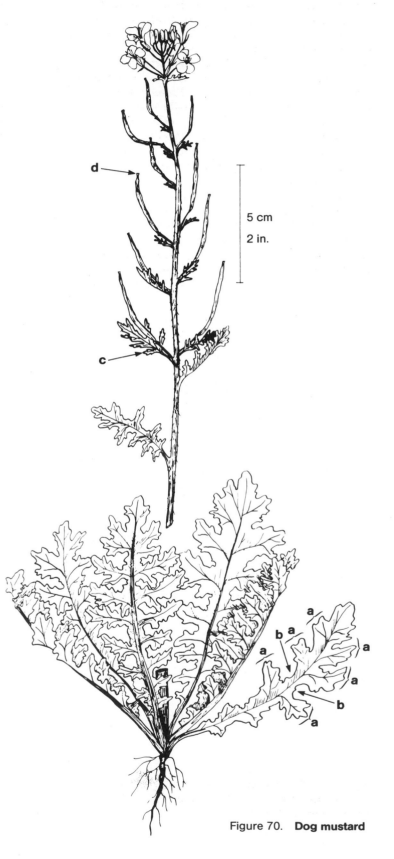

Figure 70. **Dog mustard**

Stinking wall-rocket, *Diplotaxis muralis* (L.) DC., (Figure 71A) [DIPMU, diplotaxis des murailles, Sand-rocket, diplotaxis des murs] Annual, reproducing only by seed. **Stems** 20 - 50 cm (8 - 20 in.) long, spreading erect or nearly horizontal, much-branched, smooth; **leaves** mostly clustered in a basal rosette and on the lower part of the stem, alternate (1 per node), elongated, deeply lobed or toothed; **flowers** like Wild mustard but lighter lemon yellow and on stalks 1 - 1.5 cm (2/5 - 3/5 in.) long; **pods** 2 - 3.5 cm (4/5 - 1½ in.) long with a very short beak but not developing a short stipe (see Narrow-leaved wall-rocket); flower stalks spreading at an angle from the stem. The whole plant has a distinctly unpleasant odour, somewhat resembling that of rotting turnips. Flowers from May to September.

Stinking wall-rocket usually occurs in coarse soils along roads, railways, beaches, around buildings and in waste places in southern Ontario.

It is distinguished by its leaves being mostly clustered near the base, the upper part of its stem being usually more or less branched and spreading, its lemon yellow flowers followed by short seedpods, and the very unpleasant odour from all parts of the plant.

Narrow-leaved wall-rocket, *Diplotaxis tenuifolia* (L.) DC., (Figure 71B) [DIPTE, diplotaxis à feuilles ténues, diplotaxe à feuilles ténues] A perennial, similar to but usually somewhat larger than Stinking wall-rocket. Perennial, reproducing only by seed; plants persisting for several years with a rough, semi-woody, perennial base. It differs from Stinking wall-rocket by having most of its **leaves** along the stems rather than clustered in a rosette at the ground surface, the stalks of its **seedpods** being longer, 2 - 3 cm (4/5 - 1¼ in.) long, and having a short stipe or secondary stalk (a) about 2 mm (1/12 in.) long between the base of the seedpod and the thickened receptacle where the sepals, petals and stamens have fallen off. It may flower earlier, but its distribution is similar to Stinking wall-rocket.

5 cm

2 in.

A

B

Figure 71. **Stinking wall-rocket** A. Base of annual plant. **Narrow-leaved wall-rocket** B. Upper part of stem with flowers and seedpods.

Garlic mustard, *Alliaria petiolata* (Bieb.) Cavara & Grande, (Figure 72) [ALAPE, alliaire officinale, *A. officinalis* Andrz. ex Bieb.] Annual, winter annual or biennial, reproducing only by seed. **Stems** up to 1 m (40 in.) tall, simple or little branched, smooth or with a few simple hairs; winter annual and biennial forms produce **rosettes** of leaves (A); these leaves varying from few to many, from kidney-shaped with a broad, rounded tip (a) to narrower and ovate with a rounded or nearly acute tip (b), their margins toothed with shallow, rounded to deep, coarse, pointed teeth; **lower stem leaves** alternate, broad and kidney-shaped, to 10 cm (4 in.) wide and long, with coarsely toothed margins, becoming longer and narrower upward; **upper leaves** deltoid, 1 - 7 cm (2/5 - 3 in.) long and wide, or somewhat rhombic, with acute tip and coarsely toothed margins; **flowers** (c) small, white, with 4 petals 3 - 6 mm (⅛ - ¼ in.) long and wide, the lowermost 1 - 3 flowers and seedpods may be in the axils of small leaves; **seedpods** (siliques) (d, C) 0.4 - 5 cm (1/6 - 2 in.)

long, spreading, and borne on short pedicels (e) about as thick as the pods; their beaks (f) slender, 1 - 3 mm (1/25 - ⅛ in.) long; **seeds** black, 3 mm (⅛ in.). The whole plant has a distinctive onion-like or garlic-like odour. Flowers from May to June.

Introduced and naturalized from Europe, Garlic mustard is now found in moist woods, swampy areas and ditches and along roadsides and railway embankments throughout southern Ontario. It occasionally invades adjacent cultivated land.

It is distinguished by its broad leaves with rounded to coarse teeth, small white flowers and garlic-like odour. Mature plants are distinguished from Wild mustard by their seedpods being more slender and having a slender beak that is never broad or flattened, and never containing an additional seed or two, and in some plants of Garlic mustard the lowermost 1 - 3 flowers or seedpods may be in the axils of small leaves, a characteristic it shares only with Dog mustard [Figure 70(c)].

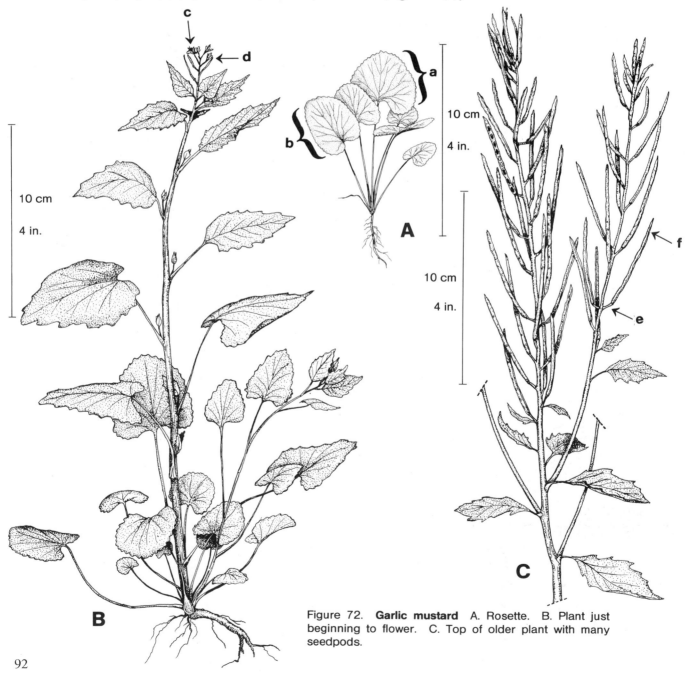

Figure 72. **Garlic mustard** A. Rosette. B. Plant just beginning to flower. C. Top of older plant with many seedpods.

92

Tumble mustard, *Sisymbrium altissimum* L., (Figure 73, Plate 51) [SSYAL, sisymbre élevé, Tumbling mustard, Tumbleweed, moutarde roulante] Annual or winter annual, reproducing only by seed. **Stems** 30 - 120 cm (1 - 4 ft) high, much-branched in the upper part, becoming rather woody and brittle as the plant matures; lower stem and leaves hairy with spreading white hair (A), but upper parts smooth (B); first **leaves** in a basal rosette (D), becoming large, hairy, shallowly toothed or deeply lobed or usually completely divided (A) into 6 or more pairs of broad, jagged-toothed segments plus a terminal lobe (a) which is never much larger than the side segments; upper leaves narrow and either shallowly toothed or pinnately divided into many very slender segments (b) which are sometimes nearly thread-like; rosette and lower leaves usually dried and gone by flowering time; **flowers** pale yellow, resembling Wild mustard but smaller, 6 mm (¼ in.) across, in loose clusters at tips of branches;

seedpods (c) very slender and very long, 5 - 10 cm (2 - 4 in.) long, stiff, wide-spreading and almost branch-like, about the same thickness as their stalks, splitting in 3 lengthwise; **seeds** about 1 mm (1/25 in.) long, oblong, yellow to reddish-yellow, olive-green, or light brown. Flowers from June to early autumn.

Tumble mustard is found throughout Ontario, usually along railway tracks, roadsides and in waste areas but it is appearing with greater frequency in grainfields, especially on sandy soils in the southern portion of the province.

When the seedpods are nearly mature, Tumble mustard is easily distinguished from all other mustards in Ontario because it is the only one with such long thin pods (c). Rosettes can be distinguished by the terminal lobe (a) of the hairy, divided leaf not being larger than the jagged-toothed lobes along the sides. Young plants up to early flowering can be distinguished by having coarsely lobed basal and lower stem leaves but finely divided upper leaves.

Figure 73. **Tumble mustard**   A. Base of plant.   B. Flowering branch.   C. Seedling, top and side views.   D. Young basal rosette.

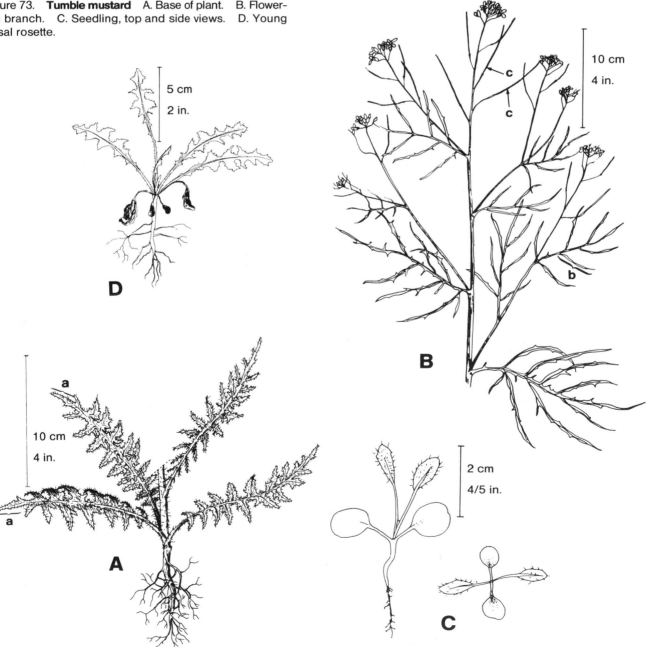

93

Hedge mustard, *Sisymbrium officinale* (L.) Scop., (Figure 74) [SSYOF, sisymbre officinal, herbe au chantre] Annual or winter annual, reproducing only by seed. **Stems** erect, 30 - 90 cm (1 - 3 ft) high, branched; rosette **leaves** with a definite stalk, divided into several, irregularly toothed, narrow segments on each side and 1 larger angular or roundish terminal segment (a), middle and upper leaves smaller, short-stalked or stalkless, less divided or with no lobes along the side, alternate (1 per node), the whole plant often with a gray-green appearance; **flowers** resembling but much smaller than Wild mustard, bright yellow, about 3 mm (⅛ in.) wide, in tight clusters at tips of stems and branches; stalks of seedpods very short (1.5 mm, 1/16 in.), at first thin (b), becoming thicker with age (c); **seedpods** closely pressed to the stem, 1 - 1.5 cm (2/5 - 3/5 in.) long, about 1.5 mm (1/16 in.) wide at the base and tapering towards the slender, seedless beak (d) at the tip, smooth or usually somewhat short-hairy; **seeds** angular, grayish-brown. Flowers from June to August.

Hedge mustard occurs throughout southern Ontario, and in a few localities in the north and northwest, being most common in waste places, gardens and edges of fields and only occasionally appearing as a weed in grainfields.

It is distinguished by the large terminal segment (a) of the divided leaf, short tapering pods on very short stalks (b) closely pressed to the stem, and the plant frequently having a gray-green appearance.

Tall hedge mustard, *Sisymbrium loesellii* L., (not illustrated) [SSYLO, sisymbre de Loesel, Loesel's hedge mustard, sisymbre élevé de Loesel] Occurs in just a few localities in Ontario. It is similar to Hedge mustard but usually is bright green; its **stems** may be taller, more branched and somewhat more hairy; **leaves** coarsely lobed as in Hedge mustard, the terminal lobe largest and somewhat triangular; **flowers** similar but the stalks of the seedpods longer (1 - 1.5 cm, 2/5 - 3/5 in.), the longer **pods** broader than their stalks, about 2.5 - 3.5 cm (1 - 1½ in.) long and not or slightly

tapered towards the tip; **seeds** oblong, 0.7 mm (1/32 in.) long, yellow-brown.

These two hedge mustards can be easily distinguished from other kinds of mustards by their coarsely lobed leaves with the large terminal lobe (a) and their small slender seedpods.

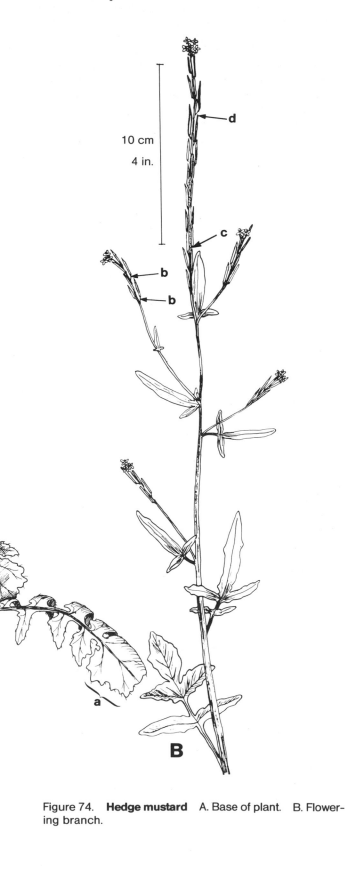

Figure 74. **Hedge mustard** A. Base of plant. B. Flowering branch.

Mouse-eared-cress, *Arabidopsis thaliana* (L.)
Heyn., (Figure 75) | ARBTH, fausse-arabette des dames,
arabidopsis de Thal] Annual or winter annual, reproducing only by seed. **Stems** slender, simple or branched,
hairy at the base, 5 - 45 cm (2 - 18 in.) high from a
slender **taproot** (a); **rosette leaves** (b) oblong to spatulate, 0.8 - 5 cm (1/3 - 2 in.) long, shallowly toothed or
lobed, with scattered fine hairs, most of which are 2-
or 3-branched; **stem leaves** (c) smaller, stalkless (d),
linear to narrowly oblong, only slightly hairy, with
mixed unbranched and branched hairs; **flowers** in
compact clusters (e) at ends of branches; the clusters
expanding into elongated racemes (f) as the flowers
mature into seedpods; petals white, spatulate, 2 - 4 mm
(1/12 - 1/6 in.) long (twice as long as sepals); **seedpods**
(g) (siliques) slender, 0.3 - 1.5 cm (⅛ - 3/5 in.) long,
less than 1 mm (1/25 in.) wide, on very slender stalks
(h) from one-half to as long as the pods; each pod
containing 48 - 60 **seeds** barely 0.5 mm (1/50 in.) long.
Flowers from April to August.

A native of Europe, Mouse-eared-cress has become
naturalized in dry fields, waste places, ditches, roadsides and around buildings in southwestern Ontario,
especially in sandy soil.

It is distinguished by its annual or, more typically,
winter annual growth habit, its slender taproot, white
petals and slender seedpods on thread-like stalks. Its
stem leaves resemble those of Mouse-eared chickweed (Figure 54) but are alternate on the stem rather
than opposite.

Figure 75.　**Mouse-eared-cress**

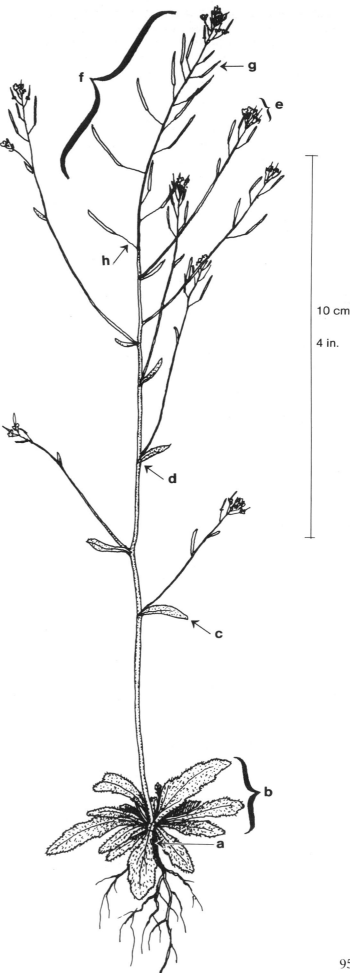

10 cm

4 in.

Flixweed, *Descurainia sophia* (L.) Webb, (Figure 76, Plate 52) [DESSO, sagesse-des-chirurgiens, Tansy mustard, sisymbre Sophia] Annual, winter annual or biennial, reproducing only by seed. **Stems** erect, 30 - 90 cm (1 - 3 ft) high, branched above; stems and leaves grayish-green from a dense covering of fine-branched hair; **leaves** alternate (1 per node), very finely dissected, almost feather-like; **flowers** individually very small and crowded at the ends of stems and branches, pale yellow; **seedpods** (a) spreading from the stem on very slender stalks, curved upwards and nearly parallel to the stem; **seeds** bright orange, oblong, about 1 mm (1/25 in.) long. Flowers from late May until the end of the summer. The whole plant has a distinctive musty odour, especially strong when cut or bruised.

Flixweed occurs in scattered localities throughout Ontario, usually in gardens, fence lines, waste places, and along roadsides, but only occasionally in grain-fields.

It is distinguished by its gray-green colour, finely divided leaves, erect seed pods on very slender stalks and its very distinctive musty odour.

Flixweed is sometimes mistakenly called Tansy mustard because it resembles and is closely related to the true tansy mustards. They are **Gray tansy mustard,** *Descurainia richardsonii* (Sweet) O. E. Schultz, (not illustrated) [DESRI, moutarde tanaisie grise, sisymbre toffu] and **Green tansy mustard,** *Descurainia pinnata* (Walt.) Britt. var. *brachycarpa* (Richards.) Fern., (not illustrated) [DESPI, moutarde tanaisie verte, sisymbre à fruits courts] Both are native plants in North America but are probably less common as weeds in Ontario than is Flixweed which was introduced from Europe. Gray tansy mustard is grayish like Flixweed but its **leaves** are less finely divided, seedpods shorter (about 10 mm, 2/5 in. long) on shorter stalks (5 mm, 1/5 in. long) and are usually held erect and very close to the stem like those of Hedge mustard (Figure 74). Green tansy mustard has **leaves** nearly as finely divided as those of Flixweed but the stem and leaves are green rather than grayish-green. Green tansy mustard has unbranched hair with a slightly enlarged head or gland at the tip, just barely visible to the naked eye, and these glandular hairs give the plant a slightly sticky texture. **Seedpods** of Gray tansy mustard are broader than those of Flixweed, somewhat cigar-shaped, about 10 mm (2/5 in.) long and nearly 2 mm (1/12 in.) wide. Green and Gray tansy mustard are more likely to be found in native situations such as open, gravelly or rocky soil, and sandy woodlands but they also occur in similar situations to those of Flixweed.

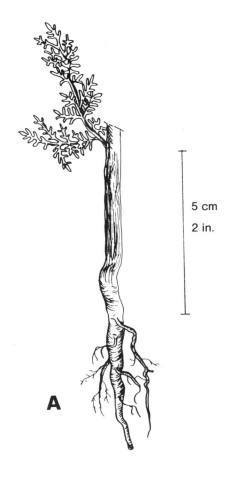

5 cm
2 in.

A

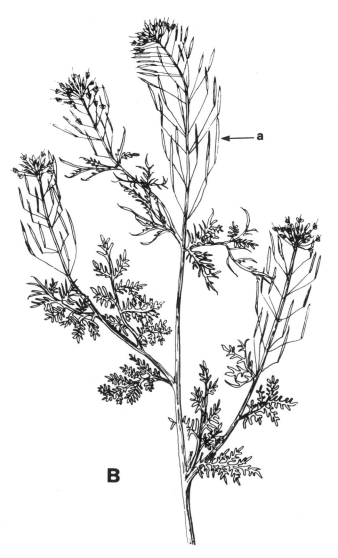

a

B

Figure 76. **Flixweed** A. Base of plant. B. Top of flowering and fruiting plant.

Dame's-rocket, *Hesperis matronalis* L., (Figure 77, Plate 53) [HEVMA, julienne des dames, Dame's-violet, Mother-of-the-evening, julienne, julienne des jardins] Perennial, reproducing only by seed. **Stems** erect, 45 - 140 cm (18 - 56 in.) high, often branched above; **leaves** lanceolate, up to 15 cm (6 in.) long, pubescent, shallowly dentate, short-stalked (a) or stalkless (b), with acuminate tips; **flowers** in elongated racemes (c), very showy and fragrant; each flower (d) 1.4 - 2.5 cm (3/5 - 1 in.) across; the 4 petals purple, or varying to shades of pink or white; **seedpods** (e) (siliques) 2.5 - 14 cm (1 - 5½ in.) long, somewhat constricted between the seeds. Flowers from May to August.

Dame's-rocket is an old-fashioned ornamental that was introduced from Europe and escaped from cultivation. It is common in damp soil along roadsides, rivers, fencerows and ditches and in waste areas, forests and abandoned orchards in southern Ontario.

It is distinguished by its tall stems, its showy purple to pink or white petals, pubescent, sharply toothed leaves and its habit of growing in scattered or thick stands in non-cultivated areas.

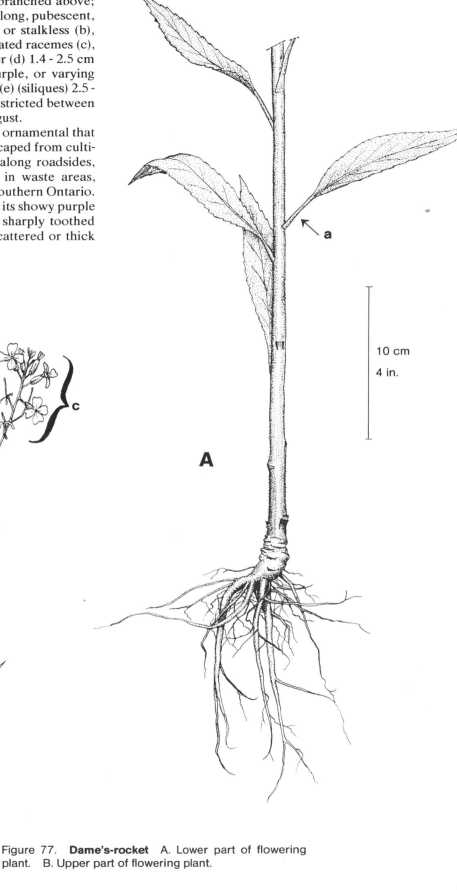

Figure 77. **Dame's-rocket** A. Lower part of flowering plant. B. Upper part of flowering plant.

97

Wormseed mustard, *Erysimum cheiranthoides* L., (Figure 78, Plate 54) [ERYCH, vélar fausse giroflée, Treacle mustard, vélar giroflée] Annual or winter annual, reproducing only by seed. **Stems** 15 - 100 cm (6 - 40 in.) high, erect, usually branched, firm, apparently hairless but slightly rough due to tiny, flat-lying, 2-branched hairs [(a) exaggerated]; **leaves** alternate (1 per node), nearly linear or broader near the middle and tapering to both ends, without teeth or with a few wavy or slightly pointed teeth, slightly rough on both surfaces with tiny 3-branched hairs [(b) exaggerated]; **flowers** similar to those of Wild mustard but paler yellow and much smaller, about 6 mm (¼ in.) across and crowded in clusters at the ends of the stems and branches, these lengthening as the pods begin to develop; **seedpods** (c) on slender stalks about 1 cm (2/5 in.) long which stand out from the stem, the pod itself standing upwards or nearly parallel to the stem, 15 - 25 mm (3/5 - 1 in.) long, usually somewhat 4-angled in cross-section and tipped by a short blunt beak; **seeds** dull reddish-yellow, very small, about 1 mm (1/25 in.) long and usually less than half as wide. Flowers from mid-June to late autumn and sheds mature seeds soon after flowering begins; plants often turning purplish at maturity.

Wormseed mustard is common throughout Ontario, growing in a very wide variety of habitats from dry, rocky, shallow soils to moist sandy shores, to rich loam and clays, and is found in grainfields, hay and pastureland, waste places, gardens, poorly kept lawns, roadsides and railways, riversides, sandy beaches and limestone talus.

Figure 78. **Wormseed mustard** A. Plant. B. Seedling. C. Young plant.

It is distinguished from other mustards by its slender leaves which do not clasp the stem, the 2-branched hairs (a) on the stems and 3-branched hairs (b) on leaves which can be seen with magnification, a slightly bluish-green cast to leaves and stems, the small, pale yellow flowers, and the slender, angular seedpods (c) about 2 cm (4/5 in.) long which are tipped with a short blunt beak. Every effort should be made to prevent Wormseed mustard from going to seed in fields of oats or barley where these cereal grains may be used for feeding pigs. Seeds of Wormseed mustard have an extremely bitter taste, and **when feed is contaminated by a very small fraction of a percentage of Wormseed mustard seeds, pigs will refuse to eat it.** Apparently cattle and horses can tolerate larger proportions of Wormseed mustard than can pigs.

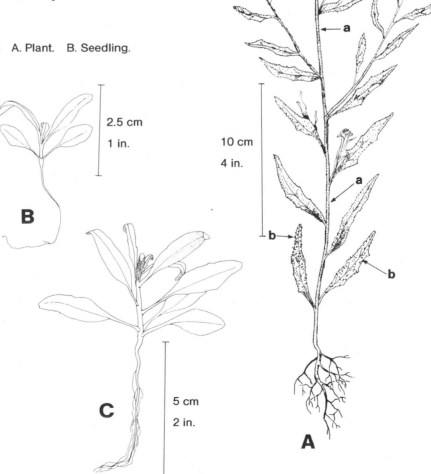

2.5 cm

1 in.

B

10 cm

4 in.

5 cm

2 in.

C

A

Tall wormseed mustard, *Erysimum hieraciifolium* L., (Figure 79) [ERYHI, vélar à feuilles d'épervière] Biennial or possibly short-lived perennial, reproducing only by seed. This is a taller, coarser plant than Worm-seed mustard; **stems** stiffly erect, 90 - 180 cm (3 - 6 ft) high, branched but with the branches also erect, similarly harsh with tiny 2-branched hairs; leaves of first-year plants in a dense rosette on the ground surface, long and narrow with the widest part usually nearer the tip end, green or sometimes purplish, their dead bases (a) obvious at ground level in the second year; stem leaves (B) alternate (1 per node) on the stem and of similar size and shape but smaller upwards, with tiny 3-branched to 4-branched hairs on both surfaces; **flowers** somewhat larger than Wormseed mustard and on shorter stalks, **seedpods** (b) erect and closely parallel to the stem. Flowers from mid-July to the end of the growing season.

Tall wormseed mustard occurs in several localities, mostly in southeastern Ontario where it grows in pastureland, waste areas, railroad embankments and river flats.

It is distinguished by its tall, erect stature, slender leaves with 3- to 4-branched hairs (seen under magnification), small yellow flowers on short stalks, and numerous seedpods closely paralleling the central stem, forming a tighter, denser inflorescence than Wormseed mustard at maturity.

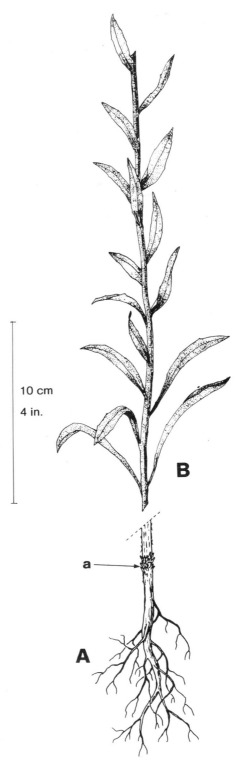

Figure 79. **Tall wormseed mustard** A. Base of second-year plant.   B. Middle portion of plant.   C. Upper portion of plant.

Creeping yellow cress, *Rorippa sylvestris* (L.) Bess., (Figure 80) [RORSY, rorippe sylvestre] Perennial, reproducing by **rhizomes** (a) and by seed. **Stems** spreading or ascending 10 - 60 cm (4 - 24 in.) high, simple to freely branched; **leaves** thin and pinnately parted almost to midrib (b), lanceolate in outline, with toothed or cut divisions that are lanceolate or linear; lower leaves up to 20 cm (8 in.) long, upper ones progressively reduced; **flowers** (c) in small clusters at ends of branches; the clusters expanding into elongated, open racemes as the flowers mature; each flower 3 - 10 mm (1/8 - 2/5 in.) wide, with 4 bright yellow petals longer than the 4 sepals; **seedpods** (d) (siliques) slenderly linear-cylindric, 2 - 15 mm (1/12 - 3/5 in.) long and 0.4 - 1.5 mm (1/50 - 1/16 in.) wide; their pedicels (e) 3 - 20 mm (⅛ - 4/5 in.) long, thread-like and spreading perpendicular to the stem; **seeds** 0.6 - 0.8 mm (1/40 - 1/30 in.) long. Many patches of Creeping yellow cress do not set seed and their seedpods remain undeveloped. Flowers from June to September.

Creeping yellow cress was introduced from Eurasia and is found throughout southern Ontario in moist soil in river beds, along sand dunes, wet meadows and in depressional areas in fields and gardens.

It is distinguished by its perennial habit of growth often resulting in dense patches with numerous intertwining rhizomes, its petals being much longer than its sepals, its lateral leaf segments often being sharply toothed and more widely spaced than in Marsh yellow cress, and the frequent absence of seed set.

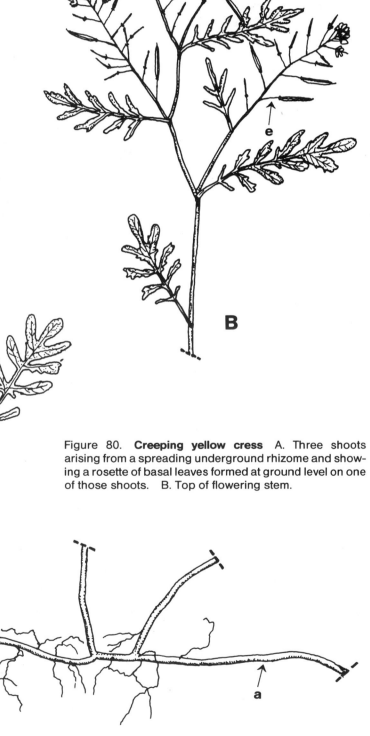

10 cm

4 in.

Figure 80. **Creeping yellow cress** A. Three shoots arising from a spreading underground rhizome and showing a rosette of basal leaves formed at ground level on one of those shoots.   B. Top of flowering stem.

March yellow cress, *Rorippa islandica* (Oeder) Borb., (Figure 81) [RORIS, rorippe d'Islande, cresson de marais, rorippe palustre] Annual or biennial, reproducing only by seed. **Stems** erect, glabrous to hairy, 0.1 - 1.3 m (4 - 52 in.) high, simple or branched, often somewhat purplish in the lower part, arising from a **taproot** (a); **leaves** alternate, pinnately lobed or merely toothed, lanceolate to oblong-ovate in outline, up to 15 cm (6 in.) long, their bases somewhat flared and partially clasping the stem (b); **flowers** (c) in small clusters at the ends of branches; the clusters expanding into fairly compact racemes as the flowers mature; each flower 1 - 5 mm (1/25 - 1/5 in.) wide, with 4 sepals about 1 - 2 mm (1/25 - 1/12 in.) long, 4 yellow petals 1 - 2 mm (1/25 - 1/12 in.) long, 6 stamens and a short but usually definite style; **seedpods** (d)

(silicles) 1.5 - 10 mm (1/16 - 2/5 in.) long and 0.5 - 4 mm (1/50 - 1/6 in.) thick, slenderly ellipsoid to almost spherical; their pedicels (e) thread-like, spreading or ascending, 2 - 7 mm (1/12 - ¼ in.) long when mature; **seeds** 0.4 - 0.9 mm (1/60 - 1/30 in.) long. Flowers from May to September.

Marsh yellow cress is a widely occurring native plant in moist or wet areas and in some areas may have been introduced from Europe. It occurs throughout Ontario in wet or moist soils along shores, in waste places and in depressions in cultivated fields.

Marsh yellow cress is distinguished by its pinnately-lobed leaves, its seedpods ranging from shorter than to twice the length of the thread-like pedicels and its annual or biennial habit.

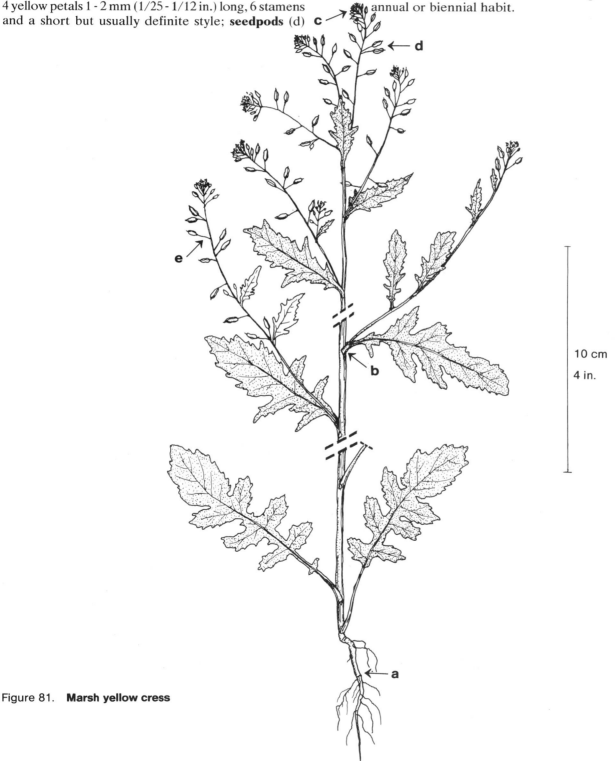

10 cm

4 in.

Figure 81. **Marsh yellow cress**

101

Yellow rocket, *Barbarea vulgaris,* R. Br., (Figure 82, Plate 55) [BARVU, barbarée vulgaire, Herb barbara, Herb of St. Barbara, Winter cress, herbe de Sainte-Barbe, cresson d'hiver] Usually biennial or perennial, but some plants flowering, setting seed and dying after their first growing season; reproducing only by seed. Root system on young plants a **taproot**, becoming much-branched and fibrous with age; young plants producing a rosette of smooth, shiny, dark green leaves during the first year, these staying green throughout the winter or turning slightly purplish by spring; **stems** forming in the spring, 1 to several stems per plant, erect, 20 - 80 cm (8 - 32 in.) high, branched; rosette and lower stem **leaves** long-stalked, hairless, divided into 1 large rounded terminal lobe (a) and smaller lobes (b) along each side; upper leaves alternate (1 per node), short-stalked or stalkless, coarsely toothed, or without teeth, or sometimes deeply lobed, but always with a pair of basal lobes (c) which clasp the stem; **flowers** similar to Wild mustard but golden-yellow and somewhat smaller, 10 - 16 mm (2/5 - 2/3 in.) across; the **seedpods** and their stalks either nearly erect and overlapping one another forming a dense raceme as in the typical botanical variety *(B. vulgaris* var. *vulgaris)* (resembling arrangement of seedpods shown in Figures 74 and 79), or as in the second botan-

ical variety *(B. vulgaris* var. *arcuata* (Opiz. Fries), the stalks spreading with the seedpods (d) standing outwards or curving upwards and usually not overlapping one another, thus forming an open raceme (as illustrated in Figure 82B); stalks 3 - 6 mm (⅛ - ¼ in.) long; pods 1.5 - 3 cm (3/5 - 1¼ in.) long with a slender, seedless beak 2 - 3 mm (1/12 - ⅛ in.) long; **seeds** egg-shaped 1 - 1.5 mm (1/25 - 1/16 in.) long, metallic grayish-brown. Flowers from mid-May to early July and sometimes again briefly in late autumn.

Yellow rocket is common throughout most of Ontario in meadows, pastures, waste areas, roadsides, railways and along watercourses, being especially common in moist rich soil and is apparently still spreading rapidly in such areas. Its occurrence in grainfields is increasing.

It is similar to Wild mustard and often mistaken for it, although the two are easily distinguished. Yellow rocket is a perennial or biennial, so flowers much earlier in the season than Wild mustard and has smaller and deeper golden-yellow flowers. Its leaves are dark glossy green or somewhat purplish, hairless, and distinctly clasp the stem, and the seedpod is tipped by a very slender beak which does not have a seed in its base.

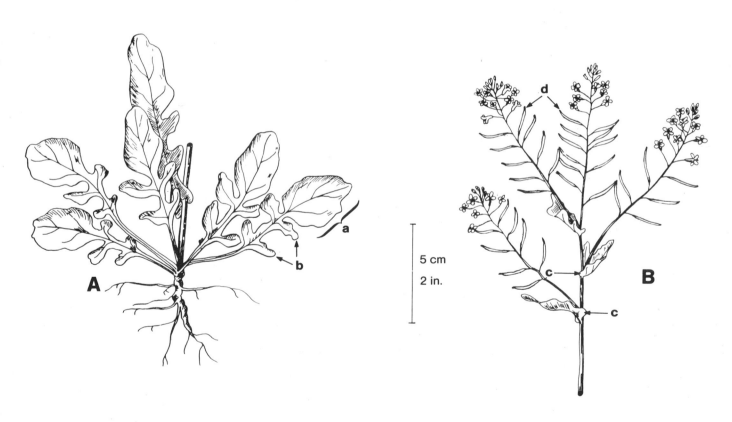

Figure 82. **Yellow rocket** A. Base of plant. B. Flowering and fruiting stem of variety with spreading seedpods.

Pennsylvania bitter cress, *Cardamine pensylvanica* Muhl., (Figure 83) [CARPE, cardamine de Pennsylvanie, cresson amer] Annual, biennial or possibly a short-lived perennial, reproducing by seed. **Stems** mostly 15 - 25 cm (6 - 10 in.) high but in wetter habitats up to 75 cm (30 in.) long, erect where growing on dry or moist soil, or if on wet soil or in standing water, weak and more or less prostrate with ascending tips, smooth, mostly light green with darker green slender parallel lines; rosette **leaves** pinnately compound with 1-6 pairs of membranous, elliptic, obovate or rounded, smooth leaflets, and a larger terminal leaflet, all with smooth to wavy or weakly toothed margins; the blade of one leaflet connected to that of the next by a very slender wing along the side of the mid-vein of the compound leaf; rosette leaves often shrivelled and brown (a) by the time the seedpods appear; stem leaves (b) similar to rosette leaves, 4 - 8 cm (1½ - 3½ in.) long, often with narrower and longer leaflets; **flowers** 4 mm (1/6 in.) wide with white petals; pedicels ascending when mature at about 45° to the stem, 2 - 15 mm (1/12 - 3/5 in.) long; **seedpods** (c) (siliques) narrowly linear, 1 - 3 cm (2/5 - 1-1/5 in.) long, spreading-erect to nearly parallel with the stem; each with a slender beak (d) 1 - 2 mm (1/25 - 1/12 in.) long; **seeds** orange, 1 - 1.5 mm (1/25 - 1/16 in.) long and 0.5 mm (1/50 in.) wide. Flowers from May to August out-of-doors but may flower any time if infesting potted plants in the greenhouse.

Bitter cress is a native plant of swamps and wet woods in Ontario but has recently become a problem in container stock in greenhouses and nurseries.

It is distinguished by its soft, nearly succulent stems and leaves, its pinnately compound leaves with the terminal leaflet being larger than the lateral ones, its small, white flowers, and its slender, nearly erect seedpods with tiny orange seeds. It is an excellent substitute for Water-cress.

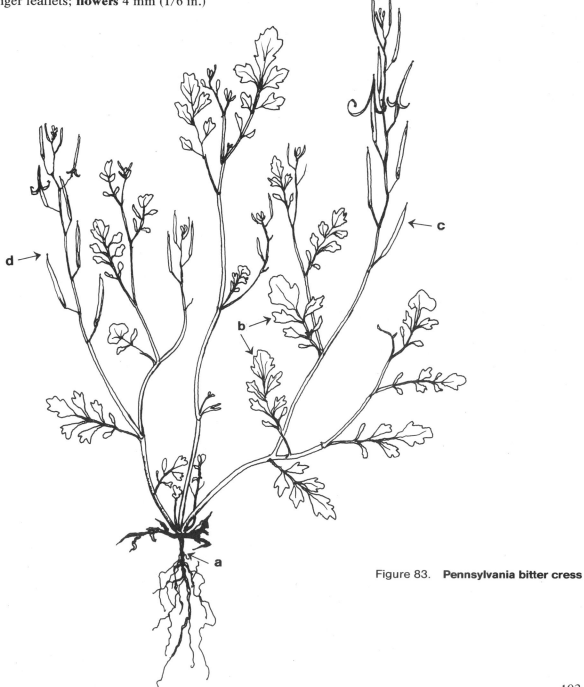

Figure 83. **Pennsylvania bitter cress**

Hoary alyssum, *Berteroa incana* (L.) DC, (Figure 84) [BEFIN, berteroa blanche, alysse] Annual or short-lived perennial, reproducing only by seed. **Stems** erect, 20 - 70 cm (8 - 28 in.) high, usually branched above and frequently purplish; green or each plant with 1 to many stems per plant; first **leaves** in a basal rosette, long-stalked, broadest near the tip; middle leaves similar but smaller; upper leaves stalkless, either elliptic or broader near the base, tapering to a long narrow point; all leaves alternate (1 per node), entire (without teeth) and not clasping the stem (a); stems, leaves, sepals and seedpods covered with very short star-shaped hairs giving the whole plant a gray hoary appearance; **flowers** like Wild mustard but smaller (3 mm, ⅛ in. across) with deeply lobed, white petals, clustered near the tips of the stems and branches; **seedpods** on erect stalks and held close to the stem; pods (b) elliptical or oval, 5 - 8 mm (1/5 - 1/3 in.) long by 3 - 4 mm (⅛ - 1/6 in.) wide, slightly flattened; septum (c) (membranous partition) as wide as the greatest width of the pod and usually remaining on the stalk after the sides of the pod have fallen off when mature; each pod containing 4 to 12 reddish-brown to brownish lens-shaped **seeds** 1 - 1.5 mm (1/25 - 1/16 in.) long with a faint suggestion of a wing around the edge. Flowers from late May to autumn, maturing and shedding seeds throughout the summer.

Hoary alyssum occurs throughout Ontario but is more common in the southern part, particularly on sandy soils. It is found in hay and pasture fields, meadows, roadsides, waste areas and occasionally in gardens or poorly kept lawns.

It is distinguished from other mustards with rounded seedpods by its stalkless, non-clasping stem leaves (a) with smooth (entire) margins, the dense star-shaped hairs that give the whole plant a hoary appearance, and the broad septum (membranous partition) (c) in the oval, hoary seedpods which are held erect and very close to the stem.

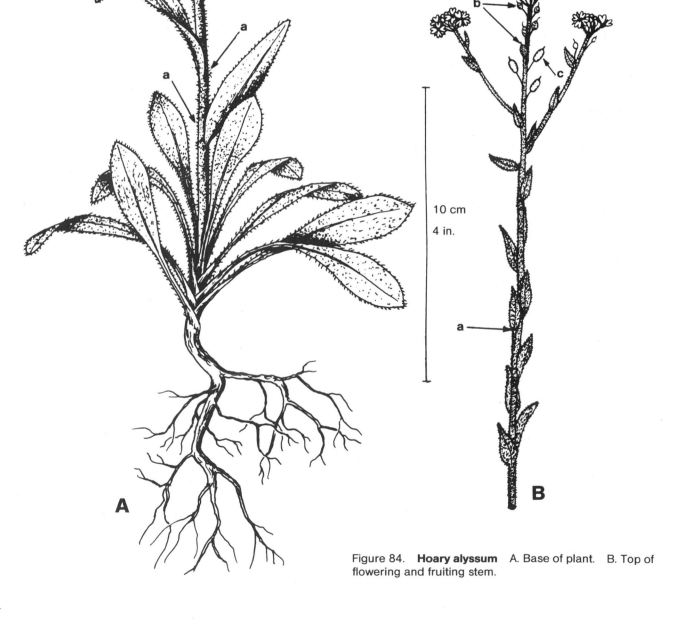

Figure 84. **Hoary alyssum** A. Base of plant. B. Top of flowering and fruiting stem.

Stinkweed, *Thlaspi arvense* L., (Figure 85, Plate 56) [THLAR, tabouret des champs, Fanweed, Field penny-cress, Frenchweed, Pennycress, thlaspi des champs, monayère] Annual or winter annual, reproducing only by seed. **Stems** 5 - 60 cm (2 in. - 2 ft) high, erect, branching in the upper part and sometimes also near the base, hairless; the first several leaves usually in a basal rosette at the ground surface, these with stalks and smooth or slightly wavy margins (A); lower stem leaves with shallow, irregular teeth, rounded towards the tip and tapering towards the narrow stalk which has 2 little lobes or auricles (a) which clasp the stem; middle and upper leaves shallowly or sometimes deeply toothed, without stalks but with a pair of lobes at the base (b) which strongly clasp the stem; **flowers** white, very small (about 3 mm, 1/8 in. across) in rounded clusters at the ends of branches; **seedpods** very flat, rounded to oval, 8 - 12 mm (1/3 - 1/2 in.) wide and usually a bit longer; the central seed-containing portion slightly thickened but surrounded by a broad flat wing with a narrow deep notch (c) at the tip, in the centre of which are the remains of the tiny style; seed-containing section divided into 2 compartments by a very narrow septum (membranous partition), each side containing 3 to 8 seeds; this white septum often remaining on the plant after the pod breaks apart to release the seeds; **seeds** reddish-brown to purplish or blackish, ovoid but somewhat flattened, 1.5 - 2 mm (1/16 - 1/12 in.) long with several rows of concentric ridges on each side. Flowers from early spring to late fall. The whole plant has a sour turnip-garlic odour which is distasteful to most people, and **causes tainted milk when dairy cattle eat it.**

Stinkweed occurs throughout Ontario in cultivated fields, waste places, roadsides and gardens.

It is distinguished from the pepper-grasses, which it closely resembles, by the complete absence of hair from stems and leaves, its unpleasant odour and its larger flat seedpods with a broad flat wing.

Figure 85. **Stinkweed** A. Base of plant. B. Flowering and fruiting stem.

The hoary cresses, *Cardaria* spp. (not illustrated) [CADSS, cranson, Perennial pepper-grass, White-top, White-weed] of which there are three species in scattered localities in Ontario, resemble Stinkweed in general appearance of stems, leaves and flowers. Their most important features are their deeply penetrating and widely spreading **roots** and **underground stems** which make them extremely difficult to eradicate. In addition to their perennial habit, they are readily distinguished from Stinkweed by being densely short-hairy (hence the common name hoary) and having wingless **seedpods** containing only 2 seeds. The mature seedpods are spherical and slightly hairy in **Globe-podded hoary cress**, *Cardaria pubescens* (C.A. Meyer) Jarmolenko, [CADPE, cranson velu]; they are lens-shaped and hairless in **Lens-podded hoary cress**, *Cardaria chalepensis* (L.) Handel-Mazzetti, [CADDC, cranson rampant]; and they are somewhat flat with a heart-shaped base in **Heart-podded hoary cress**, *Cardaria draba* (L.) Desv., [CADDR, cranson dravier, passerage velu]. All three hoary cresses flower from May to July, and occur in cultivated land, pastures, roadsides and waste areas.

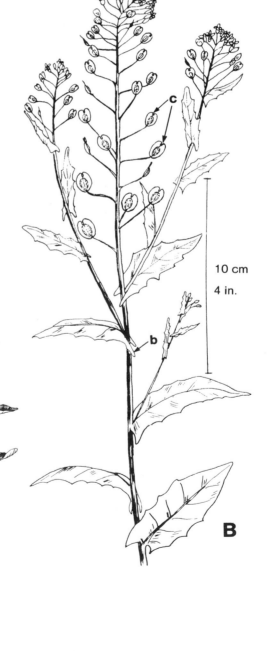

10 cm
4 in.

A

B

105

Field pepper-grass, *Lepidium campestre* (L.) R.Br., (Figure 86, Plate 57) [LEPCA, lépidie des champs, pepperweed, passerage des champs] Annual or biennial, reproducing only by seed. **Stems** 10 - 50 cm (4 - 20 in.) high, branched near the top, short hairy; **leaves** of basal rosette long-stalked, and varying from without teeth or lobes (A) to deeply lobed along each side (B); stem leaves alternate (1 per node), stalkless, short, wavy-margined, with arrowhead-shaped bases (a) that clasp the stem; stems and leaves somewhat rough in texture due to a covering of very short hair; **flowers** individually very small but forming dense, whitish, small clusters at the tips of the stems and branches; **seedpods** numerous and closely spaced along each branch, standing straight out from the stem on short stalks about 4 - 8 mm (1/6 - 1/3 in.) long; the pods flattened, oblong, 5 - 6 mm (1/5 - 1/4 in.) long, mostly held horizontally and with the tip slightly upturned (b), winged towards the outer end (c) and with a small terminal notch in which the tiny style persists as a wee spine; **seeds** 2 per pod, 1 on each side of the septum (membranous partition); septum only as wide as the fruit is thick. Flowers from May to July.

Field pepper-grass is common in pastures, roadsides, edges of woods and waste areas throughout southern Ontario; only rarely found in cultivated fields.

It is distinguished from Common pepper-grass by the clasping bases (a) of the stem leaves, and the seedpods being larger with distinct wings (c) and an upcurved tip (b).

Common pepper-grass, *Lepidium densiflorum* Schrad., (Figure 87) [LEPDE, lépidie densiflore, Green-flowered pepper-grass, Pepperweed, passerage, passerage densiflore] Annual or winter annual, reproducing only by seed. **Stems** 10 - 60 cm (4 - 24 in.) high, usually very much-branched in the upper part and sometimes towards the base as well, densely covered with very short hair; rosette **leaves** with a definite stalk, deeply lobed or divided into separate segments or merely sharply toothed; lower stem leaves alternate (1 per node), smaller and less lobed than the basal ones; upper stem leaves very narrow and either shallowly toothed or without teeth; **flowers** individually very small with the white petals extremely short or

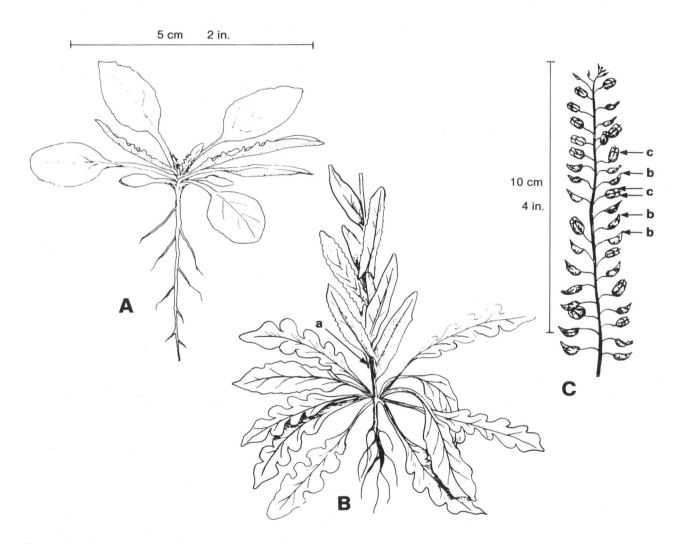

Figure 86. **Field pepper-grass** A. Young plant. B. Base of flowering plant. C. Raceme of seedpods.

Figure 87. **Common pepper-grass** A. Root. B. Stem with 4 racemes of seedpods. C. Seedling, top and side views. D. Young plant.

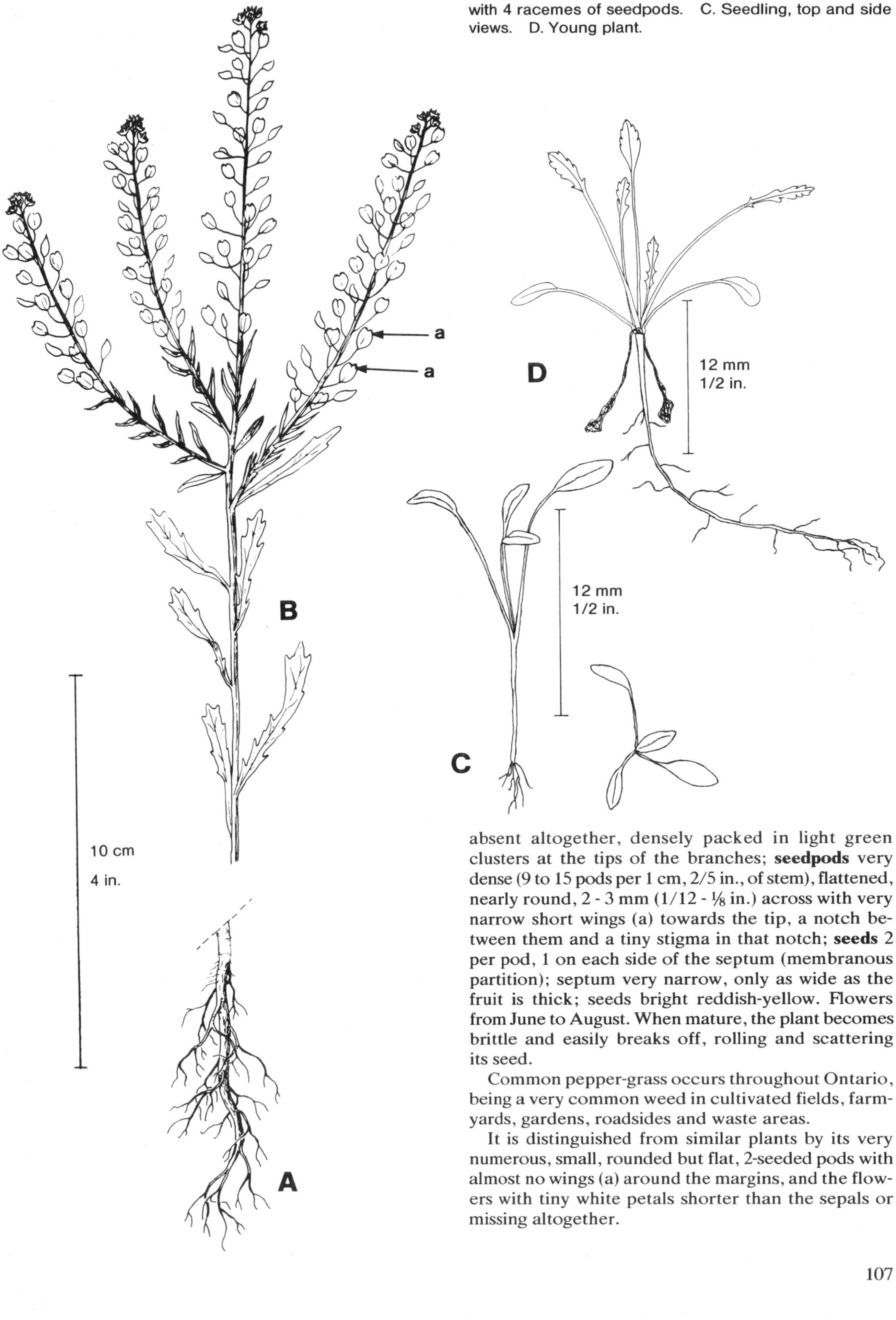

absent altogether, densely packed in light green clusters at the tips of the branches; **seedpods** very dense (9 to 15 pods per 1 cm, 2/5 in., of stem), flattened, nearly round, 2 - 3 mm (1/12 - 1/8 in.) across with very narrow short wings (a) towards the tip, a notch between them and a tiny stigma in that notch; **seeds** 2 per pod, 1 on each side of the septum (membranous partition); septum very narrow, only as wide as the fruit is thick; seeds bright reddish-yellow. Flowers from June to August. When mature, the plant becomes brittle and easily breaks off, rolling and scattering its seed.

Common pepper-grass occurs throughout Ontario, being a very common weed in cultivated fields, farmyards, gardens, roadsides and waste areas.

It is distinguished from similar plants by its very numerous, small, rounded but flat, 2-seeded pods with almost no wings (a) around the margins, and the flowers with tiny white petals shorter than the sepals or missing altogether.

Poor-man's pepper-grass, *Lepidium virginicum* L., (not illustrated) [LEPVI, lépidie de Virginie, passerage de Virginie] Nearly identical in appearance to Common pepper-grass, the most important distinguishing feature being that its small **flowers** have white petals about twice as long as the sepals. It is a native plant that occurs in scattered localities throughout Ontario in meadows, waste areas, roadsides and occasionally in cultivated land.

Clasping-leaved pepper-grass, *Lepidium perfoliatum* L., (not illustrated) [LEPPE, lépidie perfoliée, passerage à feuilles embrassantes] Similar to Common pepper-grass in general habit of growth but easily distinguished because its **flowers** are pale yellow, the basal **leaves** are finely divided, and the stem leaves have rounded or oval blades which appear to completely encircle the stem. It occurs in only a few localities in the central part of southern Ontario.

Shepherd's-purse, *Capsella bursa-pastoris* (L.) Medic., (Figure 88, Plate 58) [CAPBP, bourse-à-pasteur, capselle bourse-à-pasteur, tabouret] Annual or winter annual, reproducing only by seed. **Stems** erect 10 - 60 cm (4 - 24 in.) high, branched above or throughout; first **leaves** in rosette at the ground surface, stalked, the blades very variable, oblong, 5 - 10 cm (2 - 4 in.) long, shallowly to deeply and coarsely toothed or pinnately divided; stem leaves alternate (1 per node), usually much smaller, stalkless, with a few, shallow, scattered teeth or almost lacking teeth, and with 2 narrow, pointed basal lobes (a) which clasp the stem; stems and leaves covered and with fine star-shaped hairs or are hairless; **flowers** resemble Wild mustard in form but are white and much smaller (3 - 8 mm, ⅛ - 1/3 in. across) in rounded clusters at the ends of stems and branches; **seedpods** on short (1 -

2 cm, 2/5 - 4/5 in.) stalks which spread out from the stem, more or less triangular to heart- or valentine-shaped, the pointed end attached to the stalk and the 2 lobes at the outer end; seed-containing section divided by a narrow septum (membranous partition) with several seeds on each side; **seeds** about 1 mm (1/25 in.) long, oblong, dull orange-yellow to slightly reddish. Flowers from early spring to late fall.

Shepherd's-purse occurs throughout Ontario in grainfields, waste areas, roadsides, gardens and lawns.

It is distinguished from all other plants in the Mustard Family by its valentine-shaped seedpods, hence "purse" in its English name. In the rosette stage, it can be distinguished from other mustards with lobed basal leaves by usually being hairy, the lobes or divisions more or less uniform on each side, and its generally small size.

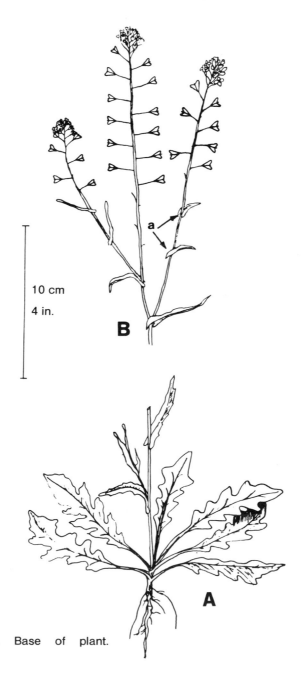

10 cm
4 in.

Figure 88. **Shepherd's-purse** A. Base of plant. B. Flowering and fruiting stem.

Small-seeded false flax, *Camelina microcarpa* Andrz. ex DC., (Figure 89, Plate 59) [CMAMI, caméline à petits fruits, caméline à petites graines] Annual or winter annual, reproducing only by seed. **Stems** erect, 30 - 90 cm (1 - 3 ft) high, somewhat branched; young winter annual plants forming a rosette of leaves in the fall but annual plants do not (A); stem **leaves** alternate (1 per node), the lower ones narrowly oval, stalkless, broadest near the middle, 2 - 10 cm (1 - 4 in.) long, somewhat clasping (a); middle and upper leaves stalkless, widest near the base, tapering towards the slender tip and clasping the stem with 2 basal lobes (b); leaves and lower portion of stems rough-hairy with star-shaped hairs; **flowers** resembling Wild mustard but smaller and pale yellow, in rounded clusters at ends of stems and branches; **seedpods** shaped like a slightly flattened teardrop, 4 - 6 mm (1/6 - ¼ in.) long, tipped with a slender beak or style 1 - 2 mm (1/25 - 1/12 in.) and on slender stalks which spread 6 - 25 mm (¼ - 1 in.) from the stem; septum (membranous partition) as wide as the greatest width of the pod and often remaining on the stalk when the sides of the pod drop off; **seeds** 0.8 - 1.2 mm (1/30 - 1/20 in.) long, reddish-brown to dark reddish-brown. Flowers from late May until early autumn, frequently dropping seed while still flowering.

Small-seeded false flax occurs throughout Ontario but is more common in the southern part of the province, infesting grainfields, seeded pastures, abandoned fields, waste places and roadsides.

Two other kinds of false flax may be found in Ontario in similar situations but are not as common as Small-seeded false flax. Both resemble it in general appearance an habit of growth, the main distinguishing features being in the seedpods and seeds. **Large-seeded false flax,** *Camelina sativa* (L.) Crantz, (not illustrated) [CMASA, caméline faux lin, caméline, caméline cultivée], has oblong **seeds** about 2 mm (1/12 in.) long in teardrop-shaped **seedpods** usually 6 mm (¼ in.) or longer, and its **stems** are not as hairy. **Flat-seeded false flax,** *Camelina parodii* Ibarra and La Porte, (not illustrated) [CMAAL, caméline à graines plates, caméline dentée, *Camelina dentata* Pers.], has large, flat **seeds** which are round in outline and about 2.5 mm (1/10 in.) in diameter in **pods** that tend to be flat across the top rather than rounded.

All three kinds of false flax are distinguished from other members of the Mustard Family with small, nearly round pods by their light yellow flowers followed by very smooth, hairless, teardrop-shaped seedpods having a broad septum (membranous partition) as wide as the pod, their narrowly triangular or somewhat arrowhead-shaped stem leaves with clasping bases, and the stems and leaves roughened with tiny star-shaped hairs.

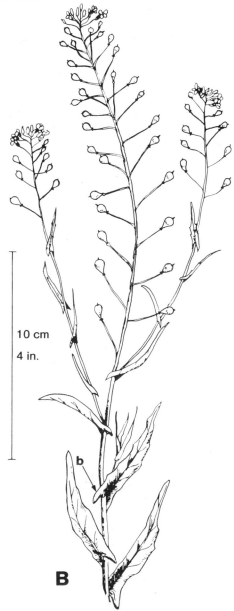

10 cm
4 in.

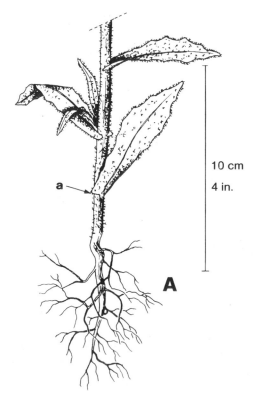

a

10 cm
4 in.

A

B

Figure 89. **Small-seeded false flax** A. Base of annual plant. B. Flowering and fruiting stem.

Ball mustard, *Neslia paniculata* (L.) Desv., (Figure 90) [NEAPA, neslie paniculée, Neslia, Yellow-weed, neslie] Annual or winter annual, reproducing only by seed. **Stems** much branched, especially in the upper part, up to 80 cm (32 in.) high, hairy with very short simple or mostly multi-branched (star-shaped) hairs (B) giving it a somewhat rough texture; **lower stem leaves** narrowly ovate without clasping bases (a), 1 - 6 cm (2/5 - 2½ in.) long; **mid-stem leaves** similar but with clasping bases (b), leaf margins mostly entire or slightly irregular; **upper leaves** smaller, arrowhead-shaped and clasping; both upper and lower surfaces of all leaves with numerous star-shaped hairs; **inflorescence** of elongated racemes with slender, spreading pedicels (c); **flowers** (d) golden yellow, 1 -2 mm (1/25 - 1/12 in.) wide; **seedpod** (e, C) (silicle) nearly spherical, 2 - 3 mm (1/12 - ⅛ in.) in diameter, prominently veined on the surface, each with a single seed; **seeds** 2 mm (1/12 in.) long and 2.5 mm (1/10 in.) wide. Flowers from June to August.

Ball mustard was introduced from Europe and is found in fields, orchards, gardens and waste places and along roads and railways in Ontario.

It is distinguished by its middle and upper leaves clasping the stem, elongated racemes with spreading pedicels, small flowers with golden yellow petals followed by small, spherical, one-seeded pods, and its stems and leaves with a rough texture due to tiny star-shaped hairs.

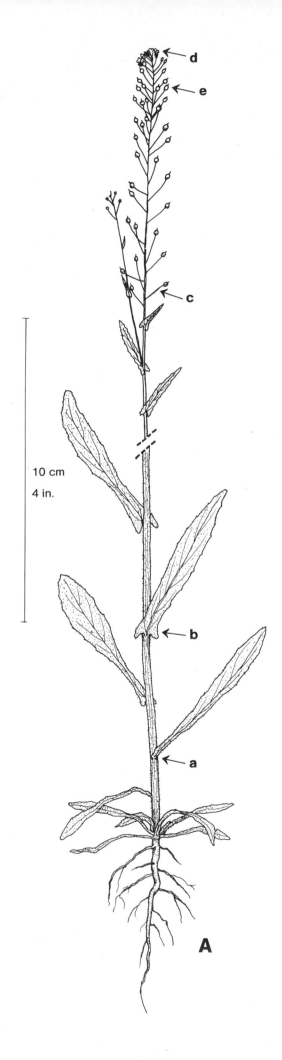

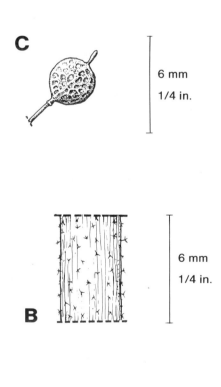

Figure 90. **Ball mustard** A. Plant. B. Portion of stem magnified to show star-shaped hairs. C. Seedpod (nearly spherical).

MIGNONETTE FAMILY (RESEDACEAE)

Yellow mignonette, *Reseda lutea* L., (not illustrated) [RESLU, mignonette jaune] Biennial or short-lived perennial from a slender taproot; reproducing only by seed. **Stems** erect or much branched, up to 80 cm (32 in.) high, round or ridged lengthwise; **lower leaves** 5 - 10 cm (2 - 4 in.) long, 6 - 25 mm (¼ - 1 in.) wide near the end and narrowing gradually towards the stem, unlobed or with one deep lobe on each side near the outer end; **middle and upper leaves** usually wider and pinnately lobed with 2 or more long narrow segments on each side of the outer 1/3 to ½ of the leaf blade; **flowers** yellow with a greenish cast in terminal racemes; young racemes dense and conical in shape but elongating with age so the older flowers and seedpods become separated; flowers 5 - 8 mm (1/5 - 1/3 in.) across; petals usually 6, as few as 4 or rarely as many as 8, each with 3 slender, finger-like lobes at its outer end; 12 - 20 **stamens**; **seedpods** 1 cm (2/5 in.) long, 4 mm (1/6 in.) in diameter, with 3 or 4 narrow wings (less than 1 mm, 1/25 in. wide) that terminate in little points around the end of the seedpod; usually containing 20 or more seeds. Flowers from May to August.

Yellow mignonette occurs as an occasional weed in pastures, waste areas, roadsides and abandoned yards where it may have been grown as an ornamental in place of the sweeter-scented **Sweet mignonette**, *Reseda odorata* L.

From a distance, Yellow mignonette may be confused with Yellow rocket, Wild mustard, or other yellow-flowered mustards, but it is distinguished from them by its flowers which usually have 6 petals, each with 3 tiny finger-like lobes, its slightly winged seedpods with 3 or 4 points or horns at the end, and the outer 1/3 to 1/2 of its middle and upper leaves with irregular narrow lobes.

ORPINE FAMILY (Crassulaceae)

Mossy stonecrop, *Sedum acre* L., (Figure 91, Plate 60) |SEDAC, orpin âcre, Hen-and-chickens, Stonecrop, Yellow stonecrop, vermiculaire âcre| Perennial, reproducing by seed, by creeping horizontal stems rooting at the nodes and by bits of broken stem with a few leaves which also root at the nodes and start new patches. **Stems** creeping, densely matted, with many short, semi-erect branches, 5 - 15 cm (2 - 6 in.) high and covered with numerous, small, alternate (1 per node), overlapping, succulent (fleshy), ovoid **leaves** (a) 2 - 10 mm (1/12 - 2/5 in.) long and round in cross-section; **flowers** (b) yellow, 8 - 10 mm (1/3 - 2/5 in.) across in small clusters, each flower with 5 green sepals, 5 yellow petals, 10 stamens and 5 pistils; most of the pistils becoming pointed seedpods containing several seeds. Flowers from June to July.

Mossy stonecrop is a common lawn weed in the central part of southern Ontario and occasionally in other regions as well. It was introduced as an ornamental for rock gardens because of its ability to grow well in coarse, sandy, shallow soils low in fertility. In these situations, it can crowd out grass and become a serious lawn weed. It also occurs in gardens, roadsides and waste areas.

It is distinguished by its low stature, short, thick, very succulent leaves and small, yellow flowers.

Several other kinds of stonecrops (*Sedum* spp.) may escape from cultivation but are usually less common. Their flowers range from white through yellows and pinks to orange or reddish-purple; their succulent leaves may be round in cross-section or quite flat, and their stems may be up to 60 cm (2 ft) high.

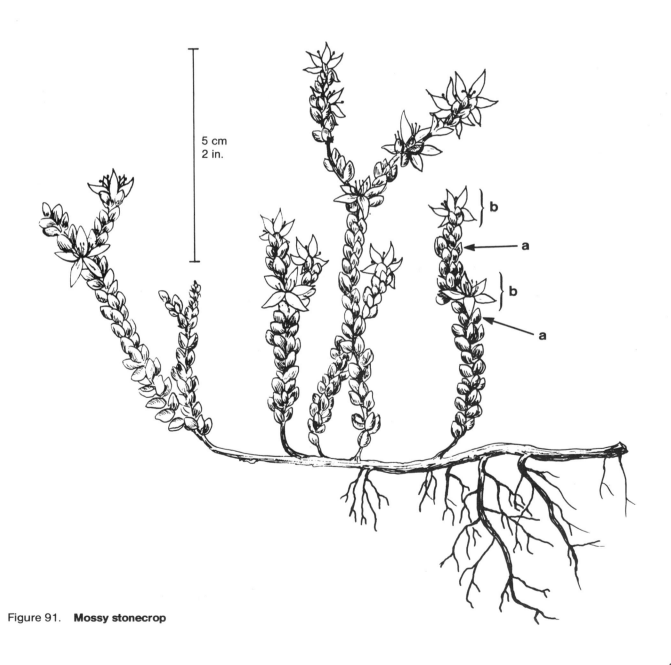

5 cm
2 in.

Figure 91. **Mossy stonecrop**

Rough cinquefoil, *Potentilla norvegica* L., (Figure 92, Plate 61) [PTLNO, potentille de Norvège, Upright cinquefoil, Yellow cinquefoil, potentille] Annual, biennial or short-lived perennial, reproducing only by seed. **Stems** 20 - 50 cm (8 - 20 in.) high, usually branched, sometimes with 2 or more stems from the same root, hairy throughout; **leaves** alternate (1 per node), compound; 1 leaf consisting of 3 leaflets (a) at the end of a leafstalk (petiole) (b) and a pair of stipules (c) at the base of the leafstalk where it joins the stem; each leaflet oblong to roundish with coarse, sharp, forward-pointed teeth; leaves in a rosette early in the growing season and, at this stage, frequently mistaken for strawberry; lower stem leaves long-stalked; uppermost leaves stalkless with the 3 leaflets and pair of stipules apparently attached directly to the stem (d); **flowers** about 6 mm (¼ in.) across, on short stalks from leafy branches in the upper part of the plant; 5 pale yellow petals about the same length as the green sepals, a ring of many stamens around the cluster of many tiny pistils which mature into a cluster of seeds; each **seed** about 1 mm (1/25 in.) long, yellowish to pale brown and ridged lengthwise. Flowers in June and July.

Rough cinquefoil occurs throughout Ontario in pastures, meadows, waste areas, roadsides, and occasionally in gardens and cultivated fields.

Rosettes of Rough cinquefoil are distinguished from strawberry plants (*Fragaria* spp.) by having teeth all around the margins of all 3 leaflets, whereas with strawberry the lower ¼ to 1/3 of each leaflet is usually without teeth. Older plants have robust, erect stems with several leaves and yellow flowers, whereas strawberry has a slender, short, nearly leafless stem with loose clusters of white flowers. It is distinguished from the yellow-flowered buttercups by its 3-leaflet leaves and the presence of a pair of stipules (c) at the base of each leafstalk (b). Rough cinquefoil is distinguished from other cinquefoils by the combination of 3-leaflet (a) leaves green on both surfaces, and small (6 - 10 mm, ¼ - 2/5 in. across), pale yellow flowers in which the sepals and petals are of about equal length.

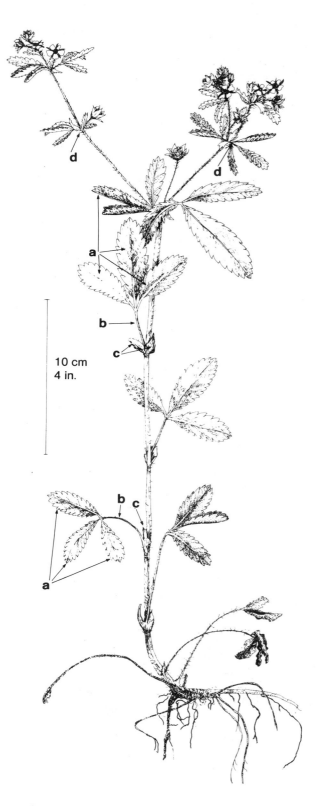

Figure 92. **Rough cinquefoil**

Sulphur cinquefoil, *Potentilla recta* L., (Figure 93, Plate 62) [PTLRC, potentille dressée, Five-finger cinquefoil, Rough-fruited cinquefoil, Upright cinquefoil, Yellow cinquefoil, potentille droite] Similar to Rough cinquefoil in general habit and appearance but distinguished by being perennial from a coarse, fibrous **root** system; usually multiple-stemmed, the **stems** often taller (20 - 80 cm, 8 - 32 in. high); **leaves** green on both sides, palmately compound with usually 5 to 7 narrow, coarsely toothed, hairy leaflets (a) at the tip of the leafstalk (petiole) (b) (like fingers from the palm of the hand) and a pair of stipules (c) at the base of each leafstalk (b); first 2 or 3 true leaves (d) on seedling not divided; **flowers** large, 2 - 2.5 cm (4/5 - 1 in.) across; petals deep yellow to sulfur-yellow, longer than the green sepals; **seeds** prominently wrinkly-ridged. Flowers from early June until fall.

Sulphur cinquefoil occurs throughout Ontario, being common in non-cultivated soils such as pastures, meadows, waste areas, clearings in woods, and road-sides.

It is distinguished by its 5 to 7 leaflets palmately arranged at the end of a leafstalk like fingers from the palm of a hand, but sometimes with only 3 leaflets per leaf or the leaves not divided on the smaller flowering branches; the leaves always green on both surfaces, and the large, deep yellow to sulfur-yellow flowers with petals longer than sepals. Sulphur cinquefoil is sometimes mistaken for **Marijuana** (CNISA, chanvre, Hemp, Cannabis, *Cannabis sativa* L.) because of its palmately compound leaves, but Marijuana is a much taller plant up to 1.2 - 3 m (4 - 10 ft.) tall, with much larger palmately compound leaves, each having 5 - 11 leaflets, the leaflets long and slender (up to 15 cm, 6 in., long or even longer, and 1.5 cm, 3/5 in., wide) with coarse teeth, the leaf petioles without stipules, and the stems and leaves somewhat rough with very short, stiff, in-curved hairs but lacking the prominent hairiness of the cinquefoils.

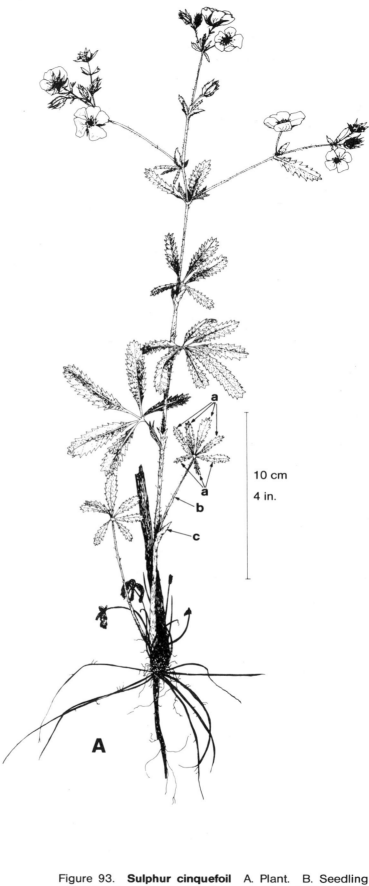

10 cm
4 in.

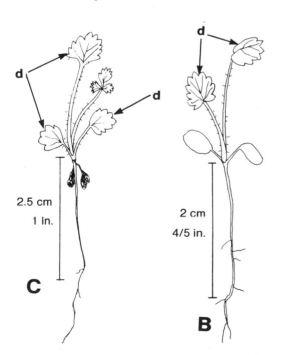

2.5 cm
1 in.

2 cm
4/5 in.

Figure 93. **Sulphur cinquefoil** A. Plant. B. Seedling with 2 true leaves. C. Seedling with 4th leaf trifoliolate.

115

Silvery cinquefoil, *Potentilla argentea* L., (Figure 94) [PTLAG, potentille argentée] Perennial, reproducing only by seed. **Stems** 10 - 50 cm (4 - 20 in.) long, 1 to several from each stout perennial crown, erect or spreading or nearly prostrate; early **leaves** in a dense basal rosette; basal and stem leaves long-stalked, palmately compound with 3 or usually 5 to 7 leaflets (a) which are dark green on the upper surface and silvery-gray on the undersurface (leaflets arranged like fingers from the palm of a hand) each leaflet shallowly and coarsely toothed to very deeply lobed; each leafstalk or stalkless upper leaf with 2 slender, pointed stipules (b) at its junction with the stem; **flowers** yellow, small (6 - 10 mm, ¼ - 2/5 in. across), in branching clusters at ends of branches; petals about the same length as sepals; and many stamens and pistils. Flowers from late May until autumn.

Silvery cinquefoil occurs throughout Ontario, usually on coarse-textured, well-drained soils in open fields, pastures, waste areas, roadsides, and occasionally in lawns.

It is distinguished by its palmately compound leaves [leaflets (a) arranged like fingers from the palm of a hand], with coarsely toothed or lobed leaflets which are green on the upper surface but silvery-gray on the undersurface, and its small yellow flowers with petals and sepals of equal length.

Silverweed, *Potentilla anserina* L., (not illustrated) [PTLAN, potentille ansérine, ansérine] Has a very different habit of growth from Silvery cinquefoil. Its long, slender reddish **stems** trail over the ground surface, like strawberry runners, with internodes often 10 - 15 cm (4 - 6 in.) long, frequently rooting and starting new plants at each node, therefore reproducing both by seed and by runners. Unlike the other cinquefoils, the **leaves** of Silverweed are pinnately compound with many leaflets along each side (as in Small burnet, Figure 96) and often with a mixture of large and small leaflets as in yellow avens (Figure 95), the leaflets silvery-gray on the undersurface and usually dark green on the upper surface; central stalk of each compound leaf and the runners often pinkish to reddish; **flowers** yellow on stalks about 2 - 10 cm (1 - 4 in.) high from nodes on the runners, 2 cm (4/5 in.) across and with petals a little longer than sepals. Flowers from early June to autumn.

It occurs throughout Ontario, usually on coarse-textured soils, on beaches, along rivers, in waste areas, roadsides and occasionally in lawns.

It is distinguished by its long runners, its pinnately compound leaves that are silvery-gray on the underside and green on top, and by its yellow flowers. Stork's-bill is similar to Silverweed with its pinnately divided leaves, but they are green on both surfaces and it has rosy-pink flowers. Also see page 142.

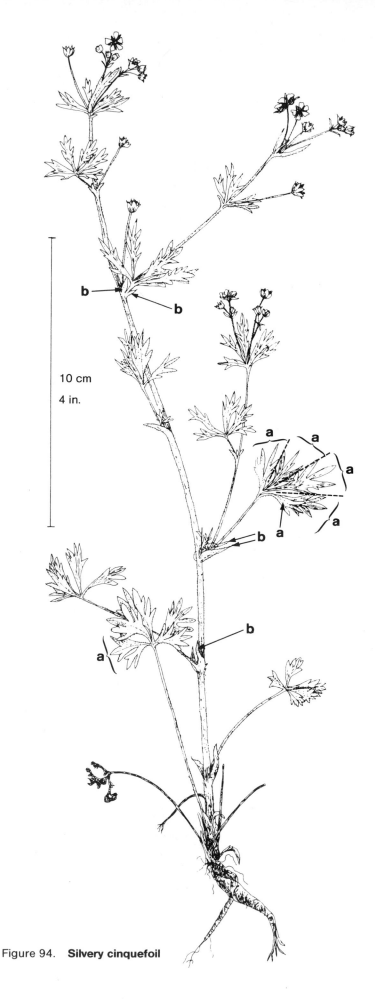

10 cm
4 in.

Figure 94. **Silvery cinquefoil**

Yellow avens, *Geum aleppicum* Jacq. var. *strictum* (Ait.) Fern., (Figure 95, Plate 63) [GEUAS, benoîte stricte, Burs, benoîte d'Alep] Perennial, reproducing only by seed. **Stems** erect, to 1 m (40 in.) high, frequently branched above. **Leaves** very variable, rosette leaves long-stalked, pinnately compound with a large terminal leaflet (a) and a mixture of large (b) and small (c) leaflets along each side of the central stalk (rachis), leaflets coarsely toothed, hairy and green on both surfaces; stem leaves alternate (1 per node), similar but with shorter stalks, especially towards the top of the stem and each with a pair of green leaflet-like stipules (d) where the leafstalk (e) joins the stem; upper leaves stalkless, sometimes just shallowly toothed or lobed without being divided into leaflets; **flowers** few in widely branching inflorescences, 1 - 2 cm (2/5 - 4/5 in.) across, with 5 deep yellow to orange-yellow petals, 5 smaller sepals, numerous stamens and pistils in a dense central cluster; at maturity each flower stalk lengthening and the cluster of pistils enlarging into a nearly spherical brown to dark brown head or bur about 2 cm (4/5 in.) in diameter; each single-seeded pistil (now a fruit or "seed") in the mature bur has a sharply hooked tip (f) which clings to fur, clothes and skin. Flowers from early June to late summer, and the burs persist into late fall or winter.

Yellow avens occurs throughout Ontario in meadows, open woods, pastures, waste areas and roadsides, but is rarely found in cultivated land.

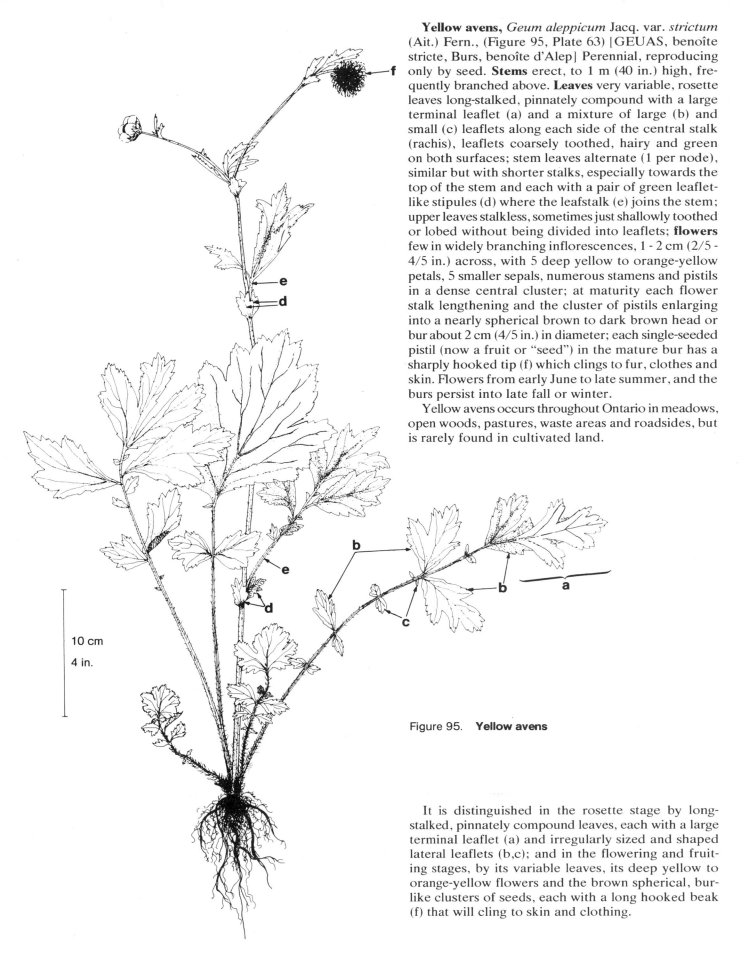

Figure 95. **Yellow avens**

It is distinguished in the rosette stage by long-stalked, pinnately compound leaves, each with a large terminal leaflet (a) and irregularly sized and shaped lateral leaflets (b,c); and in the flowering and fruiting stages, by its variable leaves, its deep yellow to orange-yellow flowers and the brown spherical, bur-like clusters of seeds, each with a long hooked beak (f) that will cling to skin and clothing.

117

Small burnet, *Sanguisorba minor* Scop., (Figure 96) [SANMI, sanguisorbe mineure, Salad burnet, petite pimprenelle] Perennial, reproducing only by seed. **Stems** 20 - 70 cm (8- 28 in.) high, spreading or erect from the short, thick underground **rootstalk**, slender, wiry, usually branched in the upper part; rosette **leaves** numerous, pinnately compound with up to 17 small oval leaflets (a), each with 3 to 7 prominent teeth on each side, usually lighter green below than above; stem leaves alternate (1 per node), scattered, shorter and have fewer leaflets; stipules small and toothed on upper stem leaves but very small or absent from rosette and lower stem leaves; **flowers** individually very small but clustered together in dense, ovoid, greenish heads (b) on long leafless branches; each flower has 4 small, green or brown sepals but no petals, the lower flowers in each head having no pistils but many stamens with long drooping filaments; the upper flowers having 2 pistils but no stamens, or being bisexual with both stamens and pistils; each pistil producing a pair of semi-ovoid hard **seeds**. Flowers from May to July.

Small burnet occurs in several scattered localities in southern Ontario, usually in coarse sandy or gravelly soils, in pastures, meadows, waste areas, and roadsides.

It is distinguished by its pinnately compound leaves with many, small, toothed leaflets, and its greenish, ovoid heads of many densely packed small flowers.

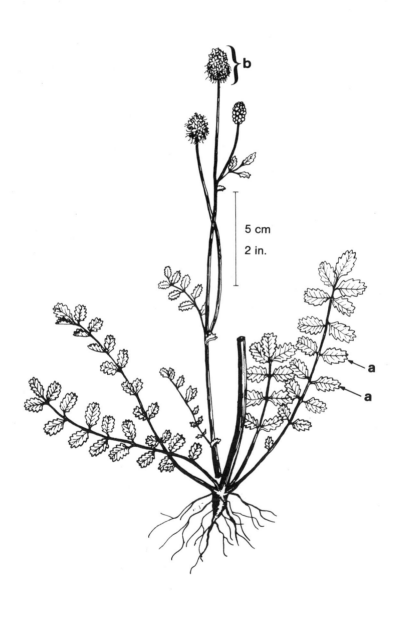

5 cm
2 in.

Figure 96. **Small burnet**

Hawthorn, *Crataegus* spp., (Figure 97) [CSCSS, aubépine, Haw, Hawes, Thorn, Thornbush, senellier] Shrubs, or small trees up to 8 - 10 m (25 - 32 ft.) high, reproducing only by seed; trunks and branches gray-brown to brownish or dull gray, usually with long (1 - 7.5 cm, 2/5 - 3 in.) stout **thorns**, the thorns (a) usually simple (unbranched) or rarely compound with 1 or more smaller, sharp-pointed spines branching sideways from the main thorn (b); **leaves** alternate (1 per node) on young, growing branch tips and clustered on short, lateral spurs on older branches, very variable but usually toothed and often lobed as well, each leaf having one main central midrib and several side veins (c) going out to the marginal teeth; **flowers** few to many in clusters along the branches; each flower with 5 small sepals, 5 larger showy white or pinkish petals and many stamens; **fruit** apple-like, reddish, 1 - 3 cm (2/5 - 1¼ in.) in diameter, with a thin coarse pulp and 1 to 5 large hard **seeds**. Flowers in late spring or early summer; fruit may remain on the branches long after the leaves have fallen in autumn.

Several species of Hawthorn are native in Ontario. Much hybridization has occurred among these, and the taxonomy of this genus is very complicated. Hawthorns occur throughout southern Ontario, often being troublesome in old pastures, cleared areas, borders of woods, along fencerows, and among ornamental shrubs around homes.

Although the Hawthorns, as a group, are easily distinguished by their long, sharp thorns (a) coming from the sides of branches (compare with European buckthorn, Figure 115, having thorns in crotches and at tips of short branches), their leaves with branching veins (c), and their large, showy, white to pinkish flowers followed by small apple-like fruits, the several individual species and varieties are difficult to identify with certainty. Hawthorns can also be distinguished from **Honey-locust,** *Gleditsia triacanthos* L., and **Black locust,** *Robinia pseudoacacia* L., both occasionally grown as ornamentals, as both have compound leaves and flowers that resemble those of the Sweet pea in shape and fragrance.

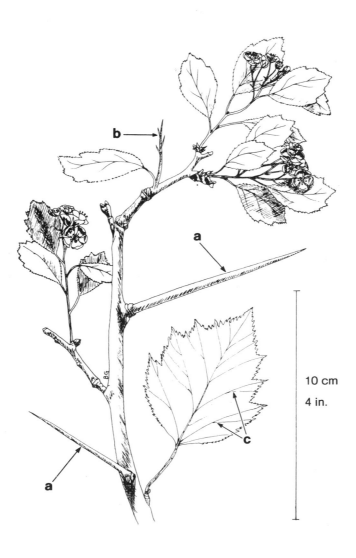

10 cm
4 in.

Figure 97. **Hawthorn**

119

LEGUME or BEAN FAMILY (Leguminosae)

Low hop clover, *Trifolium campestre* Schreb., (Figure 98) [TRFCA, trèfle agraire, Large hop clover, Hop clover, trèfle couché, *Trifolium procumbens* L.] Annual, reproducing only by seed. **Stems** erect, 10 - 40 cm (4 - 16 in.) high, usually much-branched and finely hairy; **leaves** alternate (1 per node), compound, trifoliolate, all 3 leaflets ovate in outline but with the widest part near the tip; the two lateral leaflets (a) without stalks but the terminal or central leaflet (c) with a definite stalk (b) 2 - 4 mm (1/12 - 1/6 in.) long, and with a pair of small ovate stipules (d) at the base of the leafstalk (e); most leaflets broadest near the tip and somewhat flattened across the end; **flowers** individually very small but 20 to 30 grouped together in dense, ovoid, head-like clusters on stalks from leaf axils, each small flower resembling a bean flower but yellow and with conspicuous diagonal veins on each side; the head-like clusters (f) about 1 cm (2/5 in.) in diameter, at first bright yellow but turning a drab beige-brown as they mature; **seedpods** very small, paper-thin, light brown; each splitting to release a single yellow-orange egg-shaped seed about 1 mm (1/25 in.) long. Flowers from June to August.

Low hop clover occurs in scattered localities in southern Ontario, usually in old pastures, waste places and along roadsides.

It is distinguished by its annual habit, the stalked (b) terminal leaflet (c) with ovate stipules (d) and small yellow bean-like flowers in dense ovoid clusters that turn a drab beige-brown as they mature.

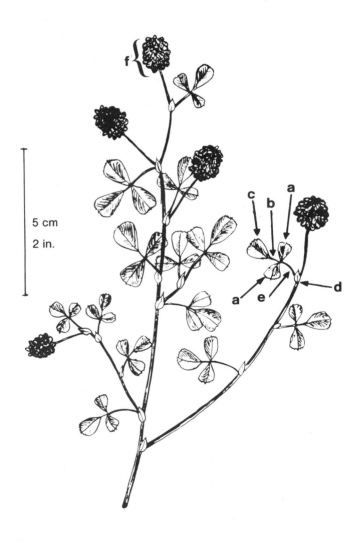

5 cm
2 in.

Figure 98. **Low hop clover**

Black medick, *Medicago lupulina* L., (Figure 99A, Plate 64) [MEDLU, lupuline, Yellow-clover, luzerne lupuline, minette] Annual, reproducing only by seed. **Stems** wiry, as much as 80 cm (32 in.) long and lying prostrate on the ground, or much shorter and erect or spreading; **root** slender but very tough and difficult to pull out or hoe off; **leaves** alternate (1 per node), compound with 3 small oval leaflets shallowly toothed at the tips, the central leaflet with a definite stalk (a), the leafstalk (b) with a pair of thick stipules (c) at its junction with the stem; **flowers** individually very small but grouped in dense head-like clusters, about 1 cm (2/5 in.) in diameter, on long stalks from leaf axils; each flower very small, yellow, similar in form to pea or bean flowers; **seedpods** black (hence the common name), slightly coiled, prominently ridged and hairy or smooth. Flowers from early spring to late autumn, dropping its seed during most of that time.

Black medick occurs throughout Ontario in most soil textures. A particularly common weed in lawns, it also grows in gardens, waste places, roadsides, pastures and sometimes in cultivated fields.

It is distinguished by its compound leaves having 3 oval leaflets, all with shallow teeth towards their tips but only the central one with a definite stalk (a); the small, nearly spherical clusters of yellow flowers on stalks usually longer than the leaves; and the small clusters of black coiled seedpods produced from those flower heads.

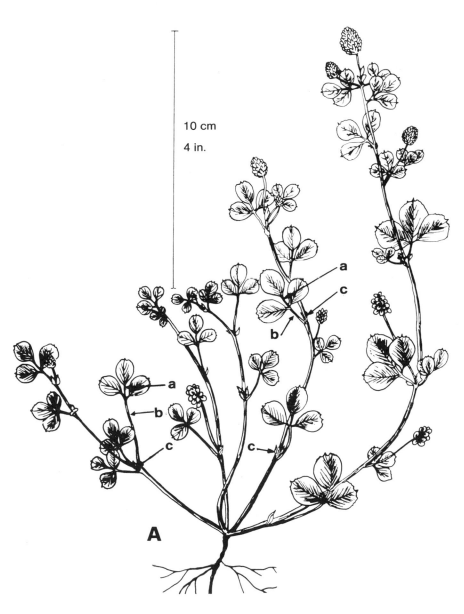

10 cm

4 in.

Figure 99. **Black medick**   A. Plant. (Cont'd.)

121

Three weeds that belong to the Oxalis Family (**Oxalidaceae**) are frequently confused with Black medick. They are **Common yellow wood-sorrel,** *Oxalis dillenii* Jacq., (Figure 99B, Plate 65) [OXAST, oxalide de Dillenius, Oxalis, Sour-clover, *Oxalis stricta* misapplied], **European wood-sorrel,** *Oxalis stricta* L., (not illustrated) [OXAEU, oxalide d'Europe, Oxalis, Sour-clover, oxalide dressée, pain d'oiseau, *Oxalis europaea* Jord.], and **Creeping wood-sorrel,** *Oxalis corniculata* L., (not illustrated) [OXACO, oxalide cornue, Oxalis, Sour-clover, oxalis corniculé]. All are low-growing perennials, rarely as much as 40 - 50 cm (16 - 20 in.) high; **leaves** gray-green to bright green or purplish-green; each leaf compound and consisting of 3 heart-shaped (valentine-shaped) leaflets attached by their pointed ends (d) to the tip of the usually erect petiole, and either hanging down or standing out horizontally in 3 directions; **flowers** (e) bright yellow, 4 - 10 mm (1/6 - 2/5 in.) across, with 5 uniformly shaped petals and 10 - 15 stamens; **seedpods** 1 - 2.5 cm (2/5 - 1 in.) long, slender; each with several seeds. **Creeping wood-sorrel** is usually purplish-green and has longer, trailing stems than the other two, these stems rooting where they touch the ground. **European wood-sorrel** is bright green; its stems have sparse to abundant long hairs, and its mature flowers and seedpods are borne on straight (not zig-zagged) stalks. **Common yellow wood-sorrel** (Figure 99B) is somewhat grayish-green because of very short, closely appressed hairs; its stems lack the long hair, and after flowering, the stalks of its seedpods (f) bend at the nodes and become more or less zig-zagged so they resemble the letters "N" or "Z" (g). Other technical differences that distinguish among these wood-sorrels are beyond the scope of this book.

All three are occasional weeds in lawns, gardens and waste areas throughout Ontario.

They are distinguished from Black medick by their leaflets being heart-shaped, the absence of a distinct stalk for one of the three leaflets (which (a) in Figure 99 shows to be characteristic of Black medick), their yellow flowers having 5 uniformly shaped petals, and their long, narrow seedpods containing several seeds. The leaves of these wood-sorrels resemble those of the shamrock (a variety of White clover, *Trifolium repens* L.) and have a characteristically sour taste (hence, one of their common names being "sour-clover").

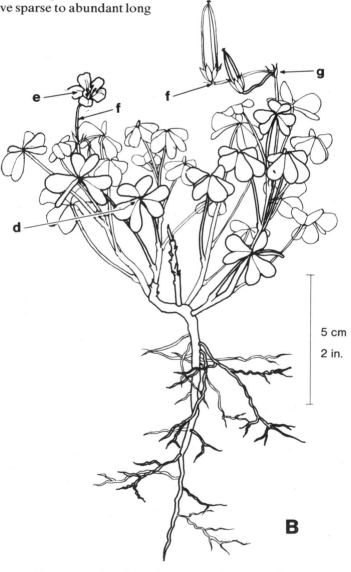

5 cm

2 in.

B

Figure 99. (Cont'd.) **Common yellow wood-sorrel** B. Plant.

White clover, *Trifolium repens* L., (not illustrated) [TRFRE, trèfle blanc, White dutch clover, trèfle rampant] Similar to Black medick but differs in being perennial, having somewhat larger **leaflets**, all of which are stalkless, each usually having a V-shaped whitish mark on the upper surface, and it has larger white **flowers.**

A plant of mixed virtue, White clover is common throughout Ontario in pastures, lawns, meadows, roadsides, waste places and cultivated land, having been intentionally planted as a forage or ground cover in many situations and persisting as an unwanted weed in others.

Bird's-foot trefoil, *Lotus corniculatus* L., (Figure 100) [LOTCO, lotier corniculé, Yellow trefoil, lotier cornu] Perennial, reproducing only by seed. **Stems** 30 - 60 cm (12 - 24 in.) long, prostrate or spreading to erect, usually several from a tough root-crown; **leaves** alternate (1 per node), pinnately compound, each consisting of 5 leaflets; the lower 2 leaflets (a) produced very close to the stem and separated from the outer 3 by a definite stalk (b), resembling stipules but true stipules not produced; **flowers** pea-like, yellow or occasionally reddish-orange, in small umbels raised above the leaves at the tips of long naked stalks; **seedpods** 2 to 4 cm (4/5 - 1-3/5 in.) long, round, slender, brownish to blackish, and hanging or spreading horizontally. Flowers from June to August.

Bird's-foot trefoil is another plant of mixed virtue: usually good but occasionally undesirable; it is a valuable cultivated forage legume but it also escapes from cultivation and may become quite common along roadsides, in uncultivated fields, waste areas and occasionally in lawns throughout most of Ontario.

It is distinguished by its tough perennial root-crown, branching stems, compound leaves with 5 leaflets, the lowermost pair (a) resembling stipules because they are produced very near the stem, its clusters of moderately sized flowers with yellow to reddish corollas 10 - 14 mm (2/5 - 5/8 in.) long and the umbel-like clusters of slender seedpods. After flowering, its umbel-like cluster of seedpods might be confused with **Crown-vetch** (CZRVA, *Coronilla varia* L.), which is often planted as a soil binder along highway rights-of-way, but crown-vetch is usually a taller, coarser plant with pink-purple flowers and usually more than 11 leaflets in each compound leaf.

Figure 100. **Bird's-foot trefoil**

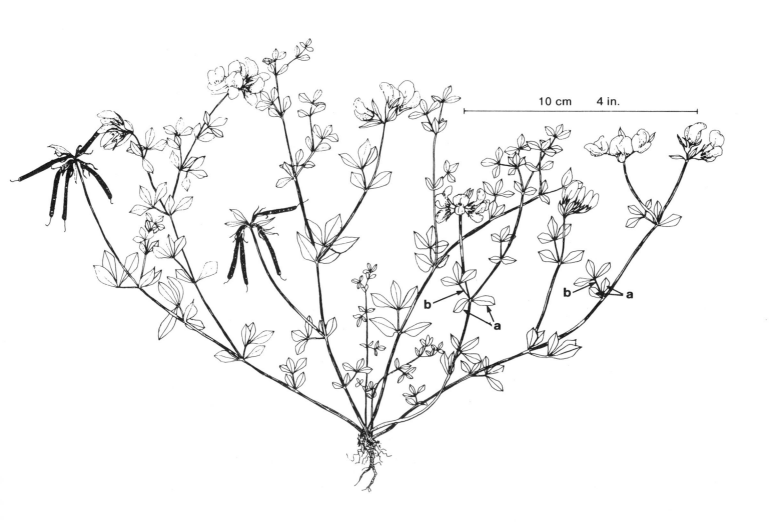

Narrow-leaved vetch, *Vicia angustifolia* Reichard, (Figure 101) [VICAN, vesce à feuilles étroites, vesce sauvage] Annual or winter annual, reproducing only by seed. **Stems** smooth, weak, at first erect but later lying on the ground or climbing on nearby plants, 40 - 100 cm (16 - 40 in.) long; **leaves** alternate (1 per node), pinnately compound with usually 2 to 5 pairs of long narrow leaflets each tipped with a hair-like point (a) and 1 - 3 curly, branched tendrils (b) at the end; **flowers** (c) 1 or 2 together on very short (up to 3 mm, ⅛ in. long) stalks in the axils of leaves, pea-like, violet to purple or rarely white, 12 - 18 mm (½ - ¾ in.) long; **seedpods** (d) about 5 cm (2 in.) long, at first flat but becoming round and black at maturity and splitting into two corkscrew-like sections (e), releasing 10 to 16 nearly spherical black **seeds**. Flowers in early summer.

Narrow-leaved vetch is found mostly in southern Ontario where it occurs in fields, waste places and fencerows.

It is distinguished from other true vetches (all having compound leaves ending in tendrils) by its annual or winter-annual habit, its leaves usually with fewer than 12 narrow leaflets and its flowers (c) occurring singly or in pairs on very short stalks in the leaf axils (angle formed between stem and petiole or leafstalk).

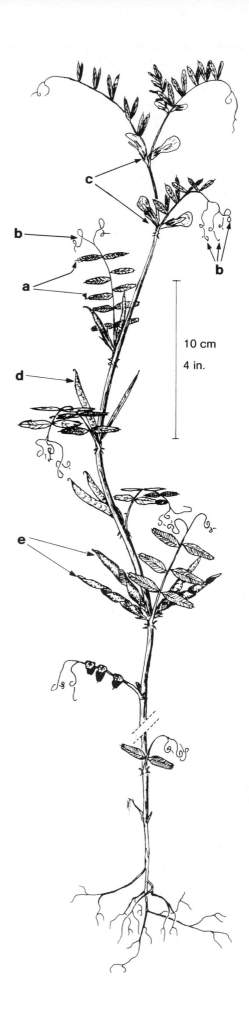

Figure 101. **Narrow-leaved vetch**

Tufted vetch, *Vicia cracca* L., (Figure 102, Plate 66) [VICCR, vesce jargeau, Bird vetch, jargeau, vesce multiflore, petits-oiseaux] Perennial, reproducing by seed and by spreading underground **rootstocks. Stems** 40 cm - 2 m (16 - 80 in.) long, weak, wiry, trailing on the ground or climbing on nearby objects; **leaves** alternate (1 per node), pinnately compound with 8 to 12 pairs of bristle-tipped leaflets (a) and branching tendrils (b) at the end; the plant climbing by means of these tendrils; **flowers** (c) bluish-purple, pea-like, about 12 mm (½ in.) long, often 30 or more crowded together on one side of a long bare stalk; **seedpods** (C) pea-like, 10 - 25 mm (2/5 - 1 in.) long by 4 - 6 mm (1/6 - ¼ in.) wide, partly flattened, light brown, containing 2 to 8 rounded to oval reddish-brown **seeds;** seeds 2.5 - 3 mm (1/10 - ⅛ in.) across and marked with a prominent, long, whitish or reddish-brown scar. Flowers from early June to late autumn.

Tufted vetch occurs throughout Ontario in cultivated fields, pastures, waste places, roadsides and gardens.

It is distinguished by its spreading underground rootstalks, compound leaves with 8 to 12 pairs of leaflets and branching tendrils (b), many flowers (c) clustered on one side of a long stalk, and its flattened, brownish seedpods (C) containing up to 8 rounded seeds, each with a scar extending ¼ to 1/3 of the way around it.

Hairy vetch, *Vicia villosa* Roth, (not illustrated) [VICVI, vesce velue, vesce de Russie] Closely resembling Tufted vetch but is distinguished by being an annual or, occasionally, biennial, and has **seedpods** 20 - 40 mm (4/5 - 1½ in.) long by 6 - 12 mm (¼ - ½ in.) wide, also containing up to 8 **seeds,** but these seeds have the scar running only 1/12 to 1/5 of the way around each seed.

Hairy vetch occurs in scattered localities throughout southern Ontario in habitats very similar to those of Tufted vetch.

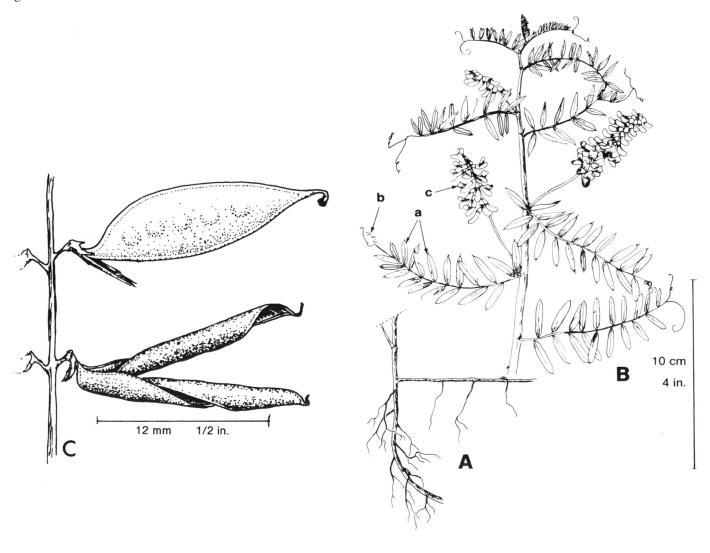

Figure 102. **Tufted vetch** A. Base of plant. B. Top of flowering stem. C. 2 seedpods.

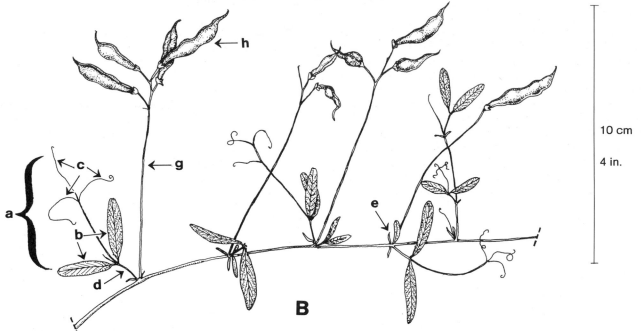

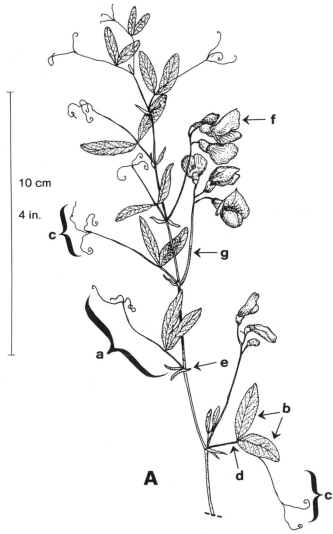

Figure 103. **Tuberous vetchling** A. Flowering stem. B. Fruiting stem with several seedpods.

Tuberous vetchling, *Lathyrus tuberosus* L., (Figure 103, Plate 67) [LTHTU, gesse tubéreuse, Earth-nut pea, Everlasting pea, Perennial pea, Vetchling, Wild pea, macusson, châtaigne de terre] Perennial reproducing by many underground tubers (like small potatoes) and by seed. **Stems** 20 - 100 cm (8 - 40 in.) long, slender, hairless, wingless, much-branched, weak and usually sprawling in a tangled mass; in spring and summer usually coming directly from small, potato-like **tubers** which may be as much as 40 cm (16 in.) deep in the ground; **leaves** (a) compound and alternate (1 per node) but appearing simple and opposite (2 per node) because each compound leaf consists of 2 stalk-less, opposite leaflets (b) and a slender, 3-branched tendril (c) (rarely 1- or 2-branched) at the end; leaf-stalk (d) (between the 2 leaflets and the stem) short, 8 - 20 mm (1/3 - 4/5 in.) long, slender, wingless, and with a pair of slender, pointed stipules (e) about 1 cm (2/5 in.) long on either side where it joins the stem; each individual leaflet narrowly elliptic, 2 - 5 cm (4/5 - 2 in.) long, pointed at both ends; **flowers** (f) pink to violet, resembling a Sweet pea in colour, shape and fragrance, in groups of about 5 (2 to 10) on long, erect stalks (g) from the leaf axils; **seedpods** (h) light brown, about 2 cm (4/5 in.) long and usually containing 2 to 3 greenish to brownish **seeds**. Flowers from June to September.

Tuberous vetchling occurs in cultivated fields, pastures, meadows, orchards, old gardens, edges of woods, roadsides and sometimes in gravel quarries in scattered locations in southern Ontario.

Before flowering, it is distinguished by its slender, non-winged, weak stems with alternate, compound leaves having just 2 opposite leaflets (b) plus a 3-branched, thread-like tendril (c), and reproducing from numerous, small, potato-like tubers. **Everlasting pea,** *Lathyrus latifolius* L., (not illustrated) [LTHLA, gesse à feuilles larges, gesse vivace], resembles Tuberous vetchling but is a larger, coarser plant with broadly winged **stems**, winged leafstalks and does not reproduce by tubers.

RUE FAMILY (Rutaceae)

Prickly-ash, *Xanthoxylum americanum* Mill., (Figure 104, Plate 68) [ZANAM, clavalier d'Amérique, frêne épineux, *Zanthoxylum americanum* Mill.] Tall shrubs or small trees up to 8 m (26 ft) high; reproducing by seed and sprouting from spreading underground **rhizomes**, often forming dense impenetrable stands. **Stems** very prickly with pairs of stout, triangular **prickles** (a) at every node, the needle-sharp tip of each prickle pointing outwards or slightly upwards; **leaves** pinnately compound with 2 to 5 pairs of leaflets (b) and 1 terminal leaflet (c); leaflets narrowly to broadly ovate with a pointed tip, dark green above and light green below, very finely hairy on the underside when young but later becoming smooth, with very small translucent dots due to the presence of oil glands, these resembling pinpricks through the leaf when viewed against the light; leaf margins very shallowly toothed to almost smooth and with a tiny yellowish gland in the base of the notch between the teeth; **flowers** unisexual, in small umbel-like clusters (d) from the nodes of branches of the previous year and appearing in May before the leaves expand; males and females on different plants; petals 4 or 5, yellowish, very small, 1 - 2 mm (1/25 - 1/12 in.) long; sepals absent; stamens 4 or 5 and longer than the petals in male (pollen-producing) flowers; pistils 3 to 5 in female (seed-producing) flowers, forming small, stalked, spherical or elliptical **pods** about 5 mm (1/5 in.) across and splitting across the top to release

2 **seeds**. Flowers in May; seeds mature in August to September.

Prickly-ash occurs in woods and moist meadows in southern and southwestern Ontario. Because the foliage may be browsed when other forage is scarce and because **it has been suspected of having poisoned cattle and sheep** in Indiana, it should be viewed with suspicion when present in areas used for pasturing livestock.

It is distinguished from wild and cultivated roses, *Rosa* spp., [rosier] by its clusters of small yellow flowers (d) on leafless branches in May, and by its pairs of triangular prickles (a) at each node of the stem, rather than irregularly scattered along the stem. Taller shrub and tree forms of Prickly-ash might be confused with **Black locust,** *Robinia* spp. [ROBSS, robinier] or **Honey-locust,** *Gleditsia* spp. [GLISS, février] which have compound leaves and may also have pairs of prickles on the stems at the base of each leaf, but it can be distinguished by its small yellow, unisexual flowers that blossom on leafless branches in May, whereas the two locusts have larger, showy, pea-like flowers that blossom after the leaves are out, and by the leaflets of its once-compound leaves having translucent dots and very shallow teeth with tiny yellow glands between the teeth. Its smooth-margined, pinnately compound, alternate leaves resemble those of Poison sumac (p. 138) but its pairs of spines and early yellow flowers are distinctive.

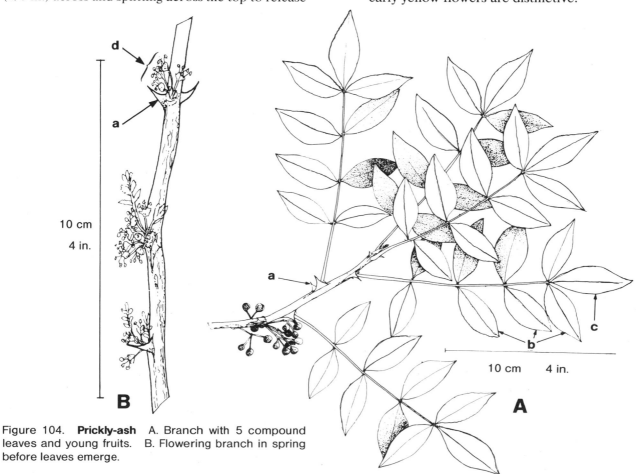

Figure 104. **Prickly-ash** A. Branch with 5 compound leaves and young fruits. B. Flowering branch in spring before leaves emerge.

127

SPURGE FAMILY (Euphorbiaceae)

Three-seeded mercury, *Acalypha rhomboidea* Raf.,
(Figure 105) [ACCRH, ricinelle rhomboide, Copperleaf, rhombic copperleaf, ricinelle de Virginie] Annual, reproducing only by seed. **Stems** erect, 7.5 -
100 cm (3 - 40 in.) high, simple or branched, slightly
hairy; **leaves** green to bronze-green, 1 - 9 cm (2/5 -
3½ in.) long, lance- to rhombic-ovate on petioles (a)
that are 1/3 the length to almost as long as the leaf
blade; margins with irregular, rounded teeth; **flowers**
in greenish clusters (B, b) in axils of leaves, each
cluster composed of one or more palmately cleft bracts
(c) with 5 to 9 lobes, one or more stalked male spikes
4 - 15 mm (1/6 - 2/5 in.) long and one or more shorter
female flowers; seedpods (d) deeply 3-lobed (similar
to those of Leafy spurge, see (h) in Figure 112B) and
containing 3 seeds; **seeds** tan coloured, 1.6 - 1.8 mm
(1/15 in.) long. Flowers from July to September.

Three-seeded mercury occurs in dry or moist soil
in open woods, fields, waste places, ditches and roadsides throughout south-central Ontario.

It resembles young plants of Redroot pigweed but
is distinguished by its flowers borne in axillary clusters
with bracts having 5 - 9 lobes and its leaves occasionally
a bronze-green colour.

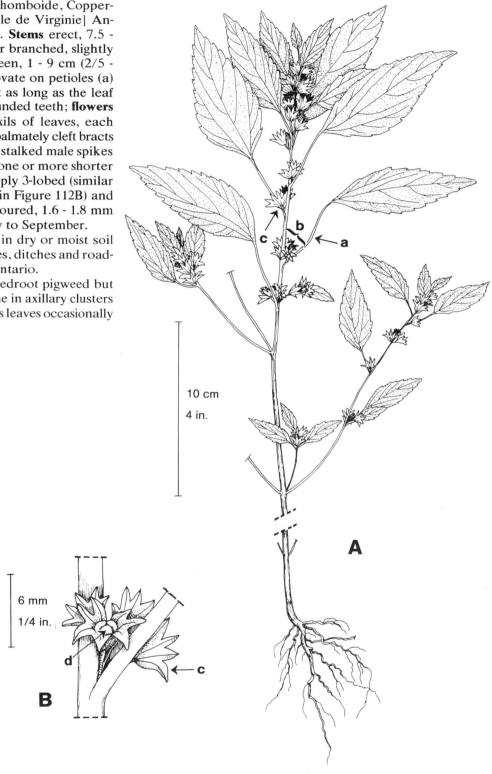

Figure 105. **Three-seeded mercury** A. Plant. B. Portion
of fruiting stem showing 1 three-seeded fruit developing
from 1 of 4 flowers in a leaf axil.

128

Thyme-leaved spurge, *Euphorbia serpyllifolia* Pers. (may include *E. glyptosperma* Engelm., **Ridge-seeded spurge**), (Figure 106) [EPHSP, euphorbe à feuilles de serpolet, euphorbe à feuilles de thym] Annual, reproducing only by seed. **Stems** smooth, prostrate to somewhat erect, 10 - 30 cm (4 - 12 in.) long, reddish to green; **leaves** 3 - 14 mm (⅛ - 3/5 in.) long and basically oblong, with almost entire margins and asymmetrical bases (a); **flowers** in complex inflorescences called cyathia (b), as described for Spotted spurge (Figure 108), each cyathium very small (0.8 - 1.2 mm, 1/30 - 1/20 in. in diameter) and producing a single **fruit** or seedpod (c) that is smooth, sharply 3-angled, about 1.5 - 2.0 mm (1/16 - 1/12 in.) long and wide, and containing 3 gray **seeds**. The entire plant, except its seeds, contains a white, milky juice. Flowers from July to September.

Thyme-leaved spurge occurs in gardens, lawns, fields, waste places, and along railway lines in sandy or alluvial soil throughout southern Ontario.

It is distinguished from other prostrate weeds by the following: from Purslane by its milky juice, less succulent stems and leaves, and its opposite leaves; from the prostrate knotweeds which often have reddish stems by having milky juice, opposite leaves and no ocrea; from Carpetweed by having opposite leaves rather than whorls of 3 to 8 leaves at each node; and from other prostrate spurges by its hairless stems and its leaves being almost entire (with rarely smooth margins).

Five other species of prostrate or nearly prostrate annual spurges also occur in Ontario. All are native plants which grow naturally in sandy or gravelly soils along lakes and streams, in sand dunes, and other open areas. However, because sometimes they may grow in cultivated fields, gardens, roadsides, railway ballast, and waste places, most of them are also considered to be weedy plants. All resemble Thyme-leaved spurge in branchiness, leaf shape, and having white milky juice. Distinctions among them are technical but include hairiness of stem and seedpod, size of seedpod, and features of the seed coat.

Figure 106. **Thyme-leaved spurge** A. Plant lying prostrate on the ground. B. End portion of flowering and fruiting stem.

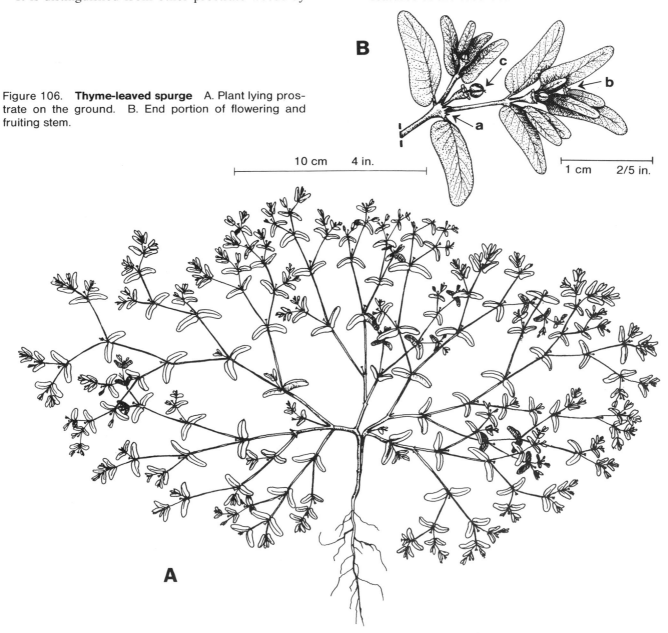

10 cm   4 in.

1 cm   2/5 in.

129

Hairy-stemmed spurge, *Euphorbia vermiculata* Raf., (Figure 107, Plate 69) [EPHVE, euphorbe vermiculée, euphorbe hirsute] Annual, reproducing only by seed. **Stems** prostrate or somewhat ascending, up to 40 cm (16 in.) long, branching from near the base and throughout (similar to Thyme-leaved spurge, Figure 106A), reddish-green, and with scattered long hairs throughout; **leaves** opposite, ovate to lanceolate, 3.5 - 20 mm (⅛ - 4/5 in.) long with minutely serrated (saw-toothed) margins and asymmetrical (uneven) bases (a); petioles 0.5 - 1 mm (1/50 - 1/25 in.); **flowers** in complex inflorescences called cyathia (b), as described for Spotted spurge (Figure 108), each cyathium very small and producing a single **fruit** or seedpod (c) that is 1 - 2 mm (1/25 - 1/12 in.) long and wide, smooth, strongly 3-lobed and containing 3 seeds; **seeds** gray or pale brown, 1 - 1.5 mm (1/25 - 3/50 in.) and sharply angled. The entire plant, except its seeds, contains a white, milky juice. Flowers from July to September.

Hairy-stemmed spurge grows in dry open soil in fields, gardens, lawns, roadsides, pathways and waste places such as along railroad lines in southern Ontario.

It is distinguished from other prostrate weeds by the following: from Purslane by its milky juice, less succulent stems and leaves, and its opposite leaves; from the prostrate knotweeds which often have reddish stems by having milky juice, opposite leaves and no ocrea; from Carpetweed by having opposite leaves rather than whorls of 3 to 8 leaves at each node; and from other prostrate spurges by its usually prostrate hairy stems and its sharply angled seeds.

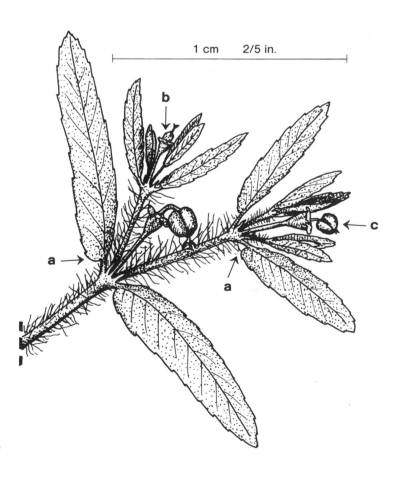

Figure 107. **Hairy-stemmed spurge**

Spotted spurge, *Euphorbia nutans* Lag., (Figure 108) [EPHMA, euphorbe couchée, Wartweed, euphorbe maculée, formerly misnamed as *Euphorbia maculata* L.] Annual, reproducing only by seed. **Stems** mostly erect and bushy-branched throughout, or nearly prostrate, finely hairy when young, smooth and somewhat succulent when older, green or reddish; **leaves** opposite (2 per node), stalkless, oblong or lanceolate, usually somewhat asymmetrical (uneven) at their bases (a), dark green above and often with a red or reddish-purple blotch near the middle, lighter green and usually somewhat finely hairy on the undersurface, margins distinctly toothed; lower leaves of upright plants often dropping early, leaving the lower stem and lower parts of the branches nearly bare. **Flowers** complex, individually very small (b) without sepals or petals and unisexual but clustered together in structures called cyathia very similar to those described for Leafy spurge (Figure 112B); each cyathium is a tiny cup about 2 - 4 mm (1/12 - 1/6 in.) across with 4 tiny wings at its margins and containing several single stamens and a single 3-lobed pistil with a 3-branched style and stigma; ovary maturing into a 3-lobed, hairless **seedpod** (c) about 2 - 2.5 mm (1/12 - 1/10 in.) long and containing 3 small **seeds** about 1.3 mm (1/20 in.) long with a few transverse wrinkles on the sides. The whole plant, including stem, roots, leaves and flowers, with the possible exception of mature seeds, contains a sticky, white milky juice which exudes freely from any cut or broken surface.

Spotted spurge is very common in the southwestern portion of southern Ontario, occurring in cultivated fields, gardens, waste areas and roadsides. It can also be found in the counties bordering the north shore of Lake Ontario.

It is distinguished by its usually bushy-branched habit, its opposite leaves with uneven bases and reddish blotches near the middle, its milky juice, and its tiny flowers with 3-lobed, 3-seeded, hairless seedpods.

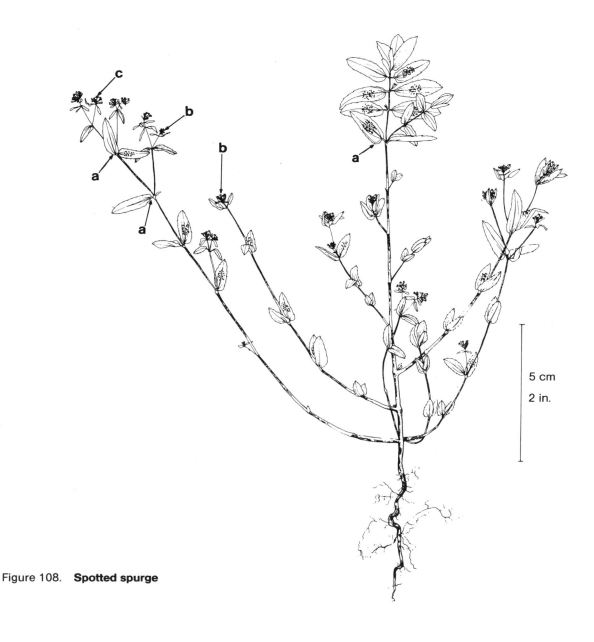

Figure 108. **Spotted spurge**

5 cm
2 in.

Dentate spurge, *Euphorbia dentata* Michx., (Figure 109) [EPHDE, euphorbe dentée] Annual, reproducing only by seed. **Stems** erect, 20 - 120 cm (8 - 48 in.) high, with ascending branches, and roughened with short hairs; **leaves** mostly opposite (a), occasionally alternate (b), linear to ovate, hairy; their margins coarsely to shallowly dentate (toothed) to almost smooth; **flowers** individually tiny and borne in a complex cup-like structure called a cyathium (c), as described for Leafy spurge (Figure 112B), the rim of the cyathium with 5 oblong, sharply dentate lobes and 1 (or more) short-stalked broad glands; **seedpods** 3-lobed (d) and containing 3 seeds; the **seeds** ovoid,

rough-tuberculate, 1 - 3 mm (1/25 - 1/8 in.). The entire plant, except its seeds, contains a white, milky juice. Flowers from July to September.

Dentate spurge is found in dry soil in cultivated fields, roadsides, railway banks and waste places in southern Ontario.

It is distinguished from most other plants by the combination of mostly opposite, coarsely toothed leaves and milky juice throughout, and from other spurges by its stem leaves being almost always opposite and hairy on both sides, and the presence of usually only one gland on the involucre.

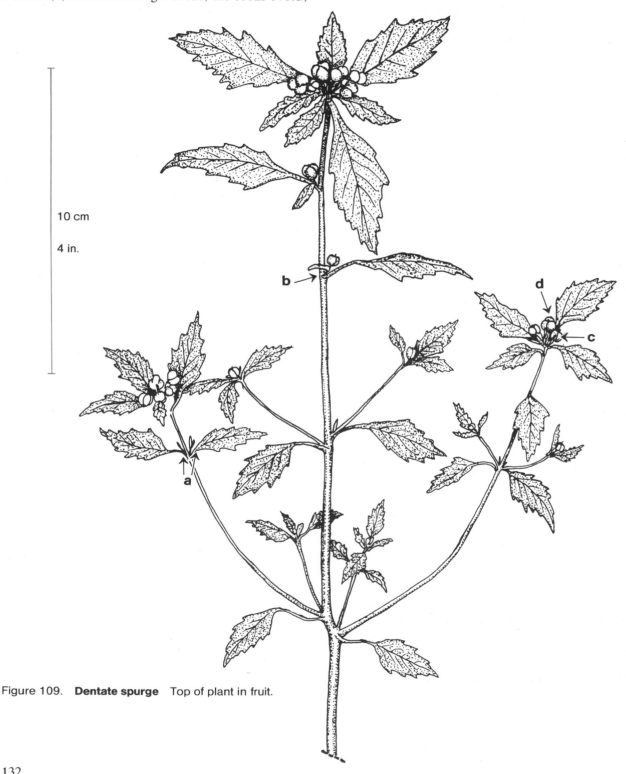

10 cm

4 in.

Figure 109. **Dentate spurge** Top of plant in fruit.

Petty spurge, *Euphorbia peplus* L., (Figure 110, Plate 70) [EPHPE, euphorbe peplus, euphorbe des jardins] Annual, reproducing only by seed. **Stems** erect, 10 -30 cm (4 -12 in.), single or branched from the base; top of each main stem 3-branched (a) at base of inflorescence; lower and middle stem **leaves** (b) alternate (1 per node), oblong to rounded, 1 - 2 cm (2/5 - 4/5 in.) long, short-stalked; leaves at tip of stem (c) in one whorl of 3 leaves (d) from the same node; leaves opposite (2 per node) in the inflorescence (e); **inflorescence** beginning as a 3-branched umbel (a) and branching repeatedly in 2's (e), with a small flower cluster(f), in the angle between each pair of branches; flowers complex in cyathia or tiny cups (f), like those described for Leafy spurge (Figure 112B); **seedpods** 3-lobed, containing 3 **seeds**; seeds about 1.5 mm (1/16 in.) long and about half as wide, somewhat 6-sided, the 2 inner faces with long, narrow depressions, the 4 outer surfaces with 2 to 4 circular depressions, gray to gray-brown. All parts contain a white milky juice which freely exudes when the plant is cut or broken. Flowers from early July until end of fall.

Petty spurge occurs throughout southern Ontario in gardens, waste areas, roadsides and occasionally in cultivated fields.

It is distinguished from other erect-growing spurges by its annual habit, by the combination of alternate leaves (b) on main stem, whorl of 3 leaves (d) at tip of stem (c), and pairs of smaller opposite leaves in the inflorescence (e), by its main umbel at the tip of the stem having only 3 branches (a), and by its small, elongated, gray to brownish, 6-sided seeds with 2 elongated depressions and 4 rows of 2 to 4 rounded depressions. There is also a tendency for the stems to be somewhat succulent, and for the 3 main branches of the inflorescence to be somewhat enlarged (g) above the nodes and taper upwards to be much thinner (h) just below the next pair of small leaves.

Sun spurge *Euphorbia helioscopia* L., (Plate 71) [EPHHE, euphorbe réveille-matin, Wartweed, réveille-matin, herbe aux verrues] very similar to Petty spurge but differs from it by usually being taller (5 - 60 cm, 2 -24 in. high) and coarser with larger leaves (1 - 5 cm, 2/5 - 2 in. long), by having a whorl of 5 **leaves** at the tip of the stem and 5 main branches to the **inflorescence** umbel, and by having **seeds** which are egg-shaped to nearly spherical, 2 - 2.5 mm (1/12 - 1/10 in.) in diameter, black and roughened by a network of prominent vein-like ridges over the entire surface.

Sun spurge has nearly the same distribution in Ontario as Petty spurge and occupies similar habitats.

Broad-leaved spurge, *Euphorbia platyphylla* L., (not illustrated) [EPHPL, euphorbe à grandes feuilles, euphorbe à larges feuilles] another erect annual spurge resembling Petty spurge. It is distinguished by having 5 branches in the main **umbel** (similar to Sun spurge in this respect) but its **leaves** are usually larger or longer and somewhat pointed, and its **seeds** are smooth, shiny, dark brown, egg-shaped and about 2 mm (1/12 in.) long.

Broad-leaved spurge also occurs in southern Ontario in similar habitats as Sun spurge but is not as common.

Figure 110. **Petty spurge**

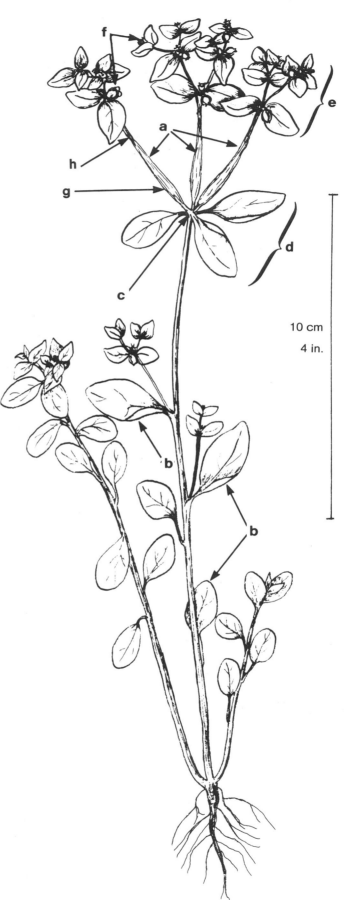

10 cm
4 in.

133

Cypress spurge, *Euphorbia cyparissias* L., (Figure 111, Plate 72) [EPHCY, euphorbe cyprès, Graveyard spurge, Graveyard weed, Poor man's-hedge, rhubarbe des pauvres] Perennial reproducing by seed and from widely spreading, much-branched underground roots with numerous pink buds and forming dense stands. **Stems** erect 10 - 80 cm (4 - 32 in.) high, usually much-branched above; **leaves** alternate (1 per node) (a), very numerous, small, narrow, linear or club-shaped; tip of stem at beginning of inflorescence (flowering branches) with a whorl of 10 or more shorter leaves (b); **flowers** yellowish-green on a many-branched umbel (usually 10 or more main branches) at the tip of the main stem and on the upper branches; leaf-like bracts (c) of the inflorescence short and broad, heart-shaped, tapering towards the pointed tip, at first light yellowish-green but usually turning reddish-green towards maturity; flowers very small, unisexual, without sepals or petals, and crowded together in a complex structure called a cyathium, like those described for Leafy spurge Figure 112B); one little cyathium between each pair of bracts throughout the inflorescence; each flower cluster producing a 3-lobed **seedpod** containing 1 to 3 egg-shaped, smooth, grayish **seeds** 1.5 - 2 mm (1/16 - 1/12 in.) long. The whole plant contains an acrid sticky white juice. Flowering begins in late spring or early summer and may continue intermittently until late autumn.

Two kinds of Cypress spurge occur in Ontario, a sterile diploid form which does not produce viable seed, and a fertile tetraploid form which produces abundant fertile seed. The sterile form, reproducing only from underground parts was once commonly cultivated in gardens and cemeteries. It has persisted in many localities and occasionally spreads vegetatively to surrounding roadsides and waste places. This form occurs throughout Ontario. The fertile form which can reproduce by seed as well as by underground parts has become a rampant and troublesome weed in Dufferin County and in the Braeside area of eastern Renfrew County, occupying hundreds of hectares of pasture, abandoned cultivated land, woodland, and roadsides.

Although sheep can be forced to eat Cypress spurge and may develop a preference for it, the literature suggests **it may be toxic to cattle and horses. The milky juice can be irritating on bare skin and cause a potentially serious rash for some people.**

It is distinguished from most other plants by its milky juice, its spreading perennial roots with pink buds, its numerous, small slender leaves, and its yellowish-green inflorescence, from the upright annual spurges (Petty, Sun and Broad-leaved) by its perennial habit, and from these and Leafy spurge by its slender stems with numerous, crowded, narrow leaves, its umbel with usually more than 10 slender branches from the tip of the main stem, its heart-shaped bracts or leaves in the inflorescence tapering towards the tip, and by the production of densely leafy branches after early summer flowering.

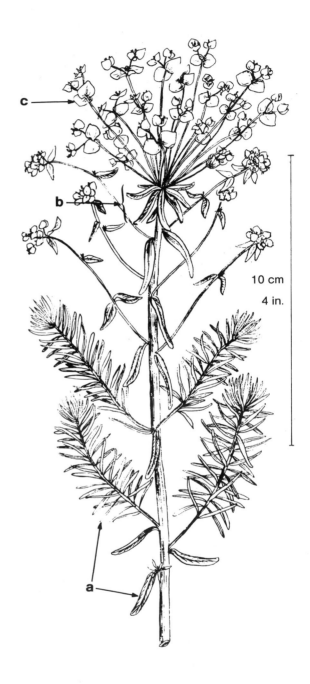

10 cm
4 in.

Figure 111. **Cypress spurge**

Leafy spurge, *Euphorbia esula* complex*, (Figure 112, Plate 73) [EPHES, euphorbe ésule, euphorbe feuillue] Perennial, reproducing by seed and by widely spreading **underground roots** having numerous small pinkish buds from which new leafy shoots are produced. Similar to Cypress spurge but taller and coarser. **Stems** erect, up to 1 m (40 in.) high; **leaves** numerous, alternate (1 per node) (a), or crowded and some appearing opposite (2 per node) (b), 3 - 7 cm (1¼ - 3 in.) long, linear or wedge-shaped, and 1 whorl of 7 or more leaves at the tip of the stem (c); **inflorescence** greenish, consisting of a large umbel-like cluster of 7 or more branches at the tip of the main stem (c) and smaller branching clusters at the ends of these and other branches (d) below the main umbel; leaves (bracts) (e) of the inflorescence very broadly ovate to almost kidney-shaped and usually abruptly tipped with a very fine point; **flowers** tiny, unisexual and very unusual; several male (pollen-producing) flowers consisting only of single, tiny stamens (f) without sepals or petals, and 1 female (seed-producing) flower consisting only of a single pistil (g) also without sepals or petals crowded in a cup-like structure (h), the rim of which has 4 yellowish U-shaped glands (j) and 4 tiny lobes (k), the whole complex of several tiny male and one female flowers in a cup being called a cyathium (B); **seedpods** (m) 3-lobed, containing 3 **seeds** about 2.5 mm (1/10 in.) long, smooth, grayish to yellowish or brownish and usually with a tiny yellow bump near the base; the seedpods exploding when dry and throwing the seeds several metres in all directions. The plants are deep green to almost bluish-green during spring, changing to yellowish-green or olive-green at flowering time during June and July, and changing back to a dull green or sometimes reddish-green after flowering; then sometimes with a secondary period of flowering in late August or September, shedding seeds while still flowering.

Leafy spurge occurs in several localities throughout Ontario, occupying a wide variety of soils and habitats, including cultivated land, meadows, pastures, waste places, open woodland, roadsides, and gardens.

It is distinguished from most other plants by having milky juice, spreading roots with pink buds, its slender green leaves that are mostly alternate, and its yellowish-green inflorescence, and from Cypress spurge by its taller, coarser habit, longer leaves, and fewer branches in the main umbel at the tip of the stem. It is distinguished from the annual erect spurges by its perennial habit, and tall, coarse stems with mostly linear leaves.

*There is still considerable confusion about the botanical name for the Leafy spurge that grows in North America. What is called Leafy spurge is actually a complex of several closely related groups of plants which seem to have physiological differences but are very similar in appearance. Insects and disease organisms can tell the difference even though people cannot! The names *E. virgata* and *E. x pseudovirgata* are also being used for this complex in current literature.

Figure 112. **Leafy spurge** A. Top of flowering plant. B. Detail of a portion of the inflorescence showing 2 oval bracts (e), each with a small branch in its axil and between the branches is 1 cyathium consisting of a cup (h) with U-shaped glands (j) and tiny lobes (k) on its rim and showing 3 male flowers (f) (3 single stamens) and 1 female flower (g) (1 single pistil) that have emerged from inside it.

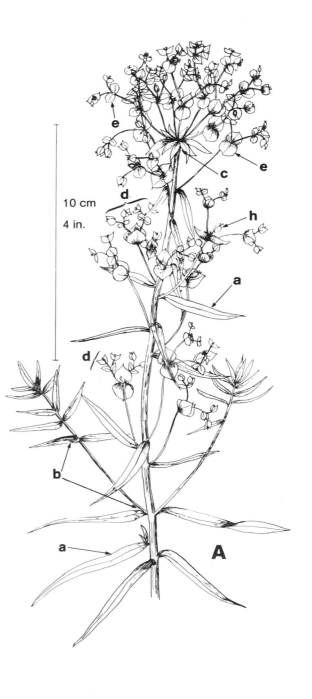

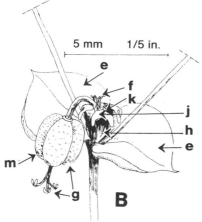

CASHEW FAMILY (Anacardiaceae)

Poison-ivy, *Rhus radicans* L., (Figure 113, Plates 74, 75) [TOXRA, herbe à la puce, sumac vénéneux, sumac grimpant, bois de chien; incorrectly called Poison-oak which is *Rhus toxicodendron* L. and does not occur in eastern Canada] Perennial, spreading by seed and by woody **rhizomes** (underground stems) which produce dense patches. **Stems** woody and of two kinds, the most frequent kind growing horizontally on or just below the ground surface with upright leafy stalks 10 - 80 cm (4 - 32 in.) high; the second kind is a climbing vine which develops aerial roots and may climb 6 - 10 m per node (a), compound, each compound leaf (b) consisting of 3 leaflets (c) at the tip of a long leafstalk (petiole) (d); the middle leaflet has a longer stalk (e) than the 2 side leaflets (f); overall leaflet shape and type of toothing highly variable between leaflets on the same stem, as well as among plants within a patch and between patches; leaflets ranging from narrow to broadly ovate with a smooth margin (A, C), to a few scattered, shallow, rounded teeth (D), to several, coarse, deep-pointed teeth which give the leaflet a lobed appearance (E); leaves purplish to reddish when unfolding in spring (May to early June), bright green and often shiny (with a varnished appearance) in summer and turning a vivid orange-red to wine-red in autumn in sunny areas, but often lacking the bright colour in shaded places; leaflet smooth and hairless on both surfaces except for small tufts of brownish hair on the underside along the mid-vein and in the angles formed by the mid-vein and some of the lower branching veins; **flowers** small, white or greenish, with 5 sepals and 5 petals (g), in branching clusters from the leaf axils (angles between leafstalk and stem); flower clusters inconspicuous because they are often hidden below the dense leaf canopy and because many plants do not flower every year; each flower in the cluster followed by a whitish to dull greenish-yellow, dry, berry-like **fruit** (h) about 5 mm (1/5 in.) in diameter with lengthwise ridges and somewhat resembling a peeled orange. Flowers in June and July; berries produced by September but often remaining on the low leafless stems all winter.

Poison-ivy occurs under forests, in edges of woodland, meadows, waste areas, fence lines, and roadsides throughout most of Ontario south of a line from North Bay to Kenora. The tall climbing vine form, however, is mainly confined to the counties bordering Lake Erie, Lake Ontario and the lower Ottawa Valley.

It is distinguished by its low growth or its occasional climbing habit, its 3 leaflets (c) in each compound leaf (b), its leaves deep green in summer, reddish in spring and fall, its clusters of whitish to greenish-yellow berries (h), and its short, erect, leafless stems which frequently retain a few berries all winter long.

All parts of Poison-ivy, including the roots, contain a poisonous substance which causes an irritating inflammation of the skin of most people, the inflamed areas frequently developing blisters and accompanied by intense itchiness. The poisonous substance is an oily resin contained in the juice of the plant. Contact with any broken part of the plant, with leaves which have been chewed by insects, or with shoes, clothing, implements, or pets which have touched broken parts of the plant may cause a person with sensitive skin to react. Dry twigs in winter or dug-up roots in summer can often cause a reaction. Burning Poison-ivy leaves and stems releases the poison in the form of tiny droplets on particles of ash and dust in the smoke, and can cause a severe reaction on exposed skin and in the breathing passages if a sensitive person breathes or

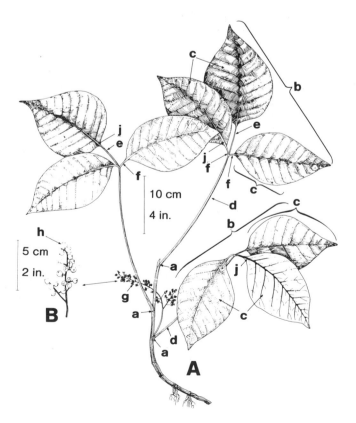

Figure 113. **Poison-ivy** A. Low-growing form with short erect stem and a flower cluster from the axil of 1 compound leaf. B. Cluster of dry white, berry-like fruits produced from the flower cluster. (Cont'd.)

passes through the smoke of such a fire. The author had a severe reaction on his arms and legs after trimming a specimen plant with hand clippers. Although the plant parts never touched his clothes, it seems that microscopic oil droplets may have squirted out while cutting the stems and vines and penetrated the cotton of his trouser legs and shirt sleeves.

In cases of suspected contact with the plant, washing the skin and clothing with a strong soap may not prevent a reaction but it will help minimize reinfection to other parts of the body or to other individuals. If a reaction does develop, one should seek the advice of a physician for proper treatment. Poison-ivy is designated as a noxious weed by the Province of Ontario, and it is the duty of every person in possession of infested land to destroy noxious weeds thereon. For more information, see Ontario Ministry of Agriculture and Food Factsheet, *Poison-ivy,* Agdex 647.

Poison-ivy is sometimes mistakenly called **Poison-oak** because some plants have very coarsely toothed or lobed leaflets. The true Poison-oak, *Rhus toxicodendron* L. (not illustrated) [TOXQU], occurs in the southern United States, but not in Canada.

Virginia creeper, *Parthenocissus* spp., (not illustrated) [PRTSS, vigne vierge, parthénocisse], a climbing vine with compound leaves, occasionally has some **leaves** with only 3 leaflets, but usually there are 5, and its **fruits** are soft and bluish. Although this plant is not poisonous to touch, as is Poison-ivy, **its blue grape-like berries are poisonous if eaten. Manitoba maple,** *Acer negundo* L., (not illustrated) [ACRNE, érable négondo, érable à Giguère, érable du Manitoba], may have 3 leaflets instead of the usual 5, but its compound **leaves** are arranged in opposite pairs (2 per node) on the stems and the **seeds** are long and winged. **Hog-peanut,** *Amphicarpa bracteata* (L.) Fern., (not illustrated) [APPBR, amphicarpe bractéolée, amphicarpe monoïque], normally has 3 leaflets like Poison-ivy, but it is a twining herbaceous vine (not woody), its purplish to whitish **flowers** are pea-like and larger than those of Poison-ivy, and each of the 3 leaflets in 1 compound **leaf** of Hog-peanut has 3 strong veins (the midrib plus 1 big vein on each side) joining the leaflet stalk, whereas Poison-ivy has only 1, the midrib (j).

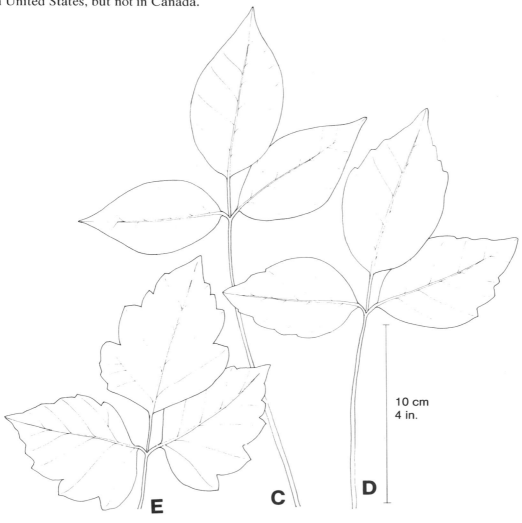

10 cm
4 in.

Figure 113. **Poison-ivy** (Cont'd.) C.-E. Variation in margin and lobing of leaflets.

Poison sumac, *Rhus vernix* L., (Figure 114, Plate 76) [TOXVX, sumac à vernis, Poison elder, Poison dogwood, bois chandelle] Coarse shrub or small tree 1.5 - 7 m (5 - 23 ft) high, often branched at the base, with brown to gray smoothish bark; **branches** hairless, very slightly roughened with tiny, wart-like surface glands, and bearing prominent leaf scars (a); **leaves** alternate on the branches (b), but each leaf (c) pinnately compound with 3 to 6 pairs of leaflets (d) that are nearly opposite each other (e), plus 1 terminal leaflet (f); each leaflet 4 - 10 cm (1½ - 4 in.) long and ½ to 2/3 as wide, somewhat rounded at the base and pointed (acuminate) at the tip (g), dark green above and lighter green below; margins of leaflets are usually smooth but occasionally may be wavy, irregularly lobed or coarsely toothed; the whole compound leaf (7 - 13 leaflets plus their central stalk) falling from the branch in autumn; **flowers** dull white, produced in 4 - 20 cm (1½ - 8 in.) long, spreading or pendulous panicle-like clusters that arise from leaf axils; **berries** (h) whitish or drab, 4 - 5 mm (1/6 - 1/5 in.) long. Flowers in July.

Poison sumac is found in southern Ontario in wet woods and edges of swamps and lakes. **The entire plant is as poisonous to most people as is Poison-ivy (see page 136). CAUTION: Because both the foliage in summer and the bare twigs in winter can cause severe dermatitis, take special care to avoid these parts touching hands or face when in damp woods.**

Poison sumac is distinguished by its appearance as a coarse shrub or small tree, its alternately arranged, pinnately compound leaves with 7 - 13 usually smooth-margined leaflets and its clusters of white flowers followed by whitish berries. Prickly-ash (page 127) and the true Ash trees, *Fraxinus* spp., [frêne] also have pinnately compound leaves with smooth margins on their leaflets, but Prickly-ash has pairs of large prickles along its branches and smaller ones at the bases of some of the leaflets, and the true Ash trees have their compound leaves in opposite pairs along the branches. **Staghorn sumac,** *Rhus typhina* L., [RHUTY, sumac vinaigrier, sumac amarante, vinaigrier], a very common shrub with velvety-hairy branches (hence its common name), sharply and coarsely toothed leaflets in pinnately compound leaves that turn vivid red in fall, and cone-shaped clusters of red fruits **is not poisonous.**

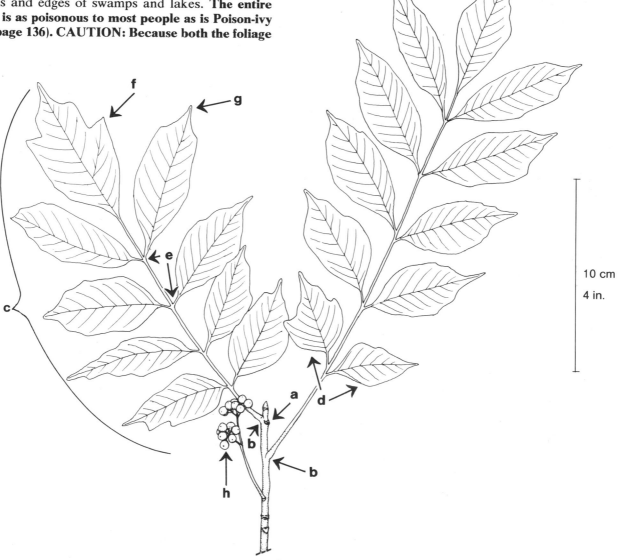

10 cm

4 in.

Figure 114.   **Poison sumac**   End portion of a twig with 2 compound leaves and 2 clusters of small white berries.

BUCKTHORN FAMILY (Rhamnaceae)

European buckthorn, *Rhamnus cathartica* L., (Figure 115, Plate 77) [RHACT, nerprun commun, Common buckthorn, nerprun purgatif, nerprun cathartique] Perennial, reproducing only by seed. Grows as a bushy small tree or several-stemmed shrub up to 6 m (20 ft) high. Most branches older than one year are tipped with a short, sharp **thorn** (a), (hence "thorn" in its English name); this thorn often present in the fork of 2 branches (b); **leaves** usually opposite (2 per node) (c), but sometimes alternate (1 per node) (d), elliptic or oblong usually with fine rounded teeth but sometimes nearly smooth, dark green above and lighter green or yellowish-green below; usually with 3 main branching veins (e) (sometimes 2 or 4) on each side of the midrib that strongly curve or arch forward towards the tip of the leaf (Plate 77A); **flowers** small, with 4 sepals and 4 petals, greenish to yellowish, short-stalked, in small clusters from the axils of leaves or on short twigs along the stem; each flower unisexual with either 4 stamens or 1 pistil but not both, and the sexes usually on different plants; **berries** (f) round, 5 - 6 mm (1/5 - ¼ in.) in diameter, purplish-black and very juicy with 4 very hard **seeds** (stones). Flowers during May and June but the berries, and often the dry leaves, persist on the tree long into winter.

European buckthorn was introduced as an ornamental shrub, but its seeds have been widely scattered by birds and other animals so it is common in fence lines, woodland, pastures and abandoned farmyards throughout southern Ontario. Because **European buckthorn is an alternate host for the fungus which causes leaf and crown rust of oats,** it must be destroyed to minimize this disease on oats.

It is distinguished by the sharp, thorn-tipped branches (a, b) in contrast to the simple or compound thorns growing from the sides of branches in the Hawthorns (Figure 97), by the prominent forward-curved side veins (e, Plate 77A) of the leaves, the clusters of purplish-black berries (f) along the stems and short twigs, and each berry usually with 4 hard seeds. **These juicy berries are very bitter and cathartic, and usually cause severe stomach cramps if eaten.**

For additional information, see Ontario Ministry of Agriculture and Food Factsheet, *Common Barberry and European Buckthorn: Alternate Hosts of Cereal Rust Diseases*, Agdex 110/632.

Alder buckthorn, *Rhamnus frangula* L., (not illustrated) [RHAFR, nerprun bourdaine, Glossy buckthorn, bourdaine] Resembling European buckthorn but its branches lack the thorny tips; its **leaf** margins are smooth or rarely slightly toothed; the side veins of the leaf are more numerous and do not curve towards the tip of the leaf; **flowers** have 5 sepals and 5 petals and the reddish to black **berry** has only 2 or 3 hard **seeds**. Alder buckthorn was also introduced as an ornamental shrub and has spread from cultivation to moist meadows and wet areas, but it is not an important alternate host for leaf or crown rust of oats.

Chokecherry, *Prunus virginiana* L., (Plate 78) [PRNVG, cerisier à grappes, cerisier de virginie] Is often confused with the buckthorns because of similar growth form, leaf shape, and fruit size and colour. However, Chokecherry does not have thorns; the side veins of its leaves do not curve forward; its blue-black or deep red fruits have only a single stone; and its young twigs and leaves have an "almond" odour when crushed. **Chokecherry leaves and branches are poisonous to livestock but the flesh of its fruits is wholly edible.**

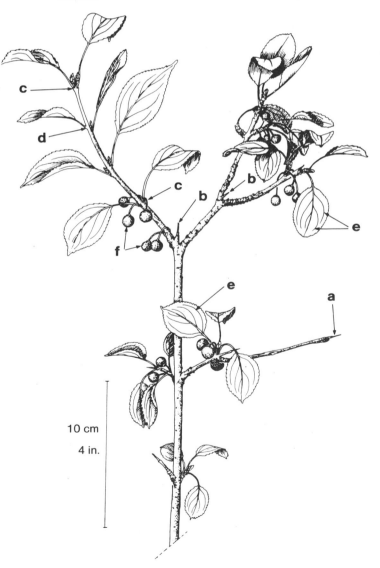

Figure 115. **European buckthorn**

MALLOW FAMILY (Malvaceae)

Musk mallow, *Malva moschata* L., (Figure 116, Plate 79) [MALMO, mauve musquée] Perennial, reproducing only by seed. **Stems** erect, 40 - 100 cm (16 - 40 in.) high, rough-hairy; **leaves** in basal tufts or rosettes and alternate (1 per node) on erect stems; rosette leaves and lowermost stem leaves (A) long-stalked, shallowly lobed and with rounded teeth but never deeply dissected or divided; mid- and upper stem leaves (B) long-stalked to short-stalked or stalkless near the top, deeply cut or divided into 5 to 7 major segments (a), each segment with numerous, irregular, rounded or sharp teeth (b); **flowers** in clusters near the ends of the stem and upper branches, and on long stalks from the upper leaves; sepals forming a 5-lobed cup (c) about 1 cm (2/5 in.) across; petals 5, united near their bases, white to rosy or pale purple, each one triangular (d) or somewhat heart-shaped, about 2.5 cm (1 in.) long so the flower is about 5 cm (2 in.) across; the filaments of the many stamens united into a thin erect column (e) around the several styles and standing like a small peg about 10 mm (2/5 in.) high in the middle of the flower (C); **fruit** a circle of slightly fused dry sections ("seeds") around a common centre (resembling Figure 117D), and usually enclosed by the persistent sepals after the petals fall. Flowers from late June until autumn.

Musk mallow, once widely cultivated as an ornamental in perennial flower gardens, has escaped to roadsides, fields and waste places throughout most of southern Ontario.

It is distinguished by its erect habit, its simple basal leaves (A) and deeply divided stem leaves (B), its large 5-petaled flowers with many stamens united into a column (e) in the centre of the flower (C), and its dry fruits arranged in a circle.

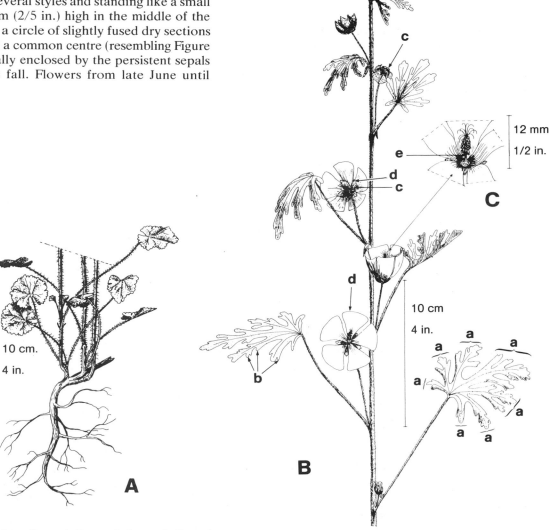

Figure 116. **Musk mallow** A. Base of plant. B. Top of flowering stem. C. Centre of flower showing several thread-like styles and stigmas protruding from the top of the central column of united stamens.

Common mallow, *Malva neglecta* Wallr., (Figure 117A-D, Plate 80) [MALNE, mauve négligée, Cheeses, Garden mallow, Round-leaved mallow, amours] Annual, biennial or short-lived perennial, reproducing only by seed. **Stems** much-branched, erect or trailing on the ground with upturned ends, hairy, 10 - 60 cm (4 - 24 in.) long, from a stout taproot; **leaves** alternate (1 per node), long-stalked; blades rounded or kidney-shaped with a deep heart-shaped base, shallowly lobed (a) and toothed (b); stipules (c) green to purplish or brownish, triangular, 2.5 - 6 mm (1/10 - ¼ in.) long; **flowers** in axils of leaves; sepals 5, in a ring; petals 5, white to pinkish or lilac, 1 - 1.5 cm (2/5 - 3/5 in.) across and with a column of stamens in the centre covering the pistil (as (e) in Figure 116C); **fruit** a circle of about 12 to 14 dry sections ("seeds"), each section (d) having flat sides but being rounded on its back, very finely hairy, and containing 1 dark brown **seed.** Flowers from June to late autumn.

Common mallow occurs throughout most of Ontario and is a very frequent weed in lawns, gardens, barnyards, roadsides, waste places and occasionally in cultivated fields.

It is distinguished by its low stature, its rounded to kidney-shaped leaves, its flowers 1 - 1.5 cm (2/5 - 3/5 in.) across with a central column of stamens and the individual sections in the ring of fruits rounded (D) and not prominently veined.

Round-leaved mallow, *Malva pusilla* Sm., (Figure 117E) [MALPU, mauve à feuilles rondes, Cheeses, Garden mallow, mauve très grêle, *Malva rotundifolia* L.] Very similar in habit and general appearance to Common mallow but differs by having smaller **flowers** with petals only about 6 mm (¼ in.) long, and the back of each "seed" section (e) flat, rather than round, and covered with a network of fine ridges and depressions. It also flowers at about the same time as Common mallow and occurs throughout most of Ontario in similar habitats but is not as abundant.

Figure 117. **Common mallow** A. Seedling. B. Base of mature plant. C. End of flowering stem. D. Fruit (ring of "seeds"). **Round-leaved mallow** E. Fruit (ring of "seeds").

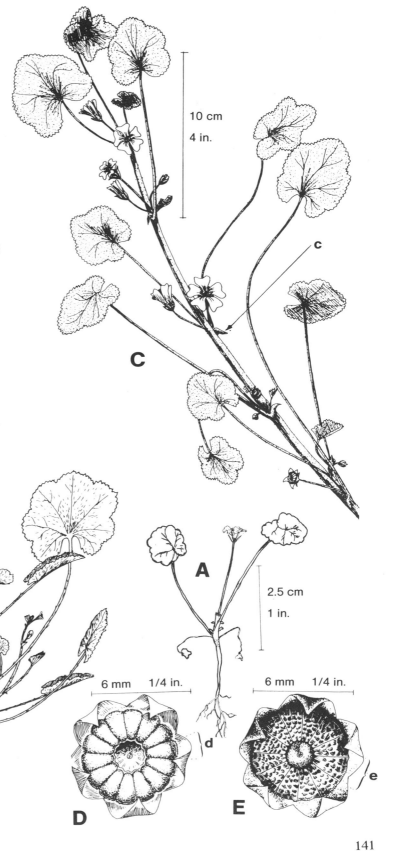

141

Several members of the Geranium Family (Geraniaceae) (not illustrated) may be confused with the mallows. Except for **Stork's-bill**, *Erodium cicutarium* (L.) L'Her., (EROCI, érodium cicutaire, érodium à feuilles de ciguë), which has pinnately divided leaves, all of the others have palmately veined leaves that range from very shallowly to very deeply palmately lobed, or in **Herb-Robert**, *Geranium robertianum* L., (GERRO, géranium de Robert, herbe-à-Robert) palmately divided. All have **pink to rosy-purple flowers** with 5 petals, but only 10 (rarely 5) **stamens** that are **not united into a central column** as in the Mallow Family. All have a long, slender fruit, about 1 - 3 cm (2/5 - 1 1/5 in.) long and 2 -3 mm (1/12 - ⅛ in.) in diameter, that is surrounded at the base by a ring of 5 almost spherical lobes, each lobe about 2 - 3 mm (1/12 - ⅛ in.) in diameter and containing one seed. Six or 7 species of wild geraniums (GERSS, *Geranium* spp., géranium), sometimes also called "Crane's-bill" because of the long, slender fruit, may occasionally be encountered as weeds in some situations in Ontario but they can be distinguished from each other only on technical characteristics that are beyond the scope of this book.

Velvetleaf *Abutilon theophrasti* Medic., (Figure 118, Plate 81) [ABUTH, abuliton, Butter-print, Elephant-ear, Indian-mallow, Pie-marker, abutilon feuille de velours] Annual, reproducing only by seed. **Stems** 1 - 2 m (3 - 6½ ft) tall and occasionally taller, much-branched in the upper part, finely soft-hairy; **leaves** alternate (1 per node), broadly heart-shaped, large, 7 - 20 cm (3 - 8 in.) wide with a sharp-pointed apex, shallowly round-toothed, soft-hairy and very velvety to the touch; **flowers** single or in small clusters from the leaf axils, each with 5 large sepals and 5 yellow to yellow-orange petals, 1.3 - 2.5 cm (½ - 1 in.) wide when open; the filaments united to form a central column as in the mallows (as (e) in Figure 116C); the **fruit** from each flower is a circular cluster of 12 to 15 seedpods about 1.3 - 2.5 cm (½ - 1 in.) long (B), at first green (Plate 81B) but turning dark brown to black at maturity, each individual pod (a) opening with a vertical slit down its back and containing several purplish-brown, V-shaped **seeds** about 1 mm (1/25 in.) thick and 2 - 3 mm (1/12 - ⅛ in.) long. Flowers from late July until autumn.

Velvetleaf occurs in southern Ontario where it is increasing in corn, soybeans and other annually tilled crops and in waste places.

It is distinguished by its erect habit of growth, large, alternate, valentine-shaped leaves which are very soft-velvety to the touch, its yellow to yellow-orange flowers, each with a central column of stamens, its ring of several seedpods (B) produced from each flower, and in late autumn by the rather grotesque appearance of its erect, branched, brownish to blackish stem with many erect clusters of seedpods.

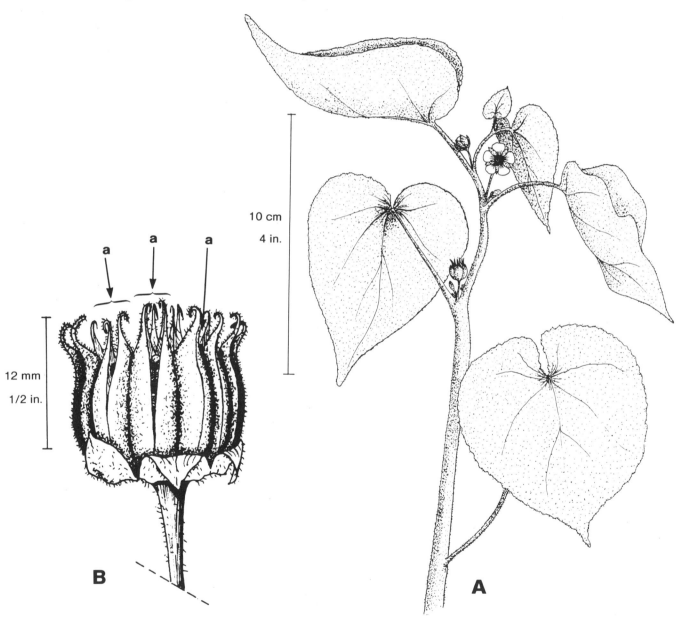

Figure 118. **Velvetleaf** A. Upper part of flowering stem.
B. Cluster of seedpods.

Flower-of-an-hour, *Hibiscus trionum* L., (Figure 119, Plate 82) [HIBTR, ketmie trilobée, fleur d'une heure, ketmie enflée] Annual, reproducing only by seed. **Stems** at first erect but soon much-branched and spreading, 30 - 50 cm (12 - 20 in.) high, rough-hairy; **leaves** alternate (1 per node), leaf-stalks about as long as the blades, leaf blades deeply 3-parted with each division coarsely lobed; **flowers** 2 - 4 cm (¾ - 1½ in.) in diameter with a ring of several linear bracts (a) below the calyx; calyx of 5 papery-thin united sepals (b), coarsely hairy on the prominent, purplish, lengthwise veins; petals yellowish with a dark or purplish-brown centre or eye; filaments united into a central column as in the mallows (as (e) in Figure 116C); **seedpod** globular, opening at the top, with many purplish-brown, V-shaped **seeds** about 2 mm (1/12 in.) long. Flowers from July to late autumn.

Flower-of-an-hour occurs only in the southwestern part of southern Ontario where it is a frequent weed in row crops, open fields and waste places.

It is distinguished by its low branching habit, bluish-green leaves which are deeply 3-parted and coarsely toothed, yellow flowers with a purplish-brown eye spot, a cluster of linear bracts (a) immediately below the calyx, and the purple-veined papery calyx (b) enclosing the globular seedpod.

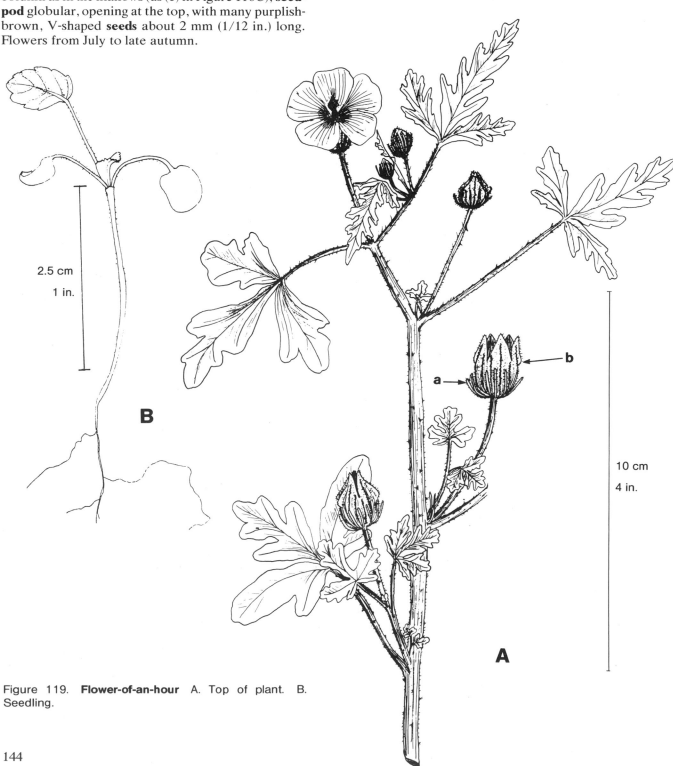

Figure 119. **Flower-of-an-hour** A. Top of plant. B. Seedling.

144

ST. JOHN'S-WORT FAMILY (Hypericaceae)

St. John's-wort, *Hypericum perforatum* L., (Figure 120, Plate 83) |HYPPE, millepertuis perforé, Goatweed, Klamathweed, millepertuis commun, herbe Saint-Jean] Perennial, reproducing by seed and by spreading underground roots or **rhizomes. Stems** of 2 kinds: upright flowering stems 40 - 80 cm (16 - 32 in.) high, tough or woody near the base, branching and smooth except for shallow ridges below the base of each leaf; and horizontal basal branches, these produced in late fall or early spring, short, densely leafy, and radiating out from the basal crown of each plant; leaves oposite (2 per node), stalkless, elliptic or linear, smooth-margined and, when viewed against the light, appear to have many small perforations or transparent dots (B, Plate 83B); **flowers** numerous in clusters at ends of branches; each flower, about 2 cm (4/5 in.) across, has 5 yellow petals with several, small, black dots along the margins, many stamens in 3 clusters and a single pistil in the centre; **seedpods** splitting from the tip; **seeds** dark brown about 1 mm (1/25 in.) long. Flowers from June to August; seedpods frequently persisting all winter.

St. John's-wort occurs throughout Ontario in pastures, edges of woodlots, roadsides, abandoned fields, waste areas and occasionally in lawns and flower borders. **If eaten by livestock, St. John's-wort may cause photosensitization, a condition in which patches of white or light-coloured skin become seriously sunburned under normal exposure to sunlight. Avoid pasturing animals where this weed is abundant or keep them under shade during normal sunny days.**

It is distinguished by its almost woody base, opposite leaves, bright yellow flowers, and leaves with transparent dots (B, Plate 83B).

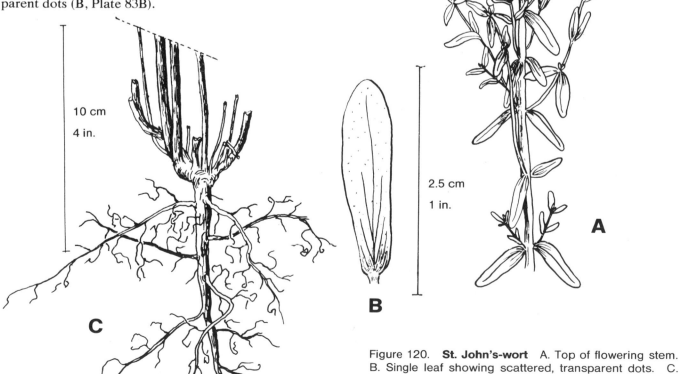

Figure 120. **St. John's-wort** A. Top of flowering stem. B. Single leaf showing scattered, transparent dots. C. Basal crown and root.

145

Field violet, *Viola arvensis* Murr., (Figure 121, Plate 84) [VIOAR, violette des champs, European field pansy, Field pansy, Wild pansy, pensée des champs] Annual or possibly living for two years, reproducing only by seed. **Stems** erect and short or much-branched and somewhat spreading, up to 30 cm (12 in.) long, somewhat fleshy or succulent, with or without fine hair; **leaves** of seedlings and young plants very small, with long stalks (a), rounded blades, a few shallow teeth, and very small stipules; stem leaves of older plants alternate (1 per node), larger, oval to oblong or nearly linear, all with a few coarse rounded teeth; **stipules** (appendages at junction of leafstalk and stem) of stem leaves large, resembling leaf blades, deeply dissected with a long, thin, terminal lobe (b) and several, narrow, shorter segments on either side (c); **flowers** (d) on long thin stalks (e) from axils of leaves, pale yellow or white and yellow, resembling those of the cultivated pansy but much smaller, about 1 - 1.5 cm (2/5 - 3/5 in.) long, and with a very short spur (2 mm, 1/12 in.) at the base of the lower petal; **seedpods** splitting into 3 divisions (f) and scattering numerous, small, brownish **seeds**. Flowers from early May to midsummer and occasionally in autumn.

Field violet occurs throughout most of Ontario in gardens, cereal crops, pastures, abandoned fields and waste places.

It is distinguished by the small yellow flowers (d) resembling a miniature pansy, the lowest leaves rounded with very small stipules but upper leaves oblong and with large, prominent, deeply dissected stipules (b, c) so that the stem appears to have tufts of tiny narrow leaves at each node.

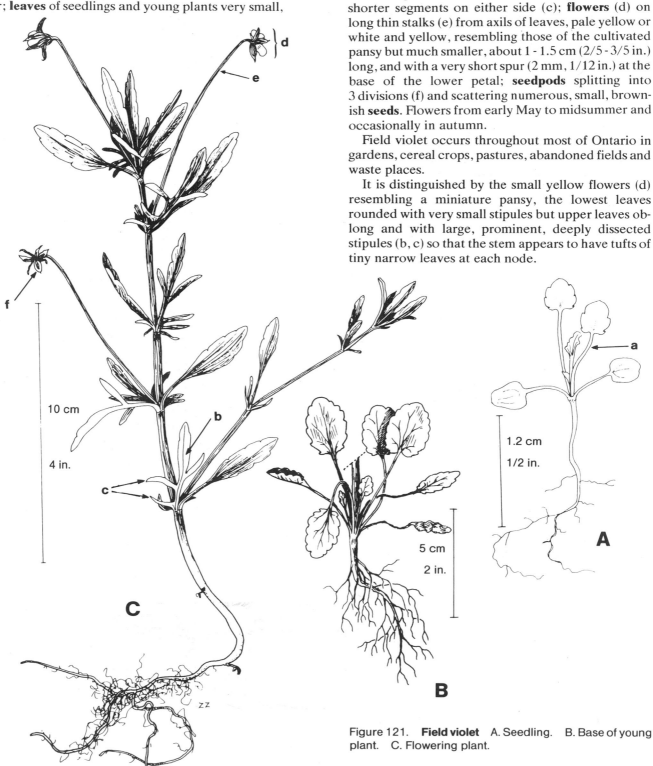

Figure 121. **Field violet** A. Seedling. B. Base of young plant. C. Flowering plant.

LOOSESTRIFE FAMILY (Lythraceae)

Purple loosestrife, *Lythrum salicaria* L., (Figure 122, Plate 85) [LYTSA, salicaire, Spiked loosestrife, salicaire commune, lythrum salicaire] Perennial, reproducing only by seed. **Stems** tall, erect, 60 - 120 cm (24 - 48 in.) high, somewhat branched, usually finely hairy, more or less square in cross-section, especially where the leaves are opposite; **leaves** opposite (2 per node) or sometimes whorled (3 or more per node), stalkless, broad near the base and tapering towards the tip, 3 - 10 cm (1¼ - 4 in.) long, finely hairy; upper leaves and those in the inflorescence usually alternate (1 per node) and smaller than the lower ones; **flowers** in dense terminal spikes; sepals united into a column with 8 to 10 or 12 prominent green veins and ending in several, long, thin, pointed lobes; petals 5 to 7, red-purple, 7 - 10 mm (¼ - 2/5 in.) long, very showy; stamens several and 1 pistil; **seedpod** small, containing many tiny **seeds**. Flowers from June to autumn.

Purple loosestrife was introduced from Europe but is now widely naturalized in wet meadows, river floodplains, and damp roadsides throughout most of Ontario.

Its opposite leaves and square stems resemble plants of the Mint Family but it is distinguished by having separate petals, a seedpod with many fine seeds, and it lacks the minty odour.

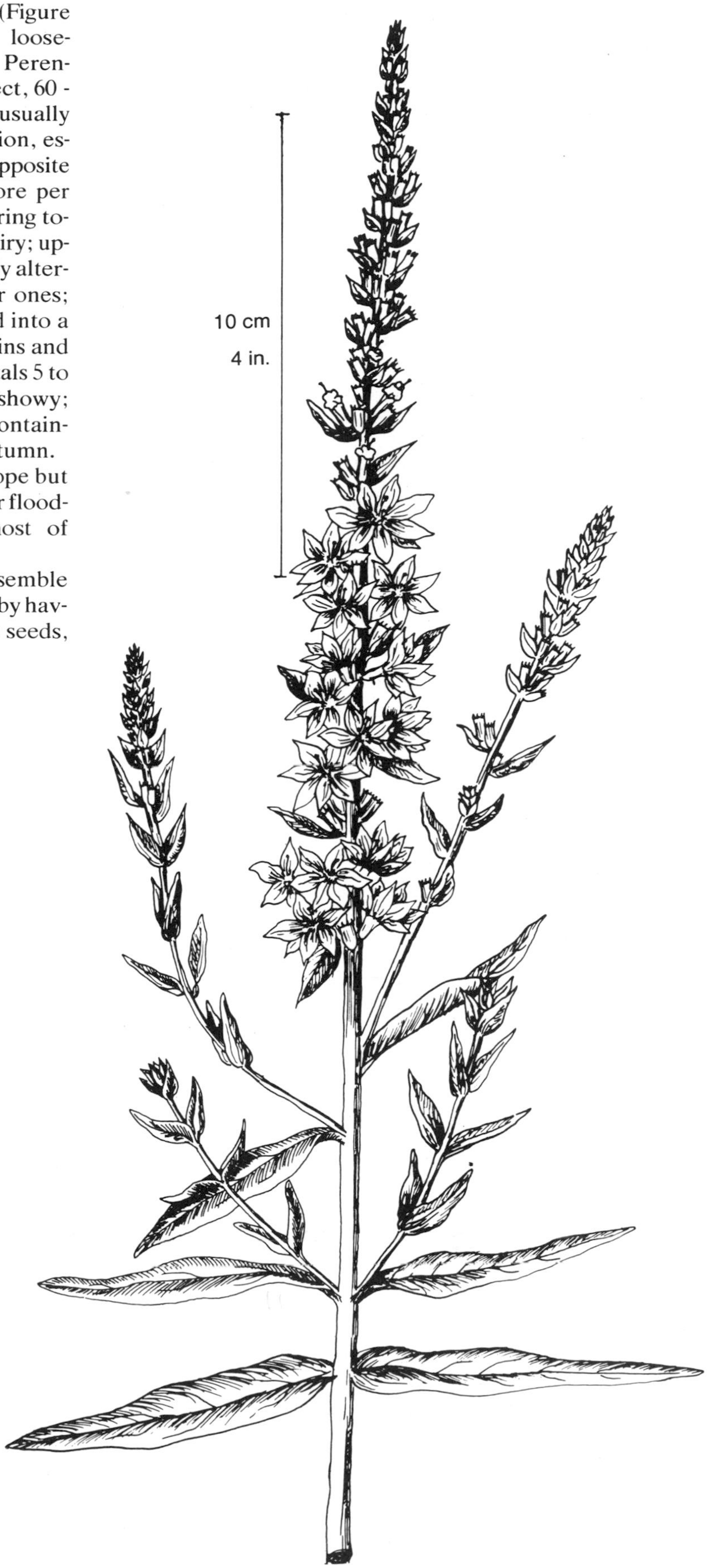

10 cm
4 in.

Figure 122. **Purple loosestrife**

EVENING-PRIMROSE FAMILY (Onagraceae)

Yellow evening-primrose, *Oenothera biennis* L., (Figure 123, Plate 86) |OEOBI, onagre bisannuelle, Evening-primrose, onagre commune, herbe aux ânes| Biennial or short-lived perennial, or rarely annual, reproducing only by seed. **Taproot,** especially of biennial plants, becoming thick, fleshy and deeply penetrating (A); **stems** erect, up to 2 m (6½ ft) high, usually somewhat branched, the branches spreading and becoming erect, often hairy, either green or purple-tinged; **leaves** of first-year plants in a rosette, their short stalks (a) gradually broadening into the elliptical to oblong leaf blades, green or with a reddish cast, midrib often pinkish to reddish, margins irregular or weakly toothed; stem leaves alternate (1 per node), stalkless, similar to the basal leaves but gradually smaller upwards, with wavy or toothed margins; **flowers** in long spikes on stems and branches; each flower in the axil of a small leafy bract (b) which resembles the upper stem leaves and is usually much shorter than the flower; flowers stalkless but mistakenly appear short-stalked, the lowermost portion (c) of the apparent "stalk" being the ovary and the thinner portion (d) above this being the hypanthium (floral tube) at the top of which are 4 narrow green sepals (e), 4 large yellow petals 1 - 2.5 cm (2/5 - 1 in.) long, and 8 stamens; edges and tips of sepals (f) united in unopened flower bud; **seedpod** (g, C) 1 - 3.5 cm (2/5 - 1½ in.) long, nearly cylindrical but tapering towards the tip, the inside divided into 4 chambers by 4 lengthwise partitions, and the outer wall splitting downwards from the tip into 4 valves (h) to release the seed; **seeds** irregular in shape, dark reddish-brown to black with rough surfaces. Flowers from July to September.

Yellow evening-primrose occurs throughout Ontario in waste areas, roadsides, lakeshores, river valleys and occasionally in fields of winter wheat or fall rye where its long spikes of bright yellow flowers are very conspicuous.

It is distinguished by its tall, erect stems with long spikes of large, bright yellow flowers followed by short seedpods splitting downward on 4 sides; its rosette plants distinguished by the usually pinkish to reddish midribs of their elongated, elliptic to oblong leaf blades.

Small-flowered evening-primrose, *Oenothera parviflora* L., (not illustrated) |OEOPF, onagre parviflore, and in error, Yellow evening-primrose, onagre muriquée| A very similar plant but differs by having slightly smaller **flowers,** the petals of which are usually not more than 1.5 cm (3/5 in.) long; longer leafy **bracts** below each flower, these about as long as the whole flower; purplish hair with slightly enlarged or bulbous bases on the leaves and stem; and the tips of the **sepals** in the unopened flower buds being very thin and not united. Small-flowered evening-primrose occurs throughout Ontario in similar habitats.

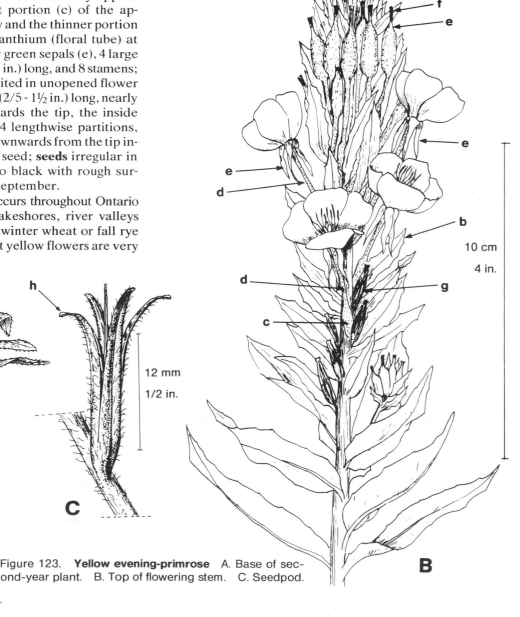

Figure 123. **Yellow evening-primrose** A. Base of second-year plant. B. Top of flowering stem. C. Seedpod.

148

CARROT or PARSLEY FAMILY (Umbelliferae)

Wild carrot, *Daucus carota* L., (Figure 124, Plate 87) [DAUCA, carotte sauvage, Bird's-nest, Queen Anne's-Lace, carotte] Biennial or, occasionally, annual and sometimes a short-lived perennial, reproducing only by seed. **Seedlings** emerge during spring and early summer, with 2 long, narrow, thin cotyledons (seed leaves) (a); first true **leaf** is compound with 3 main divisions (A); later leaves compound with many divisions; first-year plant usually stemless, with a deeply penetrating, tough **taproot** and a rosette of stalked, very finely dissected (lacy), hairy leaves virtually identical in appearance and smell to leaves of the cultivated carrot; bases of leafstalks broad and flat (b); stem produced in the second year on biennial plants, erect, to 1 m (40 in.) tall, branching, grooved, rough-hairy or bristly; stem leaves similar to basal leaves but smaller and on shorter stalks; base of leafstalk broadened and more or less circling the stem at each node (c); **flowers** white in compound umbels (large umbels made up of many smaller umbels) at tips of stem and branches (Plate 87); a whorl of several 3- to 5-branched bracts (d) at the base of each compound umbel; most flowers white or occasionally pinkish, but the single flower (e) arising from the centre of the compound umbel is often dark purple; after flowering the umbel closes, forming what is commonly called a "bird's-nest"; **fruits** ("seeds") grayish to brownish with several rows of spines by which they cling to clothing and animal fur. Flowers from June to September. Stems, leaves and root have the familiar carrot odour.

Wild carrot occurs throughout most of Ontario in old pastures, waste places, roadsides, meadows and occasionally as a weed in gardens and flower borders. The cultivated carrot was developed from Wild carrot, which has a coarse, woody, fibrous, unpalatable taproot, by selecting strains having soft juicy edible roots.

It is distinguished by its finely divided leaves, its erect, hairy stem, its white to pinkish compound umbels surrounded at their bases by whorls of slender 3- to 5-branched bracts, its bird's-nest cluster of fruits and its typical carrot odour, and a coarse, fibrous, unpalatable root.

Caraway, *Carum carvi* L., (not illustrated) [CRYCA, anis canadien, carvi, anis] Resembling Wild carrot, being about the same height, having finely dissected **leaves** and compound **umbels** of small white flowers but lacking the carrot odour. It is also a biennial but flowers in spring and early summer; its **stems** are not hairy, the bracts below the inflorescence are small and usually not branched, and its **fruits** ("seeds") are smooth (without hooked spines) and have a caraway flavour. Caraway occurs along roadsides, in waste places and near old building sites in scattered localities throughout Ontario.

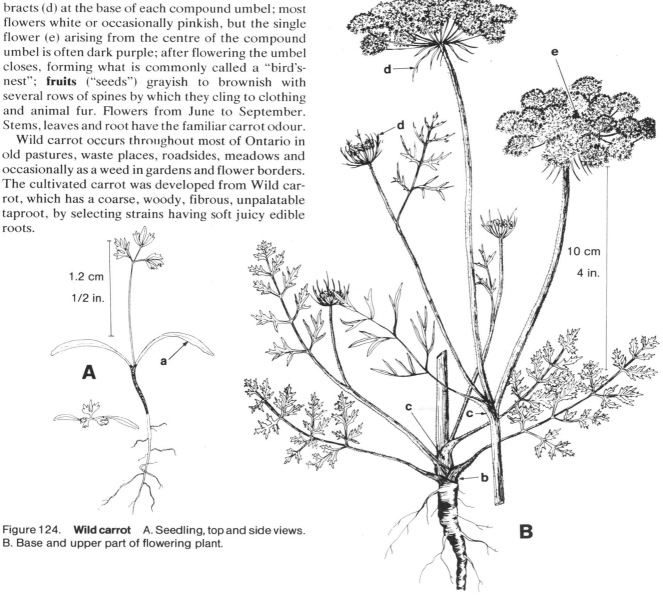

Figure 124. **Wild carrot** A. Seedling, top and side views. B. Base and upper part of flowering plant.

Goutweed, *Aegopodium podagraria* L., (Figure 125, Plate 88) [AEOPO, égopode podagraire, Bishop's goutweed, herbe aux goutteux] Perennial, reproducing by seed and by widely spreading, much-branched, whitish underground stems (**rhizomes**) (a) producing dense patches. Flowering **stems** erect, 40 - 90 cm (16 - 36 in.) high, branched in the upper part but seldom seen when the weed infests lawns or gardens; basal **leaves** arise directly from the rhizomes at the ground surface (b); these and the leaves arising from below the ground surface (c) (called "radical leaves") are all long-stalked, divided in 3 main parts (d) but quite vari-able as each part may be redivided into as many as 5 subdivisions, a single leaf therefore consisting of from 3 to as many as 15 broad, flat, somewhat oval leaflets, the separation often incomplete giving the lobed leaflet a "mitten-like" appearance (e); all leaflets irregularly coarsely to finely toothed; base of terminal leaflet symmetrical (f); base of lateral leaflet not symmetrical (g); stem leaves alternate (1 per node), similar to basal leaves but usually smaller, with fewer divisions and with a short stalk; bases of leafstalks (h) broad, flat and winged so they more or less encircle the stem at the node; **flowers** individually very small, white, in compound umbels without any bracts immediately below the umbel (j). Flowers from June to August.

Goutweed was widely cultivated as a vigorous perennial ground cover because of its strong spreading rhizome system, but the same characteristics enable it to escape from cultivation and invade lawns, hedges, gardens, roadsides and waste places, the habitats in which it occurs throughout most of southern Ontario. Some cultivated forms have variegated leaves, the leaflets being green near the centre but whitish around their margins. These are usually less aggressive than forms with entirely green leaves.

Goutweed is distinguished by its very vigorous, aggressive spreading habit, its widely spreading whitish rhizomes, and its compound leaves consisting of 3 to 15 broad leaflets which usually have a symmetrical base (f) on the terminal leaflet but non-symmetrical bases (g) on the lateral leaflets.

Figure 125. **Goutweed** A. Non-flowering plant with 2 basal leaves and 1 radical leaf. B. Top of flowering stem.

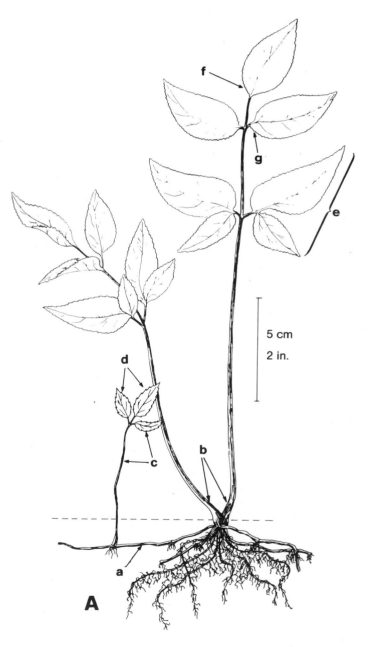

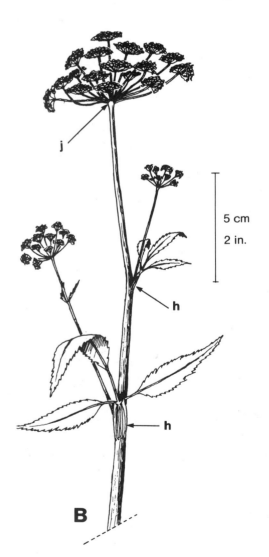

Poison hemlock, *Conium maculatum* L., (Figure 126, Plate 89) [COIMA, ciguë maculée, Deadly hemlock, Poison parsley, ciguë tachetée] Biennial, reproducing only by seed. **Stems** freely branched to 3 m (10 ft) in height and smooth, with reddish-purple spots or blotches (a); **leaves** finely divided, consisting of 3, 5 or 7 main divisions (b), each of which is divided and redivided, the ultimate divisions (c) toothed or incised; the complete leaf (d) from 3.5 - 40 cm (1½ - 16 in.) long, broadly triangular-ovate, smooth and hairless; leafstalks (e) often marked with reddish-purple spots or blotches like the stems; **flowers** small, crowded in compound umbels (f, B) 2 -8 cm (4/5 - 3½ in.) wide; the terminal umbel (g) blooming first but soon overtopped by others on the ends of branches arising from axils of leaves lower on the stem (h); the base of each main umbel surrounded by several small, ovate-pointed bracts (i) (involucre) 1 - 3 mm (1/25 - ⅛ in.) wide and up to 10 mm (2/5 in.) long, and the bases of each of the smaller umbellets (j) (simple umbels) in each compound umbel with still smaller bracts (k), but these on one side of the umbellet only; individual flowers (l) white, broadly ovoid and 2 - 4 mm (1/12 - 1/6 in.) across; mature **fruits** almost spherical, 2 - 3 mm (1/12 - ⅛ in.) long and equally wide, smooth except for 5 prominent light-coloured, rounded or wavy, lengthwise ribs on each of the 2 halves or "seeds" (C). Flowers from June to August.

All parts of this plant are very poisonous. It was introduced from Eurasia and is now found in a few locations in southern Ontario along roads and in woodlots and waste places. A recent introduction through contaminated forage seed resulted in its occurrence in a few cultivated fields.

It is distinguished from other members of the Carrot or Parsley Family by the combination of these characteristics: its finely-divided leaves, the reddish-purple spots or blotches on its smooth stems and leaf petioles, and its small (up to about 8 cm or 3½ in. across) compound umbels with the tiny bractlets only on one side of each umbellet.

Wild chevril, *Anthriscus sylvestris* (L.) Hoffm., (not illustrated) [ANRSY, anthrisque des bois, cerfeuil sauvage] Resembles Poison hemlock with its finely-divided leaves and umbels of white flowers. However, it differs by being a smaller plant, rarely as much as 1 m (40 in.) tall; having green stems and leaf petioles

that are completely without red-purple mottling; by having small bracts at the base of the rays of the simple umbels [umbels of individual flowers, as illustrated at (k) in Figure 126B], but no bracts around the base of the rays of each compound umbel [compare with those of Poison hemlock illustrated at (i) in Figure 126B]; and by each fruit (pair of "seeds") being smooth and somewhat "banana-shaped," about 5 mm (1/5 in.) long and 1 mm (1/25 in.) wide. Wild chevril is also sometimes mistaken for Wild carrot. It occurs along roadsides, edges of woods and in waste places. It is not poisonous.

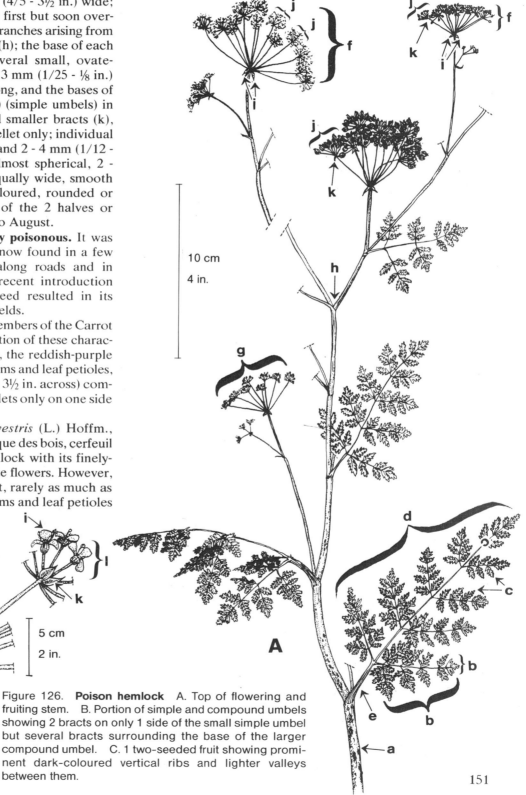

Figure 126. Poison hemlock A. Top of flowering and fruiting stem. B. Portion of simple and compound umbels showing 2 bracts on only 1 side of the small simple umbel but several bracts surrounding the base of the larger compound umbel. C. 1 two-seeded fruit showing prominent dark-coloured vertical ribs and lighter valleys between them.

151

Water-parsnip, *Sium suave* Walt., (Figure 127, Plate 90) [SIUSU, berle douce, berle à larges feuilles] Perennial, reproducing only by seed. **Roots** coarsely fibrous or cord-like (A) but never tuberous. **Stems** erect, 60 - 200 cm (2 - 6½ ft) high, branching above, hollow except for a partition at each node; **leaves** alternate (1 per node), pinnately compound with usually 5 to 15 leaflets, these arranged in 2 to 7 pairs of opposite leaflets (a) along the leaf axis (rachis) (b) plus 1 terminal leaflet (c), the base of the leafstalk broad, thin-winged (d) and encircling the stem at the node (e), leaflets variable in shape from very narrow and linear to lance-shaped but always sharply saw-toothed; basal leaves growing submerged in water are 2 or more times pinnately divided (C) and quite unlike the stem leaves which grow above the water surface (B); **flowers** (f) individually very small, white, in compound umbels [1 large umbel (g) made up of several small umbels (h)] varying 3 - 12 cm (1¼ - 4½ in.) across, with several, narrow, pointed bracts (j) at the base of each large umbel; **fruits** (pairs of "seeds") oval, 2 - 3 mm (1/12 - ⅛ in.) long. Flowers from July to September.

Water-parsnip is a native plant throughout Ontario and grows in low wet areas, often in standing water as deep as 1 m (40 in.). Water-parsnip has been reported to be poisonous to livestock and, although experimental feeding trials have not proven it to be harmful, livestock growers should be cautioned against the potential danger of this native plant.

It is distinguished from Water-hemlock, known to be very poisonous, by its stem leaves above the water surface being once-pinnately compound, its several thin bracts (j) at the base of each compound umbel (g), its numerous thin or cord-like roots at the base of each stem (A), and by the absence of well-defined cross-partitions in the base of the stem which are characteristic of Spotted water-hemlock (Figure 128C).

Circumstantial evidence suggests that Water-parsnip may be poisonous to hogs and cattle so it must be regarded with suspicion.

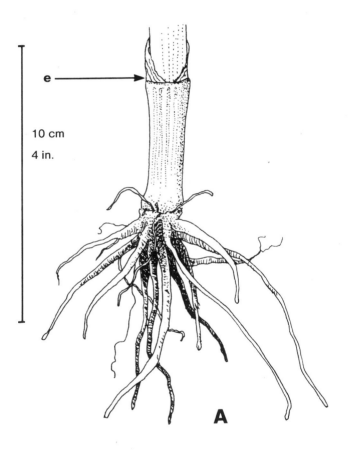

e →

10 cm
4 in.

A

Figure 127.   **Water-parsnip**   A. Base of plant. (Cont'd.)

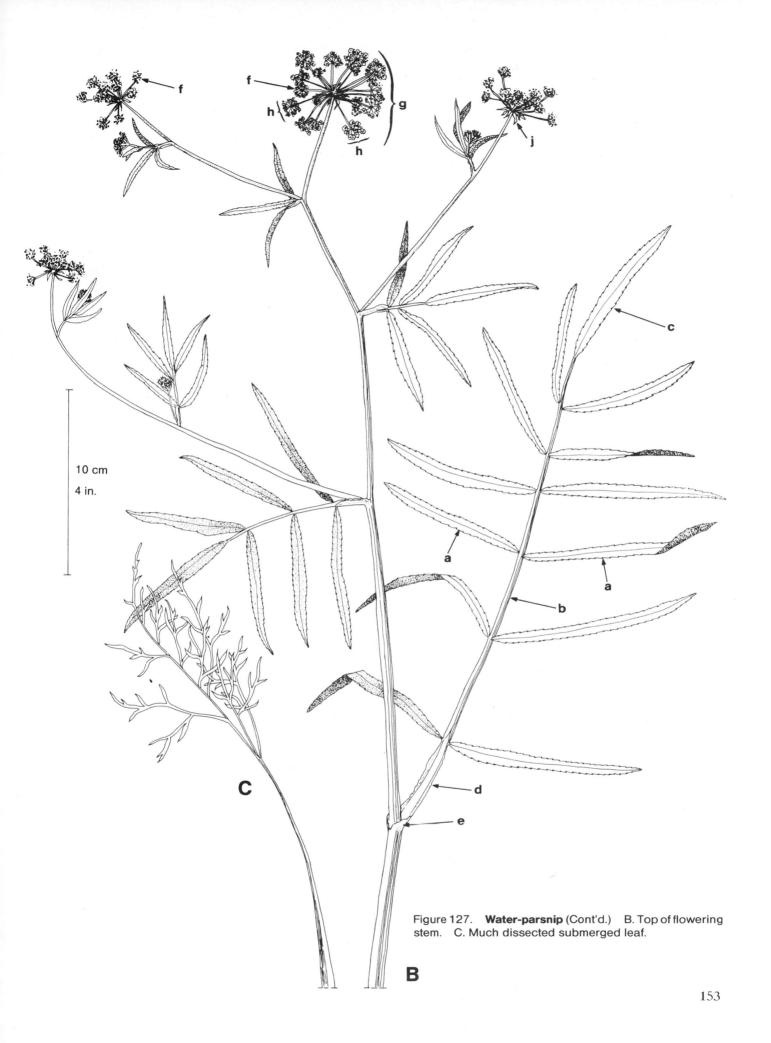

Figure 127. **Water-parsnip** (Cont'd.) B. Top of flowering stem. C. Much dissected submerged leaf.

153

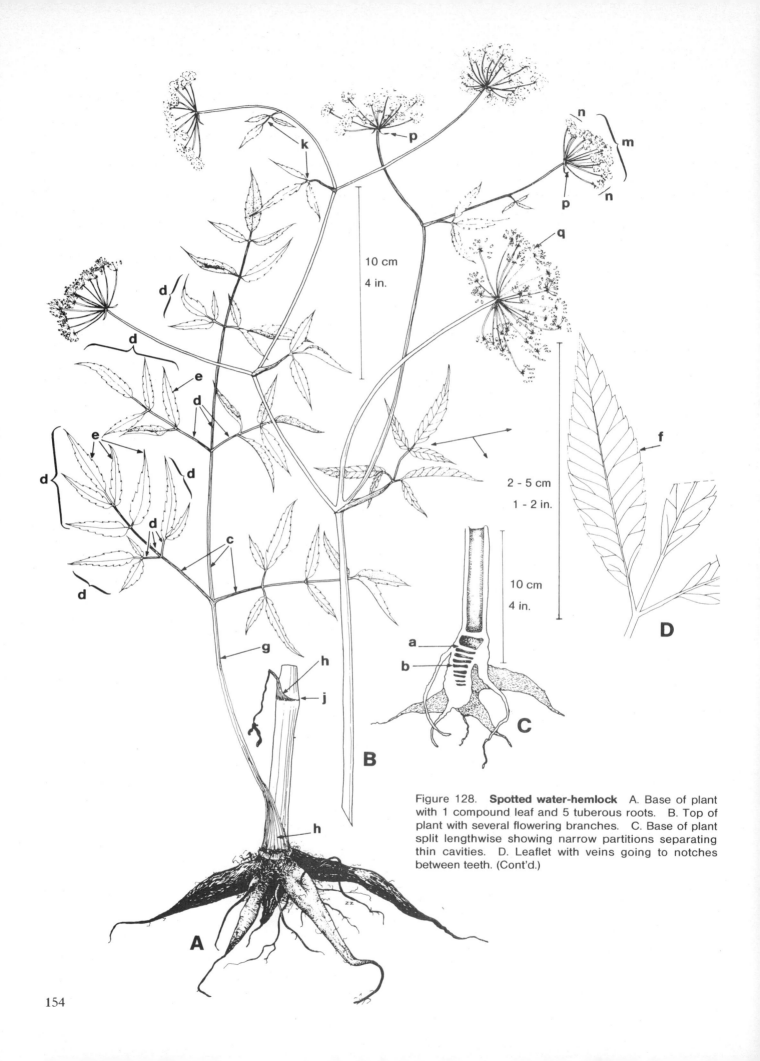

10 cm
4 in.

2 - 5 cm
1 - 2 in.

10 cm
4 in.

Figure 128. **Spotted water-hemlock** A. Base of plant with 1 compound leaf and 5 tuberous roots. B. Top of plant with several flowering branches. C. Base of plant split lengthwise showing narrow partitions separating thin cavities. D. Leaflet with veins going to notches between teeth. (Cont'd.)

Spotted water-hemlock, *Cicuta maculata* L., (Figure 128 A-D, Plate 91) |CIUMC, carotte à Moreau, Beaver poison, Musquash-root, Poison parsnip, Spotted cowbane, Spotted-hemlock, Water-hemlock, cicutaire maculée| Perennial, reproducing only by seed. **Stems** erect, 1 - 2 m (3 - 6½ ft) high, hollow except for a partition at each node, round or slightly angular with purplish lengthwise streaks; base of stem slightly swollen (C) and usually with several, narrow cross-partitions (a) separating thin cavities (b), these visible by splitting the lower stem lengthwise downwards through the base; the freshly split surfaces usually soon developing little droplets of an amber or yellowish oily secretion; the swollen base usually surrounded by 3 or more fleshy, thickened, tuber-like **roots** which taper into long thin strands (A); basal **leaves** at least twice compound, that is, each leaf divided once into 3 or more parts (c) and each of these parts divided again into smaller parts or leaflets (d), occasionally these again redivided into still smaller parts or leaflets (e); the veins in each leaflet going to the notches (f) between teeth on the margins (D); leafstalk (g) long, thin, often somewhat channeled and always broadened at the base (h) and partly surrounding the stem at the node (j); stem leaves alternate (1 per node), usually twice compound but leaves in the inflorescence frequently only once compound into 3 or 5 leaflets (k); **flowers** individually small, white, in compound umbels at ends of the stems and branches, 1 large umbel (m) made up of several small, simple umbels or umbelets (n); each compound umbel flattish or rounded across the top and up to 12 cm (5 in.) in diameter but never spherical, usually without bracts or with only 1 or 2 bracts (p) at its base; **fruit** a pair of oval or oblong, yellowish-brown "seeds" (q) 2 - 4 mm (1/12 - 1/6 in.) long with prominent, rounded, brown-

ish, lengthwise ribs on the outer surface. Flowers from June to August.

Spotted water-hemlock is a native plant throughout Ontario, occurring in wet meadows, pastures, ditches, edges of streams and rivers, and swampy areas. **Spotted water-hemlock is the most poisonous of all Canadian plants to both human beings and livestock, all parts of the plant being poisonous. Extreme care must be taken when pasturing areas where this plant grows, and in collecting wild greens, roots or seeds for human consumption.**

It is distinguished by the combination of its twice-compound leaves, base of split stem showing alternate narrow cross-partitions (a) and thin cavities (b), and thickened tuberous roots (A) surrounding base of stem; also by its white flowers in flattish compound umbels (m) up to 12 cm (5 in.) across, these without any or sometimes with 1 or 2 bracts (p) immediately below the umbel and the veins in each leaflet going to the notches (f) between teeth on the margins (D).

Angelica, *Angelica atropurpurea* L., (Figure 128E-F, Plate 92) |ANKAT, angélique, Purple angelica, angélique noir pourpré| Similar to Spotted water-hemlock but usually grows much taller (up to 2.5 m, 8½ ft) with thicker purplish **stems** (up to 5 cm, 2 in. in diameter) lengthwise ridged and smooth or pebbled, has larger 2 to 3 times compound **leaves** (E) with broader leaflets (often 2 - 5 cm, 4/5 - 2 in. wide), and much larger, coarser, compound **umbels** which are spherical and often up to 30 cm (12 in.) in diameter. It may have alternate partitions and chambers in the base of the stem and a yellowish oily secretion on cut surfaces like Spotted water-hemlock (see a, b in Figure 128C), but usually does not have thickened or tuberous roots like those (see Figure 128A) that are characteristic of Spotted water-hemlock. The veins in leaflets of Angelica go to the tips of the teeth (r) on the margins (F) rather than to the notches between the teeth as in Spotted water-hemlock |compare with (f) in Figure 128D|.

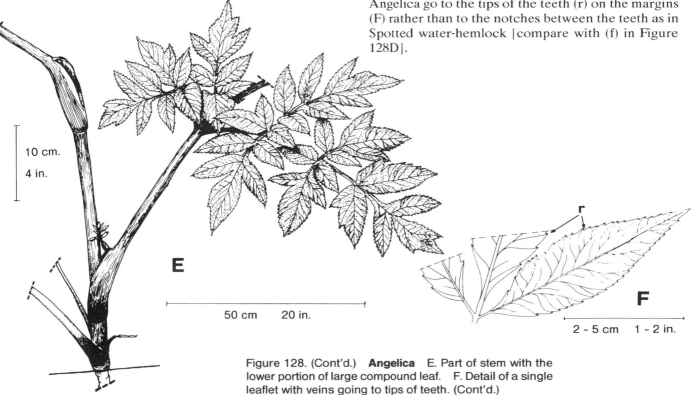

10 cm.
4 in.

E

50 cm   20 in.

r

F

2 - 5 cm   1 - 2 in.

Figure 128. (Cont'd.) **Angelica** E. Part of stem with the lower portion of large compound leaf.   F. Detail of a single leaflet with veins going to tips of teeth. (Cont'd.)

155

Cow-parsnip, *Heracleum lanatum* Michx., (Figure 128G) [HERMA, berce laineuse, Bamboo, poglus, *H. maximum* Bartr.] Biennial or sometimes perennial; similar in form to Spotted water-hemlock but usually taller (1 - 3 m, 3 - 10 ft), and much coarser in general appearance; **stems** hollow, 1 - 5 cm (2/5 - 2 in.) in diameter, often hairy (a) below the nodes, often somewhat woolly or hairy throughout; basal **leaves** long-stalked, 50 - 100 cm (20 - 40 in.) high, divided into 3 large, broad leaflets, these deeply lobed, sometimes the central one redivided, jagged-toothed with the veins mostly going to the tips of the teeth; stem leaves similar but smaller; lower portion of each leafstalk much expanded (b), almost balloon-like, circling the stem at the node; **flowers** white in large, nearly flat-topped, compound umbels 10 - 20 cm (4 - 8 in.) or more across; **seeds** large, flat, elliptic in outline, 7 - 14 mm (¼ - ⅝ in.) long. Flowers from June to September. Occurs throughout Ontario in meadows and edges of moist woods. Not considered poisonous.

It is distinguished by its large, broad trifoliolate leaves, its slightly woolly or hairy stems, and its large, coarse umbels of white flowers.

Cow-parsnip is not considered to be poisonous.

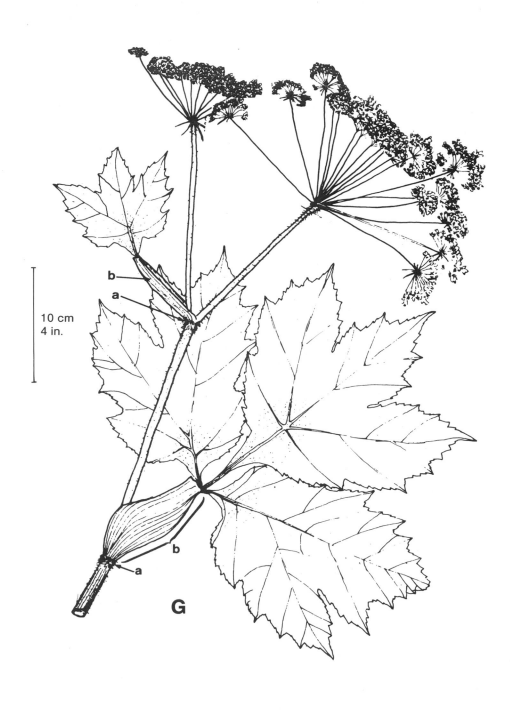

Figure 128. (Cont'd.) **Cow-parsnip** G. Top of flowering stem.

156

Giant hogweed, *Heracleum mantegazzianum* Somm. & Lev., (Figure 129, Plate 93) [HERMZ, berce du Caucase] Biennial or perennial, flowering only once in its lifetime and reproducing only by seed. Plants forming rosettes to 1 m (40 in.) high the first year; in the second year, either sending up a flowering stem, or remaining vegetative and producing a very large rosette of huge leaves, these including their petioles, up to 2 m (80 in.) high, and flowering in the third year; **flowering stems** up to 5 m (16 ft) high and up to 10 cm (4 in.) in diameter, hollow except at the nodes; both stems and petioles having conspicuous reddish-purple flecks throughout and sometimes nearly solid purple near the base; lower stem often very rough with sharp-pointed, irregularly-spaced bumps; leaf blades of **rosette leaves** very large, up to 1 m (40 in.) across, compound with 3 large deeply cut leaflets, each leaflet (a) with deep irregular lobes and coarse, sharp teeth on all margins; their petioles often with sharp-pointed bumps similar to those on the flowering stems; **leaves on the flowering stem** of similar shape but smaller, the upper ones often not divided but just deeply 3-lobed; **inflorescence** a compound umbel up to 120 cm (4 ft)

across, consisting of many (approximately 30 to 50) branches, each branch ending in a simple umbel with approximately 30 to 40 flowers; the whole compound umbel with a flat bottom and gently rounded top; petals white or rarely pinkish and up to 12 mm (½ in.) long; **fruit** oval in outline, 7 - 13 mm (¼ - ½ in.) long, 6 - 10 mm (¼ - 2/5 in.) wide and 1 - 3 mm (1/25 - ⅛ in.) thick, smooth to softly hairy, with usually 4 prominent dark-coloured oil tubes. Flowers from June to August.

Giant hogweed was introduced from Europe, presumably as an ornamental, and has escaped along roadsides, streambanks and waste areas in scattered localities in southern Ontario. **It has been implicated as a cause of severe dermatitis in a few susceptible individuals.**

It is distinguished by its huge size, its very large, compound leaf blades, its tall, thick, hollow, often sharply roughened stems, and its large flat-topped compound inflorescence with white flowers and large, flat fruits with prominent dark-coloured oil tubes. Flowering inflorescences are often heavily infested by aphids.

1 m
40 in.

Figure 129. **Giant hogweed** Second-year plant with rosette leaves up to 125 cm (50 in.) high plus a central stem with 2 leaves emerging through the top of the rosette. The central stem will later produce a very large umbel of flowers.

Bulbous water-hemlock, *Cicuta bulbifera* L., (Figure 130) [CIUBU, cicutaire bulbifère, ciguë bulbifère] Perennial, reproducing by seed and by bulblets. **Stems** slender, 30 - 100 cm (12 - 40 in.) high, hollow except at the nodes, round, basal portion not swollen but usually with alternate slender partitions and narrow cavities as in Spotted water-hemlock (Figure 128C); main **roots** somewhat thickened and fleshy or slender and cord-like; basal and lower stem **leaves** alternate (1 per node), 2 to 3 times compound, each leaf divided into 3 or more parts (a), with each of these parts divided again (b) and sometimes re-divided a third time (c), but the leaflets very slender and appearing almost like thin branches (B); upper leaves less divided, and those of the true branches (d) not divided at all (e), bearing in their axils (angle between leaf and stem) clusters of small bulblets (f); **flowers** individually very small, arranged in small compound umbels (g) at the ends of the main stem and a few branches, sometimes the white flowers inter-spersed with small bulblets similar to those in the axils of leaves. Flowers from July until autumn.

Bulbous water-hemlock is a native plant which occurs throughout Ontario in wet habitats similar to where Spotted water-hemlock may also be found. Like Spotted water-hemlock, **Bulbous water-hemlock is also poisonous to both livestock and human beings. Considerable care must be exercised when allowing livestock to pasture in areas where either of these two native plants grows or when collecting wild plants for human consumption.**

It is distinguished by its variation in leaf complexity: those on the lower stem having many slender leaflets, those on middle and upper stems having fewer leaflets, and those on the uppermost branches being simple (neither compound nor divided); by the tiny bulblets in the axils of these simple leaves, and by its small, compound umbels that usually contain a mixture of flowers and bulblets.

Figure 130. **Bulbous water-hemlock** A. Base of plant. B. Compound leaf from lower stem. C. Upper part of stem with slender, simple leaves and bulblets in their axils.

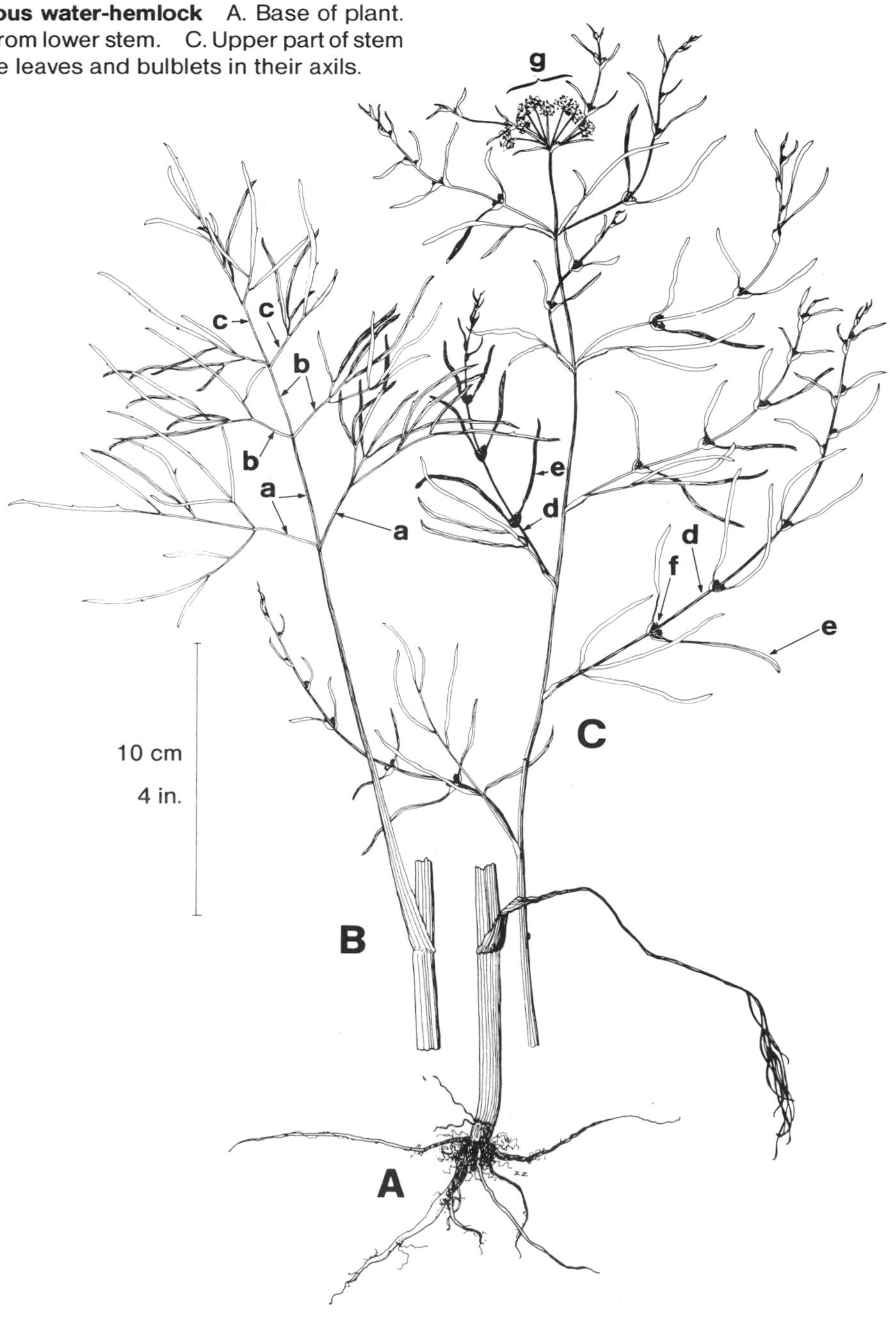

158

Wild parsnip, *Pastinaca sativa* L., (Figure 131) [PAVSA, panais sauvage, Yellow parsnip, panais, panais cultivé] Biennial, reproducing only by seed. **Stems** erect, 50 - 150 cm (20 - 60 in.) high, branched, hollow except at the nodes (a); **seedlings** with small ovate leaves on long stalks, later rosette leaves pinnately compound with broad leaflets; plants remaining as a rosette during the first season and developing a thick white to yellowish **taproot** (B); stem **leaves** alternate (1 per node), pinnately compound with usually 2 to 5 pairs of opposite (2 at a place), sharply toothed, relatively broad leaflets (b) that may be somewhat mitten-shaped, and 1 somewhat diamond-shaped leaflet (c) at the tip; all leafstalks broad (d) and completely encircle the stem; uppermost leaves reduced to narrow bracts (e) with flowering branches from their axils; **flowers** yellow, small, clustered in compound umbels 10 - 20 cm (4 - 8 in.) across; **seeds** round in outline, flat and winged. Flowers from May to late autumn. The whole plant has a distinctive parsnip odour.

Wild parsnip occurs throughout Ontario in abandoned yards, waste places, meadows, old fields, roadsides and railway embankments. It is very similar to the cultivated parsnip and some stands may merely be the cultivated parsnip which escaped or persisted from earlier plantings. **Some people develop a severe skin irritation from contact with the leaves of Wild parsnip, but the root of this plant is edible.**

It is distinguished from other members of the Carrot Family by its pinnately compound stem leaves with broad, sometimes coarsely-lobed leaflets (b, c), yellow flowers and distinctive odour.

Figure 131. **Wild parsnip** A. Seedling. B. Taproot. C. Top of flowering stem.

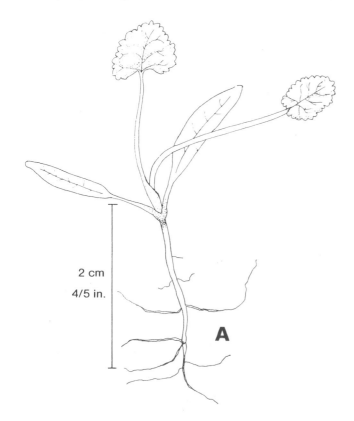

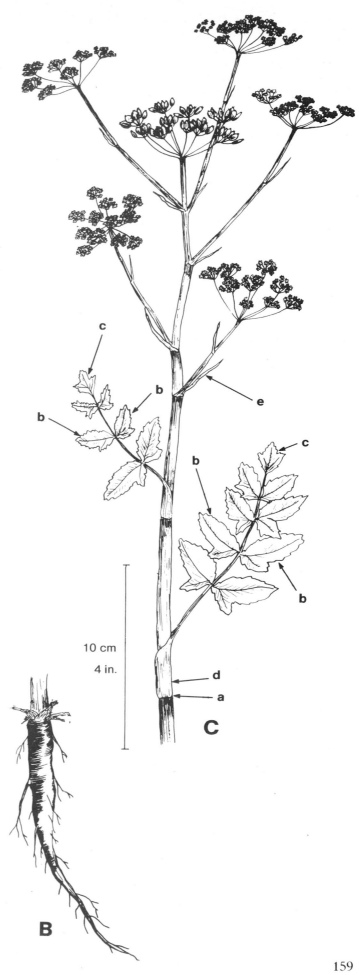

159

DOGBANE FAMILY (Apocynaceae)

Spreading dogbane, *Apocynum androsaemifolium* L., (Figure 132A, B, Plate 94) [APCAN, apocyn à feuilles d'androseme, Indian hemp, fausse herbe à la puce] Perennial, reproducing by seed and by spreading underground rhizomes. **Stems** erect or leaning, occasionally unbranched but usually repeatedly branched in the upper part, 20 - 75 cm (8 - 30 in.) high, slender, smooth, often reddish; **leaves** opposite (2 per node), oblong to ovate, often drooping, on short stalks (a); upper surface bright to dark green, undersurface lighter green to whitish-green and finely hairy at least along the mid-vein, young leaves at ends of branches distinctly whitish; **flowers** (b) in branched clusters at ends of stems and small branches; calyx lobes short and triangular; corolla whitish to pinkish, bell-shaped, 6 - 10 mm (¼ - 2/5 in.) long; **seedpods** (c) usually in pairs, 7 - 20 cm (3 - 10 in.) long, thin, pencil-like but more tapered towards the tip, straight or slightly curved, splitting lengthwise with a single slit to release the small, slender **seeds**, each with a long, white, silky parachute. All parts of the plant contain milky juice. Flowers from June to August.

Spreading dogbane is a native plant that occurs throughout Ontario in pastures, edges of woodlands, waste areas, fields and roadsides, usually in dry areas or on shallow soils.

It is distinguished by its slender somewhat fleshy appearance, its leaves opposite, short-stalked (a), often drooping, undersurface slightly hairy and lighter green, the younger ones whitish-green; its clusters of pinkish flowers (b) usually 6 mm (¼ in.) or longer, its pencil-like seedpods (c), and milky juice.

Indian hemp, *Apocynum cannabinum* L., (not illustrated) [APCCA, apocyn chanvrin, Dogbane, chanvre du Canada] Very similar to Spreading dogbane but often grows up to 1 - 1.5 m (40 - 60 in.) high, usually has broader ovate to elliptic leaves on longer stalks and its whitish or greenish-white flowers are usually less than 5 mm (1/5 in.) long. Indian hemp flowers at about the same time as Spreading dogbane and occupies similar habitats but is not as common, and is found mainly in southern Ontario. **Both Spreading dogbane and Indian hemp may be poisonous to livestock.**

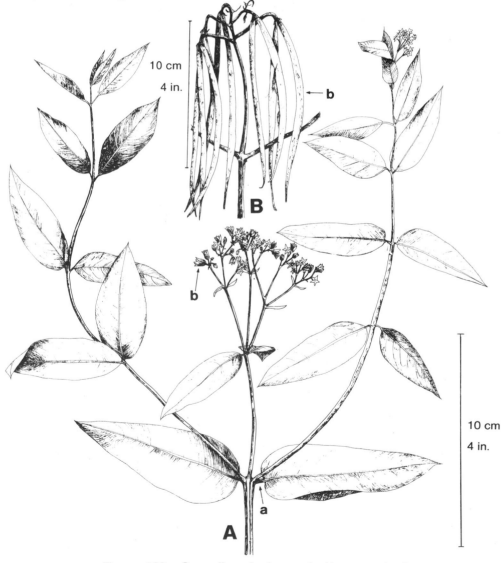

10 cm
4 in.

10 cm
4 in.

Figure 132. **Spreading dogbane** A. Upper part of flowering plant. B. Cluster of seedpods. (Cont'd.)

Clasping-leaved dogbane, *Apocynum sibiricum* Jacq., (Figure 132C, Plate 95) [APCVE, apocyn à feuilles embrassantes, Indian hemp, Prairie dogbane, chanvre sauvage] resembles both Spreading dogbane and Indian hemp and before flowering is easily confused with Common milkweed. Perennial from deeply penetrating and widely spreading coarse roots (d), these often 20 - 30 cm (8 - 12 in.) below the surface; **stems** coarse, erect, up to 1 m (40 in.) tall, arising from buds (e) on the roots; the main stem with branches throughout its length, smooth and hairless, green or with a slight pinkish cast; **leaves** usually opposite (f) but occasionally alternate (g), mostly sessile or with very short petioles (usually not more than 3 - 5 mm, ⅛ - 1/5 in. long), up to 5 cm (2 in.) wide and 12 cm (4¾ in.) long or sometimes larger, oblong to broadly elliptic with a somewhat abruptly pointed tip and a broadly rounded to heart-shaped base, smooth and hairless on both surfaces, the undersurface lighter green than the upper; the basal lobes of the larger leaves somewhat clasping the stem; **inflorescence, flowers** and **seedpods** similar to those of Spreading dogbane except that the calyx lobes of Clasping-leaved dogbane are narrow and 3 - 5 times longer than wide, and its corolla is white and usually only 3 - 6 mm (⅛ - ¼ in.) long. All parts of the plant contain milky juice. Flowers from July to September.

Clasping-leaved dogbane is also a native plant with much the same distribution and abundance as Spreading dogbane and **may also be poisonous to livestock.**

It is distinguished from both Spreading dogbane and Indian hemp by the lower leaves on its main stem and lower branches having heart-shaped bases that more or less clasp the stem, and the petioles of all leaves being very short or almost absent; and, from Spreading dogbane by the undersides of its leaves being virtually hairless, even along the midribs, as well as by its smaller white flowers having very narrow sepals. It is distinguished from Common milkweed by its lighter green leaves having abruptly pointed tips and being virtually hairless (those of milkweed being somewhat bluish-green, more rounded at the tip, and finely velvety hairy on the undersurface); by its loosely branching inflorescence (not an umbel) with small white flowers, and by its pencil-thin seedpods.

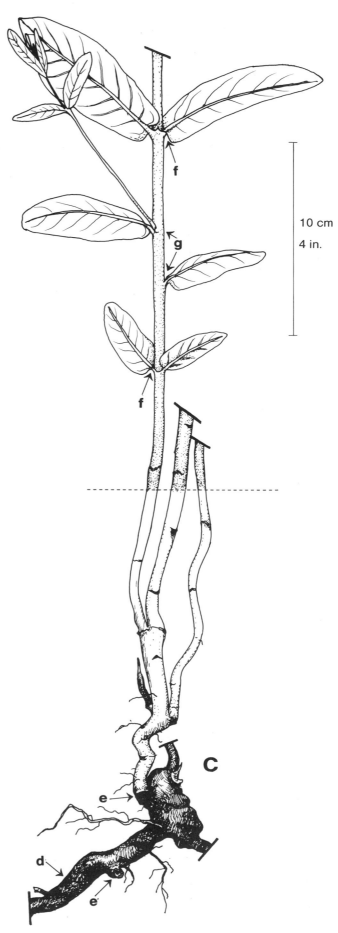

10 cm
4 in.

Figure 132. (Cont'd.) **Clasping-leaved dogbane** C. 3 shoots from a deep, coarse perennial root (dotted line represents ground surface), and leaves on lower portion of 1 shoot.

MILKWEED FAMILY (Asclepiadaceae)

Swamp milkweed, *Asclepias incarnata* L., (Figure 133) [ASCIN, asclépiade incarnate] Perennial, reproducing by seed and possibly by rhizomes. **Stems** erect, stout, 30 - 150 cm (12 - 60 in.) high, with little milky juice and few, if any, hairs; **leaves** opposite, rather numerous, lanceolate to elliptic, 4.5 - 20 cm (1¾ - 8 in.) long with fine veins clearly visible on the underside; **inflorescence** broad, usually formed from several umbels (a) of flowers; **flowers** (b) pink to rose-purple (rarely whitish), similar to those of Common milkweed but more slender; **fruits** slender pods (C) with elongated tips, rusty-green, splitting lengthwise at maturity; **seeds** brown, flat, with winged margins and tufts of long, silky, white hair. Flowers from June to August.

Swamp milkweed is found in swamps, ditches and other wet areas in woods, fields and roadsides in southern and central Ontario. **It is considered poisonous to livestock.**

It is distinguished from other milkweeds by its numerous, slender leaves, its pink to rose-purple flowers and its slender, non-warty pods, and from other narrow-leaved plants by its smooth stems, slender, opposite leaves and somewhat milky juice.

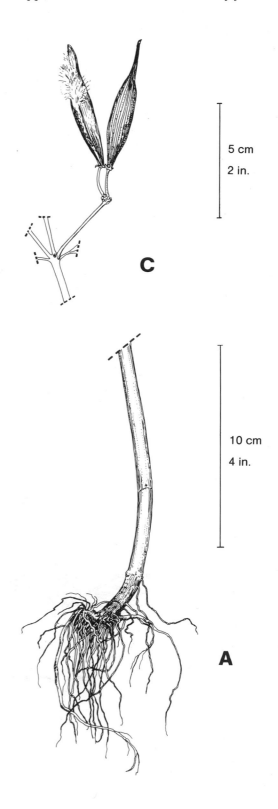

Figure 133. **Swamp milkweed** A. Base of plant. B. Flowering stem with 10 simple umbels. C. Two seedpods from 2 flowers of 1 umbel.

Common milkweed, *Asclepias syriaca* L., (Figure 134, Plate 96) [ASCSY, asclépiade de Syrie, cotonnier, petit-cochon] Perennial, reproducing by seed and by horizontally spreading underground roots which produce new leafy stems. **Stems** erect, 1 - 2 m (3 - 6½ ft) high, stout, unbranched or sometimes with 1 or 2 branches near the top, usually several stems close together from the underground root system; **leaves** opposite (2 per node) or whorled (3 or more per node), oblong with a rounded or tapered base and a rounded to somewhat pointed tip, without teeth, underside covered with fine velvety hair, upper surface usually without hair and deeper green; **flowers** in dense, nearly spherical clusters or umbels at tip of stem and from axils of upper leaves, each flower 8 -10 mm (¼ - 2/5 in.) across, greenish to purplish or whitish, with 5 thin sepals and 5 larger petal lobes (a) bent back along the flower stalk and an unusual arrangement of 5 hoods and horns forming a crown or "corona" (b) around the top of each flower. The flowers are uniquely adapted for insect pollination, having waxy pollen in tiny wishbone-shaped structures which hook onto an insect's leg but come off when transferred to the flower of a different plant. **Fruits** (B) at first green, fleshy,

7 - 10 cm (2½ - 4 in.) long and ¼ to ½ as wide, covered with soft, warty protuberances (c), later turning brown, splitting lengthwise along a single opening and releasing numerous seeds; usually only 1 or 2 (rarely up to 5) seedpods develop from the many flowers of a single flower cluster; **seed** flat, oval, with a tuft of long silky hair at one end. The whole plant, root, stem, leaves, flowers and fruit, contain abundant, thick, white, milky juice. Flowers from mid-June to August, and matures seed from August to October.

Common milkweed occurs throughout southern Ontario in pastures, meadows, waste places, roadsides and cultivated land. It is especially common in the Manitoulin Islands and the east-central portions of southern Ontario, but it seems to be increasing in most other portions of the province as well. **Other species of milkweed have been found to be highly toxic to livestock, and circumstantial evidence suggests Common milkweed may, under some circumstances, also be toxic.**

It is distinguished by its pairs of broad, oval, softly hairy leaves, umbels of purplish to whitish flowers with their peculiar arrangement of parts, and the large, thick, softly warty (c) seedpods (B).

Green milkweed, *Asclepias viridiflora* Raf., (not illustrated) [ASCVI, asclépiade à fleurs vertes] Similar to Common milkweed but with slender stems, nearly linear leaves usually less than 2.5 cm (1 in.) wide but up to 20 cm (8 in.) long and small, spherical umbels about 4 cm (1½ in.) in diameter on very short lateral stalks from upper leaf axils, followed by 1 to 3 slender, smooth seedpods. Flowers in June and July. Green milkweed is a native plant on coarse soils in southwestern Ontario.

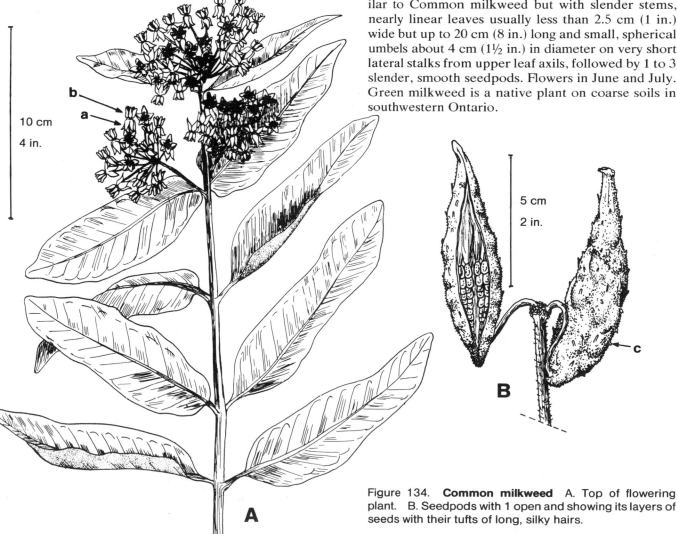

Figure 134. **Common milkweed** A. Top of flowering plant. B. Seedpods with 1 open and showing its layers of seeds with their tufts of long, silky hairs.

163

Whorled milkweed, *Asclepias verticillata* L., (Figure 135) [ASCVE, asclépiade verticillée] Perennial, reproducing only by seed. **Stems** erect, 20 - 90 cm (8 - 36 in.) high, sparingly branched in the upper part, slender, 1 or several from a cluster of fibrous **roots**; bases of old stems often persisting (a); **leaves** very narrow, in whorls of 3 to 6 at each node of the stem; flowers and seedpods (b) similar to Common milkweed but the clusters are smaller and fewer-flowered, **flowers** smaller and greenish, and the **seedpods** smaller, thinner, and lacking the soft, warty bumps. Flowers from July to September.

Whorled milkweed occurs in dry open areas in pastures, around woods, and along roadsides in the western portion of southern Ontario. **It is poisonous to livestock.**

It is distinguished by its slender, erect stems with whorls of 3 - 6 narrow leaves, its flowers in umbels and all plant parts containing a milky juice.

Figure 135. **Whorled milkweed**

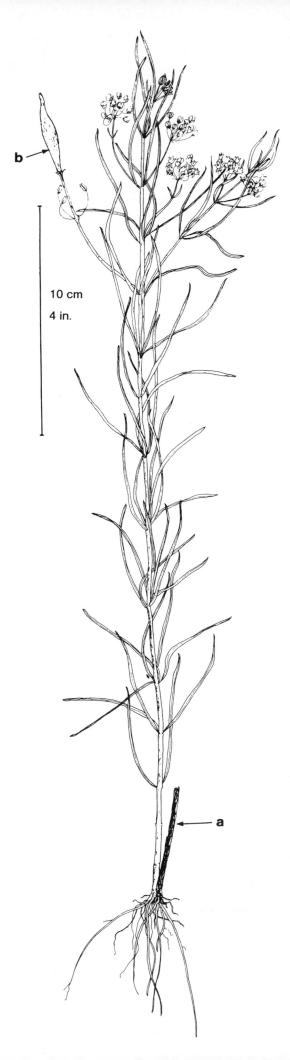

10 cm

4 in.

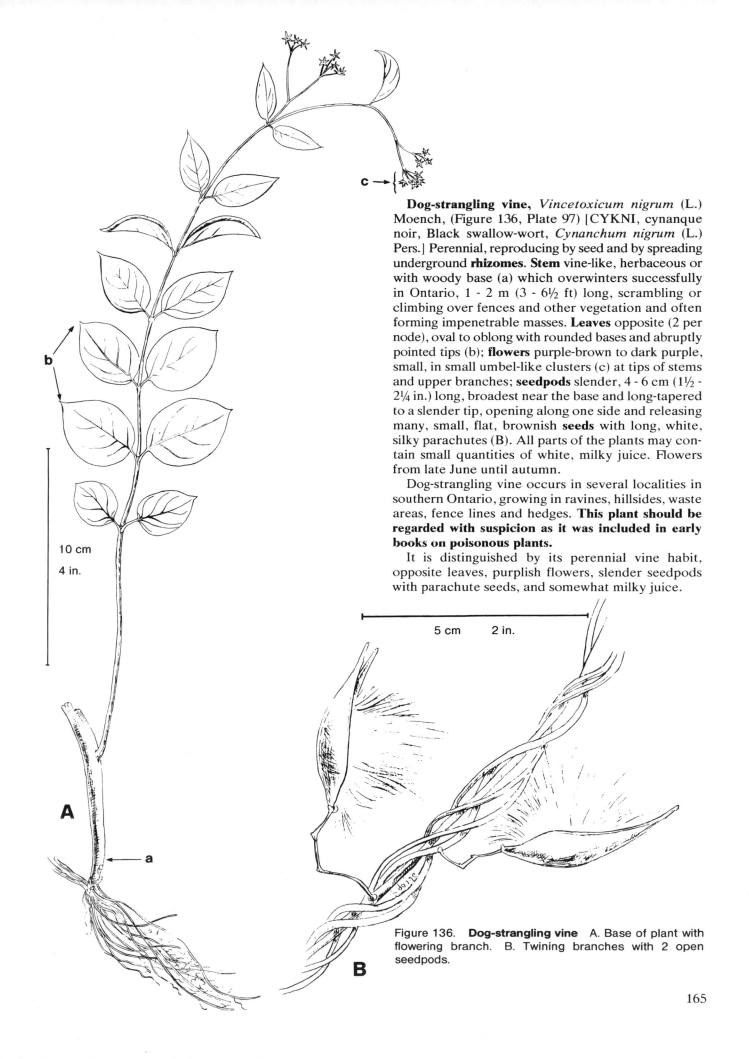

Dog-strangling vine, *Vincetoxicum nigrum* (L.) Moench, (Figure 136, Plate 97) [CYKNI, cynanque noir, Black swallow-wort, *Cynanchum nigrum* (L.) Pers.] Perennial, reproducing by seed and by spreading underground **rhizomes. Stem** vine-like, herbaceous or with woody base (a) which overwinters successfully in Ontario, 1 - 2 m (3 - 6½ ft) long, scrambling or climbing over fences and other vegetation and often forming impenetrable masses. **Leaves** opposite (2 per node), oval to oblong with rounded bases and abruptly pointed tips (b); **flowers** purple-brown to dark purple, small, in small umbel-like clusters (c) at tips of stems and upper branches; **seedpods** slender, 4 - 6 cm (1½ - 2¼ in.) long, broadest near the base and long-tapered to a slender tip, opening along one side and releasing many, small, flat, brownish **seeds** with long, white, silky parachutes (B). All parts of the plants may contain small quantities of white, milky juice. Flowers from late June until autumn.

Dog-strangling vine occurs in several localities in southern Ontario, growing in ravines, hillsides, waste areas, fence lines and hedges. **This plant should be regarded with suspicion as it was included in early books on poisonous plants.**

It is distinguished by its perennial vine habit, opposite leaves, purplish flowers, slender seedpods with parachute seeds, and somewhat milky juice.

10 cm
4 in.

5 cm   2 in.

Figure 136. **Dog-strangling vine** A. Base of plant with flowering branch. B. Twining branches with 2 open seedpods.

165

MORNING-GLORY FAMILY (Convolvulaceae)

Field bindweed, *Convolvulus arvensis* L., (Figure 137, Plate 98) [CONAR, liseron des champs, European bindweed, Small-flowered morning-glory, Wild morning-glory, liseron] Perennial, reproducing by seed and by an extensively spreading and very persistent, whitish underground **root** system (a). **Stems** slender, smooth or pubescent or very finely hairy, usually twining or curling (b), prostrate or climbing on any nearby object; **leaves** alternate (1 per node), with short or long stalks, very variable in form but commonly arrowhead-shaped with 2 basal lobes (c) and smooth margins, sometimes long and narrow (d), or broader (e) or nearly round except for the 2 basal lobes; **flowers** on long stalks (f) from axils of leaves, always with a pair of small, narrow, green bracts (g) on the flower stalk some distance below the flower; flowers with 5 small green sepals (h) and a white to pinkish funnel-shaped corolla 2 - 2.5 cm (4/5 - 1 in.) in diameter when fully opened; **seedpods** roundish, about 5 mm (1/5 in.) long containing 1 to 4 **seeds** each of which is about 3 mm (⅛ in.) long, pear-shaped and 3-angled with 1 side rounded and with tiny grayish bumps. Flowers from mid-June until autumn.

Field bindweed occurs throughout Ontario in cultivated fields, gardens, lawns, roadsides, and waste places.

It is distinguished from Hedge bindweed (page 167), which also has perennial roots, by its smaller leaves, flowers usually not over 2.5 cm (1 in.) in diameter, and the 2 small bracts (g) near the middle of the flower stalk (f), these tiny bracts never enclosing the base of the flower. It is distinguished from Wild buckwheat (page 58) by being perennial with extensively creeping, white, cord-like, fleshy roots (a) which produce new shoots and form dense patches; by its white or pinkish, funnel-shaped flowers with long stalks, and by the absence of an ocrea (membranous sheath) surrounding the stem at the base of each leafstalk [see (a) in Figure 36C].

Figure 137. **Field bindweed** A. Plant reproducing from horizontally spreading root. B. Portion of flowering stem twining around an erect support.

Hedge bindweed, *Convolvulus sepium* L., (Figure 138) [CAGSE, liseron des haies, Hedge morning-glory, Large morning-glory, Wild morning-glory, gloire du matin, grand liseron] Perennial reproducing by seed and by rhizomes. **Stems** to 3 m (10 ft) long, twining or creeping with extensive branching, smooth or rarely somewhat hairy; **leaves** arrowhead-shaped with very prominent basal lobes (a) more or less parallel to the petiole; 4 - 15 cm (1½ - 6 in.) long, with long petioles (b); **flowers** on long (5 - 15 cm, 2 - 6 in.) pedicels (c) from leaf axils; the base of each flower enclosed by a pair of leaf-like bracts (d) 1 - 3.5 cm (2/5 - 1½ in.) long and half as wide; sepals (e) 5, green, usually smaller than the 2 bracts; corolla pink or white, trumpet-shaped, 4 - 8 cm (1½ - 3½ in.) long and nearly as wide; **seedpod** nearly spherical and containing 1 to 4 angular dark brown to black **seeds**. Flowers from May to September.

Hedge bindweed is a native plant in Ontario and is found in edges of woods, waste places, fencerows and occasionally in cultivated fields.

It is distinguished by its trailing or twining stems, its large, single, trumpet-shaped flowers on long pedicels and the 2 large bracts that enclose the base of the flower.

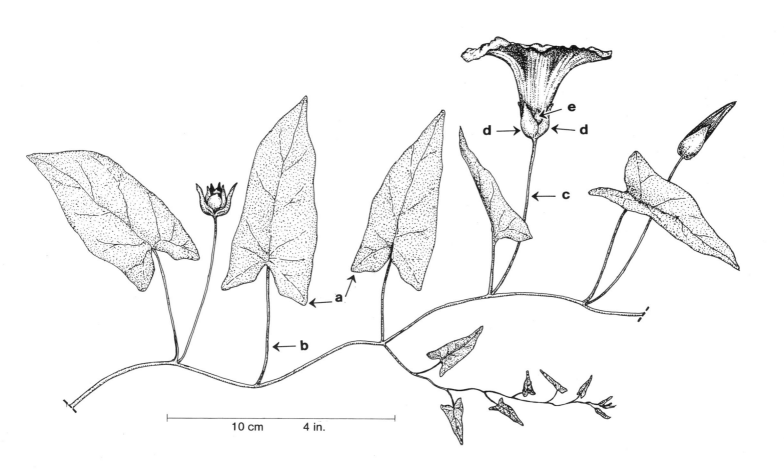

Figure 138. **Hedge bindweed** Portion of flowering and fruiting stem.

167

Dodder, *Cuscuta* spp., (Figure 139, Plate 99) [CVCSS, cuscute] Annual, reproducing only by seed. The Dodders are parasitic plants with leafless, thread-like, orange or reddish **stems** twisting and twining (a) around other plants (b), often forming dense stringy masses. Being totally without chlorophyll, they must obtain all of their growth requirements (water, minerals, carbohydrates) from other living green plants around which they wind and become attached (c). Dodder seed germinates in the soil and sends up a slender, thread-like, orange or reddish stem without any cotyledons (seed leaves). This slender stem sways or rotates slowly until it touches the stem or leaf of another plant and begins to wind around it. If this plant is susceptible to attack by Dodder (and many are not), the Dodder stem immediately begins to form **haustoria** (tiny sucker-like roots). These penetrate the tissues of the host plant and extract all of the Dodder's subsequent growth requirements from it. If the seedling is unable to contact a susceptible host, it soon withers and dies. Once attached to a susceptible host, the lower end withers and breaks its connection with the ground, while the upper end of the stem grows rapidly, branching and rebranching. Numerous small clusters of tiny whitish **flowers** (d) form along these twining stems from July to September. Each flower is followed by a small, globular **seedpod** (e) with up to 8 **seeds**.

It is distinguished by its thread-like, yellowish or orange stems that occasionally form masses of tangled threads as they twine and sprawl over other plants. On susceptible plants they curl around the individual stems and produce root-like haustoria that penetrate inside. It is also distinguished by its small, dense clusters of white flowers followed by small, round seedpods.

Several species of Dodder are native to Ontario, but they occur chiefly in moist or swampy areas where they parasitize native plants. **Field dodder,** *Cuscuta campestris* Yunker, (Figure 139) [CVCCA, cuscute des champs, cuscute de la vigne], is the most important of these as a parasite on agricultural crops, attacking carrots, petunias, tomatoes, etc.

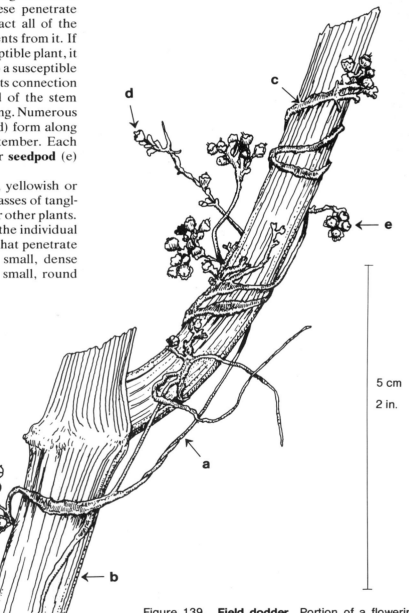

5 cm

2 in.

Figure 139. **Field dodder** Portion of a flowering and fruiting plant tightly twined around a susceptible host. Enlarged segments of the dodder stem indicate where its haustoria have penetrated the tissues of the host.

BORAGE FAMILY (Boraginaceae)

Small bugloss, *Lycopsis arvensis* L., (Figure 140) [LYCAR, lycopside des champs, lycopsis des champs, petite buglosse] Annual, reproducing by seed. **Stems** erect, 10 - 60 cm (4 - 24 in.) high; **leaves** 4 - 8 cm (1½ - 3 in.) long, lanceolate, their margins entire or with slightly irregular teeth; stems and leaves harsh and bristly due to scattered hairs 1 - 2.5 mm (1/25 - 1/10 in.) long with bulbous bases. **Flowers** in dense, short, leafy clusters (a) at the ends of short, upper branches; the clusters elongating into raceme-like inflorescences at maturity; corolla blue; the 5 united petals forming a slender tube (b) terminating in 5 small rounded lobes; the tube and lobes 6 - 8 mm (¼ - 1/3 in.) long and 5 mm (1/5 in.) wide; each flower producing 1 to 4 **nutlets**, each containing 1 **seed**; the nutlets very hard, somewhat triangular, coarsely ridged and pebbled on the surface and beige to brown in colour. Flowers from June to September.

Small bugloss is a native plant of Europe and occurs in dry or sandy soils and waste places in Ontario.

It is distinguished by its harsh, bristly-hairy stems and leaves (similar to Blueweed, Figure 141), its small blue tubular flowers with 5 small, rounded lobes, and its beige to brown, coarsely wrinkled nutlets without hooked bristles.

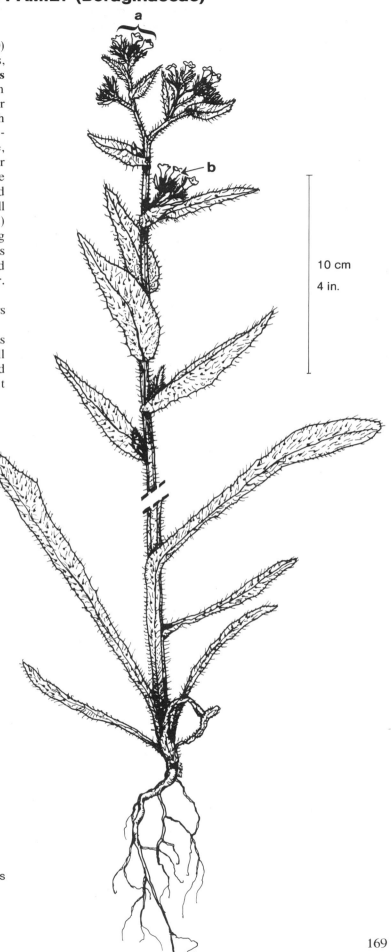

10 cm
4 in.

Figure 140. **Small bugloss** Basal and upper portions of a flowering plant.

Figure 141. Blueweed

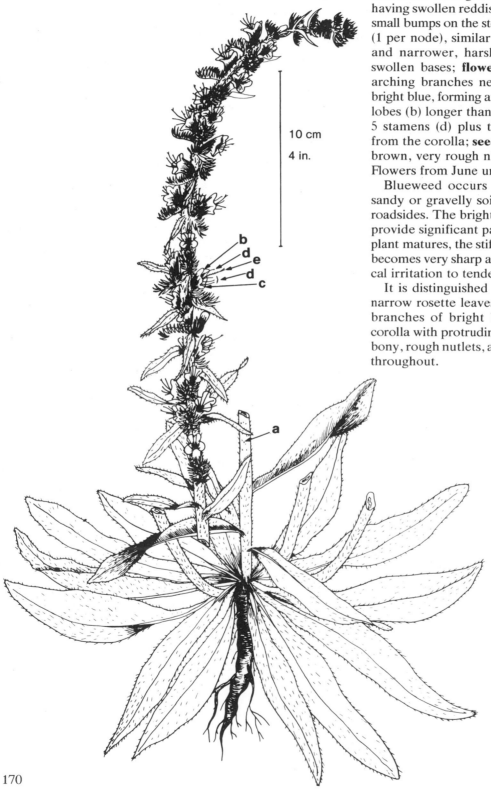

10 cm
4 in.

b
d e
d c
a

Blueweed, *Echium vulgare* L., (Figure 141, Plate 100) [EHIVU, vipérine, Blue devil, Blue-thistle, Viper's bugloss, vipérine vulgaire, herbe aux vipères] Biennial, occasionally annual or short-lived perennial, reproducing only by seed. First-year plant producing a **rosette** of long, narrow, harshly hairy leaves and a deeply penetrating fleshy **taproot**; flowering stems produced in the second year, or rarely in the first year and the plant acting as an annual; **stems** erect 30 - 90 cm (12 - 36 in.) high, 1 to several from each taproot, harshly hairy with a mixture of a few, scattered, long, stiff hairs among dense short hair, the longer hair having swollen reddish or blackish bases (a) visible as small bumps on the stem surface; **stem leaves** alternate (1 per node), similar to the basal leaves but smaller and narrower, harshly hairy, most hair stiff with swollen bases; **flowers** numerous in 1-sided, short, arching branches near the top of the stem; petals bright blue, forming an irregular corolla with the upper lobes (b) longer than the lower ones (c) and 4 of the 5 stamens (d) plus the hairy stigma (e) protruding from the corolla; **seeds** in the form of 4 hard, gray or brown, very rough nutlets about 3 mm (⅛ in.) long. Flowers from June until autumn.

Blueweed occurs throughout Ontario in coarse sandy or gravelly soil in pastures, waste places and roadsides. The bright blue flowers are attractive and provide significant pasture for honeybees. When the plant matures, the stiff hair of stem, leaves, and sepals becomes very sharp and hard and causes severe physical irritation to tender skin.

It is distinguished by its deep thick taproot, long narrow rosette leaves, erect stem with short 1-sided branches of bright blue flowers, unequally lobed corolla with protruding stamens, its clusters of 4 hard, bony, rough nutlets, and by being harshly rough-hairy throughout.

Corn gromwell, *Lithospermum arvense* L., (Figure 142) [LITAR, grémil des champs, Bastard alkanet, buglosse des champs] Annual, winter annual or biennial, reproducing only by seed. **Stems** slender, 9 - 80 cm (3¾ - 32 in.) high, often branched at the base, arising from a small **taproot** (a); **leaves** alternate, linear or lanceolate, 1.3 - 5 cm (½ - 2 in.) long, 1 - 15 mm (1/25 - 3/5 in.) wide, with a distinct midrib (b) but no obvious lateral veins; both stems and leaves densely covered with short, stiff, ascending hairs, about 0.5 mm (1/50 in.) long, giving a rough texture; **flowers** (c) solitary in the axils of the crowded upper leaves, white or bluish-white, tubular, 2 - 8 mm (1/12 - 1/3 in.) long and 1 - 5 mm (1/25 - 1/5 in.) wide; **nutlets** 3 mm (⅛ in.) long, ovoid, dull, pale brown to gray, deeply wrinkled and pitted. Flowers from May to June.

Introduced from Eurasia, Corn gromwell is found in waste places, fields and open woods and beside roads and railways in south-central Ontario.

It is distinguished by its linear to lanceolate, alternate leaves without lateral veins, its stem and leaves roughened with short, stiff ascending hairs, its small, tubular white or bluish-white flowers and its rough-wrinkled, gray-brown, dull nutlets.

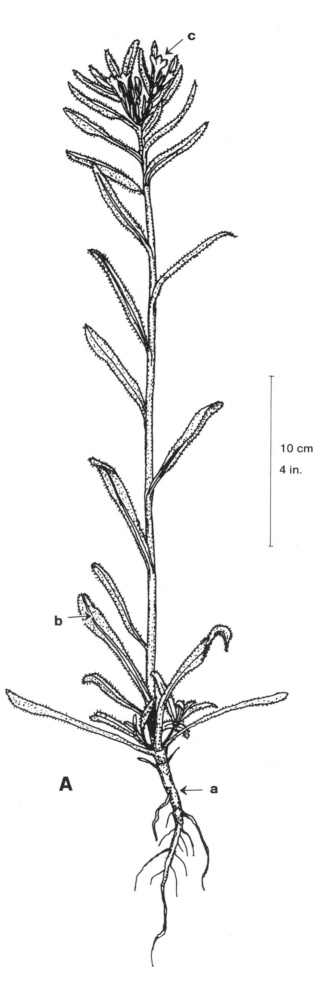

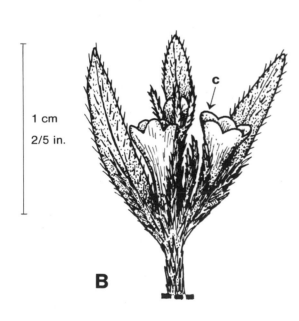

Figure 142. **Corn gromwell** A. Plant. B. Tip of a branch with 2 open flowers and a flower bud.

171

Hound's-tongue, *Cynoglossum officinale* L., (Figure 143) [CYWOF, cynoglosse officinale, langue-dechien] Biennial, reproducing only by seed. First-year plant producing a rosette of leaves and a thick, deep **taproot**; flowering stem rising in the second year; **stem** 30 - 120 cm (1 - 4 ft) high, branching in the upper part, soft-hairy; rosette **leaves** soft and velvety, narrowly elliptic or broadest towards the end, 10 - 30 cm (4 - 12 in.) long and 2 - 5 cm (1 - 2 in.) wide with rather long stalks; stem leaves shorter, oblong or broadest near the stalkless base (where they are attached to the stem) and tapered towards the tip, not toothed; **flowers** in racemes from the upper leaf axils; sepals 5, united, with triangular lobes forming a star-shaped calyx (a); corolla reddish-purple or maroon, cup-shaped and about 10 mm (2/5 in.) across; **fruit** of 4 nutlets ("seeds") (b), rounded-triangular with a somewhat flattened upper surface and roughened by numerous very short barbed prickles. Flowers from late May until August.

Hound's-tongue occurs in southern Ontario in pastures, edges of woods, waste places and roadsides.

It is distinguished by its rosette of large, softly hairy leaves; maroon flowers; and cluster of 4 rough-prickly, flattish nutlets (b).

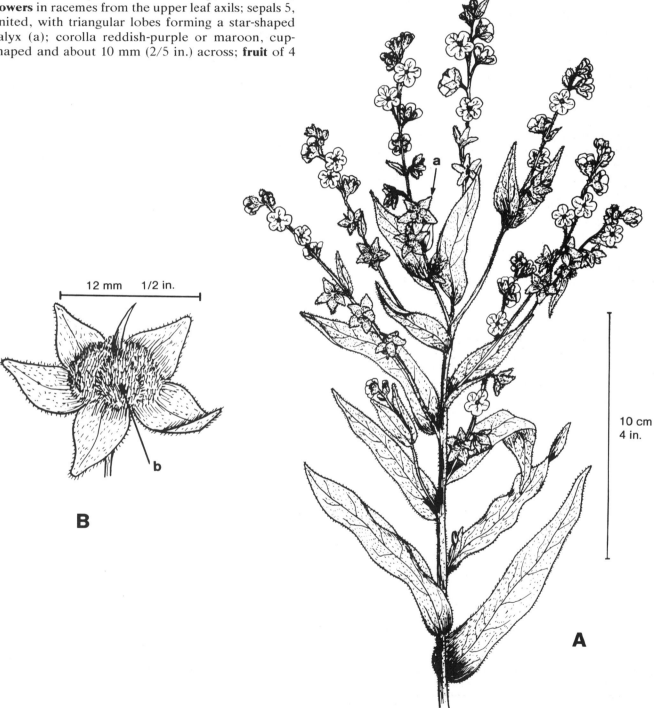

Figure 143. **Hound's-tongue** A. Top of flowering plant. B. Fruiting cluster of 4 nutlets ("seeds").

172

MINT FAMILY (Labiatae)

Germander, *Teucrium canadense* L., (Figure 144) [TEUCA, germandrée du Canada, Wood-sage, American germander, germandrée] Perennial, reproducing by seeds and by rhizomes. **Stems** erect, 15 - 100 cm (6 - 40 in.) high, stiff, hairy, square in cross-section, usually arising from the upturned ends of rhizomes (a); **rhizomes** (b) nearly white, producing numerous roots (c) from their prominent nodes (d) and varying from slender to nearly as thick as one's little finger; the thicker ones succulent and brittle; **leaves** opposite, on petioles 5 - 15 mm (1/5 - 3/5 in.) long, thick, lanceolate to narrowly elliptic, sometimes with margins nearly parallel, 0.7 - 13 cm (¼ - 5¼ in.) long and 0.2 - 6 cm (1/12 - 2½ in.) wide, dark green on the upper surface, lighter green below, somewhat hairy on both surfaces; margins irregularly toothed, the teeth varying from fine to coarse; **inflorescence** spike-like with crowded flowers at the ends of the main stem and upper branches, 4 - 20 cm (1-3/5 - 8 in.) long; 1 or 2 flowers on each side of the stem at each node (e), rarely more; calyx (f) 6 - 9 mm (¼ - 3/8 in.), 5-lobed but 2-lipped; the 3 upper lobes wider and blunter than the 2 lower; corolla purplish, pink or creamy, 1 - 2 cm (2/5 - 4/5 in.) long and appearing as a single petal with a rounded end (g) and two small lobes (h) on each side near the base. Flowers from July to September.

Germander forms dense patches in poorly drained areas in fields in southwestern Ontario.

It is distinguished from most other plants with opposite leaves by its square stems, its thick, white, brittle rhizomes, and its spike-like inflorescence of pink to purplish or creamy flowers; and from other members of the Mint Family, all of which also have square stems and opposite leaves, by its lanceolate leaves frequently with somewhat parallel margins and by the unique shape of its corolla.

Figure 144. **Germander** A. Portion of underground rhizome system with the base of 1 aboveground shoot arising from it, and upper part of a flowering shoot. B. Tip of a flowering shoot with several open flowers showing their very irregular corollas.

173

Catnip, *Nepeta cataria* L., (Figure 145) [NEPCA, herbe à chat, chataire, népète chataire] Perennial, reproducing by seed and by very short underground **rhizomes**. **Stems** erect, 40 - 100 cm (16 - 40 in.) high, square, densely white-hairy; **leaves** opposite (2 per node) on different sides of the square stem at successive nodes, heart-shaped, longer than wide, densely covered with short, soft, white hair, especially on the underside; margins coarsely toothed, each tooth with rounded sides and a blunt point; petioles about half as long as leaf blades; **flowers** dull white, in dense, whorled clusters in axils of leaves near ends of stems and branches; calyx short, tubular, of 5 united sepals forming a short tube with 15 parallel veins and ending in 5 narrow, sharply pointed soft teeth; corolla dull white with purplish dots, formed from 5 united petals, 10 - 12 mm (2/5 - ½ in.) or sometimes longer and about 6 mm (¼ in.) wide, irregular, trumpet-shaped but 2-lipped at the end, the upper lip with 2 lobes (a), the lower lip with 3 lobes; each flower producing a cluster of 4 nutlets ("**seeds**") which are smooth, reddish-brown with 2 white spots at the lower end. All parts of the plant have a characteristic odour resembling mint, and the whole plant is frequently gray-green due to a dense covering of fine white hair. Flowers from July to September.

Catnip was widely cultivated throughout Ontario and has escaped from cultivation in all parts of the province so it now occurs in open forests, meadows, pastures, waste places, roadsides, around buildings and in gardens.

It is distinguished by its erect habit of growth, square stems, the opposite, stalked, coarsely toothed, heart-shaped leaves, its dense, whorled clusters of dull white flowers, its prominent trumpet-shaped 5-lobed corolla about 12 mm (½ in.) or longer, and its distinctive odour that is so attractive to cats.

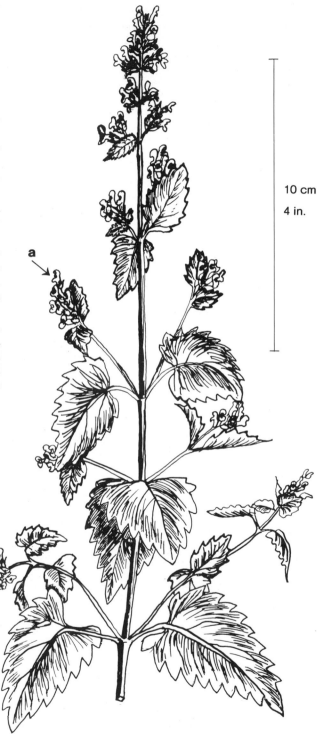

10 cm
4 in.

a

Figure 145. **Catnip**

174

Ground-ivy, *Glechoma hederacea* L., (Figure 146, Plate 101) [GLEHE, lierre terrestre, Creeping Charlie, Gill-over-the-ground, gléchome lierre, lierre-terrestre panaché] Perennial, reproducing by seed and by creeping stems. **Stems** prostrate, rooting at every node (a) which touches the ground, producing short, erect, leafy branches 10 - 30 cm (4 - 12 in.) high and slightly hairy; **leaves** opposite (2 per node), long-stalked, hairy, green or somewhat purplish; margins coarsely round-toothed to wavy-toothed; **flowers** 1 to several (usually in pairs) in axils of upper leaves; calyx short, tubular with 5 short, sharp, soft points; corolla blue-violet to purplish, about 10 - 23 mm (2/5 - 7/8 in.) long and 6 - 10 mm (¼ - 2/5 in.) wide, of 5 united petals, irregular, tubular, 2-lipped at the end, the upper lip with 2 shallow lobes (b) and the lower lip with 3 larger lobes

(c); each flower producing 4 tiny nutlets ("**seeds**"). The leaves and stems have a strong, disagreeable, almost rancid mint-like odour but the flowers are sweeter and they are sometimes used as a garnish when icing cakes. Flowers from late spring until autumn.

Ground-ivy occurs throughout Ontario but is much more common in the southern parts of the province, infesting gardens, roadsides, waste areas, pastures, open woods and occasionally edges of cultivated fields.

It is distinguished from other low-growing plants by its creeping square stems, opposite, long-stalked, rounded to kidney-shaped leaves with round or wavy teeth, prominent axillary blue to purplish flowers and strong, rather rancid, mint-like odour.

5 cm
2 in.

Figure 146. **Ground-ivy** Portion of a "creeping" stem lying on the ground surface, rooting from every node, as well as producing leaves and upright shoots from most nodes.

Heal-all, *Prunella vulgaris* L., (Figure 147, Plate 102) [PRUVU, prunelle vulgaire, Self-heal, prunelle, prunelle commune, herbe au charpentier, brunelle commune, brunelle vulgaire] Perennial, reproducing by seed and by somewhat creeping stems. **Stems** prostrate to nearly erect, 10 - 50 cm (4 - 20 in.) high, rooting at nodes (a) touching the soil, square, sharply ridged on the angles, rough-hairy; **leaves** opposite (2 per node), ovate to elliptic or round, the lower ones usually broader and with longer stalks, green or with a purplish cast; margins smooth or shallowly and irregularly toothed; **flowers** in dense spikes or head-like clusters at ends of stems (B), usually in 3's in axils of very broad ovate or kidney-shaped bracts (b); calyx a 10-veined tube ending in 1 broad, scoop-shaped upper tooth (c) and 4 thin, bristle-like lower teeth (d), often purplish; corolla blue-violet to purplish or rarely pinkish or whitish, 10 - 20 mm (2/5 - 4/5 in.) long, of 5 united petals, irregular, tubular, 2-lipped at the end, the upper lip (e) rounded and arched, the lower lip with 2 small side lobes (f) and 1 larger central

lobe (g); each flower producing 4 nutlets ("**seeds**"), these brownish to blackish, oval lengthwise but triangular in cross-section with 2 flat sides and the third rounded. Flowers from June to August.

Heat-all occurs both as a native plant and an introduced ornamental which has escaped from cultivation in most areas of Ontario. It is found in open woodland, meadows, pastures, waste areas, roadsides, lawns, and around buildings. Where subject to mowing or trampling such as in lawns or pastures, Heal-all will grow as a prostrate plant with stems rooting at nearly every node and producing only a few erect flowering branches; but where it grows without disturbance or in crowded situations, the stem may be erect and up to 50 cm (20 in.) high.

It is distinguished by its square stems, leaves opposite, stalked and with smooth or irregularly toothed margins, its compact head-like inflorescence with broad ovate or kidney-shaped bracts (b), green or purplish calyx having the 1 upper lobe (c) very broad, and its usually blue-violet flower with 2-lipped end.

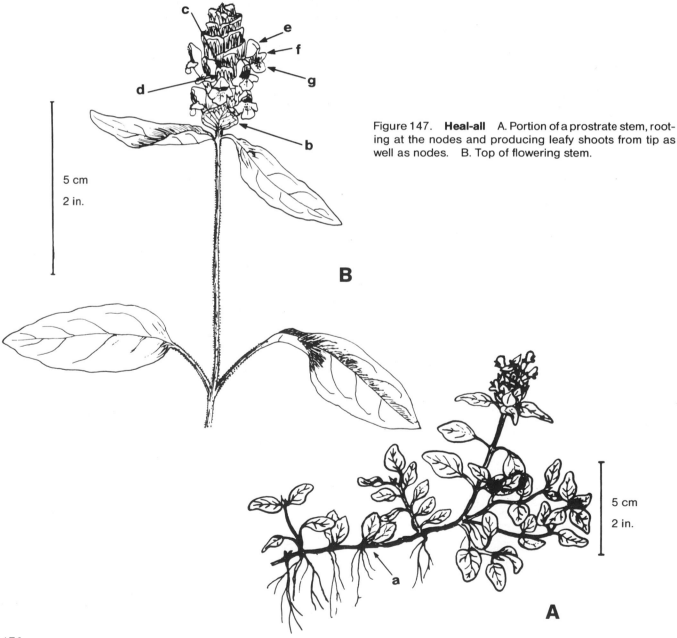

Figure 147. **Heal-all** A. Portion of a prostrate stem, rooting at the nodes and producing leafy shoots from tip as well as nodes. B. Top of flowering stem.

5 cm
2 in.

5 cm
2 in.

B

A

Hemp-nettle, *Galeopsis tetrahit* L., (Figure 148) [GAETE, ortie royale, Bee nettle, Dog nettle, Flowering nettle, chardonnet, galéopside à tige carrée] Annual, reproducing only by seed. **Stems** erect, 30 - 80 cm (12 - 32 in.) high, branched, square, usually swollen at the nodes (a), covered with rather harsh, straight, long, somewhat downward-pointing hair (b); **leaves** opposite (2 per node), ovate to elliptic with stretched-out tips (c), stalked, sparsely hairy, margins with rounded teeth, veins mostly ending in notches between the teeth; **flowers** in dense clusters in the axils of leaves near the ends of stems and branches; calyx short, tubular, 10-ribbed, ending in 5 equal, narrow, sharp, spine-like teeth (d) about 5 mm (1/5 in.) long; these very spiny when mature (e); corolla pinkish to light purplish or whitish, often variegated, and usually with 2 yellow spots, 12 - 23 mm (½ - ⅞ in.) long, of 5 united petals, irregular, tubular, 2-lipped at the end, the upper lip (f) 2-lobed (g), lower lip (h) 3-lobed (j), each flower producing 4 egg-shaped nutlets ("**seeds**"), narrowed and somewhat triangular towards the basal end, about 3 mm (⅛ in.) long and grayish-brown. Flowers from mid-July to mid-August.

Hemp-nettle occurs throughout Ontario, especially in central and northern areas, forming dense stands in grainfields and also present in seeded pastures, gardens, waste areas and along roadsides.

It is distinguished by being an annual with erect square stems covered with harsh downward-pointing hair (b), frequently with a prominent swelling (a) below each node, opposite leaves with stretched-out tips (c), leaf margins with rounded teeth, and dense clusters of pinkish or light purplish flowers with slender, sharp calyx lobes (d) which become hard and very spiny (e) at maturity.

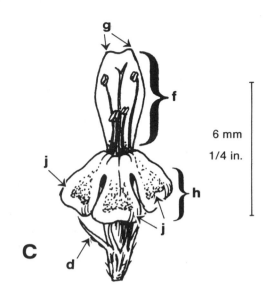

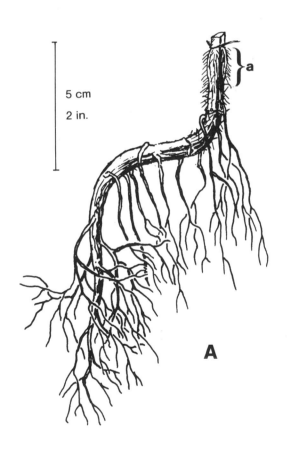

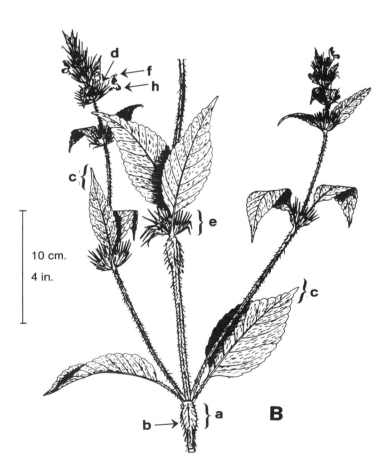

Figure 148. **Hemp-nettle** A. Base of plant. B. Portion of stem with 2 flowering branches. C. Flower.

Henbit, *Lamium amplexicaule* L., (Figure 149, Plate 103) [LAMAM, lamier amplexicaule, pain de poule] Annual or winter annual, reproducing only by seed. **Stems** erect, 10 - 40 cm (4 - 16 in.) high, much-branched near the base, the branches spreading and becoming erect, square, finely hairy; **leaves** opposite (2 per node), lower ones long-stalked (a), broad, rounded to somewhat heart-shaped with coarsely lobed or irregularly toothed margins; upper leaves stalkless, broad-based, more or less clasping the stem; **flowers** in clusters in axils of these broad, stalkless, upper leaves; calyx (b) small, tubular, 5-ribbed, with 5 small, sharp but soft teeth; corolla pinkish or purplish, 12 - 18 mm (½ - ¾ in.) long, of 5 united petals, irregular, tubular, 2-lipped at the end, the upper lip (c) arched and with a tuft of hair on the top but not lobed, lower lip (d) 2-lobed. Flowers in spring and early summer and occasionally again in late summer and autumn.

Henbit occurs throughout southern Ontario in gardens, waste places and roadsides.

It is distinguished by its annual, erect branching habit, its square stems, its opposite leaves, the lower ones long-stalked (a), the upper ones stalkless, broad, and clasping the stem, and its clusters of pinkish to purplish flowers in the axils of the broad upper leaves.

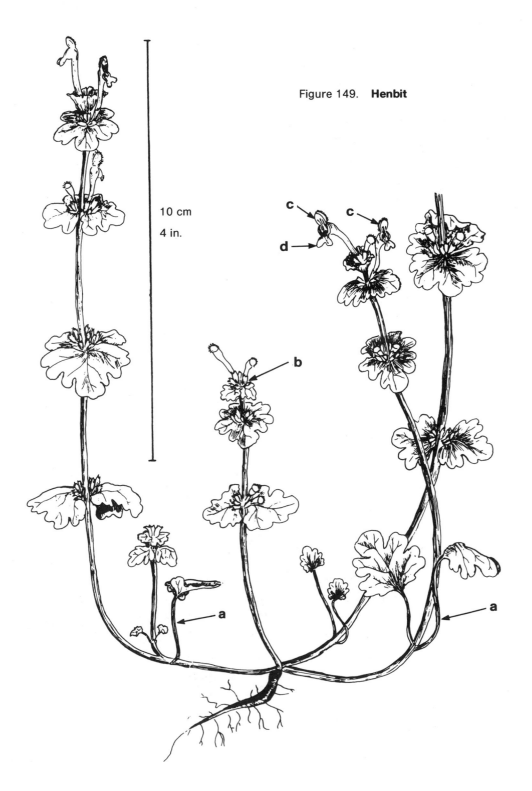

10 cm
4 in.

Figure 149. **Henbit**

178

Motherwort, *Leonurus cardiaca* L., (Figure 150, Plate 104) [LECCA, agripaume cardiaque, agripaume, herbe piquante] Perennial, reproducing only by seed. **Stems** erect, 40 - 180 cm (16 - 70 in.) high, square, somewhat hairy along the angles, branched, frequently several stems from 1 coarsely fibrous root crown; **leaves** opposite (2 per node), lower ones long-stalked, rounded in outline, palmately cleft into usually 5 or more main lobes which are coarsely or irregularly toothed, upper leaves on shorter stalks, smaller, and only 3- or 5-cleft; **flowers** in the axils of small upper leaves; calyx (B) tubular with 5 slender, sharp lobes, 3 pointing upwards (a) and 2 downwards (b), becoming hard, sharp, and spiny at maturity; the calyx breaking off and clinging as a bur to clothing or fur; corolla pink to pale purple or whitish, upper lip conspicuously white-hairy, not lobed, lower lip 3-lobed; each flower producing 4 nutlets ("**seeds**") which are triangular, dark brown and hairy at the apex. Flowers from June to August.

Motherwort occurs throughout southern Ontario in yards, waste places, fence lines, and roadsides.

It is distinguished in non-flowering stages by its palmately lobed leaves (almost like maple leaves) in geometrically precise arrangement in 4 vertical planes around the square stem. Flowering and fruiting plants are distinguished by their palmately lobed leaves, clusters of pinkish flowers in leaf axils, and the calyx of each flower with 5 very sharp lobes, 3 pointing upwards and 2 downwards, these becoming spiny bur-like clusters on mature and dry stems.

Figure 150. **Motherwort** A. Top of plant before flowers open. B. Mature calyx with its 5 slender, spiny-tipped lobes.

179

Marsh hedge-nettle, *Stachys palustris* L., (Figure 151, Plate 105) [STAPA, épiaire des marais, Woundwort, stachyde des marais] Perennial, reproducing by seeds and by rhizomes. **Stems** erect, 20 - 100 cm (8 - 40 in.) high, simple or loosely branching, square in cross-section, pubescent on the sides as well as on the angles, arising from upturned ends of rhizomes (a); **rhizomes** (b) creeping, whitish, often much-branched, occasionally with thickened, succulent, brittle sections (c); **leaves** opposite, stalkless (d) or on petioles usually not over 3 mm (⅛ in.) long; the main leaves lanceolate to elliptic, 3.3 - 15 cm (1¼ - 6 in.) long and 1 - 4 cm (2/5 - 1½ in.) wide, hairy on both surfaces, and margins with somewhat rounded teeth; **inflorescence** 2.5 - 25 cm (1 - 10 in.) long, composed of whorls of flowers in axils of upper leaves (B) and becoming spike-like towards the ends of branches (similar to Germander, Figure 144), each whorl usually with 6 flowers; calyx short-hairy, 6 - 9 mm (¼ - ⅜ in.) long, the 5 lobes about equal and narrowed to fine, almost hair-like points (e); corolla rose-purple, mottled with paler and darker tones, 11 - 16 mm (½ - ¾ in.) long, hairy, with the large 3-lobed lower lip (f) longer than the 2-lobed upper lip (g); each flower producing 4 hard **"seeds"** or nutlets; these dark brown, 1.8 - 2.2 mm (1/12 in.) long x 1.2 - 1.8 mm (1/20 - 1/15 in.) broad. Flowers from June to September.

Marsh hedge-nettle occurs as both naturalized and native species in Ontario. The weedy form usually occurs in dense patches in poorly drained areas of fields.

It is distinguished from most other plants with opposite leaves by its square stems, its thick, white, brittle rhizomes, and its spike-like inflorescence of rose-purple flowers; and from other members of the Mint Family, all of which also have square stems and opposite leaves, by its thick, brittle, whitish rhizomes, its leaves having petioles not more than 3 mm (⅛ in.) long, its distinctly hairy leaves, its inflorescence of mostly 6-flowered whorls and the corolla being distinctly 2-lipped.

Figure 151. **Marsh hedge-nettle** A. Leafy shoot from the upturned end of a fleshy horizontal underground rhizome.   B. Tip of flowering stem.

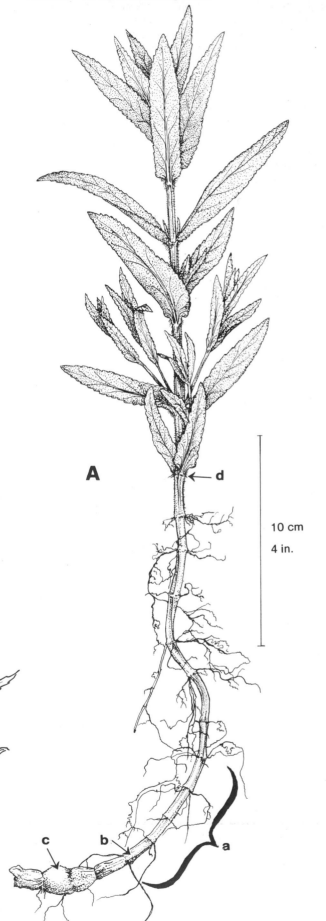

10 cm
4 in.

5 cm
2 in.

180

Field mint, *Mentha arvensis* L., (Figure 152) [MENAR, menthe des champs, menthe du Canada] Perennial, reproducing by rhizomes (a) and by seed. **Stems** erect or ascending, 15 - 80 cm (6 - 32 in.) long, often branching, square in cross-section, pubescent at least on the 4 angles; **leaves** opposite, the pairs on alternate sides at successive internodes up the stem, short-stalked, ovate or lanceolate, 1 - 9 cm (2/5 -3½ in.) long by 2 - 40 mm (1/12 - 1½ in.) wide, with toothed margins and somewhat hairy; **flowers** (b, B) in small, compact clusters in the axils of the middle and upper leaves; calyx pubescent (c), 1 - 7 mm (1/25 - ¼ in.); corolla (d) white to light purple or pink, 3 - 9 mm (⅛ - ⅜ in.) long, tubular with very short lobes. Flowers from July to September.

Field mint is a native plant occurring in wet or damp soils in open and shaded areas throughout Ontario.

It is distinguished by its square stems being pubescent at least on the angles, its shallowly toothed, opposite leaves, its small, dense clusters of white to pink flowers and its strong mint odour.

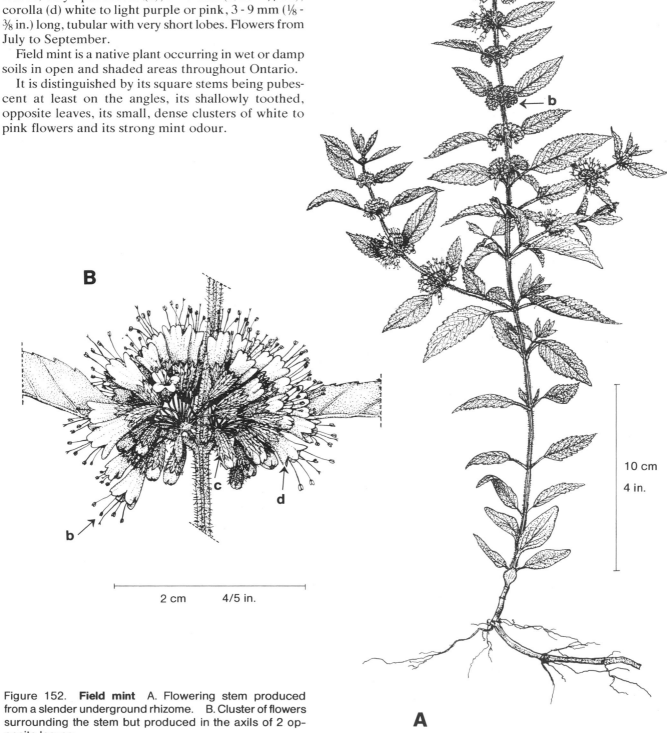

Figure 152. **Field mint** A. Flowering stem produced from a slender underground rhizome. B. Cluster of flowers surrounding the stem but produced in the axils of 2 opposite leaves.

181

NIGHTSHADE or POTATO FAMILY (Solanaceae)

Clammy ground-cherry, *Physalis heterophylla* Nees. (Figure 153) [PHYHE, coqueret hétérophylle, cerise de terre] Perennial, reproducing by seed and by deeply penetrating and widely spreading **roots. Stems** erect, 20 - 90 cm (8 - 36 in.) high, branched in the upper part, often apparently branching in 3's (2 branches and 1 leaf petiole) with a flower in the centre; **leaves** alternate (1 per node), long-stalked, ovate to somewhat rounded or diamond shaped in outline, margins smooth or with shallowly and irregularly rounded teeth; stems and leaves covered with sticky hairs; **flowers** borne singly in the angles where 2 or 3 stems and leaves come together (a), drooping on short stalks; calyx at first tubular with 5 short blunt lobes; petals united forming a trumpet-shaped corolla, mostly yellow with a dark purple centre; after blossoming, the calyx expands and becomes bladder-like (b) enclosing a small, sperical, green **berry** which turns yellowish when ripe; the berry resembles a small tomato and contains many small **seeds**. Flowers from June to September.

Clammy ground-cherry occurs in southern Ontario under dry open woodland, in pastures, cultivated fields waste areas and roadsides, especially in well-drained coarse soils.

It is distinguished by its very deep perennial root, the clammy texture of its sticky stem and leaves, its yellow and purplish flowers produced in the angles between usually 3 or more stems and leaves (a), and its bladder-like inflated calyx (b) containing a small greenish or yellowish berry.

Smooth ground-cherry, *Physalis virginiana* Mill. var. *subglabrata* (MacKenz. & Bush) U.T. Waterfall, (Plate 106) [PHYSU, coqueret glabre, *Physalis subglabrata* MacKenz. & Bush] Very similar in habit and form to Clammy ground-cherry, but the whole plant is nearly or quite hairless and lacks the clammy texture. Smooth ground-cherry occurs in similar situations to those occupied by Clammy ground-cherry, especially in southwestern Ontario.

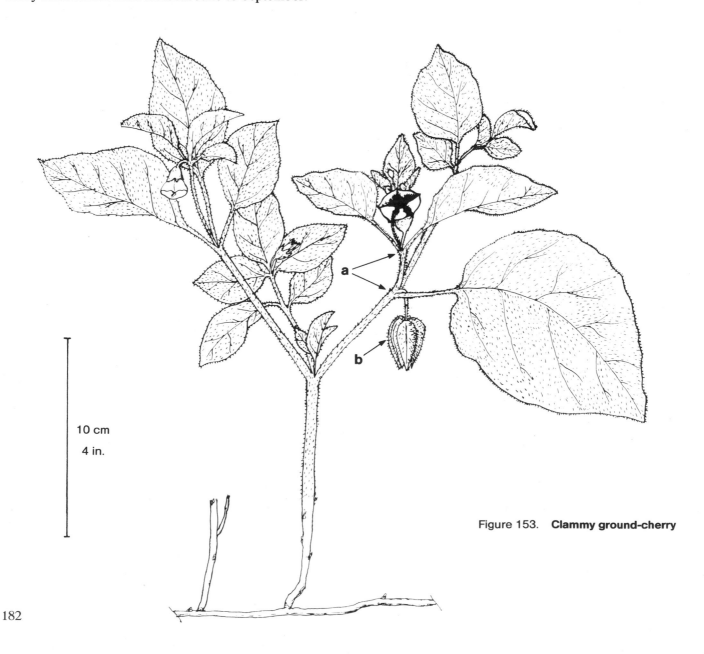

10 cm

4 in.

Figure 153. **Clammy ground-cherry**

Climbing nightshade, *Solanum dulcamara* L., (Figure 154, Plate 107) [SOLDU, morelle douce-amère, Bitter nightshade, Bittersweet, Climbing bittersweet, Deadly nightshade, douce-amère] Perennial, reproducing by seed and by spreading underground **rhizomes. Stems** partially woody, weak, erect or vine-like and climbing over fence lines and other vegetation, 1 - 3 m (3 - 10 ft) long, usually dying back close to the ground each year but in milder areas or if protected by snow becoming thick and woody in the lower part, hairless or short-hairy, with lengthwise-shredding, light gray bark; **leaves** alternate (1 per node), simple (a) or lobed with 1 or more lobes (b) near the base giving them a mitten-like appearance; **flowers** in much-branched clusters; each flower star-shaped (c) with a 5-pointed light blue to violet or rarely white corolla, in the centre of which is a slender pyramid of 5 united bright yellow stamens (d); flowers followed by oblong green **berries** (e) 8 - 12 mm (1/3 - ½ in.) long which turn bright red (Plate 107B) and juicy when ripe. Flowers in June and July; berries ripening in August and often remaining on the stems into the winter. Stems, roots, leaves and sometimes the green berries have a disagreeable civet-cat odour when bruised.

Climbing nightshade occurs throughout Ontario in open woods, edges of fields, fence lines, roadsides, and occasionally in hedges and gardens. **Stems and leaves are poisonous to livestock. The attractive, bright red berries have a bitter and sweet flavour, and, although some people can apparently eat them without harm, children have reputedly been poisoned by eating them.**

It is distinguished by its vine habit, its shredding light gray back on older stems, its usually mitten-shaped flowers (c), its juicy red berries (e), and its strong disagreeable odour.

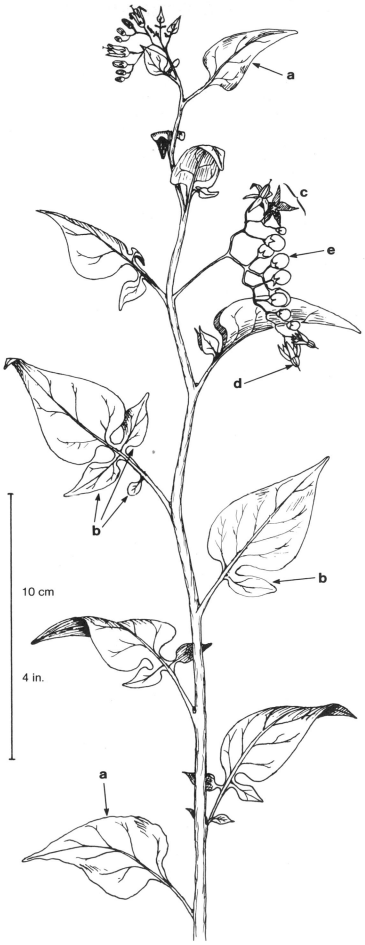

Figure 154. **Climbing nightshade**

183

Eastern black nightshade, *Solanum ptycanthum* Dun. (Figure 155, Plate 108) [SOLPT, morelle noire de l'est, Black nightshade, Deadly nightshade, often mistaken as *Solanum nigrum* L., and in the previous edition included under the name American nightshade, morelle d'Amerique, *Solanum americanum* Mill.] *Annual, reproducing only by seed.* **Stems** erect, 5 - 100 cm (2 - 40 in.) high, usually much-branched in the upper part, mostly hairless; **leaves** alternate (1 per node), ovate or rhombic (diamond-shaped), pale green, soft, thin and nearly translucent; **flowers** small, usually 2 to 5 grouped together in a small umbel (flower stalks all from 1 point) (a) on a short stalk sticking out from the side of the stem (b) rather than from the axil of a leaf (angle between leaf and stem) as in most other plants; calyx of 5 united sepals with 5 pointed lobes, small and not enlarging with the fruit (c); petals white or white tinged with purple, united into a star-shaped corolla with 5 sharp lobes resembling the flower of a potato but much smaller, about 9 - 15 mm (1/3 - 2/5 in.) in diameter; the short anthers (d) about 1.3 - 2 mm (1/20 - 1/12 in.) long, united and forming a yellow column in the centre of the flower; **fruits** are berries, always larger than the calyx, green at first but turning black and juicy when mature, 5 - 9 mm (1/5 - 1/3 in.) in diameter, containing several, small, flat **seeds** and 4 to 8 small, hard, irregular stone-like crumbs. Flowers from June until late autumn.

Eastern black nightshade occurs throughout southern Ontario in open dry woods, edges of pastures, waste places, and in cultivated land, especially in row crops. **The berries of Eastern black nightshade are reputed to be poisonous and thus the plant is sometimes called "deadly nightshade," a name belonging to a different plant. Until more information is available about their palatability, it is advisable not to eat these attractive berries. Feeding experiments have demonstrated that this plant can be toxic to cattle if it comprises about 25% or more of the forage intake.**

It is distinguished by being annual plant with thin, ovate to diamond-shaped leaves, small umbels of flowers on short stalks from sides of stems (not from leaf axils), small, white flowers, and small, black berries that are not partly enclosed by their expanded calyxes.

Black nightshade, *Solanum nigrum* L., (not illustrated) [SOLNI, morelle noire, Deadly nightshade, Garden huckleberry, crêve-chien] Very similar to Eastern black nightshade in habit, height and general appearance. It is distinguished by its thicker, dark green or purplish-green **leaves** which are opaque to transmitted light, its **flowers** about the same size but with larger anthers, these being 1.8 - 2.6 mm (1/15 - 1/10 in.) long, usually more flowers (5 to 10) in each cluster and these not in an umbel but in a short raceme (the flower stalks not all coming from 1 point), and its **berries** about the same size or half again larger and mostly without the hard, irregular stone-like crumbs among the seeds. Although some strains of this species are cultivated under the name "Garden huckleberry," **because of uncertainty of identification, it is not**

advisable to use the berries of any of these wild nightshades for human consumption.

Black nightshade occurs as a weed in cultivated land in scattered localities in southern Ontario.

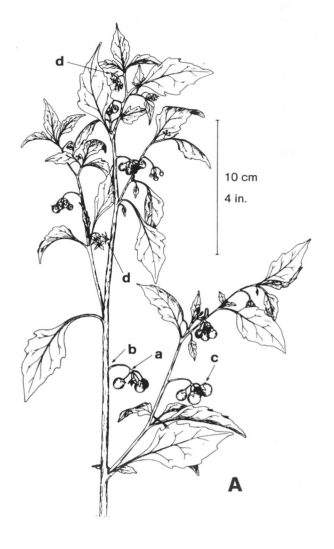

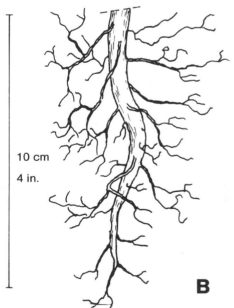

Figure 155. **Eastern black nightshade** A. Upper part of plant. B. Portion of annual root system.

Hairy nightshade, *Solanum sarachoides* Sendt., (Figure 156) [SOLSA, morelle poilue, morelle sarachoide, Cupped nightshade, Potatoweed] Annual, reproducing only by seed. **Stem** branching and softly hairy, up to 1 m (40 in.) long, spreading or erect; **leaves** alternate, ovate (a), to nearly triangular (b) (resembling some leaves of Lamb's-quarters), dull green to gray-green, thick and opaque to transmitted light, 1.5 - 10 cm (3/5 - 4 in.) long, usually finely hairy, especially along margins and main veins; some of these hairs with tiny glandular tips (c) (seen under magnification), giving the plant a slightly sticky or clammy texture; margins of leaves usually smooth but occasionally with coarse, irregular, rounded teeth; **inflorescence** (B) of 3-9 flowers in a short raceme (d, B) sticking out from the side of the stem (e) rather than from the axil of a leaf; corolla (f) white or tinged with bluish-purple; calyx at first small but enlarging with age to 4 - 9 mm (1/6 - 2/5 in.) across at maturity and acting as a cup (g) around the lower half (stem end) of the fruit (h); **fruit** a greenish berry turning yellowish-brown to brown at maturity. Flowers from July to October.

A native of South America, Hairy nightshade is found in southern Ontario in cultivated fields on both mineral and muck soils.

It is distinguished by its relatively small, thick, non-translucent leaves, its stem and leaves being finely hairy and slightly sticky or clammy, its inflorescence a short raceme, its calyx enlarging with age and partially enclosing the base of the fruit, and its fruit turning yellowish-brown to brown at maturity.

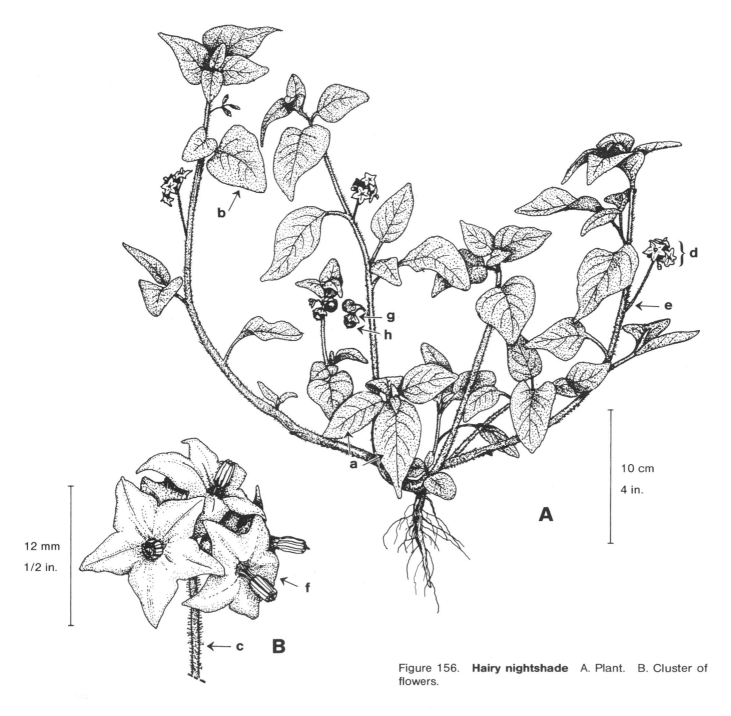

Figure 156. **Hairy nightshade** A. Plant. B. Cluster of flowers.

185

Horse-nettle, *Solanum carolinense* L., (Figure 157A,B, Plate 109) [SOLCA, morelle de la Caroline, ortie de la Caroline] Perennial, reproducing by seed and by underground **rhizomes** (B). **Stems** erect, 60 - 100 cm (24 - 40 in.) high, with a few branches near the top, covered with tiny, star-shaped hairs, each having 1 point longer than the rest (visible only with magnification), and scattered, long, hard, sharp spines (a) often 5 mm (1/5 in.) long; **leaves** alternate (1 per node), elliptic in outline but shallowly to deeply lobed with 2 to 5 rounded or sharp-pointed lobes on each side, finely hairy on both surfaces with star-shaped hairs plus several, long, hard spines (b), at least on the underside along the midrib and main veins; **flowers** arranged in 1 or more short racemes at the ends and sides of branches in the upper part, corolla pale purplish to white, 1.5 - 2 cm (3/5 - 4/5 in.) across, with 5 stamens joined in a central column about 6 mm (¼ in.) long; **berry** smooth, yellow at maturity and about 1.5 cm (3/5 in.) in diameter. Flowers from July until autumn.

Horse-nettle is found in scattered localities throughout southern Ontario, usually in sandy soils, in grainfields, pastureland, waste areas and occasionally in gardens.

It is distinguished by its harshly spiny stems (a) and leaves (b), lobed leaves, large, white to purplish flowers, smooth yellow berries, and its spreading perennial rhizomes (B) which enable this plant to form thick patches.

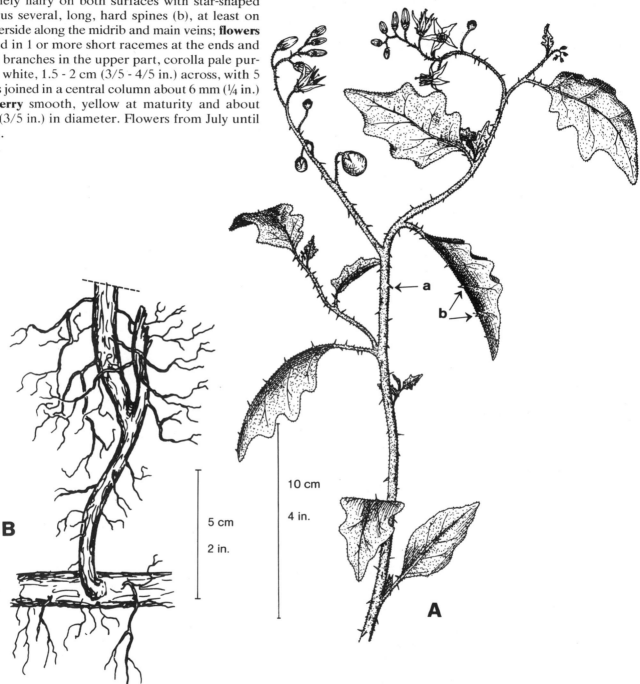

Figure 157. **Horse-nettle** A. Top of plant. B. Portion of horizontal rhizome producing new aboveground shoot. (Cont'd.)

186

Buffalobur, *Solanum rostratum* Dunal., (Figure 157C,D,E) [SOLCU, morelle rostrée] Similar in general appearance to Horse-nettle, and a close relative, botanically. **Annual**, reproducing only by seed. **Stems** erect, 50 - 100 cm (20 - 40 in.) high, usually much-branched, densely covered with hard, sharp, straight, yellowish spines (c) that stand perpendicular from the surface, these spines varying in length from less than 1 mm to more than 15 mm (1/25 - 3/5 in.) long, some of the shorter ones with star-shaped tips (d) and, on the surface, very short, small, star-shaped spines or hairs, each with 5-7 points (e) (these best seen with magnification); leaves alternate, ovate in outline but deeply pinnately lobed with the margins of the larger segments having somewhat rounded lobes (f) and rounded spaces between the lobes (g), spiny on both upper and lower surfaces, the long, straight spines (h) arising only from the veins, but the tiny, star-shaped spines or hairs more or less covering the entire leaf surfaces; **flowers** yellow, in spiny, several-flowered racemes on the upper stems and branches (as in Horse-nettle in Figure 157B); **corolla** funnel- or saucer-shaped (D), 2 - 3.5 cm (4/5 - 1½ in.) wide, with 5 points; **stamens** 5, prominent in the centre of the flower, 4 of them about 6 mm (¼ in.) long, the fifth (j) about 10 mm (2/5 in.) long; **calyx** covered with long straight spines and short star-shaped spines, tubular with 5 lobes (k), fully enclosing the berry and enlarging around it to form an extremely spiny bur-like **fruit** (E) 3 - 4 cm (1¼ - 1⅝ in.) at maturity. Flowers from July until autumn.

Buffalobur is a native plant in the western United States but has been introduced as a weed or occasional ornamental in gardens and waste places in scattered localities throughout Ontario.

It resembles Horse-nettle but is distinguished from it by being an annual, having leaves more deeply lobed, yellow flowers, its berry enclosed in a large spiny bur, and the whole plant being much more spiny. It is distinguished from the thistles by its yellow, funnel- or saucer-shaped flowers, the rounded lobes of its leaves, and its juicy berry enclosed inside the bur-like fruit.

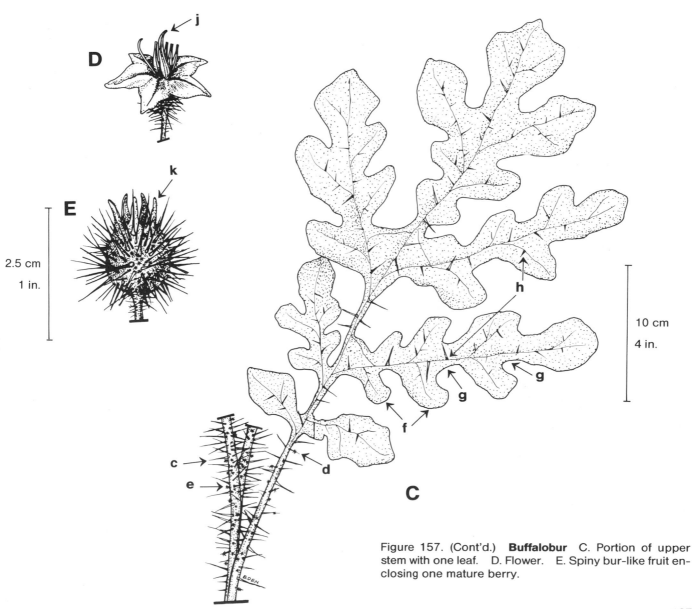

Figure 157. (Cont'd.) **Buffalobur** C. Portion of upper stem with one leaf.   D. Flower.   E. Spiny bur-like fruit enclosing one mature berry.

187

Jimsonweed, *Datura stramonium* L., (Figure 158, Plate 110) [DATST, stramoine commune, Stinkweed, Thornapple, pomme épineuse, herbe du diable] Annual, reproducing only by seed. **Stems** stout, erect, 90 - 200 cm (3 - 6½ ft) high, usually much-branched in the upper part, smooth and hairless, larger plants with the main stem often 5 cm (2 in.) or more in diameter; **cotyledons** (seed leaves) long-oval, 2 - 4 cm (4/5 - 1½ in.) long, shriveling (a) but persisting on the developing seedling; first true **leaves** (b) ovate with pointed tips and few or no lobes; later leaves distinctly alternate (1 per node), usually somewhat coarsely and sharply toothed or lobed, 10 - 20 cm (4 - 8 in.) long and long-stalked; **flowers** and seedpods short-stalked, borne singly in the angles (c) between 2 or more stems and a leaf; calyx tubular or urn-shaped; corolla (d) white or light purple, very long, tubular or trumpet-shaped, 7 - 10 cm (3 - 4 in.) long, the flared end with 5 points; **seedpod** (e) at first green and fleshy with sharp, soft spines, becoming (C) a large (2 - 5 cm, 4/5 - 2 in. across), dry, hard seedpod covered with very sharp, harsh spines and containing numerous black, flat, round **seeds**. Flowers from July to autumn. The whole plant has a sour repulsive odour and **all parts of the plant are poisonous.**

Jimsonweed occurs in the warmer parts of southern Ontario in cultivated fields and around farmyards.

It is distinguished by its tall, stout, branched stem (like small trees), large leaves, large, white or purplish trumpet-shaped flowers (d), large spiny seedpod (e, C) and sour repulsive odour.

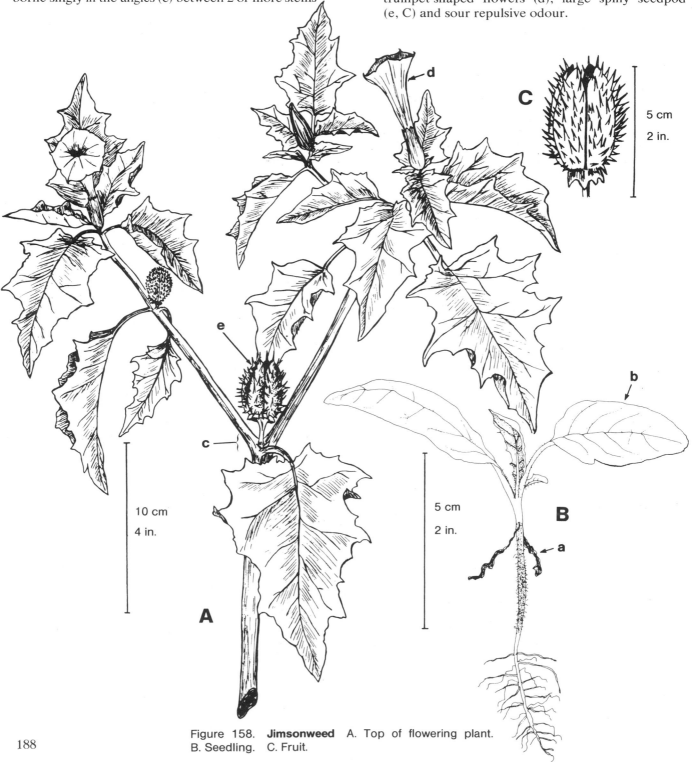

Figure 158. **Jimsonweed** A. Top of flowering plant.
B. Seedling.   C. Fruit.

FIGWORT or SNAPDRAGON FAMILY (Scrophulariaceae)

Common mullein, *Verbascum thapsus* L., (Figure 159, Plate 111) [VESTH, grande molène, Candelabra, Candlesticks, Devil's-tobacco, bouillon-blanc, tabac du diable] Biennial, reproducing only by seed. First-year plant a rosette of large, gray, woolly leaves on a deep, thick **taproot**; tall erect stems the second year. **Stem** 1 - 2 m (3 - 6½ ft) high, stout, unbranched or with 1 or 2 branches near the top, somewhat winged by edges of leaves (a) which run down the stem below their nodes; stem and leaves densely woolly; rosette **leaves** many, often 30 cm (12 in.) long and 10 cm (4 in.) wide, oblong or broadest beyond the middle, narrowed towards the stalk; stem leaves of similar shape but gradually smaller upwards and changing from widest beyond the middle to widest before the middle and without leafstalks; **flowers** in a very dense, compact, elongated, thick spike; petals 5, yellow, united into a saucer-shaped corolla 12 - 20 mm (½ - 4/5 in.) wide with 5 lobes (b), stamens with 3 small anthers and 2 long ones; **seedpods** nearly spherical, about 1 cm (2/5 in.) in diameter but obscured by the mass of woolly bracts and sepals; **seeds** brownish, very small, about 0.7 mm (1/40 in.) long. Flowers from early July to September.

Common mullein is widespread throughout southern Ontario but rather rare in the northern part of the province, occurring usually in dry sandy or gravelly soils, along roadsides, waste places and poor pastures.

It is distinguished by its densely white or gray woolly leaves during the first year, almost resembling white felt insoles, its stiffly erect stem in the second year, tipped with yellow flowers (hence one local name, "Candelabra"), its leaf margins (a) continuing down the stem as narrow wings, its very dense, thick, woolly spike with yellowish flowers (b) and nearly spherical seedpods and its erect, dry, brownish stalks which may remain standing for one or two years.

Figure 159. **Common mullein** A. Rosette of basal leaves. B. Top of flowering stem.

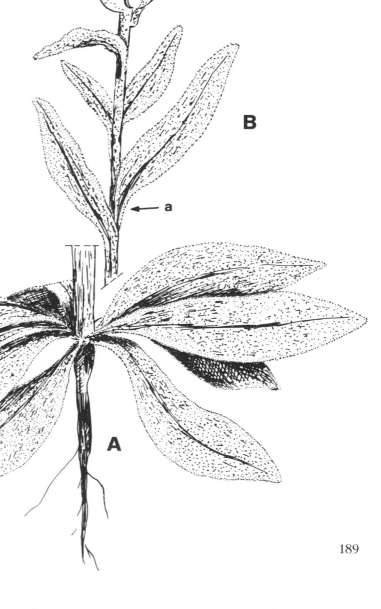

10 cm

4 in.

189

Moth mullein, *Verbascum blattaria* L., (Figure 160) [VESBL, molène blattaire, herbe aux mites] Biennial, reproducing only by seed. Similar in habit to Common mullein but shorter, thinner and not white woolly; **stems** 75 - 150 cm (30 - 60 in.) high, slender, lower part usually hairless, upper part rough or slightly sticky with short gland-tipped hairs; rosette **leaves** of the first year up to 20 cm (8 in.) long, oblong, narrowed to the base, irregularly shallowly or deeply toothed or deeply lobed; stem leaves in the second year similar to those of the rosette but smaller and shorter, the upper ones stalkless with a broad base and somewhat clasping (a) the stem; **flowers** in an elongated, loose raceme with distinct slender flower stalks 1 - 2.5 cm (2/5 - 1 in.) long; petals 5, yellowish or whitish with a purplish base, united into a saucer-shaped corolla 2 - 2.5 cm (4/5 - 1 in.) across; **seedpods** nearly spherical, about 8 mm (1/3 in.) in diameter, with a single partition across the centre, and each half containing numerous small brownish **seeds**. Flowers from June to August.

Moth mullein occurs in scattered localities in southern Ontario on dry sandy, gravelly soils along roadsides, in waste places and open pastureland.

It is distinguished by its rosette of irregularly toothed, hairless leaves during the first year, and in the second year by its stiffly erect stem, upper leaves stalkless, somewhat triangular, broad based and somewhat clasping (a) the stem but the stem not winged; its numerous but not crowded yellowish to whitish flowers with purple bases, each with a distinct flower stalk, and its spherical seedpods with a single partition across the centre.

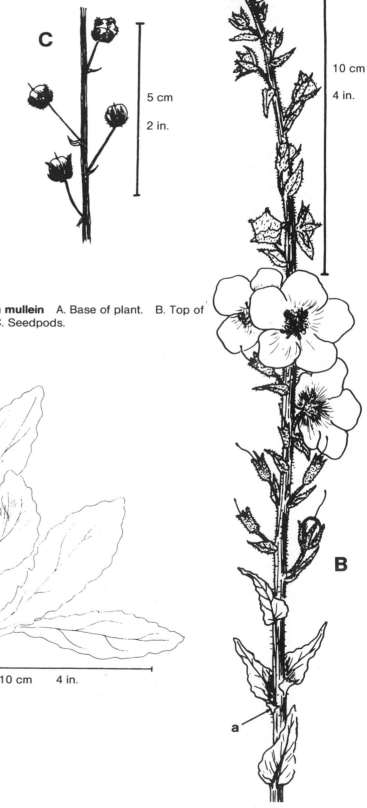

5 cm
2 in.

10 cm
4 in.

Figure 160. **Moth mullein** A. Base of plant. B. Top of flowering stem. C. Seedpods.

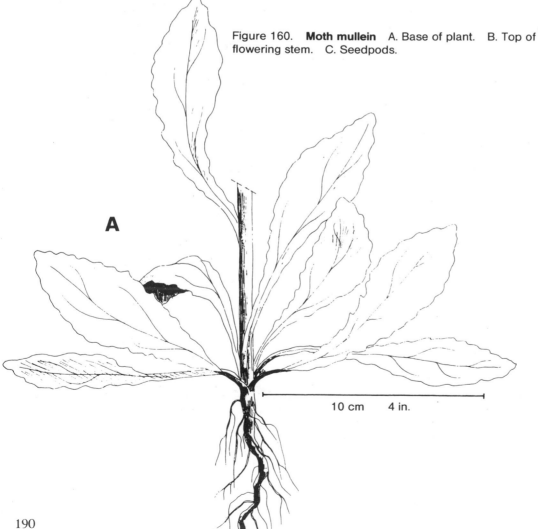

10 cm   4 in.

Toadflax, *Linaria vulgaris* Mill., (Figure 161, Plate 112) [LINVU, linaire vulgaire, Butter-and-eggs, Common toadflax, Yellow toadflax, Wild snapdragon, linaire commune] Perennial, reproducing by seed and by extensively creeping **roots** (a) which produce new shoots and form very dense patches. **Stems** erect, 20 - 90 cm (8 - 36 in.) high, usually branched in the upper part, smooth and hairless; **leaves** alternate (1 per node) but often so numerous and crowded they appear opposite (2 per node), or whorled (3 or more per node), very narrow; **flowers** in racemes at ends of stems and branches, each flower short-stalked; sepals (b) 5, narrow; corolla 2 - 3 cm (4/5 - 1¼ in.) long, of 5 united petals, yellow with an orange spot on the lower lip, very irregular with a long spur (c) at the lower end and 2-lipped at the top, the upper lip with 2 small lobes (d), the lower lip with 3 larger lobes (e), the flower resembling the cultivated snapdragon in shape; **seedpods** egg-shaped, containing many dark brown or black, flat, winged **seeds.** Flowers from June to autumn.

Toadflax is widely distributed throughout Ontario, occurring in many habitats including roadsides, fence lines, waste places, pastures, edges of woods, and cultivated fields.

It is distinguished by its perennial spreading root system; its short, smooth stems with numerous, alternate, smooth, very narrow leaves with watery juice (contrasts with Leafy spurge and Cypress spurge) and its bright yellow and orange snapdragon-like flowers, the lips of which will open if the sides of the flower are gently squeezed between thumb and finger. The seedpods of Toadflax are often very warty in appearance due to an insect which lives inside eating the developing seeds.

Dalmatian toadflax, *Linaria dalmatica* (L.) Mill., (not illustrated) [LINDA, linaire à feuilles larges, Broad-leaved toadflax, Wild snapdragon, linaire de Dalmatie, *Linaria genistifolia* (L.) Mill. ssp. *dalmatica* (L.) Maire & Petitmengin, *Linaria macedonica* Griseb.] Has flowers and seedpods very similar to Toadflax but **stems** usually taller, and more branched, **leaves** broader and often clasping the stem with rounded bases and its seeds are angular rather than round and flat. Dalmatian toadflax is also a perennial reproducing by seed and underground roots but its stands are usually not as dense as Toadflax. In late autumn it usually produces numerous, very leafy horizontal stems around the base of each plant, these leaves being ovate to nearly round, clasping, very closely spaced, and often remaining green or purplish-green throughout the winter. Dalmatian toadflax occurs throughout Ontario in old gardens, cemeteries, along roadsides, in waste places, and sandy pastures.

It is distinguished by its yellow, 2-lipped flowers with long spurs and its broad leaves with rounded bases that may clasp the stem.

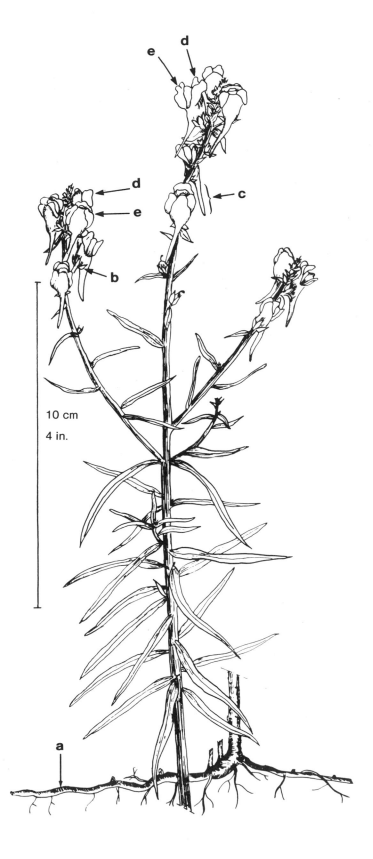

10 cm
4 in.

Figure 161. **Toadflax**

Dwarf snapdragon, *Chaenorrhinum minus* (L.) Lange, (Figure 162, Plate 113) |CHNMI, chénorhinum mineur, Dwarf toadflax, Small toadflax, linaire mineure, *Linaria minor* L.| Annual, reproducing only by seed. **Stems** erect, 10 - 40 cm (4 - 16 in.) high, usually much-branched throughout, glandular-hairy; **leaves** alternate (1 per node), sometimes in tufts along the stem, short and very narrow; flower stalks slender (a), 1 - 2 cm (2/5 - 4/5 in.) long, from leaf axils throughout the plant; **flowers** (b) resembling Toad-flax in shape but much smaller (6 - 8 mm, ¼ - 1/3 in. long), and light blue to purplish with a yellow spot; **seedpods** (c) nearly spherical, about 5 mm (1/5 in.) in diameter. Flowers from June to September.

Dwarf snapdragon occurs throughout Ontario usually in cinders and gravel along railway rights-of-way but occasionally in other waste places, cultivated fields and gardens, and has recently become a common weed in many strawberry fields.

It is distinguished by its small, erect, much-branched, somewhat sticky-hairy stems with short, narrow leaves often in tufts, and very small, light blue to purplish snapdragon-like flowers (b).

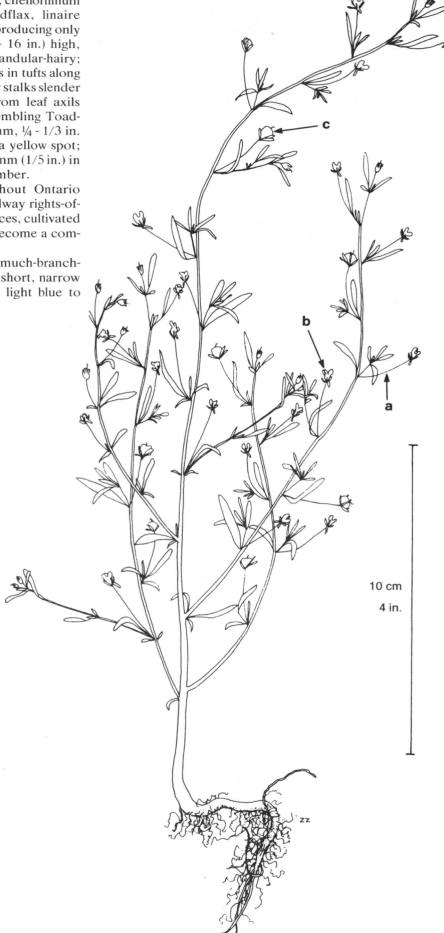

10 cm
4 in.

Figure 162. **Dwarf snapdragon**

192

Thyme-leaved speedwell, *Veronica serpyllifolia* L., (Figure 163, Plate 114) [VERSE, véronique à feuilles de serpolet, Veronica, véronique à feuilles de thym] Perennial, reproducing by seed and by spreading underground rhizomes and rooting stems. Plants tufted with spreading branches which soon curve upwards into erect stems, or with horizontal stems rooting at nodes (a) touching the ground and producing short erect branches, or occasionally just single erect stems from underground **rhizomes; stems** 10 - 30 cm (4 - 12 in.) high, somewhat fleshy, very finely hairy; **leaves** on horizontal stems (b) and lower parts of erect stems (c), opposite (2 per node), oval to roundish or broadly ovate, lacking teeth or with very fine teeth, stalkless, with 3 to 5 main veins arising from the base of the leaf, the side veins curving in towards the tip; on the upper parts of the stems the **leaves** (or flower bracts) (d) with flowers in their axils (angle between leaf and stem) are usually alternate (1 per node) and smaller than the lower opposite leaves; flowerstalk (e) usually shorter than its leafy bract (d); sepals 4, small; corolla flat with 4 lobes, pale bluish-white with blue lines or bright blue; stamens 2; **seedpods** (f) flat, appearing soon after the blossom falls, deeply notched at the tip, appearing 2-lobed, 4 - 8 mm (1/6 - 1/3 in.) wide, broader than long. Flowers from late spring until late autumn.

Thyme-leaved speedwell occurs throughout Ontario in waste places, pastures, roadsides, meadows and lawns. There are at least eight different kinds of speedwell in Ontario and identification may be difficult.

It is distinguished by its perennial habit, lower leaves opposite, somewhat roundish and lacking teeth or with very fine teeth, its short-stalked (e) flowers with white or bluish 4-lobed corolla, its flowers stalk usually shorter than the leafy bract (d) just below it, and its seedpod notched at the end.

Figure 163. **Thyme-leaved speedwell** A. Plant. B. Flower. C. Seedpod.

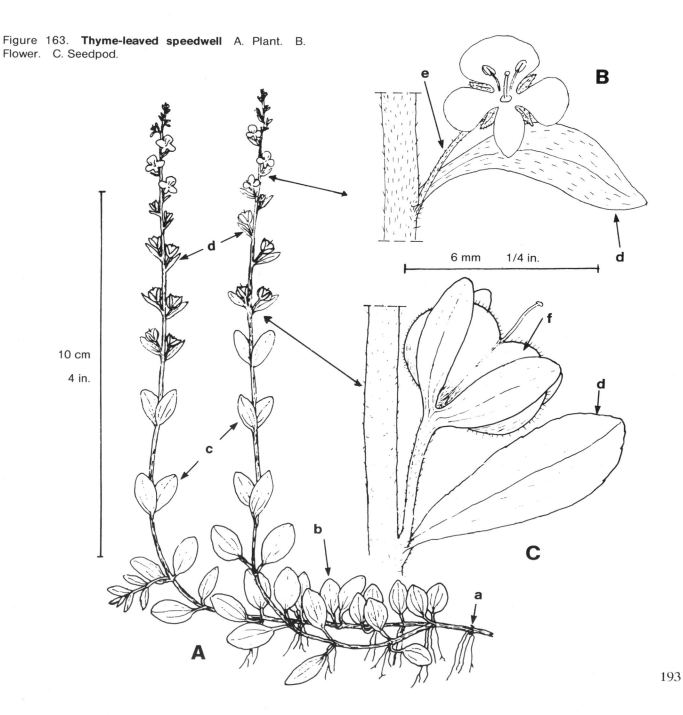

10 cm
4 in.

6 mm   1/4 in.

Purslane speedwell, *Veronica peregrina* L., (Figure 164) [VERPG, véronique voyageuse, Neckweed, Veronica] Annual, reproducing only by seed. **Stems** erect or much-branched near the base and becoming erect, smooth or with fine, slightly sticky hair; stems and leaves with a somewhat fleshy texture (hence "purslane" in the English name); lower and middle **leaves** (a) opposite (2 per node), oblong or somewhat linear, smooth or irregularly toothed, lower ones short-stalked, middle and upper ones stalkless; upper leaves (b) alternate (1 per node), smaller and narrower, each with a **flower** (c) in its axil; flower stalks extremely short; corolla flat, 4-lobed, 2 mm (1/12 in.) across, white or whitish (similar to Figure 163B); **seedpods** (d)

flat, heart-shaped with a notch at the top; each leafy bract usually much longer than its flower or seedpod. Flowers from early May to July, and occasionally again in autumn.

Purslane speedwell occurs throughout Ontario but is most common in the southern portion of the province in gardens, orchards, lawns, waste places, roadsides, railways, stony areas and occasionally in greenhouses.

It is distinguished by its somewhat smooth and fleshy stem and leaves, its lower leaves (a) opposite and narrow, upper ones (b) alternate, smaller, and its tiny white flowers (c) on very short stalks, followed by small heart-shaped seedpods (d).

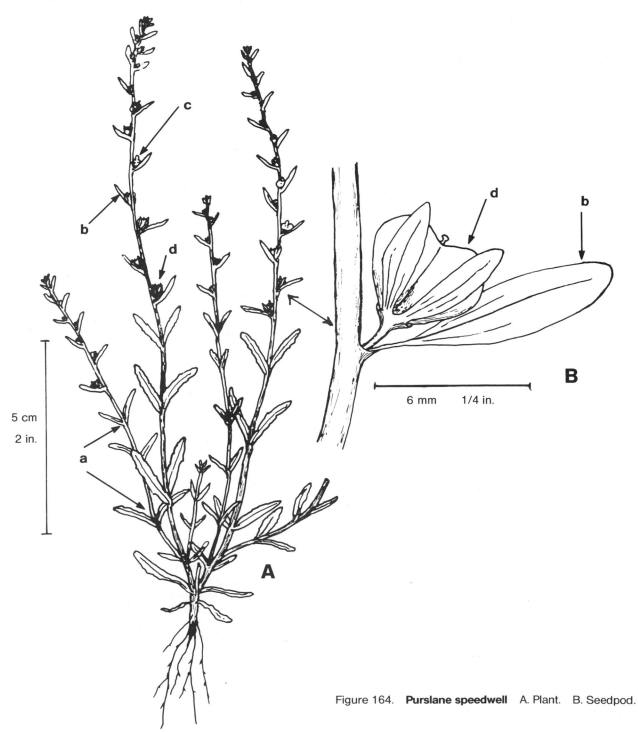

5 cm
2 in.

6 mm   1/4 in.

Figure 164. **Purslane speedwell** A. Plant. B. Seedpod.

Corn speedwell, *Veronica arvensis* L., (Figure 165, Plate 115) [VERAR, véronique des champs, Veronica] Annual or possibly winter annual, reproducing only by seed. **Stems** erect, or spreading from the base and becoming erect, 5 - 30 cm (2 - 12 in.) long, somewhat hairy; lower and middle **leaves** (a) opposite (2 per node), lowermost pairs with short stalks but the middle ones stalkless, ovate or elliptic, palmately veined (with 3 or more veins fanning out from the base), hairy on both surfaces; margins with slightly rounded teeth; upper leaves (b) alternate (1 per node), smaller, narrower, without teeth, each with a flower in its axil; **flowers** (c) on very short stalks; sepals 4, small; corolla blue-violet, flat, 2 - 2.5 mm (1/12 - 1/10 in.) wide with 4 lobes and 2 tiny stamens (similar to Figure 163B); **seedpods** (d, B) roundly heart-shaped, with a deep notch at the top. Flowers in late May and June and again in autumn.

Corn speedwell occurs in southern Ontario in pastures, waste places, roadsides, lawns and cultivated fields.

It is distinguished by its annual or winter annual habit, its somewhat rounded, toothed leaves, its tiny blue-violet flowers (c) and its almost stalkless, rounded, heart-shaped seedpods (d, B).

Bird's-eye speedwell, *Veronica persica* Poir., (Figure 166) [VERPE, véronique de Perse, Bird's-eye, Veronica, véronique de Tournefort] Annual, reproducing only by seed. Similar to Corn speedwell but **stems** longer (10 - 40 cm, 4 - 16 in.), weakly upright or often lying on the ground and rooting from nodes touching the soil; lower **leaves** (a) opposite (2 per node), short-stalked, rounded to ovate, coarsely toothed; upper leaves (b) similar in shape to the lower ones but alternate (1 per node), stalkless, each alternate leaf with a long-stalked (c) **flower** (B) in its axil; calyx deeply 4-lobed (d), 6 - 8 mm (¼ - 1/3 in.) long; corolla (e) blue, 8 - 11 mm (1/3 - ½ in.) across, flat, 4-lobed; stamens 2; **seedpods** (f, C) flat, broadly heart-shaped, the lobes pointing outwards with a shallow notch, and a persistent, long thin style (g). Flowers and seeds from May to autumn.

Bird's-eye speedwell occurs throughout Ontario in lawns, gardens, cultivated fields and waste places.

It is distinguished by its rather coarse habit of growth, large roundish leaves on the upper as well as lower parts of the plant, its long-stalked (c) large blue flowers (B) and its flat, broadly heart-shaped seedpods (f, C) with spreading lobes and persistent, long style (g). In the fruiting stage, it is sometimes confused with Shepherd's-purse, but is clearly distinct by having each long flower stalk from the axil of a rounded leafy bract (b) and the deeply 4-lobed calyx (d) remaining around the base of each seedpod; whereas in Shepherd's-purse both bracts and sepals being absent from below the seedpods.

Field speedwell, *Veronica agrestis* L., (not illustrated) [VERAG, véronique rustique, Veronica, véronique agreste] Also an annual, is very similar to Bird's-eye speedwell but is generally smaller; its blue **flowers** not over 8 mm (1/3 in.) across, on stalks of medium length which rarely exceed 12 mm (½ in.) long when the seedpods develop. Field speedwell occurs in scattered localities throughout Ontario in lawns, gardens and waste places.

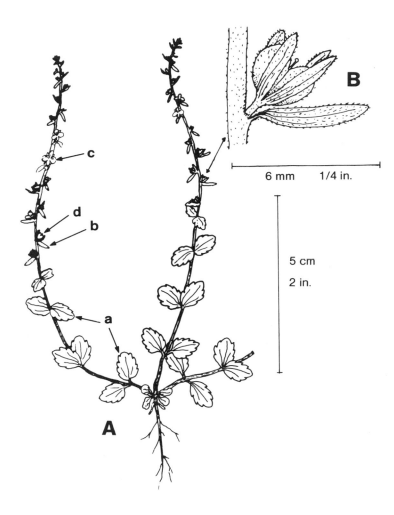

6 mm   1/4 in.

5 cm
2 in.

Figure 165.   **Corn speedwell**   A. Plant.   B. Seedpod.

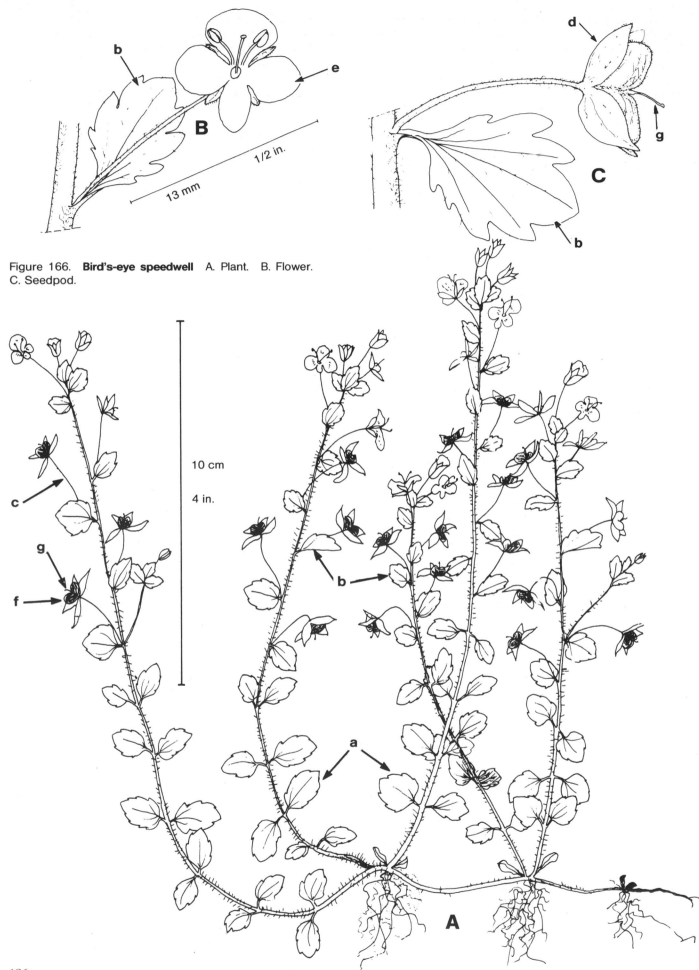

Figure 166. **Bird's-eye speedwell** A. Plant. B. Flower. C. Seedpod.

Creeping speedwell, *Veronica filiformis* Sm., (Figure 167) [VERFI, véronique filiforme, Veronica] Perennial, reproducing by seed and by slender underground **rhizomes**. Plant small and delicate; **stems** slender, creeping, often rooting at the nodes (a); some branches horizontal and others erect and bearing flowers; **leaves** small, mostly less than 10 mm (2/5 in.) across, short-stalked, with a few rounded teeth, opposite (2 per node) (b) on horizontal stems and lower parts of upright stems, but alternate (1 per node) (c) towards the ends of upright stems; alternate leaves bearing flowers (d) and, later, sometimes seedpods (e) in their axils; **flowers** bluish-white, 4-lobed, about 8 mm (1/3 in.) across on very slender thread-like stalks (f) 2 - 3 cm (about 1 in.) long. Flowers in May and June but rarely produces seedpods.

Creeping speedwell occurs in a few localities in southern Ontario in lawns and edges of woods.

It is distinguished by its perennial habit, very slender stems, small leaves and small bluish-white flowers (d) on very slender long stalks (f).

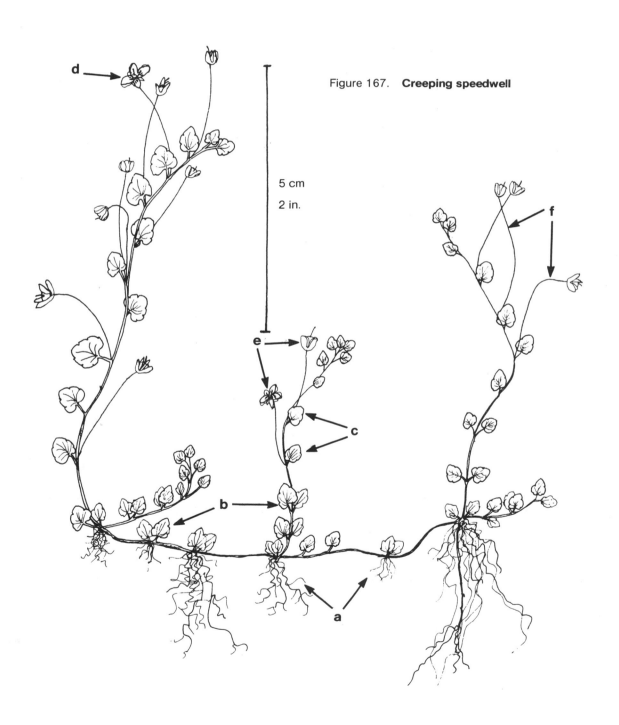

Figure 167. **Creeping speedwell**

5 cm
2 in.

Common speedwell, *Veronica officinalis* L., (Figure 168) [VEROF, véronique officinale, Gypsyweed, Veronica, thé d'Europe] Perennial, reproducing by seed and by spreading **rhizomes. Stems** hairy, more or less horizontal, much-branched, rooting at the nodes, often forming densely matted patches with short erect branches; **leaves** opposite (2 per node) (a), elliptic, up to 5 cm (2 in.) long, finely toothed, somewhat rough-hairy on both surfaces; towards the ends of the stems the axils of these opposite leaves (b) bear short, slender, dense, erect spikes (c) of light blue **flowers;** corolla 4 - 8 mm (1/6 - 1/3 in.) across; **seedpods** (d) small, flat, broadly heart-shaped, about 4 mm (1/6 in.) across, resembling those of Purslane speedwell (as in Figure 164 B, d). Flowers from May to July.

Common speedwell occurs throughout Ontario in pastures, meadows, open woodlots, waste areas and occasionally lawns and cultivated fields.

It is distinguished by its densely matted habit of growth, its coarse stems with large, rough-hairy, opposite leaves, its short spikes (b) of dense, bright blue flowers arising from axils of opposite leaves, and by the absence of flower-bearing alternate leaves towards the ends of the main stems, a feature that is characteristic of most other Speedwells.

Germander speedwell, *Veronica chamaedrys* L., (not illustrated) [VERCH, véronique germandrée, Bird's-eye, petit-chêne] Another rhizomatous perennial with prostrate stems, but it does not grow as dense as Common speedwell. Its **leaves** are opposite (2 per node), ovate to somewhat triangular, nearly stalkless with broad bases, coarse rounded teeth, softly hairy on both surfaces; **flowers** in loose, open racemes originating from axils of opposite leaves rather than at the ends of stems; flowers blue, 8 - 12 mm (1/3 - 1/2 in.) across, on very slender stalks 5 - 10 mm (1/5 - 2/5 in.) long. Flowers from May to August.

Germander speedwell occurs in a few areas of southern Ontario as a weed in lawns, pastures, and waste areas.

It is readily distinguished by its broadly triangular leaves with coarse teeth and its loosely elongated racemes of blue flowers on very slender stalks.

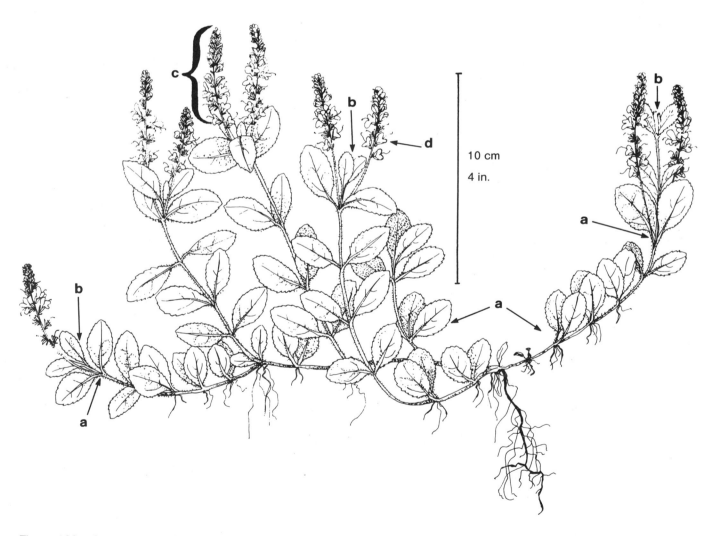

Figure 168. **Common speedwell**

PLANTAIN FAMILY (Plantaginaceae)

Broad-leaved plantain, *Plantago major* L., (Figure 169) [PLAMA, plantain majeur, Common plantain, Doorweed, Dooryard plantain, Plantain, Whiteman's-foot, grand plantain] Perennial, reproducing only by seed. Plant stemless, except for the leafless flowering stalks; **leaves** all in a basal rosette, oval or elliptic, 5 - 30 cm (2 - 12 in.) long, the blade about as long as its thick green stalk, smooth or somewhat rough-hairy, with 3 to several prominent veins radiating from the leafstalk towards the tip, margins smooth or irregularly toothed; **root** system thick and fibrous; **flowers** in compact spikes on erect, leafless stalks from among the basal leaves; each spike (a) about the size and shape of a lead pencil but consisting of many, tiny, stalkless, greenish flowers giving it a coarsely granular texture; each flower about 2 - 3 mm (1/12 - 1/8 in.) across, with 4 sepals, 4 petals, 2 stamens and 1 pistil; the egg-shaped **seedpod** (b) developing beneath the withering flower; this mature seedpod splitting apart with a circular fracture around its middle so that the top part drops off and releases the 5 to 16 dark brown or nearly black angular **seeds**, each about 1 mm (1/25 in.) long. Flowers and sets seed from spring until late autumn.

Broad-leaved plantain is very common in all but the most remote unsettled areas of Ontario occurring in cultivated land, pastures, meadows, waste places, roadsides, lawns and gardens.

It is distinguished by its rosette of dull green, oval leaves with thick green stalks, and its elongated spikes (a) of tiny green flowers each followed by a small egg-shaped pod (b) with usually more than 5 tiny dark brown or nearly black seeds.

Rugel's plantain, *Plantago rugelii* Dcne., (not illustrated) [PLARU, plantain de Rugel, Pale plantain, plantain pâle] Very similar to Broad-leaved plantain, differing mainly by having reddish or purplish bases on the **leafstalks**, cylindrical **seedpods** which contain fewer seeds and its **seeds** somewhat larger (up to 2.5 mm, 1/10 in. long). Rugel's plantain is a native plant in moist depressions and river valleys throughout southern Ontario, but it has spread to lawns, gardens, pastures, roadsides and waste areas.

Hoary plantain, *Plantago media* L., (not illustrated) [PLAME, plantain moyen, plantain intermédiaire] Also similar to Broad-leaved plantain, being distinguished by densely short-hairy **leaves** which are thick but soft in texture and usually lie flat on the ground, its short dense spikes of tiny **flowers** raised high above the leaves on long, slender, leafless stems, the flowers with long slender stamens having whitish or purplish anthers, and **seedpods** containing only 2 to 4 **seeds** each. Hoary plantain occurs in southern Ontario in lawns and waste places but is not common.

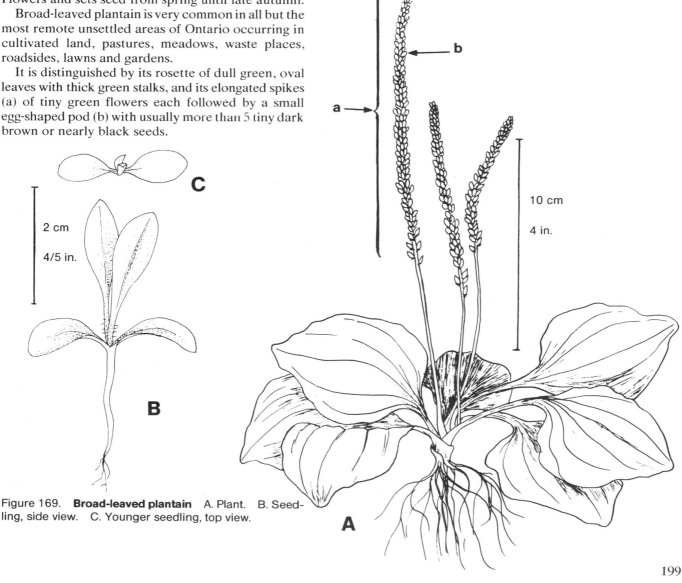

Figure 169. **Broad-leaved plantain** A. Plant. B. Seedling, side view. C. Younger seedling, top view.

Narrow-leaved plantain, *Plantago lanceolata* L., (Figure 170, Plate 116) [PLALA, plantain lancéolé, Buckhorn plantain, English plantain, Ribgrass, plantain à feuilles lancéolées, herbe à cinq coutures] Perennial, reproducing only by seed. Very similar to Broad-leaved plantain in general habit of growth; differing mainly in having long, narrow **leaves** which have very prominent, almost parallel veins or ribs which run the length of the leaf, sometimes the blade being strongly folded lengthwise along each rib, and the very short, compact, somewhat oval spike (a) of tiny **flowers** at the ends of long, thin, leafless stems; at flowering, the spike surrounded by a halo of anthers (b) at the ends of long thin stamens protruding from the flowers; **seedpod** contains only 1 or 2 **seeds**, each about 3 mm (⅛ in.) long. Flowers from spring until late autumn and the plant may act as an annual or perennial.

It occurs throughout Ontario in pastures, meadows, roadsides, cultivated fields, lawns and gardens.

It is distinguished by its rosette of long, narrow leaves with prominent, parallel veins, and its slender, leafless stems tipped with short, dense, oval spikes of tiny flowers.

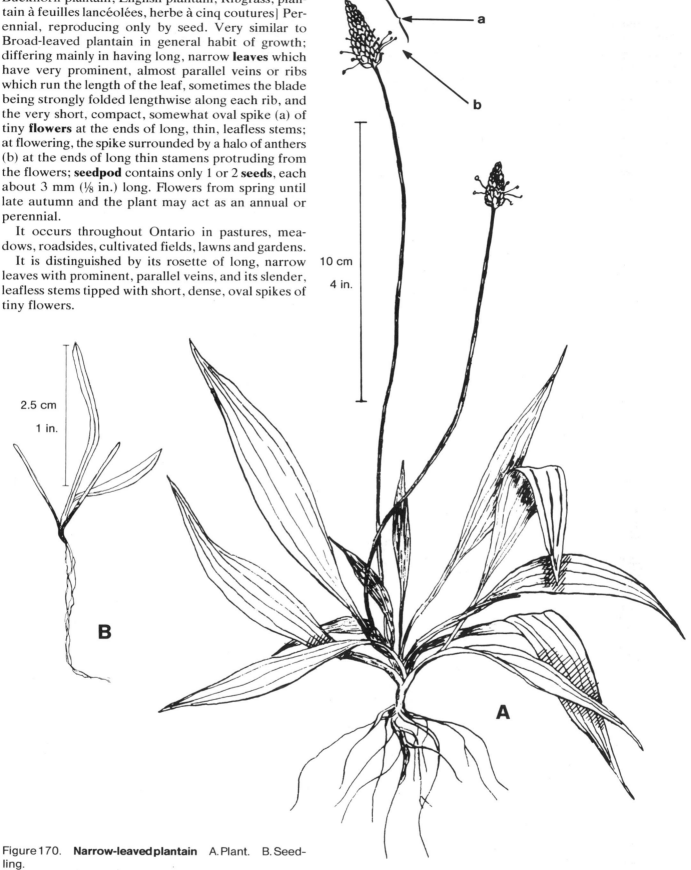

10 cm
4 in.

2.5 cm
1 in.

Figure 170. **Narrow-leaved plantain** A. Plant. B. Seedling.

200

MADDER FAMILY (Rubiaceae)

Smooth bedstraw, *Galium mollugo* L., (Figure 171, Plate 117) [GALMO, gaillet mollugine, gaillet] Perennial, reproducing by seed and by spreading underground rhizomes. **Stems** slender, soft, smooth, much-branched, at first erect but soon matted or spreading over nearby vegetation; **leaves** in whorls of 6 to 8 per node (a), narrowly oblong or wider towards the end, 1 - 3 cm (2/5 - 1¼ in.) long, bright green; **flowers** in loosely branching clusters at the ends of stems and on short branches throughout the plant; each flower with 4 tiny white petals (b), 2 - 4 mm (1/12 - 1/6 in.)

across, sitting on top of a small spherical ovary which develops into the **fruit** ("seed"). Flowers from June to August.

Smooth bedstraw occurs throughout Ontario in pastures, meadows, river flats, roadsides and occasionally in lawns and gardens. There are several other kinds of perennial white-flowered bedstraws in Ontario but they are rarely considered weedy.

It is distinguished by having usually 6 or 8 leaves per node on the smooth stems and branches.

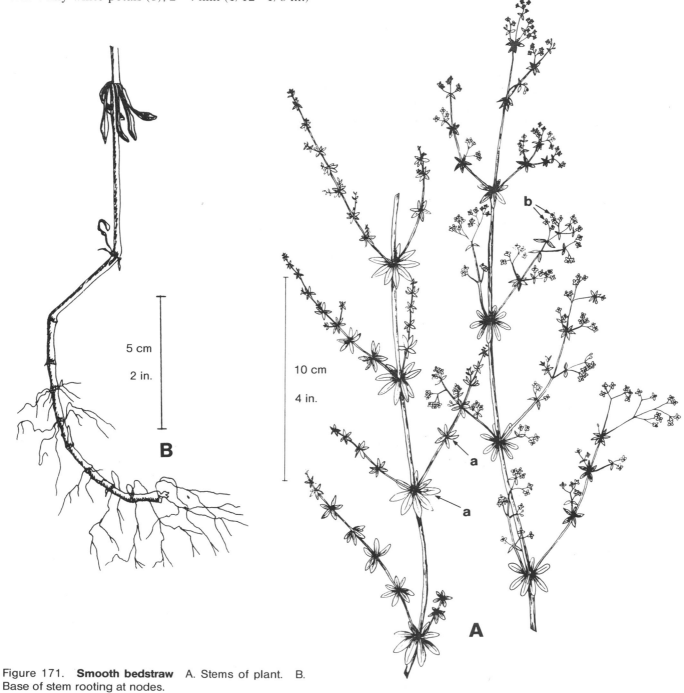

5 cm
2 in.

B

10 cm
4 in.

a

a

b

a

A

Figure 171. **Smooth bedstraw** A. Stems of plant. B. Base of stem rooting at nodes.

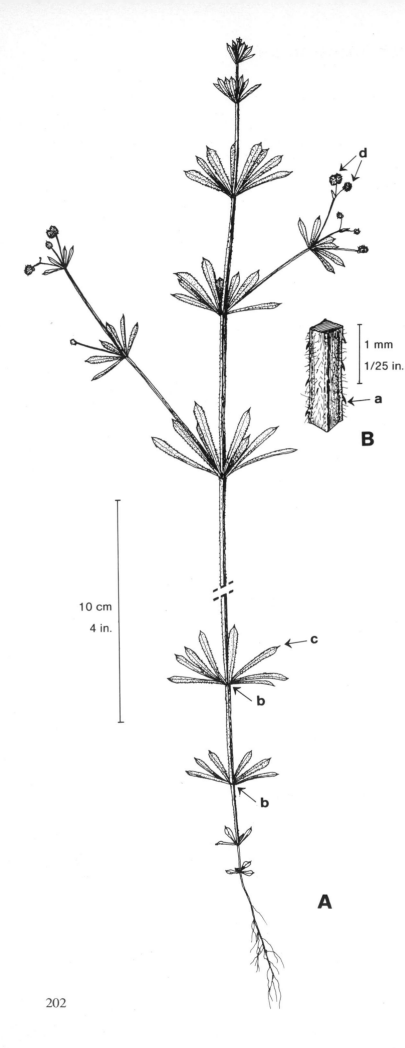

Cleavers, *Galium aparine* L., (Figure 172, Plate 118) [GALAP, gaillet grateron, Spring cleavers, Goose-grass, gratteron] Annual, reproducing only by seed. **Stems** weak or reclining, 10 - 121 cm (4 - 48 in.) long, square in cross-section (B) with strongly ribbed corners, with very short, downward- or backward-pointing, firm, hair-like, curved bristles (a); **leaves** usually 3 to 8 in a whorl (b), linear, tapering at the base, mostly 1 - 8 cm (2/5 - 3-2/5 in.) long, with bristles at the pointed tip (c), somewhat hairy on both surfaces and with many very short, backward-pointing bristles on the margins. These tiny hook-like bristles on stems and leaves cause them to cling together in masses and to cling to clothing, skin or fur, hence the common name, "cleavers." **Inflorescence** mostly 1- to 5-flowered; flowers very small and soon replaced by the small spherical fruits (d); **fruits** bristly, 1.5 - 4 mm (1/16 - 1/6 in.) in diameter. Flowers from May to August.

Cleavers is found in southern Ontario in woods, meadows, compost heaps, gardens and fields, and along roadsides and riverbanks.

It is distinguished by its square, weak, clinging stems, its bristle-tipped leaves that also cling with backward-pointing bristles on the margins, and all leaves arranged in whorls of 3 to 8 at each node of the stem.

Yellow bedstraw, *Galium verum* L., (not illustrated) [GALVE, gaillet vrai, Our Lady's bedstraw, gaillet jaune] Individual stems resemble Smooth bedstraw but are thinner and firmer so they tend to stand more erect than those of Smooth bedstraw. It is also a perennial with 6 or 8 leaves in each whorl, but its **leaves** are very narrow and the **flowers** are bright yellow. The plant has a pleasant aroma, and was widely used as a packing for mattresses (hence "bedstraw"). It occurs in scattered localities throughout Ontario in pastures, roadsides and waste places.

Figure 172. **Cleavers** A. Lower and upper parts of a mature plant. B. Portion of stem enlarged to show the backward-pointing bristles (a).

TEASEL FAMILY (Dipsacaceae)

Teasel, *Dipsacus sylvestris* Huds., (Figure 173, Plate 119) [DIWSI, cardère des bois, cardère sylvestre] Perennial, reproducing only by seed. First-year plants becoming large **rosettes**, the leaves long, tapering towards both ends, somewhat toothed along the margins, with scattered, stout prickles (a) on the upper surface, especially along the midrib and with each side vein (b) curving forward and joining the next vein above it; **stems** of second-year plants erect, to 2 m (6½ ft) high, usually branched near the top, very prickly; **stem leaves** similar to rosette leaves but smaller, stalkless, broader towards the stem and tapering towards the tip, opposite (2 per node), their bases occasionally united and forming a cup around the stem which may hold a quantity of rainwater; **flowers** in egg-shaped, dense, spiny heads (B) with long, slender, stiff, prickly bracts (c) below the head and numerous, short, stiff bristles (d) within the head; individual flowers small, corolla tubular, 10 - 15 mm (2/5 - 3/5 in.) long, whitish near their bases, pale to deep purplish towards their 4-lobed ends, 3 - 4 mm (⅛ - 1/6 in.) across, with usually 4 stamens protruding from the corolla tube; flower heads maturing into hard, brown, stiff-spined structures (Plate 119B) that were used for teasing and carding wool (hence the common name); **seeds** 4-angled, ridged, light brown, about 5 mm (1/5 in.) long. Flowers from July to September.

Teasel occurs throughout southern Ontario in waste areas, meadows, roadsides, and sometimes in cultivated land, usually in moist areas and on coarse soils.

It is distinguished by its large rosette of shiny green leaves with stout prickles (a) on the upper surface, its prickly stems with pairs of opposite leaves often having cup-like bases, its egg-shaped heads (B) of flowers at the ends of stems and branches, these maturing into hard, brown structures completely surrounded by firm, sharp bristles (d).

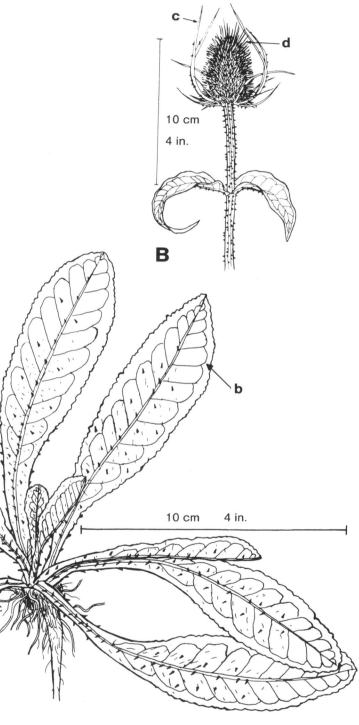

Figure 173. **Teasel** A. First-year plant with rosette leaves. B. Top of flowering branch.

GOURD or MELON FAMILY (Cucurbitaceae)

Wild cucumber, *Echinocystis lobata* (Michx.) T. & G., (Figure 174, Plate 120) [ECNLO, concombre grimpant, échinocystis lobé, concombre sauvage] Annual, reproducing only by seed. **Stems** vine-like, much-branched, climbing over fences, shrubs and trees to a height of 5 m (17 ft) or higher, soft and somewhat fleshy, lengthwise grooved, hairless or sometimes hairy at the nodes; **leaves** bright green, long-stalked, usually 5-lobed, resembling the cultivated cucumber, the margin of each lobe smooth or with scattered slender teeth; the lobes deep and the petiole attached in the broadly rounded heart-shaped leaf base, each leaf usually paired with a long, curly, branching tendril (a) on the opposite side of the stem at the same node (B); **flowers** with sexes separate, male flowers (b) in long, showy, branching panicles from the axil of each leaf, their petals small, white or greenish-white with prominent yellow anthers but with no pistil or ovary; female flowers (c) short-stalked, one in the axil of the tendril opposite the petiole of the leaf immediately below each cluster of male flowers; female flowers with no stamens but with a small, spherical, weakly spiny ovary (d) below the 6 small, yellow-green petals (e); **fruit** (C) fleshy, oblong 2.5 - 5 cm (1 - 2 in.) long, weakly prickly, after maturity dying and opening at the blossom end, releasing 4 large, flat, brown to blackish mottled **seeds**; the dry empty seedpod hanging from the branch during fall and winter as a small spiny mesh bag. Flowers from July to late autumn.

Wild cucumber occurs throughout southern Ontario in river bottoms, meadows, edges of woods, fence lines and waste areas, usually in low moist areas, but occasionally in drier sites as well.

It is distinguished by its vine habit, its branched tendrils opposite the bright green leaves, its long clusters of male flowers (b), its female flowers borne singly and its large, fleshy, weakly spiny 4-seeded fruits (C), also borne singly.

Goldencreeper, *Thladiantha dubia* Bunge, (not illustrated) [THDDU, thladianthe douteuse, Thladianthe] Resembling young plants of Wild cucumber. It is a perennial reproducing almost exclusively from fleshy, underground, potato-like **tubers**. Its **stems** are slender and somewhat twining, 1 - 2 m (40 - 80 in.) long but mostly climbing over other plants by means of tendrils; **leaves** alternate (1 per node), short-stalked, broadly heart-shaped, about 7.5 - 15 cm (3 - 6 in.) long, with a deep, rounded, U-shaped base, smooth margins, a slender, stretched-out tip, and rough-hairy on both surfaces; **flowers** showy, bright yellow, 15 - 25 mm (3/5 - 1 in.) across, somewhat resembling the shape of the male (pollen-producing) flowers of the cultivated cucumber. Canadian plants have only male (pollen-producing) flowers; the female (seed-producing) plant apparently has not been introduced. Flowers from July to September.

Goldencreeper occurs in scattered localities in southern Ontario, persisting in old gardens where it was introduced as an ornamental, spreading through lawns, gardens, along roadsides, in waste places and into cultivated fields.

It is distinguished by its rough-hairy, heart-shaped leaves with deep, rounded, U-shaped bases and stretched-out tips, climbing by tendrils, its bright yellow flowers, and reproducing only by very persistent, widely spreading, fleshy, underground, potato-like tubers which make it extremely difficult to eradicate.

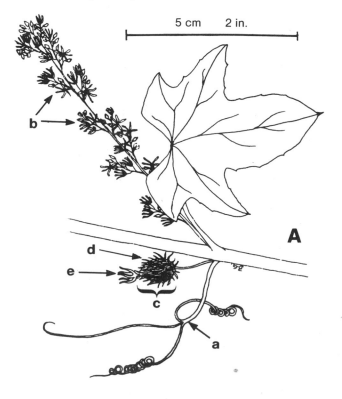

Figure 174. **Wild cucumber** A. Branch with cluster of male flowers and 1 female flower. B. Portion of branch with 1 fruit. (Cont'd.)

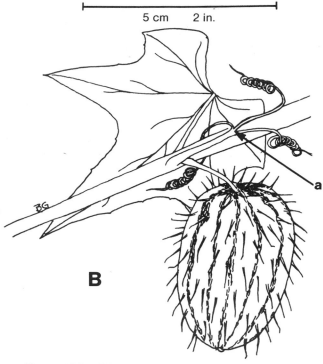

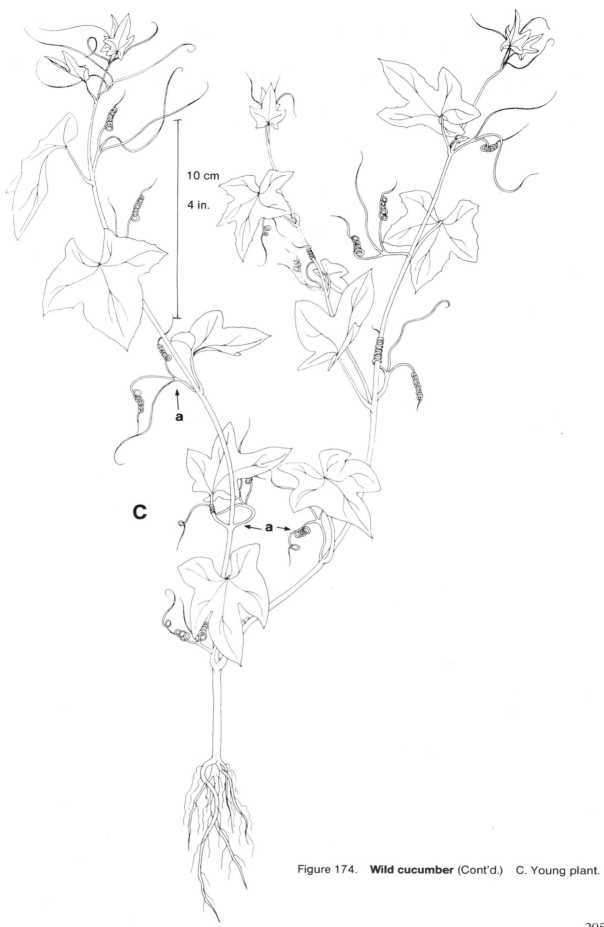

10 cm

4 in.

C

a

a

Figure 174.   **Wild cucumber** (Cont'd.)   C. Young plant.

Bur-cucumber, *Sicyos angulatus* L., (Figure 175) [SIYAN, sicyos anguieux, Bur cucumber, figue sauvage] Annual, reproducing only by seed. Creeping or climbing; **stems** sometimes several metres (several yards) long, hairy, with branched tendrils (a) opposite each leaf; **leaves** broad with 3 to 5 pointed angles or shallow lobes and deeply heartshaped at the petiole end; margins with widely spaced, very shallow teeth; petioles attached in the narrow space (b) between the lobes of the heart-shaped leaf base; **flowers** of two kinds: male, pollen-producing flowers in open-branched clusters (c) on long stalks, their corolla (d) white or greenish and 5-lobed; female, seed-producing flowers in small, head-like clusters (e) on shorter stalks; individual **fruits** ovoid, up to 23 mm (7/8 in.) long and 10 mm (2/5 in.) wide, not inflated and not succulent, covered with fine cobwebby hair and several to many, long (4 mm, 1/6 in.), slender, yellow, hard, sharp, barbed spines; 3 to 10 fruits usually clustered together in a spiny bur (f). Flowers from July to September.

Bur-cucumber occurs in damp soil along river banks and in yards and fields in southern Ontario, sometimes almost completely covering the plants with which it is growing.

It is distinguished by its vine habit with branched tendrils opposite each leaf, the narrow space between the lobes of the heart-shaped leaf base, and its non-inflated, sharply spiny fruits borne in clusters of 3 to 10 together.

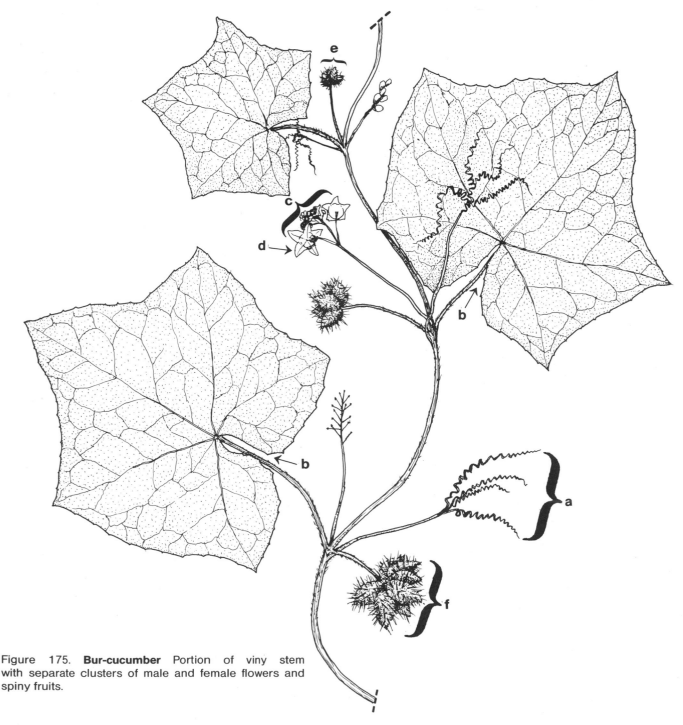

Figure 175. **Bur-cucumber** Portion of viny stem with separate clusters of male and female flowers and spiny fruits.

HAREBELL or BELLFLOWER FAMILY (Campanulaceae)

Creeping bellflower, *Campanula rapunculoides* L., (Figure 176, Plate 121) [CMPRA, campanule fausse raiponce, Bellflower, Rover bellflower, campanule raiponce] Perennial, reproducing by seed and by the extremely persistent, widely spreading, fleshy, whitish underground **rhizomes** (a) and thickened storage **tubers** (Plate 121B). **Stems,** when present, erect, up to 1 m (40 in.) high, smooth or finely hairy, usually without branches; **leaves** mostly arising singly or in clusters directly from rhizomes below the ground surface (b), these long-stalked and called "radical" leaves (root leaves) (A, Plate 121A, B); the blades round to nearly heart-shaped at the base, ovate, pointed towards the tip, irregularly toothed, usually finely hairy; leaves (c) on developing stems (B) alternate (1 per node), similar to radical leaves but stalks progressively shorter and blades smaller, less heart-shaped and more regularly toothed; uppermost leaves (d) narrow and stalkless; **flowers** in elongating racemes at the ends of the stems, blue, bell-shaped, 2 - 3 cm (4/5 - 1¼ in.)

across, ending in 5 uniform points (e); flower stalks frequently curved and giving the whole inflorescence an attractive 1-sided appearance; **seedpods** (f) formed below the calyx and corolla, somewhat spherical, containing many very fine **seeds.** Flowers from June until autumn.

Creeping bellflower occurs throughout Ontario in lawns, gardens, fence lines, roadsides, waste places and occasionally in cultivated fields. It is sometimes planted in ornamental gardens but spreads into adjacent areas by underground rhizomes as well as by seed and is a very persistent weed.

Non-flowering plants are distinguished by their many heart-shaped, irregularly toothed leaves arising from at or below the ground surface (A), the whitish, fleshy, underground rhizomes (a) and tubers; flowering plants have characteristic bell-shaped blue flowers with a 5-pointed rim (d), and their seedpods develop between corolla and main stem.

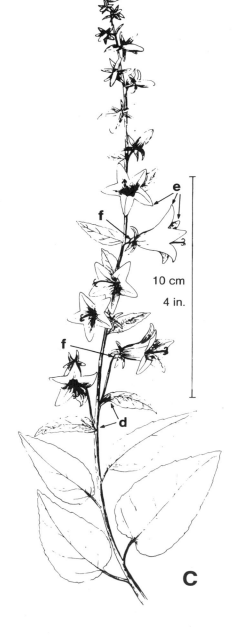

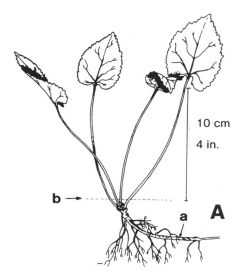

Figure 176. **Creeping bellflower** A. Stemless plant with cluster of radical leaves from upturned rhizome. B. Basal leaves and short leafy stem from horizontal rhizome. C. Top of flowering stem.

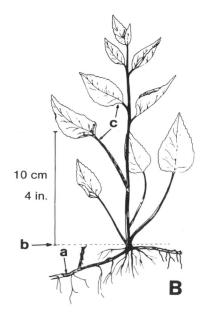

207

COMPOSITE or ASTER FAMILY (Compositae)

The Composite Family includes many of our weedy plants. Some have large, bright, showy flower heads such as Black-eyed Susan, Dandelion, Ox-eye daisy and the thistles. Others, such as ragweeds and worm-woods, have small inconspicuous flower heads. **The Composite "Flower Head"** (Figure 177).

What most people call "a flower" in the Composite or Aster Family is really a head, that is, a whole inflorescence of many small flowers tightly clustered together and resembling one single larger flower, hence the family name "Composite." The individual small flowers are called florets and may be of two types: (1) **disk** or **tubular florets** (A, C, D) which have their 5 petals united into a tubular corolla with 5 lobes (a) at the end [Figures 178(d), 204(d), 213(f)], and (2) **ray** or **ligulate** (strap-shaped) **florets** (A, B, C, E) which have their 5 petals united but forming a flat corolla (b), the outer end of which may be pointed [Figure 178 (c)], round [Figure 189 (a)], square or 2-lobed, 3-lobed [Figure 180 (b)], or 5-lobed [Figure 224 (b)]. The sepals of the individual florets are not recognizable as such. They may have been modified into soft hair (Figure 225, Dandelion), or bristles [Figure 182C,(d), Beggarticks], or scales (Figure 124, Chicory), or may be completely absent [as at (c) in Figure 177D, Ox-eye daisy, and Figure 186, Stinking mayweed]. Instead of being called "sepals,"

these hairs or bristles or scales are called "**pappus**" (c). The ovary (d) of each individual floret is below the corolla and pappus. It matures into a firm-shelled fruit, an achene, containing a single seed, but the whole unit including the firm shell is often called a "seed" (for example, sunflower seed). All the florets of a single flower head are very compactly arranged side by side on a single, flat, rounded or elongated receptacle (e). If some or all of the florets in the head have a small bract (chaffy scale) or bristle adjacent to each, the receptacle is said to be "**chaffy**," but if there are no chaffy scales or bristles among the florets, the receptacle is said to be "**smooth**" or "**naked**" (e). Immediately below and surrounding the entire group of florets is a ring of bracts (f) usually green but sometimes white or amber called the "**involucral bracts**" or "**tegules**" or "**phyllaries**" [Figures 189B, (c), 204B, (e)]. These involucral bracts around the base of the flower head are often mistakenly thought to be sepals around the base of a single flower as in most other plant families. Sepals in flowers belonging to other families enclose and protect the delicate petals, stamens and pistil in single flowers before blossoming. In the same way, involucral bracts enclose and protect all of the individual florets of each flower head before the head opens and blossoming begins.

Figure 177. **The Composite "Flower Head"** of Ox-eye daisy.   A. Flower head viewed from above.   B. Flower head viewed from below.   C. Vertical section through flower head and stalk.   D. Side view of one disk or tubular floret.   E. Front view of one sterile ray or ligulate floret (without either stamens or stigma).

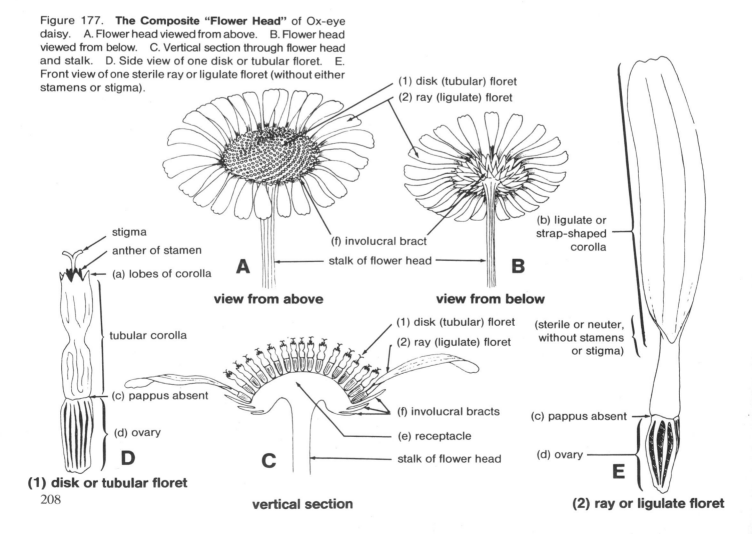

208

Classification of plants in the Composite Family is based partly on whether each flower head contains **both ray and disk florets** as in the illustrations of Ox-eye daisy [Figures 177, 189 (a), (b)], and Black-eyed Susan [Figure 178 (c), (d)], **only disk florets with no ray florets** as in the ragweeds (Figures 183, 184) and the thistles (Figures 207 - 211), or **only ray florets with no disk florets** as in Dandelion (Figure 225) and Chicory (Figure 224).

Black-eyed Susan, *Rudbeckia serotina* Nutt., (Figure 178, Plate 122) [RUDHI, rudbeckie herissée, Coneflower, Yellow-daisy, marguerite jaune, marguerite orangée] Perennial or sometimes biennial, reproducing only by seed. **Stems** erect, 30 - 100 cm (12 - 40 in.) high, single or with a few branches in the upper parts, more or less rough-hairy throughout; **leaves** alternate (1 per node); lower leaves long-elliptic, tapering to a long stalk (a); upper leaves (b) narrow, stalkless, smooth-margined or somewhat coarsely toothed; all leaves rough-hairy and usually dark green; **flower heads** (see page 208) large and showy at the ends of long, thin, erect branches, 2.5 - 7.5 cm (1 - 3 in.) in diameter with ray florets (c) orange to orange-yellow and spreading like spokes of a wheel; disk florets (d) dark purple or blackish, individually very small and tightly packed on a conic receptacle forming a prominent, hard, dark, raised centre in the head, like the hub of a wheel; **seeds** black, 4-angled with fine lengthwise lines. Flowers from mid-June to September.

Black-eyed Susan is a native plant in the Great Plains but was introduced into Ontario and has spread aggressively throughout the province in meadows, pastures, edges of woods, river valleys, lakeshores and roadsides, usually in coarse-textured soils.

It is distinguished by its long-elliptic, rough-hairy leaves, and showy, long-stemmed flower heads with bright yellow ray florets (c) and dark purplish to blackish disk florets (d).

Tall coneflower, *Rudbeckia laciniata* L., (not illustrated) [RUDLA, rudbeckie laciniée, Cut-leaved coneflower, Great coneflower, rudbeckie à feuilles dentelées] A taller plant than Black-eyed Susan with larger, broad, 3- to 7-lobed or divided **leaves** and larger **flower heads** with bright yellow ray florets and dull greenish-yellow disk florets. It is native throughout southern Ontario in meadows and river valleys.

The cultivated ornamental perennial, Golden-glow, *Rudbeckia laciniata* L. var. *hortensis* Bailey, (not illustrated) [rudbeckie laciniée cultivée], a horticultural selection from Tall coneflower, occasionally escapes from cultivation into waste places and along roadsides.

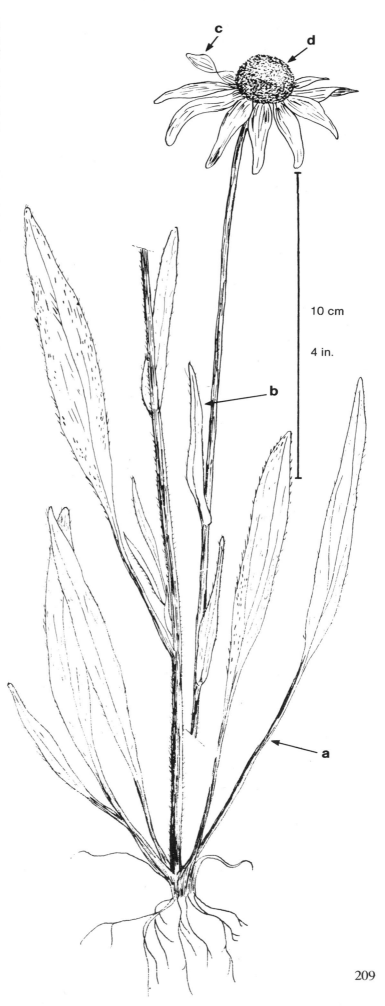

Figure 178. **Black-eyed Susan**

Jerusalem artichoke, *Helianthus tuberosus* L., (Figure 179, Plates 123, 124) [HELTU, topinambour, Tuberous sunflower, hélianthe tubéreux] Perennial, reproducing both by seed and by spreading, fleshy, underground **tubers** (a) resembling slender potatoes; **stems** erect, 1 - 3 m (40 in. - 10 ft) high, with few branches except near the top or occasionally bushy-branched throughout; lower **leaves** opposite (2 per node), stalked, ovate or broadest near the roundish base and tapering towards the pointed tip (b), 10 - 25

cm (4 - 10 in.) long, somewhat toothed, harshly hairy on the upper surface but smooth or softly hairy on the lower surface, usually with 3 main veins from the tip of the leafstalk; middle leaves similar and either opposite or alternate (1 per node); upper leaves smaller and usually alternate but occasionally opposite; **flower heads** (c) (see page 208) bright yellow, resembling the cultivated sunflower but smaller, 5 - 10 cm (2 - 4 in.) across; flower heads also resembling those of Black-eyed Susan but ray florets longer and more upright, and disk florets larger, not as crowded and yellowish rather than purplish to blackish; **seeds** similar to cultivated sunflower but somewhat smaller (about 3 - 4 mm, ⅛ - 1/6 in. long and only 1 - 2 mm, 1/25 - 1/12 in. wide). Flowers from August to late autumn.

Jerusalem artichoke occurs in moist meadows and valleys in southern Ontario; it has occasionally been cultivated as an ornamental and for its edible tubers, persisting after cultivation in old gardens, and spreading to cultivated fields, fence lines and roadsides.

It is distinguished by its tall, erect stems producing numerous, fleshy tuberous roots like slender potatoes, its medium to large leaves broad near the base and harsh on the upper surface, and its bright yellow, sunflower-like flower heads.

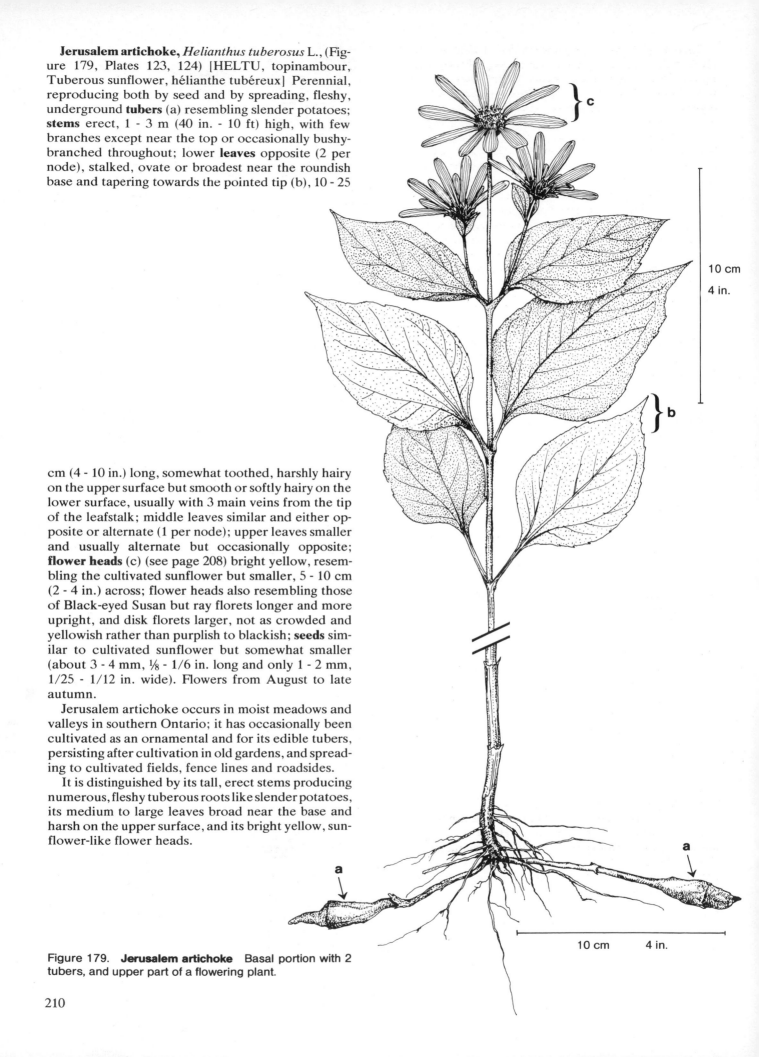

10 cm
4 in.

Figure 179. **Jerusalem artichoke** Basal portion with 2 tubers, and upper part of a flowering plant.

210

Sneezeweed, *Helenium autumnale* L., (Figure 180) [HENAU, hélénie, hélénie automale] Perennial, reproducing only by seed. **Stems** 30 - 150 cm (1 - 5 ft) high from a fibrous **root**, smooth or finely hairy; **leaves** numerous, alternate (1 per node), linear to narrowly elliptic, stalkless, somewhat toothed, the edges of the leaves continuing down the stem as narrow leaf-like wings (a); **flower heads** (see page 208) bright and showy, 2.5 - 5 cm (1 - 2 in.) across, several to many on erect branches; ray florets (b) 10 to 20 on each head, bright yellow, 3-lobed at the end, soon bending back towards the stem; disk florets (c) lighter yellow, very compact, forming a raised, rounded centre in the flower head; head surrounded by very narrow involucral bracts (d). Flowers from August to late autumn.

Sneezeweed occurs in southern Ontario in moist meadows, low places in woods and thickets, wet depressions and along lakes and streams. **It is poisonous to livestock, especially cattle and sheep.**

It is distinguished by its winged stems (a) with long narrow leaves, and its large bright yellow flower heads, with the ray florets (b) 3-lobed and bent back, and surrounded by narrow bracts (d).

Hairy galinsoga, *Galinsoga ciliata* (Raf.) Blake, (Figure 181, Plate 125) [GASCI, galinsoga cilié, Galinsoga, Quickweed, galinsoga] Annual reproducing only by seed. **Stems** erect, often much-branched with opposite branches (usually 2 per node), 20 - 70 cm (8 - 28 in.) high, usually covered with coarse spreading hair; **leaves** opposite (2 per node), lower ones long-stalked, upper nearly stalkless, blades oval, pointed towards the tip, coarsely toothed; **flower heads** (a) (see page 208) small, about 3 - 7 mm (⅛ - ¼ in.) across on short to long stalks from axils of leaves, the stalks usually hairy with slightly glandular hair; ray florets (b) white, small, about 5 per head, only slightly longer than the yellowish-green to whitish disk florets; pappus-scales present on both ray and tubular florets and as long as the corolla tubes of the ray florets. Flowers from June to late autumn.

Hairy galinsoga is common throughout southern Ontario in gardens, roadsides and waste places, especially near towns and cities.

It is distinguished by its opposite, oval, coarsely toothed leaves on opposite-branched stems and its small flower heads (a) each with 5 white tiny rays (b) and a yellow disk.

Small-flowered galinsoga, *Galinsoga parviflora* Cav., (not illustrated) [GASPA, galinsoga à petites fleurs, galinsoga] Very similar to Hairy galinsoga and distinguished from it only on technical characteristics (ray florets without pappus). It also occurs in similar situations in Ontario but is much less common than Hairy galinsoga.

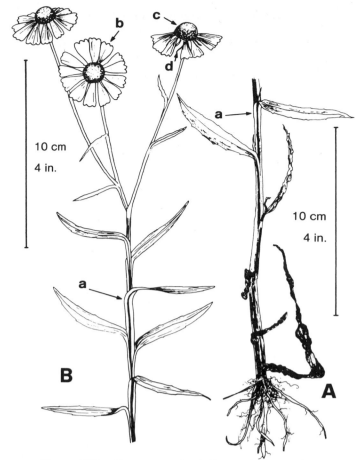

Figure 180. **Sneezeweed** A. Base of plant. B. Top of flowering stem.

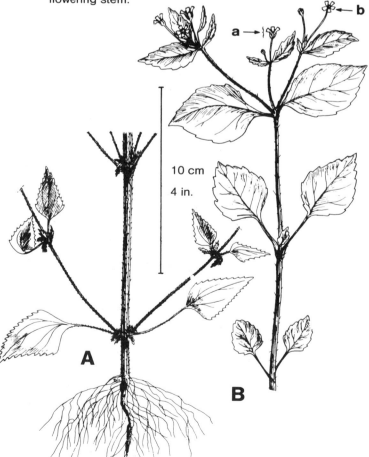

Figure 181. **Hairy galinsoga** A. Base of plant. B. Top of flowering plant.

211

Nodding beggarticks, *Bidens cernua* L., (Figure 182A) [BIDCE, bident penché, Beggar's-ticks, Bur-marigold, fourchettes] Annual, reproducing only by seed. **Stems** erect, branched, 10 - 100 cm (4 - 40 in.) high; **leaves** opposite (2 per node), undivided, narrowly ovate to linear, sharply toothed to almost smooth, leaf bases sometimes united around stem; **flower heads** (see page 208) showy, 2.5 - 5 cm (1 - 2 in.) across, ray florets (a) bright yellow, up to 1.5 cm (3/5 in.) long, usually 8 per head but occasionally fewer or absent altogether; disk florets (b) yellowish-green, many, densely crowded together; head surrounded by several, long, leafy, green involucral bracts (c); **seeds** brownish, flat, long-oval, with 2 downward-barbed awns [as in (D, d)] on top. Flowers from July to late autumn.

Nodding beggarticks occurs throughout Ontario in moist places, usually in meadows, river valleys, road-side ditches, and depressions in cultivated land.

It is distinguished by its opposite undivided leaves, its large flower heads with usually 8 yellow ray florets (a) and long, leafy, green involucral bracts (c), and its seeds with 2 downward-barbed awns.

Tall beggarticks, *Bidens vulgata* Greene, (Figure 182B, C, Plate 126) [BIDVU, bident vulgaire, Bur-marigold, fourchettes] Similar in form and habit to Nodding beggarticks but distinguished by having com-pound **leaves** (e) with 3 or 5 leaflets (f), (just 1 leaflet resembling the whole leaf of Nodding beggarticks); **flower heads** usually lacking the large yellow ray florets (see A, a), and surrounded by 10 to 16 or more long, thin, involucral bracts (g). Like Nodding beggar-ticks, its **seeds** also have 2 backward-barbed awns (d). Tall beggarticks has a similar distribution to that of Nodding beggarticks.

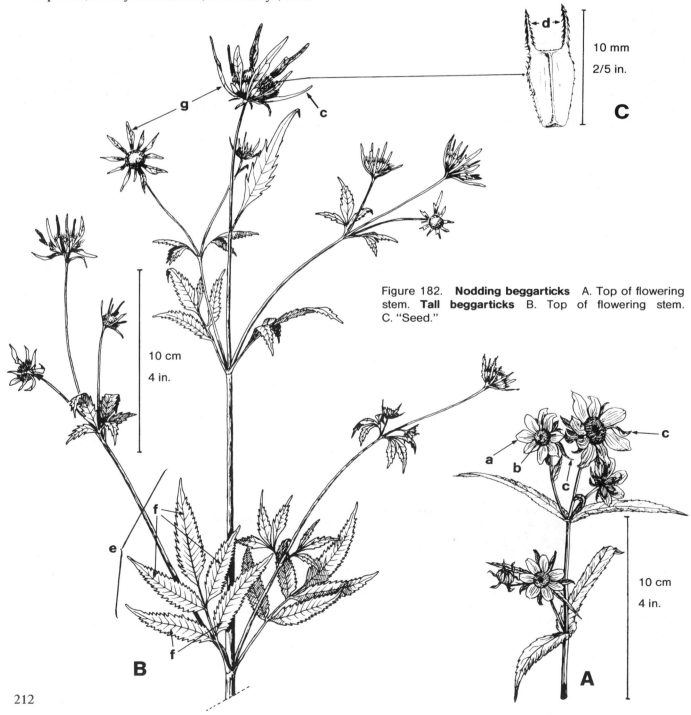

Figure 182. **Nodding beggarticks** A. Top of flowering stem. **Tall beggarticks** B. Top of flowering stem. C. "Seed."

Common ragweed, *Ambrosia artemisiifolia* L., (Figure 183, Plate 127) [AMBEL, petite herbe à poux, Short ragweed, ambrosie à feuilles d'armoise] Annual, reproducing only by seed. **Stems** erect, 15 - 150 cm (6 - 60 in.) high, usually much-branched, hairless or hairy throughout; lower **leaves** opposite (2 per node) but becoming alternate (1 per node) (B) higher on the plant, bright green to slightly yellowish-green on young plants, becoming grayish-green on older plants, compound and finely divided, the final divisions (a) usually coarsely toothed; **flower heads** (see page 208) not showy, individually small, 2 - 5 mm (1/12 - 1/5 in.) across, green and inconspicuous but very numerous and forming distinctive inflorescences (C, D, E); individual florets either male or female, but never both; all flowers within one flower head either only male or female, but both male flower heads and female flower heads usually present on the same plant; heads of male (pollen-producing) flowers (D) in raceme-like elongated clusters at ends of branches (Plate 127B), each male head (b) hanging downwards on a short stalk like a tiny inverted umbrella; female (seed-producing) flower heads (E) in axils of short, narrow, green bracts (c) near the base of each long cluster of male flower heads, each female head (d) with only a single flower and producing a single, hard, somewhat triangular or diamond-shaped **seed** with several, short, sharp spines

(e) around the upper shoulder, the whole seed 3 - 5 mm (⅛ - 1/5 in.) long. Flowers from August to October.

Common ragweed is one of the most abundant weeds of cultivated land throughout southern Ontario, but is rare or absent in northern and northwestern parts of the province. It also occurs in gardens, flower borders, poorly kept lawns, edges of sidewalks, roadsides, fencelines, waste places, and in disturbed areas in pastures and meadows.

It is distinguished by its finely divided leaves, which are opposite in the lower part and alternate (B, C) in the upper part of the plant, these being yellow-green at first, later gray-green with age, and its very numerous, tiny, non-showy, greenish male flower heads (b) clustered along slender branches (D) in the upper part of the plant (C).

Common ragweed is the most important cause of hay fever during August and September. Although inconspicuous and not recognized by most people, the tiny male flower heads (b) hanging on their slender stalks produce huge quantities of very light pollen. As the pollen falls from these hanging flowers, it is caught by the wind and may be carried for distances greater than 200 km (125 miles). Hay fever sufferers, therefore, may be affected by pollen from ragweed plants far away.

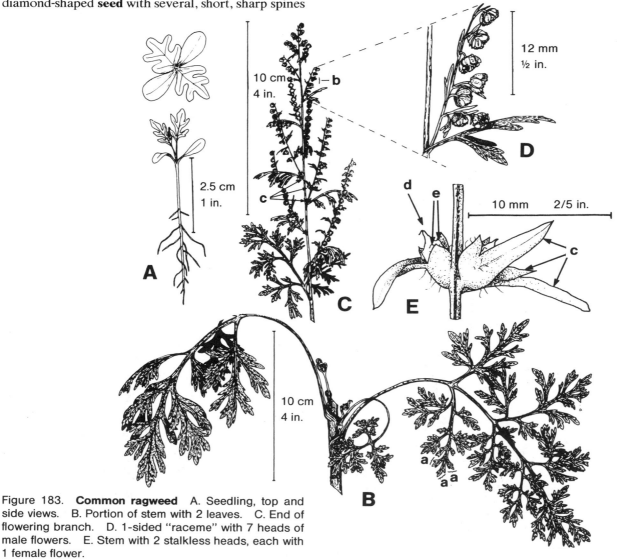

Figure 183. **Common ragweed** A. Seedling, top and side views. B. Portion of stem with 2 leaves. C. End of flowering branch. D. 1-sided "raceme" with 7 heads of male flowers. E. Stem with 2 stalkless heads, each with 1 female flower.

213

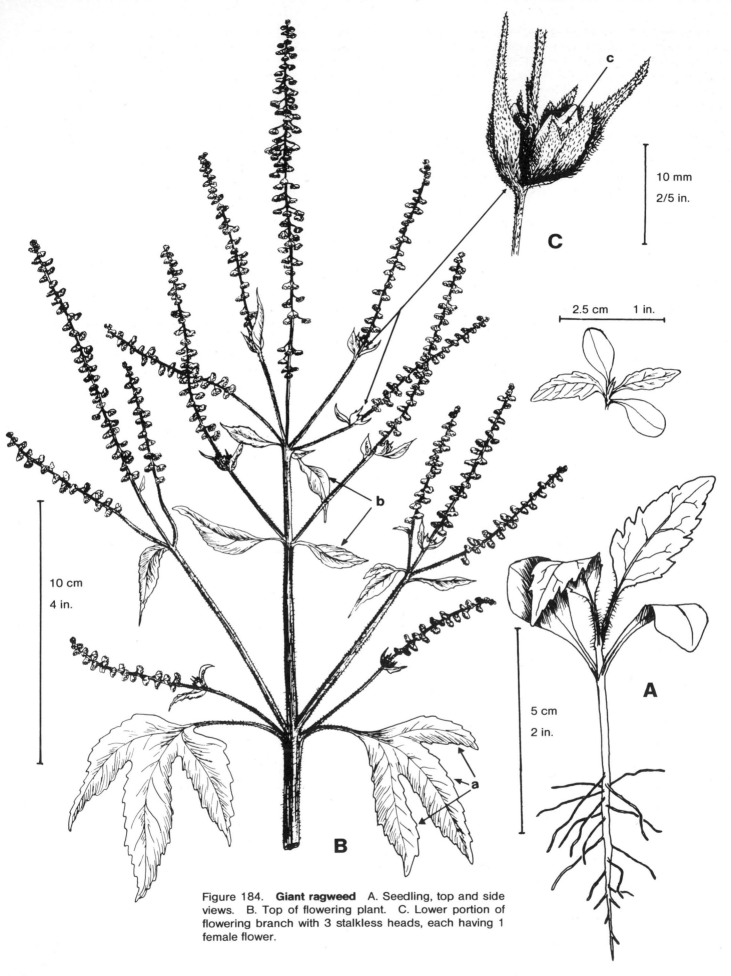

Figure 184. **Giant ragweed** A. Seedling, top and side views. B. Top of flowering plant. C. Lower portion of flowering branch with 3 stalkless heads, each having 1 female flower.

10 mm
2/5 in.

2.5 cm   1 in.

10 cm
4 in.

5 cm
2 in.

It is essential that **Goldenrod,** *Solidago* spp., (Plate 140) [verge d'or, solidage], not be confused with Common ragweed. Several species of Goldenrod occur throughout Ontario in meadows, pastures, woodland, river flats and roadsides, and have very conspicuous bright yellow inflorescences during the ragweed hayfever season of late summer and autumn. Goldenrods do produce pollen but only in small quantities, and their pollen is heavy and sticky. It is not carried on the wind and the plants are pollinated by insects. Because Goldenrod pollen is not carried on the wind, it must not be blamed as the source of irritation for ragweed hay fever sufferers.

Giant ragweed, *Ambrosia trifida* L., (Figure 184, Plate 128) [AMBTR, grande herbe à poux, Great ragweed, Kinghead, Tall ragweed, ambrosie trifide] Annual, reproducing only by seed. **Stems** erect, 0.4 - 4 m (16 in. - 13 ft) tall, usually much-branched and somewhat hairy; **leaves** opposite (2 per node) throughout the plant except towards the ends of the smaller branches at flowering time where they may be alternate (1 per node); leaves large, rounded in outline and 3- to 5-lobed (a), the lobes smooth or coarsely toothed; uppermost small leaves usually not lobed (b); in some plants most or all leaves not lobed but ovate with acuminate tips and only shallowly toothed; leaf surfaces usually rough (like medium sandpaper); **flower heads** (see page 208) unisexual as in Common ragweed; male (pollen-producing) flower heads and female (seed-producing) flower heads similar to those described for Common ragweed except that the female head is much larger and usually 2 to 4 are grouped together (C); **seed** much larger than Common ragweed, 5 - 10 mm (1/5 - 2/5 in.) long with several, prominent, lengthwise ridges ending in short blunt spines (c) around the upper shoulder of the seed. Flowers from August to October.

Giant ragweed occurs in river valleys, meadows, roadsides and occasionally in cultivated fields in the southwestern portion of southern Ontario.

It is distinguished by its very tall stature (up to 4 m or 13 ft), its large, lobed but not divided leaves, its long, slender spikes of pollen-producing flower heads and its large, angular seeds with spines around the upper shoulder.

The pollen of Giant ragweed is an important cause of hay fever during August and September, especially in southwestern Ontario (also see comments on hay fever under Common ragweed and Canada goldenrod, pages 213 and 226).

Cocklebur, *Xanthium strumarium* L., (Figure 185, Plate 129) [XANST, lampourde glouteron, Bur, Clotbur, glouteron] Annual, reproducing only by seed. **Stems** erect, usually much-branched, 30 - 120 cm (12 - 48 in.) high, rough-hairy, often with lengthwise ridges and spotted; **cotyledons** (seed leaves) (a) long, narrow, smooth, often persisting at the base of a developing stem and sometimes still present at maturity; **leaves** stalked, oval or triangular, somewhat angular heart-shaped at the base with the edges of the lowermost main branching veins usually exposed in a broad V or M (b) (not enclosed within the leaf blade as in the leaves of most other plants), margins coarsely toothed and surfaces harsh or rough-hairy; lower leaves frequently opposite (2 per node), but upper leaves alternate (1 per node); **flower heads** (see page 208) clustered in axils of leaves and at ends of branches; sexes in separate heads but both sexes on the same plant; heads of male (pollen-producing) flowers (c) small, more or less spherical, not spiny, usually several in small clusters above the larger, spiny heads of female (seed-producing) flowers; seedpod or "bur" actually 1 complete flower head (d) containing 2 female flowers, becoming very hard and woody, covered with numerous slender, hooked spines (e) and terminating in 2 very hard, hooked, beak-like spines (f), and turning brown at maturity. Each bur contains 2 **seeds,** usually 1 a bit larger than the other. Flowers from August to October.

Cocklebur occurs throughout Ontario around farmyards, in fields, along roadsides and river flats. It is particularly common in low areas which may be wet only during spring and fall, and is usually more common in fine-textured soils such as clays and clay loams than on coarser soils. **Seedlings (B) of Cocklebur are poisonous to livestock, especially to young pigs which seem to relish their taste.**

Mature plants of Cocklebur are readily distinguished by the large coarse burs (d) and their harsh leaves. Young and non-flowering plants are distinguished by their oval or broadly triangular, rough-textured leaves which have the characteristic V- or M-shaped base with the edges of the main lower branch veins (b) exposed; the lowermost leaves opposite, upper ones alternate. Seedlings of Cocklebur are distinguished by their large, long, narrow, smooth cotyledons (seed leaves) (a) and by the remnant of the bur (g) usually attached to the root at or below the ground surface. Plants of Cocklebur are highly variable in height, amount of branching, overall shape of leaves, arrangements of inflorescences and size and shape of each bur. This group is not well understood taxonomically so, although several botanical names have been used for various groups of cockleburs, all of the Ontario plants can be referred to as *Xanthium strumarium* in the broad sense.

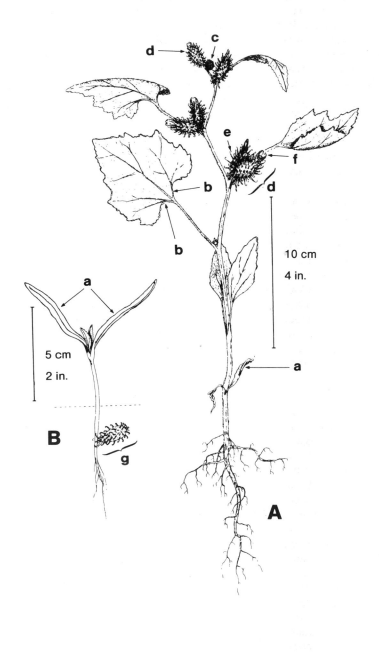

Figure 185.   **Cocklebur**   A. Plant.   B. Seedling.

Stinking mayweed, *Anthemis cotula* L., (Figure 186, Plate 130) [ANTCO, camomille des chiens, Dogfennel, Stinking chamomille, camomille puante, camomille maroute] Annual, reproducing only by seed. **Stems** usually erect, but low and bushy-branched, 10 - 60 cm (4 - 24 in.) high, usually hairless in the lower part but finely hairy (a) just below the flower heads; **leaves** very finely dissected, soft, alternate (1 per node), numerous, or sparse where plants are crowded; **flower heads** (see page 208) daisy-like, 15 - 30 mm (3/5 - 1¼ in.) across; ray florets (b) white, spreading; disk florets (c) yellow; **seeds** grayish to brownish, longer than wide, surface rough with lengthwise rows of tiny bumps. All parts of the plant, when crushed, have an offensively disagreeable odour resembling evaporating urine, hence the common name. Flowers from June to late summer.

Stinking mayweed occurs throughout Ontario in waste places, along roadsides, around dwellings and farmyards and, occasionally, in cultivated fields.

It is distinguished by its offensive odour, its finely dissected leaves, and its finely hairy stems (a) below the white and yellow flower heads.

Corn chamomile, *Anthemis arvensis* L., (not illustrated) [ANTAR, camomille des champs, anthemis des champs, camomille sauvage, fausse camomille] Almost identical to Stinking mayweed but its aromatic odour is not offensive. It has escaped from cultivation to roadsides and waste places in a number of areas in counties near Lake Ontario.

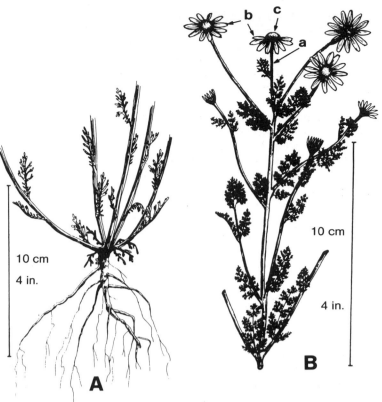

Figure 186. **Stinking mayweed** A. Base of plant. B. Flowering stem.

Pineappleweed, *Matricaria matricarioides* (Less.) Porter, (Figure 187, Plate 131) [MATMT, matricaire odorante, matricaire suave, *Chamomilla suaveolens* Rydb.] Annual, reproducing only by seed. **Stems** erect, much-branched, 5 - 40 cm (2 - 16 in.) high, smooth, hairless; **leaves** very finely dissected, light green, smooth, hairless and slightly fleshy, alternate (1 per node); **flower heads** (a) (see page 208) small, conic or egg-shaped, 5 - 9 mm (1/5 - ⅜ in.) across, yellowish-green, and without ray florets. The whole plant, and especially the flower heads, when crushed has a distinct pineapple-like odour, hence the common name. Flowers from spring until autumn.

Pineappleweed occurs throughout Ontario, especially around farmyards, waste places and roadsides. It is an occasional weed in the compacted soil along the edges of pathways. Also see Prostrate knotweed.

It is distinguished by its small stature, its small flower heads (a) without white ray florets, its smooth hairless stems below the flower heads, and its pineapple odour.

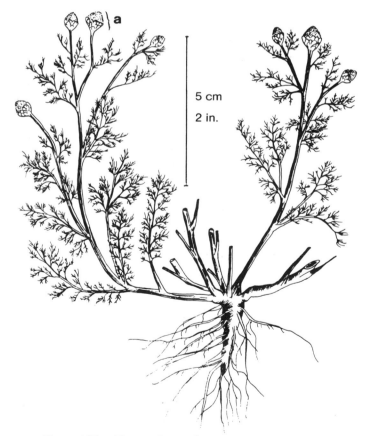

Figure 187. **Pineappleweed**

217

Scentless chamomile, *Matricaria perforata* Merat, (Plate 132) [MATMG, matricaire inodore, Scentless mayweed, matricaire maritime, *Matricaria maritima* L. var. *agrestis* (Knaf) Wilmott, *Matricaria inodora* L.] Very similar to both Pineappleweed and Stinking mayweed. It is a short-lived perennial or sometimes annual, closely resembling Stinking mayweed with its large yellow-centred **flower heads** with white ray florets, but it is usually taller (up to 75 cm, 30 in.) and more branched, its **stems** below the flower heads are smooth and hairless, and the whole plant is virtually without odour. It occurs sporadically in Ontario in waste places and roadsides, but is becoming a significant weed in pastures and some cultivated fields.

Yarrow, *Achillea millefolium* L., (Figure 188, Plate 133) [ACHMI, achillée mille-feuille, Common yarrow, Fernweed, Milfoil, herbe à dinde, mille-feuille, *Achillea lanulosa* Nutt.] Perennial, reproducing by seed and by spreading underground rootstalks (A), often forming very dense feathery- or ferny-leaved patches; **stems** erect, usually covered with fine woolly hair, about 60 cm (2 ft) tall but up to 100 cm (40 in.) in fertile situations, or very short in lawns or trampled situations; **leaves** very numerous at base of plant (A) but fewer and smaller upwards on the stem (B), finely divided or feather-like, lower ones long-stalked, the upper stalkless, alternate (1 per node), green to grayish-green, finely woolly to silky-hairy; **flower heads** (see page 208) very small but numerous in dense, flat-topped to rounded clusters, each head 3 - 7 mm (⅛ - ¼ in.) across, ray florets (a) usually only 5 per head, white or rarely pinkish; disk florets (b) more numerous, whitish; **seeds** small, flat, grayish with whitish margins. The whole plant has a characteristic sage-like odour which is offensive to some people but attractive to others. Flowers from June to late autumn.

Yarrow is very common throughout Ontario in natural areas, meadows, pastures, waste places, roadsides, and frequently in lawns.

It is distinguished by its very finely divided, feather-like or ferny leaves, the dense patches from its spreading underground root system, its flat-topped clusters of small flower heads, each head with usually 5 tiny white ray florets (a), and its characteristic sage-like aroma. Forms with pinkish to purplish or yellow flowers are cultivated as ornamental perennials and may escape to lawns and roadsides.

Figure 188. **Yarrow** A. Base of plant from horizontal underground rootstalk. B. Flowering stem.

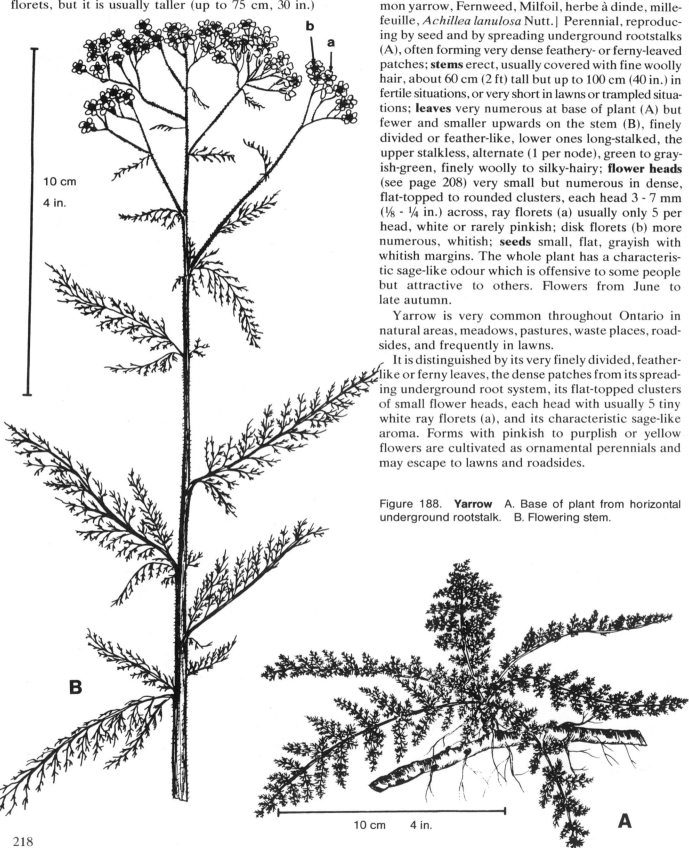

10 cm
4 in.

10 cm   4 in.

Ox-eye daisy, *Chrysanthemum leucanthemum* L., (Figure 189, Plate 134) [CHYLE, marguerite blanche, Field daisy, White daisy, grande marguerite, marguerite, chrysanthème leucanthème] Perennial, reproducing by seed and by underground rhizomes. **Stems** erect or curving upwards 20 - 90 cm (8 - 36 in.) high, single from upturned ends of **rhizomes**, or few to many from a stout **root-crown**; lower **leaves** broadly spoon-shaped, deeply and coarsely dissected or toothed, stalked, smooth, dark green, often glossy and fleshy; upper leaves narrower, similarly dissected or deeply toothed, stalkless and often clasping the stem, alternate (1 per node); **flower heads** (see page 208) large and showy, daisy-like, 2.5 - 5 cm (1 - 2 in.) across, borne singly at ends of stems and main branches; ray florets (a) usually 15 to 30 per head, white, 1 - 2 cm (2/5 - 4/5 in.) long; disk florets (b) bright yellow, short, numerous, densely packed, forming a slightly rounded centre; involucral bracts (c) at base of each head numerous, firm, overlapping, light green with brownish margins; **seeds** top-shaped with a knob-like projection on the upper end, ridged, and with alternate black and white stripes. When crushed, all parts of the plant have a disagreeably sour odour. Flowers from early June to late autumn.

Ox-eye daisy is very common and conspicuous throughout Ontario, often forming dense infestations in pastures, meadows and waste places, but also occurring in cultivated land, roadsides, gardens and lawns.

It is distinguished by its dark green, smooth, somewhat fleshy, dissected or coarsely toothed leaves, its large, conspicuous, daisy-like flower heads with white rays (a) and yellow centres (b), its rhizomatous and fibrous-rooted underground system, and its disagreeable odour.

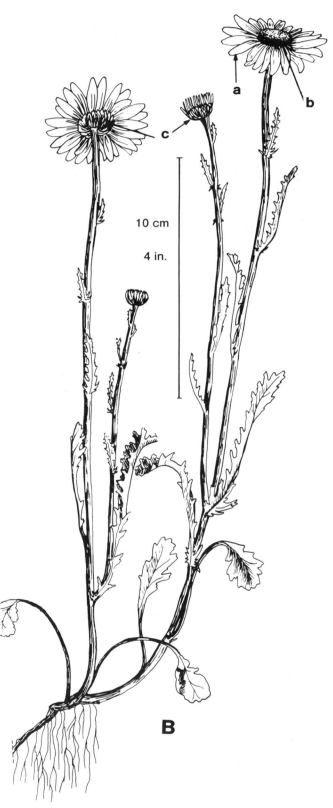

10 cm
4 in.

Figure 189. **Ox-eye daisy** A. Young rosette. B. Older plant with flowering stems.

Tansy, *Tanacetum vulgare* L., (Figure 190, Plate 135) [CHYVU, tanaisie vulgaire, Common tansy, tanaisie commune] Perennial, reproducing by seed and by spreading underground **rhizomes. Stems** coarse, erect, tall (40 - 150 cm, 16 - 60 in.), hairless; **leaves** pinnately divided and redivided, at first resembling leaves of Yarrow but becoming larger and coarser with the ultimate divisions not as fine; basal leaves large and long-stalked, often forming large dense clumps; stem leaves numerous, smaller and stalkless towards the top, alternate (1 per node); **flower heads** (see page 208) in dense, rounded or flat-topped clusters at ends of stems and branches; each head firm, button-like, 5 - 10 mm (1/5 - 2/5 in.) across,

without ray florets but with numerous, small, densely packed yellow disk florets. All parts of the plant have a strong, characteristic "tansy" aroma. Flowers from July to September.

Tansy occurs sporadically throughout Ontario in waste places, edges of fields, roadsides and old gardens.

It is distinguished by its large, pinnately divided and redivided leaves which resemble but are coarser than Yarrow, its small button-like yellow flower heads crowded in rounded or flat-topped clusters, and its characteristic aroma.

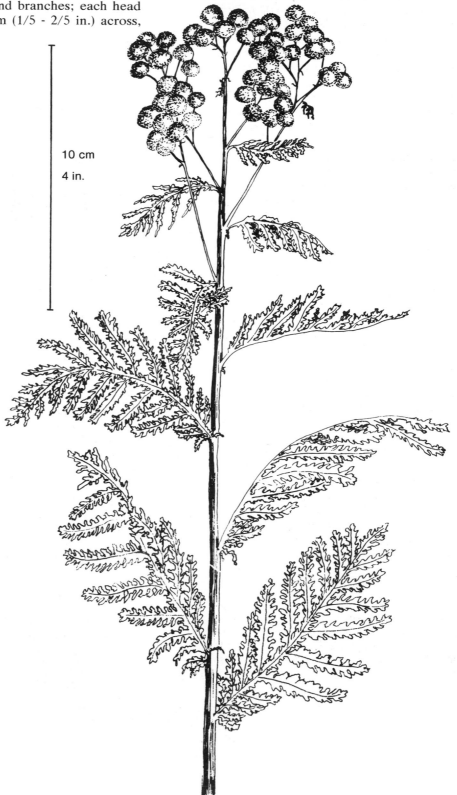

10 cm
4 in.

Figure 190. **Tansy**

220

Mugwort, *Artemisia vulgaris* L., (Figure 191) [ARTVU, armoise vulgaire, armoise commune, herbe Saint-Jean] Perennial, reproducing by seed and by the upturned ends of short, stout, horizontal, branching rhizomes (a). **Stems** erect, corrugated lengthwise, smooth to slightly hairy, simple or branched to a height of 0.5 - 2 m (1½ - 6½ ft); their colour from green to green with purplish ridges to entirely purple, especially in the upper parts. **Leaves** dark green and slightly hairy above, silvery-white beneath due to a dense covering of white-woolly hair, 1 - 10 cm (2/5 - 4 in.) long and 3 - 7.5 cm (1¼ - 3 in.) wide, principal leaves more or less divided into several segments, each of which (in lower stem leaves) may be again divided into smaller segments (b), or (in middle stem leaves) merely coarsely toothed (c), or (in upper stem leaves) with few or no teeth, or not divided (d); **flowers** in flower heads (see page 208) borne in small to elongated, spike-like clusters (e) in axils of upper leaves (f); the whole inflorescence elongated, with several to many branches and usually leafy in its lower part; each flower head 2 - 4.5 mm (1/12 - 1/6 in.) long, surrounded by an involucre of almost clear, papery bracts covered by whitish woolly hairs. The whole plant with a distinctive sage-like odour. Flowers from July to September.

Mugwort is a native plant of Europe, but has been naturalized in fields and waste places, and along roadsides, riverbanks and railway tracks in Ontario.

It is distinguished by its upright habit, the coarse divisions of the principal leaves, all of which are dark green above and silvery-white below, its short, strong, branching rhizomes without slender stolons, and its distinctive sage-like odour.

Absinth, *Artemisia absinthium* L., (not illustrated) [ARTAB, armoise absinthe, Absinthe, Vermooth, absinthe], is similar to Mugwort but is a finer, more branching plant that is silvery-silky throughout. **Stems** 40 - 150 cm (16 - 60 in.) high, gray-woolly, often many from a single root crown, very hard or almost woody at the base; **leaves** silvery-silky on both surfaces, roundish in outline but compound, 2 to 3 times divided, the final divisions flat, narrow, 2 - 4 mm (1/12 - 1/6 in.) wide, and with round tips; lower leaves long-stalked, upper ones stalkless; **flowers** in flower heads (see page 208) in spike-like clusters; both the flower heads and the clusters similar to but only about half the size of those in Mugwort; flower heads also similar in size and shape to those of Biennial wormwood (Figure 192C), but silvery-gray rather than green. The whole plant has a strong, sour, sage-like odour. Flowers from July to September.

Figure 191. **Mugwort** A. Portion of underground rhizome having produced 1 stem last year from its upturned tip plus a rhizome branch that produced this year's leafy stem. B. Middle portion of stem with a flowering branch. C. Tip of flowering stem.

Absinth occurs in scattered localities in Ontario in pastures, waste places and roadsides. The strongly aromatic foliage causes severe taint in milk when eaten by dairy cows. This plant has also been used to flavor certain alcoholic beverages, but **this practice is discouraged because the plant contains a poisonous alkaloid.**

It is distinguished in the rosette stage by its much-divided, silky-hairy leaves that are silvery-gray on both upper and lower surfaces and have a strong, sour, sage-like odour, and in the flowering or fruiting stage by its inflorescence of small, gray-woolly flower heads scattered along the longer branches in the upper part of the plant, as well as by its silvery-gray leaves and characteristic odour.

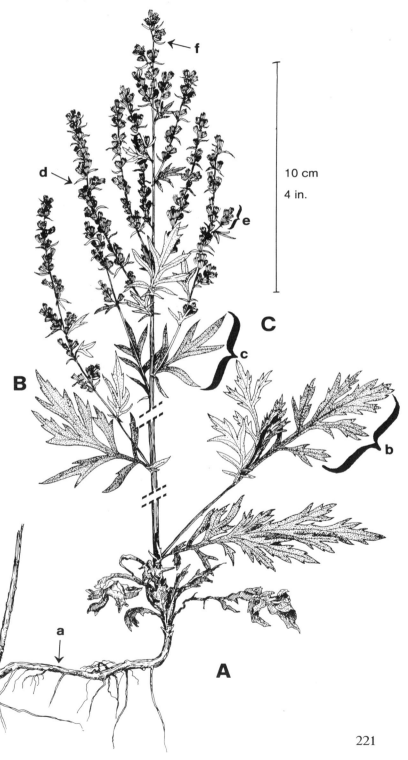

10 cm
4 in.

221

Figure 192. **Biennial wormwood** A. Lower portion of plant. B. Top of flowering stem. C. Flower heads on short branch from leaf axil.

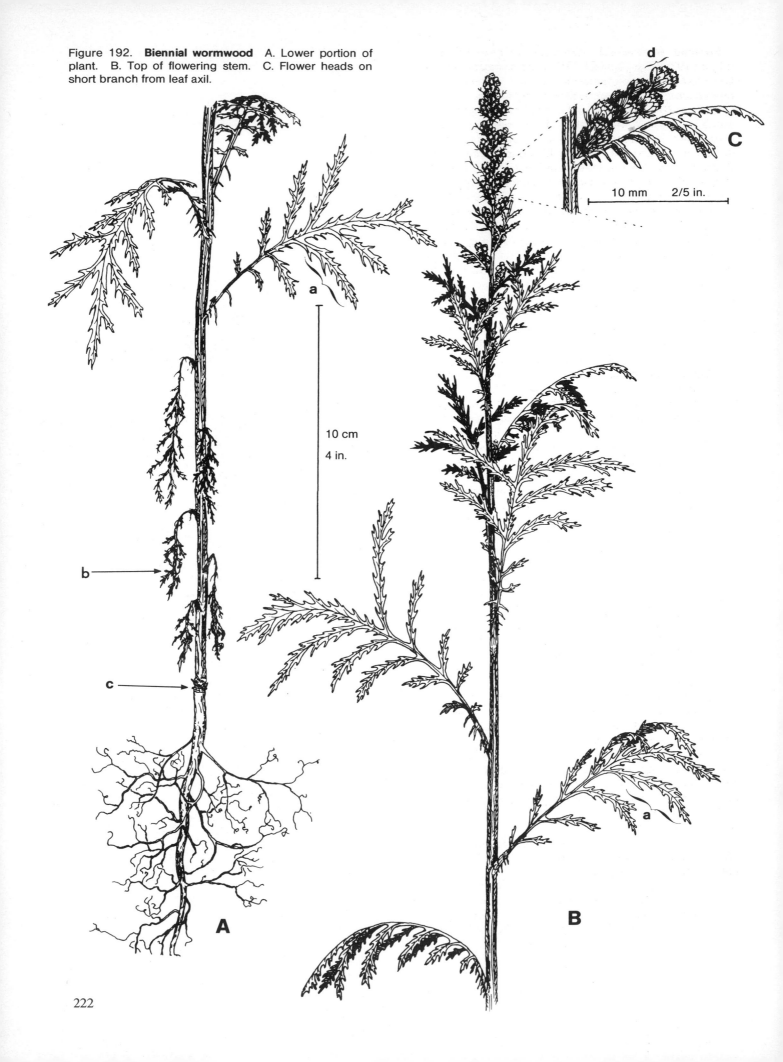

10 cm
4 in.

10 mm   2/5 in.

A

B

C

d

a

b

c

a

Biennial wormwood, *Artemisia biennis* Willd., (Figure 192, Plate 136) [ARTBI, armoise bisannuelle, Carrotweed, fausse tanaisie] Annual or biennial, reproducing only by seed. **Stems** erect, little or not branched, 10 - 150 cm (4 - 60 in.) tall or occasionally much taller, smooth, hairless, firm; first **leaves** of young plant in a basal rosette, short-stalked, pinnately divided and redivided, the final divisions coarsely and sharply toothed; stem leaves similar to basal leaves but usually only once-divided with each division (a) coarsely and sharply toothed, alternate (1 per node); by flowering time the lower stem leaves usually dying (b), and the basal rosette of leaves gone, only their scars (c) remaining; **flower heads** (d) (see page 208) greenish and inconspicuous, clustered on many short branches in the axils of small leaves towards the top of the stem, forming a slender, elongate inflorescence; each individual flower head very small, about 2 mm (1/12 in.) across, yellowish-green, without ray florets; **seeds** numerous and very small. Upper leaves, stem and flower heads, and to a lesser extent the basal leaves, when crushed have an odour resembling a combination of sage and carrot. Flowers from August to October.

Biennial wormwood occurs throughout Ontario in old fields, waste places, fence lines, meadows, around buildings, and occasionally in cultivated land. **It can cause tainted milk when eaten by dairy cows.**

It is distinguished by its erect habit, its sharply toothed (a) pinnately divided leaves, its numerous short clusters of tiny flower heads (d) along the upper stem forming a slender, elongate inflorescence, and its odour of mixed sage and carrot.

Common groundsel, *Senecio vulgaris* L., (Figure 193) [SENVU, séneçon vulgaire, séneçon commun] Annual, reproducing only by seed. **Stems** erect or somewhat reclining, often branched, 10 - 60 cm (4 - 24 in.) high, smooth, somewhat fleshy; **leaves** alternate (1 per node), slightly fleshy, variable in shape from smooth and almost without teeth to shallowly or deeply lobed, with the lobes (a) finely to coarsely and irregularly toothed; lower leaves stalked, upper ones stalkless and often clasping (b) the stem; **flower heads** (c) (see page 208) stalked in clusters at the end of stems and branches; each flower head 5 - 10 mm (1/5 - 2/5 in.) across, cylindrical or conic, without ray florets; disk florets yellowish; involucral bracts (surrounding each flower head) small, overlapping, usually with distinct black tips (d); **seeds** small, short-hairy, with a prominent, white, hairy pappus. Flowers from June to late autumn.

Common groundsel occurs throughout Ontario, often very abundantly, in gardens, row crops, waste places and roadsides.

Young plants can be distinguished by their irregularly lobed (a) and toothed leaves without white milky juice; older plants by their small conic-cylindrical flower heads (c) with black-tipped involucral bracts (d) around the base of each head.

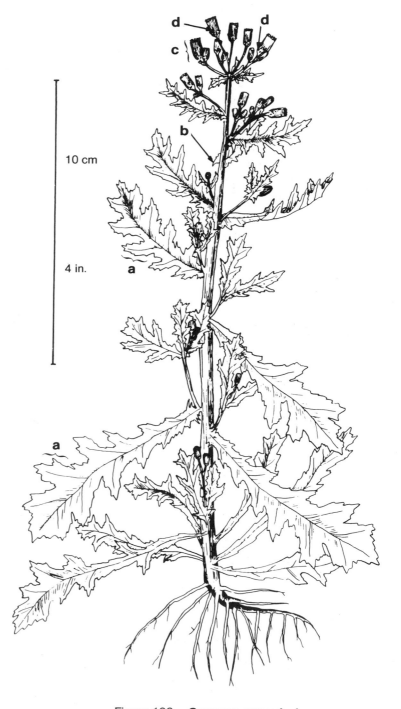

Figure 193. **Common groundsel**

223

Tansy ragwort, *Senecio jacobaea* L., (Figure 194, Plate 137) [SENJA, séneçon jacobée, Stinking Willie, herbe de Saint-Jacques, jacobée] Biennial or short-lived perennial closely related to Common groundsel. It is usually a taller plant (20 - 100 cm, 8 - 40 in.) with **leaves** broader in outline and cobwebby-hairy below, more finely divided, not as fleshy, and with their surfaces curled or crisped and wavy like leaf lettuce; **flower heads** (see page 208) in a short, broad, nearly flat-topped cluster at the end of the stem (B); each head with several, small, yellow ray florets (a) 4 - 8 mm (1/6 - 1/3 in.) long, a dense centre of yellow disk florets (b), and with involucral bracts (c) darker green but not black at their tips. Its odour is considered unpleasant by many people. Flowers from July to October.

Tansy ragwort occurs in only a few isolated localities in southern Ontario in pastures, waste places, along roadsides, and occasionally in gardens and lawns. **It is poisonous to livestock** and is responsible for Pictou disease of cattle, a serious problem in Nova Scotia where the weed is widespread.

It is distinguished by its deeply dissected leaves with curled or wavy surfaces, its erect stature with somewhat flat-topped inflorescences and its flower heads with yellow rays and yellow centres.

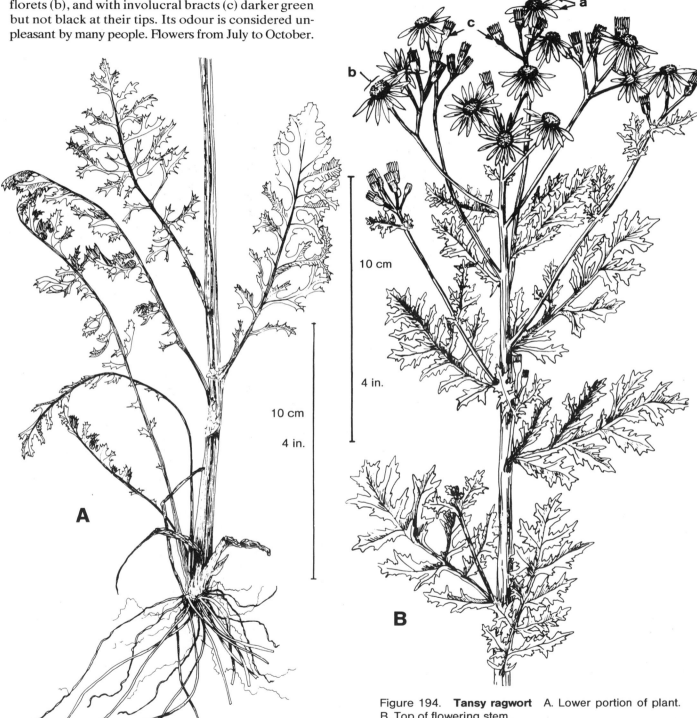

Figure 194. **Tansy ragwort** A. Lower portion of plant. B. Top of flowering stem.

Colt's-foot, *Tussilago farfara* L., (Figure 195, Plates 138, 139) [TUSFA, tussilage pas-d'âne, pas-d'âne, tussilage] Perennial, reproducing by rhizomes and by seed. Plants apparently of two types: (1) more or less leafless stems bearing flower heads in early spring (March to June), and (2) very short stems bearing large leaves in summer. **Flowering stems** 5 - 50 cm (2 - 20 in.) high, gray-woolly, with numerous short (1 - 1.5 cm, 2/5 - 3/5 in.) grayish to dark purplish bracts (a); each stem bearing a single flower head (b) (Plate 138A); **flower heads** (see page 208) at first cylindric, expanding to

A

B

3.5 cm (1-2/5 in.) wide when fully open; involucre (c) same colour as bracts on stem, 8 -15 mm (1/3 - 3/5 in.) long; ray florets (d) bright yellow, numerous, narrow (about 1 mm, 1/25 in. wide), slightly longer than the involucre, and much longer than the pappus; disc flowers (e) in centre of head, yellow, short and rounded; **seeds** produced only by ray florets, disc florets sterile; flower heads maturing in late spring to early summer, resembling dandelion heads but their pappus (parachute) is much finer and denser. Short, **non-flowering stems** producing normal leaves begin to emerge as the flower heads reach maturity. **Leaves** on long, erect petioles (f), broadly heart-shaped, usually 7.5 - 13 cm (3 - 5 in.) long by 10 - 20 cm (4 - 8 in.) wide, occasionally much larger if in very fertile soil, bright to dark green to bluish-green and hairless on the upper surface (Plate 139), white woolly on the undersurface, and palmately veined (main veins branching from the tip of the petiole); margins inwardly scalloped to variously and irregularly toothed, the tips of the teeth (g) often purplish. Flowers from March to June.

Colt's-foot was introduced from Europe and has been naturalized in forests, fields, disturbed and waste places and along roads, rivers, lakes, ravines and drainage ditches in urban and rural areas throughout southern and eastern Ontario.

In its flowering stage, Colt's-foot can be distinguished from Dandelion by its several to many purplish bracts on the flowering stem. After flowering, the vegetative plant can be distinguished from young plants of Burdock by its perennial rhizome system and its broadly heart-shaped leaves being mostly palmately veined.

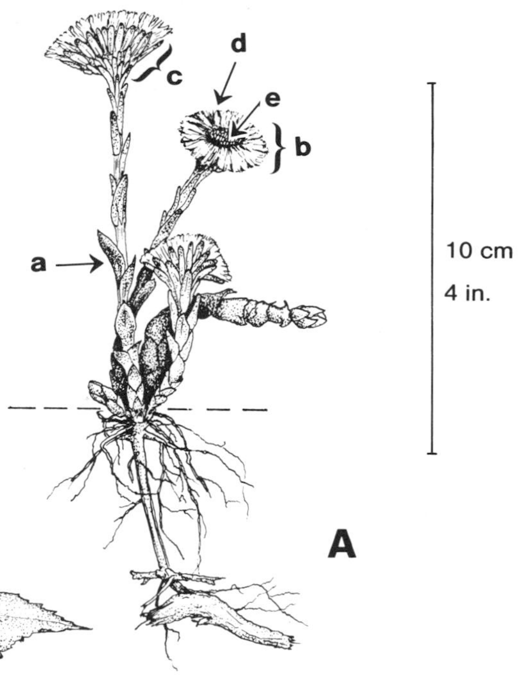

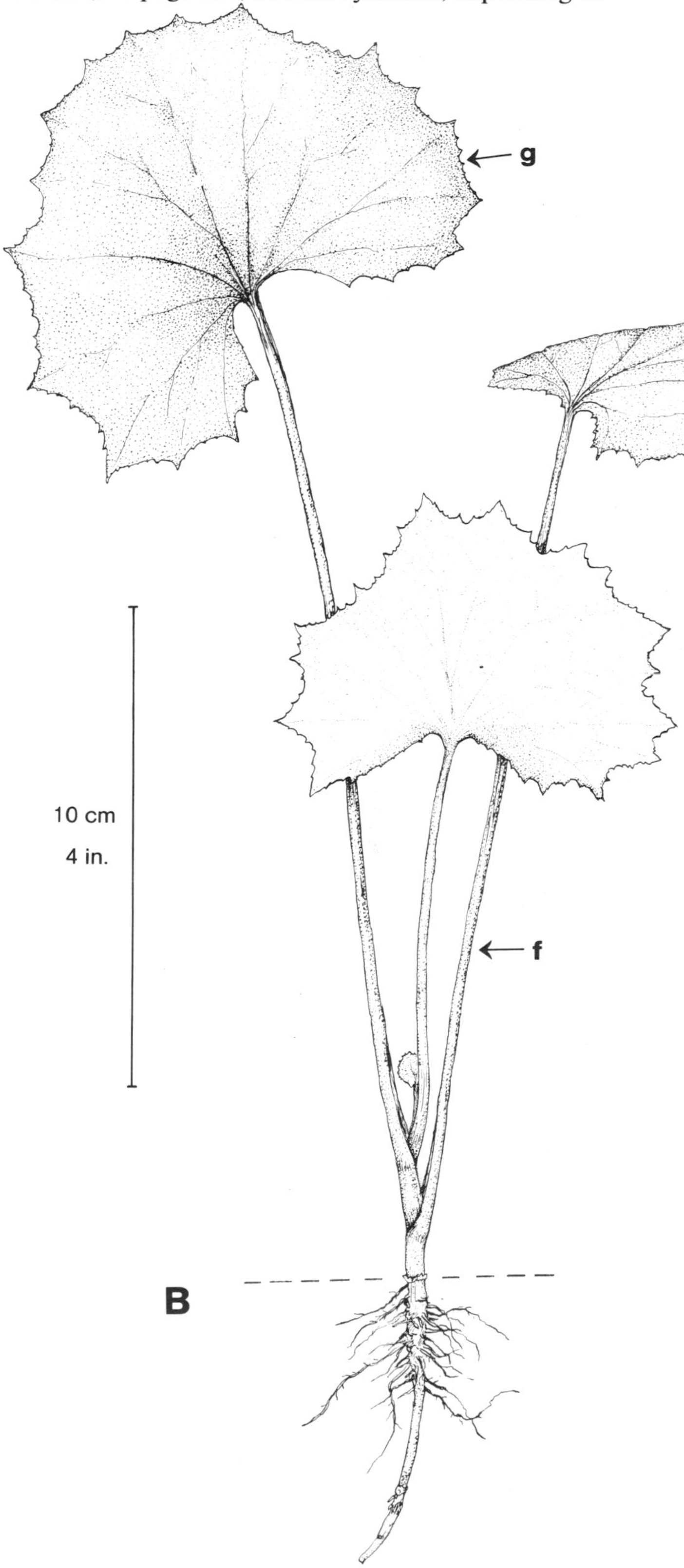

Figure 195 Colt's-foot A. Flowering stage: portion of a rhizome producing a shoot with several leafless stems and bright yellow flower heads in early spring. B. Vegetative stage: short stem with 3 leaves in midsummer.

225

Canada goldenrod, *Solidago canadensis* L., (Figure 196, Plate 140) [SOOCA, verge d'or du Canada, bouquets jaunes, solidage du Canada, verge d'or] Perennial, reproducing by rhizomes (a) and by seed. **Stems** 20 - 200 cm (8 - 80 in.) high, branching only in the upper part, hairless near the base, densely but very finely pubescent toward the top; **leaves** numerous, stalkless, sometimes crowded, 1 - 15 cm (2/5 - 6 in.) long and 1 - 22 mm (1/25 - 7/8 in.) wide, lanceolate, tapering to both ends; margins vary from nearly entire to usually having fine or sometimes coarse, widely-spaced teeth; most leaves with one prominent midvein (b) on the undersurface and two distinct lateral veins (c) that branch from it and parallel it nearly to the tip of the leaf; lower and middle stem leaves of plants in thick patches usually dying and falling off by flowering time; **inflorescence** a broad or occasionally narrow pyramidal panicle (d) 5 - 40 cm (2 - 16 in.) high and nearly as wide, with several to many horizontal branches, the upper sides of which carry numerous, densely-crowded small heads of golden yellow flowers; each individual **flower head** (e) (see page 208) about 3 mm (⅛ in.) long and wide. Flowers from mid-July to September.

Canada goldenrod is a native plant that is found throughout Ontario in moist or dry fields and meadows, edges of forests, swamps, clearings, orchards and compost piles, and along roadsides, ponds, streams, fencerows and shorelines, and recently as a weed in cultivated fields.

It is distinguished by its creeping rhizomes, its relatively narrow leaves that are widest in the middle and taper to both ends, have two lateral veins paralleling the prominent midvein and usually have widely-spaced fine to coarse teeth, and by its usually broad, pyramidal panicle.

Goldenrod is commonly accused of being the cause of hay fever allergies for many people. But it is innocent. Goldenrod is insect-pollinated and its heavy and slightly sticky pollen does not blow on the wind. Ragweed (see pages 213 - 215) is the usual culprit, but it has inconspicuous flowers whereas Goldenrod, which flowers at the same time, has highly conspicuous flowers and gets the blame.

Figure 196 **Canada goldenrod** A. Underground rhizome having produced 2 aboveground shoots. B. Top of flowering stem.

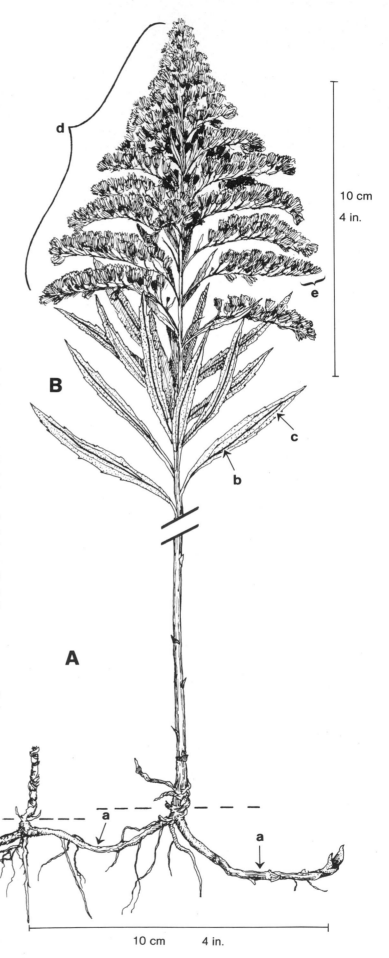

226

Narrow-leaved goldenrod, *Solidago graminifolia* (L.) Salisb., (Figure 197) [SOOGR, verge d'or à feuilles de graminée, Grass-leaved goldenrod, verge d'or à feuilles étroites] Perennial, reproducing by seed and by rhizomes (a). **Stems** 0.3 - 1.5 m (12 - 60 in.) high, branching only in the upper part, smooth to minutely hairy; **leaves** mostly linear (with parallel sides) to narrowly lanceolate (tapering gradually towards the tip), 2.5 - 15 cm (1 - 6 in.) long and 2 -12 mm (1/12 - ½ in.) wide, usually longer near the middle of the stem than at the bottom or top; each leaf with a prominent midvein on the underside and usually 1 or 2 thinner parallel veins on either side of it; leaf surfaces roughened with very short, fine, stiff hairs, especially along the veins and margins and the margins, entirely without teeth; **inflorescence** more or less flat-topped, up to 30 cm (1 ft) wide, composed of many small, 1 - 2.5 cm (2/5 - 1 in.) wide, clusters (b) of greenish-yellow **flower heads** (see page 208) that terminate each branch of the inflorescence; each tiny flower head (c) (2 - 3 mm, 1/12 - ⅛ in. long and about as wide) surrounded by greenish-yellow bracts and composed of 12 - 50 individual yellow florets. Flowers from August to September.

Narrow-leaved goldenrod is a native plant that is found in south-central Ontario in open, usually moist ground along roadsides, ditches and lakes, and in fields, pastures, swamps and waste areas.

It is distinguished by its usually linear leaves without teeth and having 1 or 2 veins parallelling the more prominent midvein, its relatively broad flat-topped inflorescence made up of many small clusters of flower heads each of which has 12 - 50 florets. The leaves of Narrow-leaved goldenrod frequently are attacked by a fungus that produces characteristic dark-brown to black, circular or oval lesions (d) about 3 - 6 mm (⅛ - ¼ in.) across.

See comments on pages 213 and 215 regarding confusion of the Goldenrods with the Ragweeds as causes of hay fever.

Figure 197 **Narrow-leaved goldenrod**

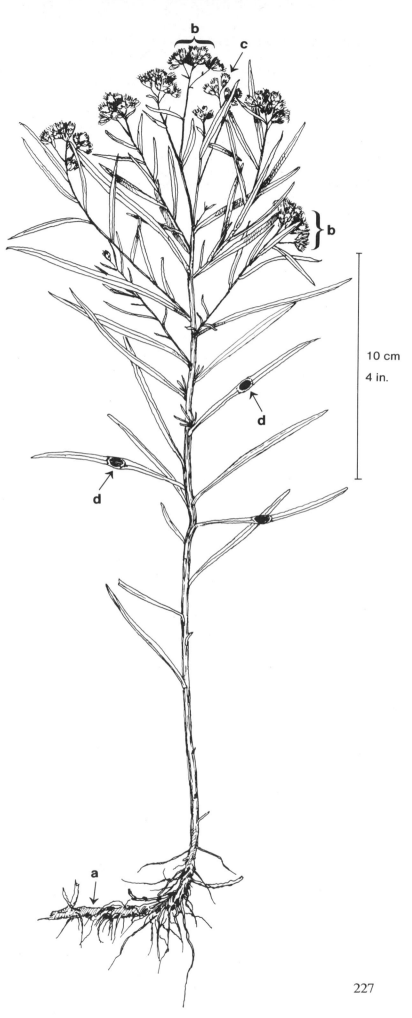

10 cm
4 in.

Annual fleabane, *Erigeron annuus* (L.) Pers., (Figure 198, Plate 141) [ERIAN, vergerette annuelle, Annual daisy fleabane, Daisy fleabane, vergerette perlée, érigéron annuel] Annual or sometimes biennial, reproducing only by seed. **Stems** erect, 20 - 150 cm (8 - 60 in.) high, short-hairy; first **leaves** in a basal rosette (B), broadly elliptic, coarsely toothed, long-stalked, bright green and usually hairy; lower and middle stem leaves similar but narrower, alternate (1 per node), mostly soft-hairy and usually not clasping the stem; upper leaves short-stalked or stalkless and sometimes partly clasping the stem (a), shallowly toothed or margins nearly smooth; **flower heads** (see page 208) in open clusters at the ends of stems and branches, each head 12 - 25 mm (½ - 1 in.) across, bright and showy; ray florets (b) white or sometimes pinkish to bluish, narrow, very numerous (up to 80 or more per head); disk florets (c) yellowish and densely packed, forming a nearly flat-topped centre. Flowers from June to late autumn.

Annual fleabane occurs throughout Ontario in pastures, meadows, waste places, gardens, roadsides and occasionally in cultivated fields.

It is distinguished by its bright green, broadly ovate, coarsely toothed, long-stalked, hairy, basal leaves (B), at least the lower and middle stem leaves distinctly toothed and soft-hairy, but not strongly clasping the stem, and its showy, white flower heads with yellow centres.

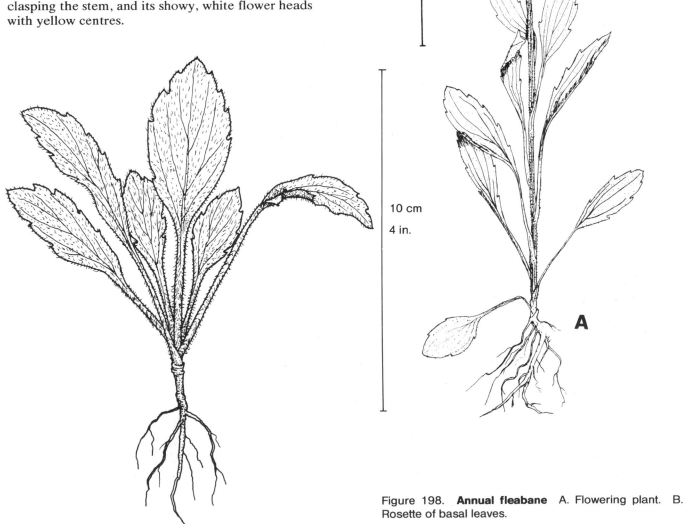

10 cm
4 in.

10 cm
4 in.

A

B

Figure 198. **Annual fleabane** A. Flowering plant. B. Rosette of basal leaves.

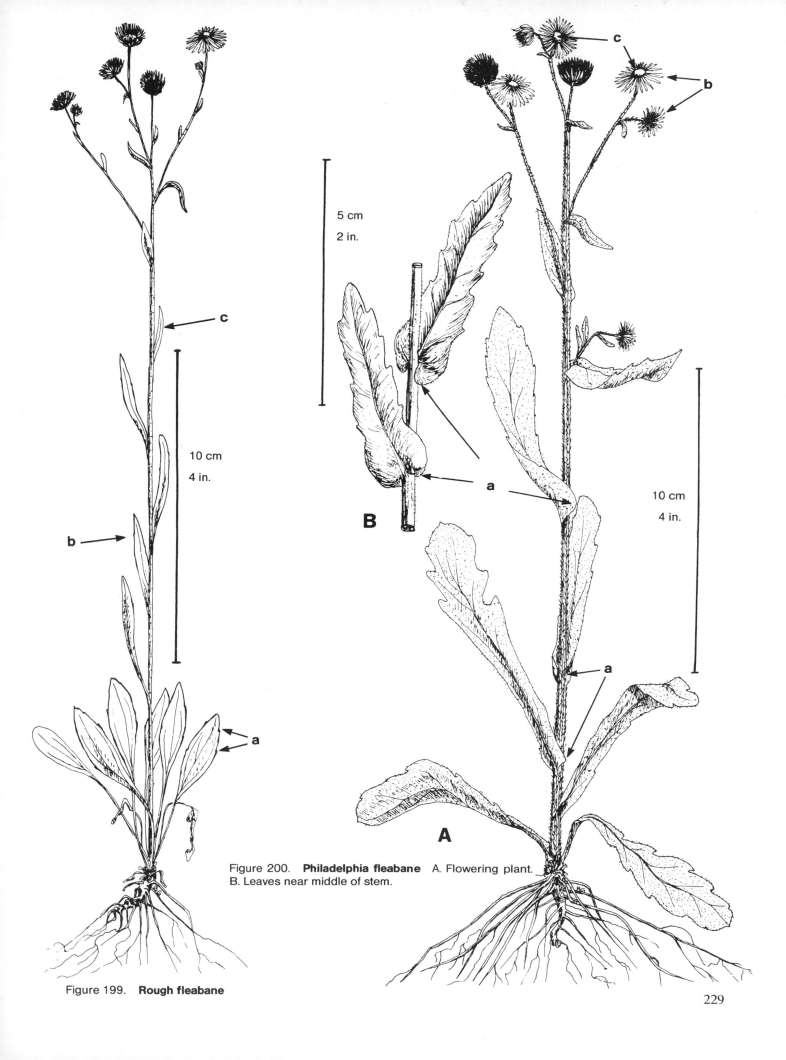

5 cm

2 in.

c

10 cm

4 in.

b

a

Figure 199. **Rough fleabane**

B

a

c

b

a

a

10 cm

4 in.

A

Figure 200. **Philadelphia fleabane** A. Flowering plant.
B. Leaves near middle of stem.

Rough fleabane, *Erigeron strigosus* Muhl., (Figure 199, Plate 142) [ERIST, vergerette rude, Daisy fleabane, Rough daisy fleabane, vergerolle rugueuse, érigéron hispide] Very similar to Annual fleabane; differing by having smaller, narrower, darker green **leaves** which are slightly rough with short stiff hair; only the basal (a) and lower stem leaves (b) having a few shallow teeth, the middle and upper leaves (c) usually very narrow and without teeth; and the **flower heads** averaging slightly smaller in size and in numbers of ray florets.

It occurs throughout Ontario and is distributed in similar habitats as Annual fleabane.

Philadelphia fleabane, *Erigeron philadelphicus* L., (Figure 200, Plate 143) [ERIPH, vergerette de Philadelphie, vergerolle de Philadelphie, érigéron de Philadelphie] Perennial, reproducing by seed, **stolons** and **basal offsets**. **Stems** erect, 30 - 100 cm (12 - 40 in.) high, soft-hairy; first **leaves** in spring in a rosette, elongated, broadest near the tip and narrowed gradually towards the base, with a few shallow teeth and often curled under along the edges; lower stem leaves similar but shorter and with somewhat broader bases, alternate (1 per node); middle and upper stem leaves (B) progressively shorter, stalkless, usually broadest near the tips and tapering gradually to broad bases which usually clasp the stem (a); **flower heads** (see page 208) similar in size and shape to Annual fleabane but usually with pinkish to light purplish ray florets (b) and yellow disk florets (c). Flowers from June to late autumn.

Philadelphia fleabane occurs throughout Ontario in pastures, waste places, roadsides, and occasionally in gardens and cultivated fields.

It is distinguished by its perennial habit, its rosette and lower stem leaves broader near their tips and tapering towards the stem, its upper stem leaves broader near their bases and strongly clasping the stem, and its flower heads with usually pinkish to light purplish ray florets.

Canada fleabane, *Erigeron canadensis* L., (Figure 201, Plate 144) [ERICA, vergerette du Canada, Bitterweed, Fleabane, Hogweed, Horseweed, Mare's-tail, vergerolle du Canada, érigéron du Canada, queue de renard, *Conyza canadensis* (L.) Cronq.] Annual or winter annual, reproducing only by seed. **Stems** erect, 10 - 180 cm (4 in. - 5 ft) high, hairy, little branched; **leaves** alternate (1 per node) but numerous and often appearing opposite (2 per node), soft-hairy at first but becoming harsh on older leaves, bright green; basal and lower stem leaves (A) narrowly oval, rarely more than 1 cm (2/5 in.) wide, tapering to a slender stalk, with a few, scattered, shallow teeth or without teeth; middle and upper leaves (B) linear, very narrow and usually without teeth; **flower heads** (see page 208) 3 - 5 mm (⅛ - 1/5 in.) across, very numerous on many short branches near the top of the main stem; ray florets white but very short and usually concealed by the slightly longer involucral bracts (a) around each flower head; disk florets yellowish; very fluffy at maturity. The leaves and other parts of the plant when crushed have a faint but distinctive odour reminiscent of carrots. Flowers from July to late autumn.

Canada fleabane occurs throughout Ontario in grainfields, pastures, waste places, roadsides and gardens.

It is distinguished by its numerous, narrow, mostly toothless bright green leaves gradually decreasing in size from base to top of plant, its numerous, small, yellow-green flower heads lacking conspicuous ray florets, its odour suggestive of carrots, and its fluffy appearance when mature.

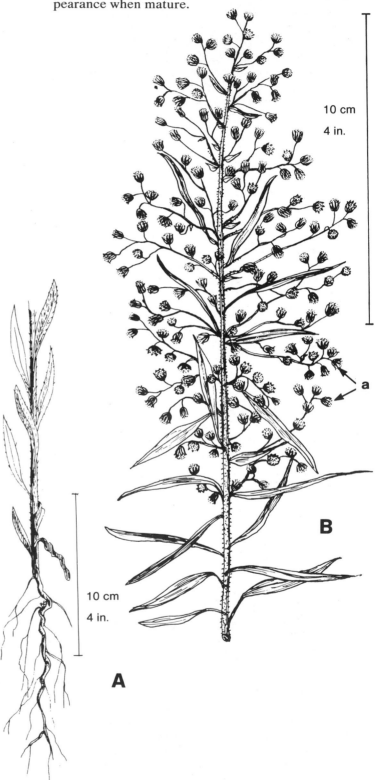

Figure 201. **Canada fleabane** A. Base of plant. B. Top of flowering stem.

English daisy, *Bellis perennis* L., (Figure 202) [BELPE, pâquerette vivace, Daisy, White daisy, pâquerette, petite marguerite] Perennial, reproducing only by seed. **Leaves** all in a basal rosette, arranged horizontally or nearly upright, short-to long-stalked, elliptic to ovate, tapering to the stalk, shallowly but irregularly toothed with rounded or small sharp teeth; **flower heads** (see page 208) on slender leafless stalks (a) raised 5 - 15 cm (2 - 6 in.) above the leafy base, showy, 2 - 4 cm (4/5 - 1½ in.) across, ray florets (b) numerous and white to purplish; disk florets (c) numerous, densely packed, yellow. Flowers from June to August.

English daisy occurs in scattered localities throughout southern Ontario where it may become a dense weed in lawns, roadsides and waste places.

It is distinguished by not having a leafy stem but only a rosette of basal leaves and a short, thin, leafless stalk (a) supporting a bright showy flower head with white to purplish ray florets (b) and a yellow centre (c).

Low cudweed, *Gnaphalium uliginosum* L., (Figure 203) [GNAUL, gnaphale des vases, immortelle des vases] Annual, reproducing only by seed. **Stems** much-branched, 5 - 25 cm (2 - 10 in.) high, densely fine-hairy to woolly; leaves **alternate** (1 per node) but numerous and appearing tufted (a) near the tips of branches, narrow and linear or a little wider near the tip, hairy, gray-green to silvery-gray. **Flower heads** (see page 208) (b) very small and crowded in small clusters near the ends of the branches and in axils of leaves, whitish to light brownish-green to straw-coloured, without ray florets; involucral bracts (c) tiny, thin, papery, tan or light brownish. Flowers from July to late autumn.

Low cudweed occurs throughout Ontario in low, moist, or poorly drained situations in meadows, pastures, depressions in cultivated fields, streams, valleys and roadside ditches. It often forms dense patches in depressions in grainfields where it can tolerate poorly drained conditions better than most cultivated plants.

It is distinguished by its low, much-branched stature with narrow leaves, its silvery-gray appearance, and its small, crowded brownish-green to straw-coloured flower heads surrounded by thin, papery involucral bracts.

Pearly everlasting, *Anaphalis margaritacea* (L.) Benth. & Hook., (not illustrated) [ANPMA, anaphale perlée, immortelle, anaphale marguerite] Closely related to Low cudweed. It differs by being perennial with **stems** up to 30 - 90 cm (1 - 3 ft) high, **leaves** larger with white-woolly undersurfaces but usually deeper green above, and dense clusters of attractive, snowy-white **flower heads**, the involucral bracts surrounding each flower head (see page 208) being white, dry, papery and remain on the plant long after it is mature. For this reason, it was widely cultivated as an everlasting flower for use in dry arrangements but now occurs throughout Ontario in waste places, meadows, roadsides and occasionally edges of cultivated fields.

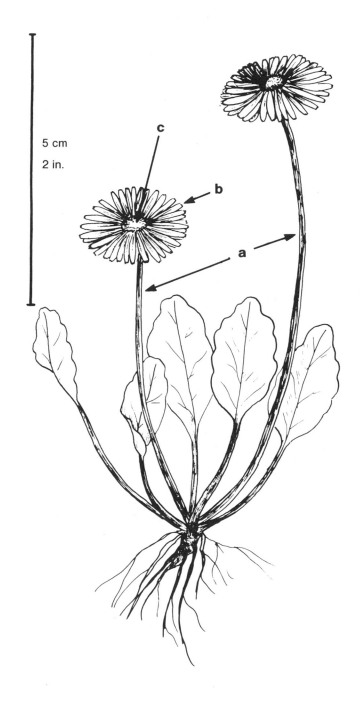

5 cm
2 in.

Figure 202. **English daisy**

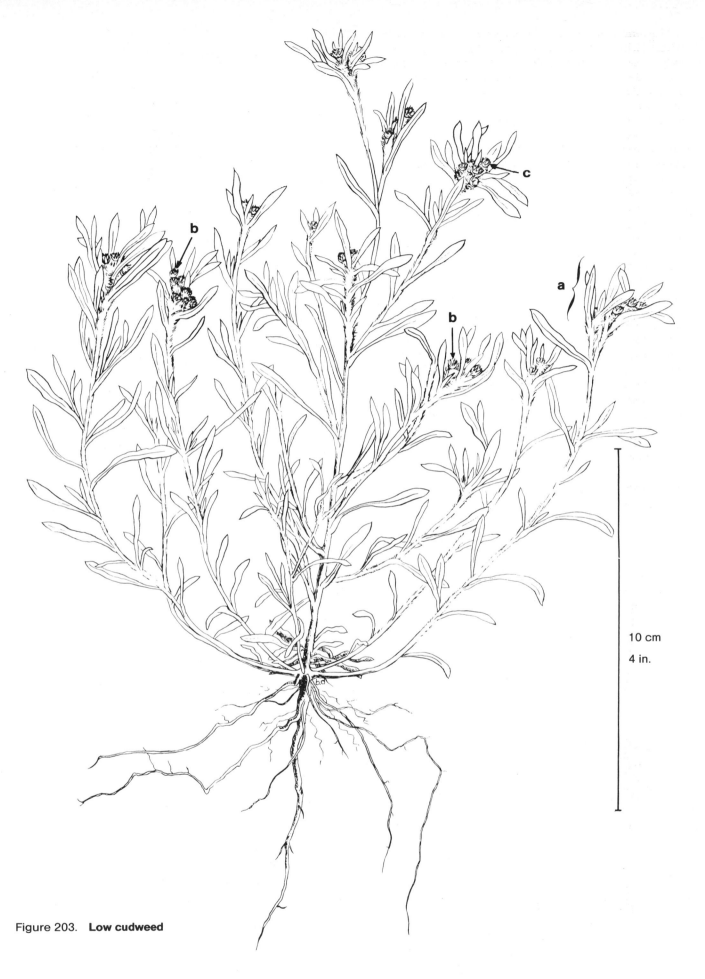

10 cm
4 in.

Figure 203. **Low cudweed**

232

Elecampane, *Inula helenium* L., (Figure 204) [INUHE, inule aunée, aunée] Perennial, reproducing only by seed. **Stems** erect, mostly without branches, 1 - 2 m (3 - 6½ ft) high, coarse, finely hairy; first **leaves** in a basal rosette with large broad blades (A) as much as 50 cm (20 in.) long, by 20 cm (8 in.) wide, ovate, usually tapering towards both tip and base, undersurface velvety-hairy, margins finely and regularly toothed with somewhat leafy-winged (a) stalks; stem leaves alternate (1 per node), similar to rosette leaves but smaller upwards on the stem, stalkless ar.d clasping (b) the stem; **flower heads** (see page 208) large, showy, coarse, 5 - 8 cm (2 - 3½ in.) across; ray florets (c) many, yellow, thin, about 2 cm (4/5 in.) long; disk florets (d) many, densely crowded, dark yellowish, forming a coarse rounded centre in the head; involucral bracts (e) around the base of the head broad, stiff, light green and finely hairy. Flowers from July to August.

Elecampane occurs in southern Ontario in meadows, moist pastures, river valleys, and roadsides.

It is distinguished by its rosette of large, ovate, finely toothed leaves (A) with velvety-hairy undersurfaces, and tapering towards both ends, its tall erect stem with alternate leaves, the upper ones clasping (b) the stem, and its large, coarse, showy, yellow flower heads. In the rosette stage, the large leaves of Elecampane may be confused with those of **Horse-radish,** *Armoracia rusticana* Gaertn., but in Horse-radish the leaves are smooth or both surfaces and the margins usually have rounded teeth. Also the stem leaves of Horse-radish do not clasp the stem, are narrower for their length, and may be deeply pinnately lobed.

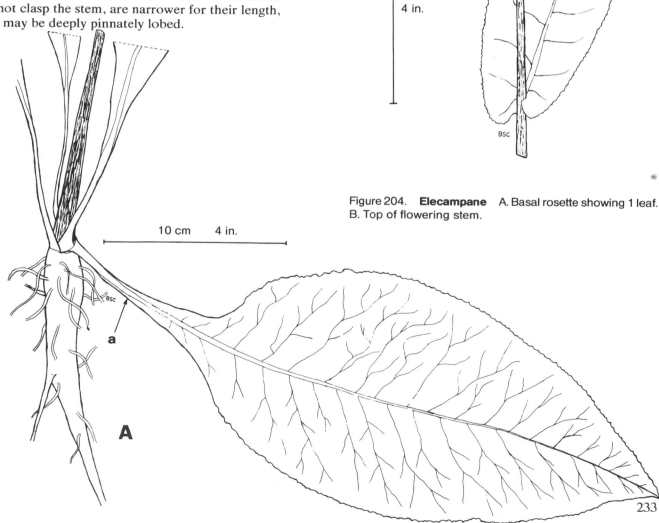

Figure 204. **Elecampane** A. Basal rosette showing 1 leaf. B. Top of flowering stem.

233

White snakeroot, *Eupatorium rugosum* Houtt., (Figure 205, Plate 145) [EUPRU, eupatoire rugueuse, eupatoire à feuilles d'ortie] Perennial, reproducing by seed and by rhizomes. **Stems** erect, slightly hairy, rising 0.2 - 1.5 m (8 - 60 in.) high from a knotty, tough **rhizome** (a); **leaves** opposite, ovate, longer than broad, the larger ones being 5 - 18 cm (2 - 7 in.) long and 3 - 12 cm (1¼ - 5 in.) wide, with sharply and coarsely toothed margins and acuminate tips; petioles (b) ¼ to 1/3 the length of the leaf blade; **inflorescence** of well-developed plants composed of several loosely branched, more or less flat-topped corymbs of flower heads (see page 208) (c) that arise from the axils of the upper leaves (d); each **flower head** (e, C) about 6 mm (¼ in.) long and nearly as wide, with 12 to 30 bright white florets (f) per head; all florets are tubular (see Figure 177 C,D) (it has no ray or ligulate florets); **"seeds"** (achenes) (D) slender, cigar-shaped, about 1.5 mm (1/16 in.) long, and tipped with a pappus of tawny hairs. Flowers from July to September.

White snakeroot is native throughout southern Ontario in rich woods, thickets, clearings, waste places, ditches, meadows and beside lakes and streams, chiefly in basic soils. **The plant is poisonous to livestock and causes "milk-sickness" in humans via consumption of milk from affected animals.**

It is distinguished by the combination of opposite, petiolate leaves with coarsely serrate margins and flat-topped inflorescences of small, white flower heads.

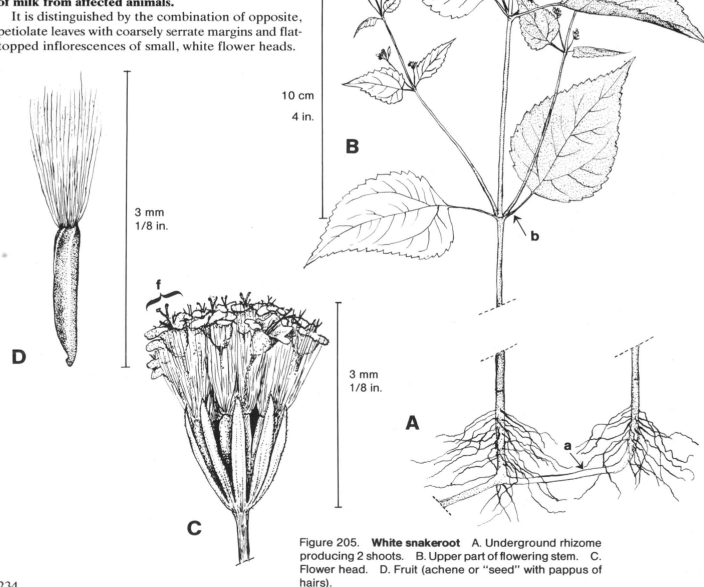

Figure 205. **White snakeroot** A. Underground rhizome producing 2 shoots. B. Upper part of flowering stem. C. Flower head. D. Fruit (achene or "seed" with pappus of hairs).

Spotted Joe-Pye weed, *Eupatorium maculatum* L., (Plate 146) [EUPML, eupatoire maculée, eupatoire pourpre, *Eupatorium purpureum* L. var. *maculatum* (L.) Darl.] and **Boneset,** *Eupatorium perfoliatum* L., (Plate 147) [EUPPE, eupatoire perfoliée, Thorough-wort, herebe à souder, herbe soudé], are closely related botanically to White snakeroot. However, they are quite different in appearance from it as well as from each other. Both are native perennials commonly found in moist or wet areas throughout most of Ontario, and both reproduce from rhizomes as well as by seed. **Spotted Joe-Pye weed** (Plate 146) grows 0.6 - 2.0 m (2 - 6½ ft) tall, with speckled or wholely purplish **stems**, these smooth or somewhat hairy; **leaves** mostly in whorls of 4 to 6, but may be only opposite or alternate near the inflorescence, narrowly to broadly ovate, narrowing gradually into long, stretched-out (acuminate) tips as well as towards the petiole, 10 - 25 cm (4 - 10 in.) long, 1 - 6 cm (2/5 - 2-1/5 in.) wide, on petioles 1 - 25 mm (1/25 - 1 in.) long; **leaf margins** toothed, the teeth ranging from coarsely and sharply forward-pointed (serrate) to shallow and somewhat rounded; **flowers** in pink to light purple **flower heads** (see page 208), each head 2 - 5 mm (1/12 - 1/5 in.) in diameter and 5 - 10 mm (1/5 - 2/5 in.) long, with 10 - 20 tubular florets (Figure 177 C,D) and no ray florets (Figure 177 C,E); the many heads clustered into a compact, broad, rounded to flat-topped, compound inflorescence. Flowers in August and September.

Spotted Joe-Pye weed is a native plant that grows in wet meadows, edges of lakes and streams, roadside ditches, and other wet places throughout Ontario.

It is distinguished by its broad, tapering leaves in whorls of 4 to 6 on speckled or solid purplish stems, and its pink to purplish flower heads in relatively compact clusters, and by usually growing in wet places.

Boneset (Plate 147) grows 40 - 150 cm (16 - 60 in.) tall; its **stems** green and usually long-hairy; **leaves** in opposite pairs, the base of each one broad and completely united to the base of the opposite leaf (perfoliate) such that the 2 leaves appear as if they were a single leaf with the stem coming up through the middle; most pairs standing out almost perpendicular to the stem; each leaf 5 - 20 cm (2 - 8 in.) long (from stem to leaf tip), 1 - 5 cm (2/5 - 2 in.) wide, somewhat long-ovate or just gradually tapering from its broad base at the stem to the stretched-out tip; **margins** shallowly or coarsely toothed, the teeth forward-pointing or somewhat rounded; **flowers** in greenish-white to white **flower heads** (see page 208); the heads 3 - 5 mm (⅛ - 1/5 in.) in diameter and about 5 mm (1/5 in.) long, with only tubular florets (Figure 177 C,D) and no ray florets (Figure 177 C,E), and clustered into a compact, rounded to flat-topped compound inflorescence. Flowers in August and September.

Boneset is a native plant that grows in moist areas in meadows, edges of lakes and streams, woodlands, roadsides and occasionally in cultivated fields.

It is distinguished by its opposite leaves being perfoliate (their bases united so they completely surround the stem with their leaf blade tissue), and its greenish-white flower heads in rounded or flat-topped compound inflorescences.

Common burdock, *Arctium minus* (Hill) Bernh., (Figure 206, Plates 148, 149) [ARFMI, petite bardane, Burdock, Burs, Clotbur, Lesser burdock, Wild burdock, Wild rhubarb, bardane mineure, rapace, rhubarbe sauvage, toques] Biennial, reproducing only by seed. **Stems** erect, 60 - 180 cm (2 - 6 ft) high, often widely branched, thick, hollow, grooved lengthwise; first **leaves** in a basal rosette (A), becoming large (up to 50 cm, 20 in. long, and 30 cm, 12 in. wide), with heart-shaped base, coarse, resembling a clump of cultivated rhubarb, but the undersides of the leaf blades are white woolly and the stout leafstalks are hollow; lower leaves on the stem of second-year plants similar to basal leaves, smaller, alternate (1 per node); middle and upper leaves gradually smaller with shorter, slender stalks and the blade tending to be less heart-shaped and more pointed towards both ends, especially among the flower heads; **flower heads** (see page 208) globular, numerous, borne singly on short stalks or in small clusters at ends of branches and from axils of leaves; each head about 2 cm (4/5 in.) in diameter, densely covered with purplish, hooked bristles (a); ray florets absent; disk florets (b) purple or occasionally white, closely packed in the centre of the head; at maturity the head or bur (hence the common name "burdock") easily breaks off its stalk and clings to clothing and animal fur, gradually scattering the brownish angular **seeds**, each about 6 mm (¼ in.) long. Flowers from July to September.

Common burdock occurs throughout Ontario in waste places, pastures, open woods, roadsides, fencerows and barnyards but seldom in cultivated land.

It is distinguished by its rosette of very large heart-shaped leaves resembling Rhubarb but woolly on the undersurface and with hollow leafstalks, and its tall, branched stem in the second year with many short-stalked flower heads or burs densely covered with hooked spines (a) and borne singly or in small clusters at ends of stems and from leaf axils, these turning brown at maturity.

Great burdock, *Arctium lappa* L., (not illustrated) [ARFLA, grande bardane, Large burdock, bardane majeure, rapace, rhubarbe sauvage, toques] Very similar to Common burdock, differing from it by having solid leafstalks in the lower part of the plant, larger **flower heads** (usually over 2.5 cm, 1 in. across) on longer stalks and arranged in flat-topped clusters rather than scattered along the stems. Great burdock is found in a few localities in southern Ontario along roadsides, fence lines, waste places and river meadows.

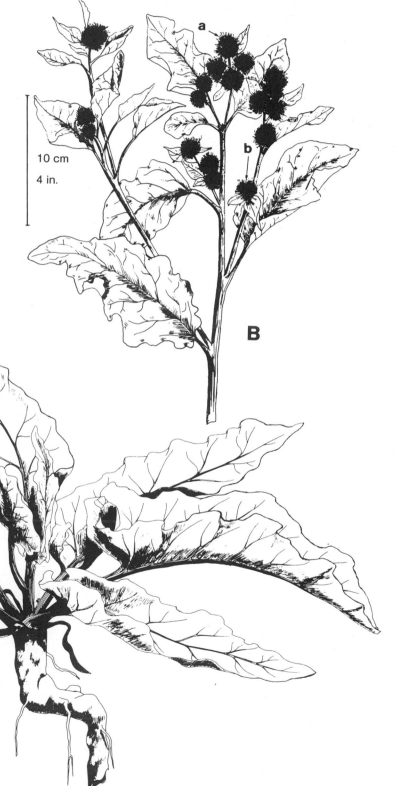

Figure 206. **Common burdock** A. Rosette of leaves. B. End of flowering branch.

Nodding thistle, *Carduus nutans* L., (Figure 207, Plates 150, 151, 156A) [CRUNU, chardon penché, Musk thistle] Biennial, reproducing only by seed. **Stems** of second-year plants erect, 30 - 180 cm (1 - 6 ft) high, with harshly spiny, irregularly lobed, leaf-like wings (a) running lengthwise on all stems and branches except just below each flower head; first-year plants forming a large, circular, nearly flat **rosette** (A), each leaf often 30 cm (12 in.) long by 10 cm (4 in.) wide, bright green to gray-green, margins deeply lobed, the lobes close together, twisted and wavy, with long, sharp spines pointing in all directions; the actual upper and lower surfaces of the leaf blade and its lobes (apart from the harshly spiny margins) finely woolly-hairy and soft to the touch; **stem leaves** of second-year plants similar to rosette leaves but gradually smaller and less lobed upwards, alternate (1 per node); **flower heads** (B) (see page 208) single on slender, smooth, long, bare (not spiny-winged) stalks (b) at ends of branches (Plate 156A) and from axils of upper leaves, each head large, 4 - 7.5 cm (1½ - 3 in.) across but occasionally smaller, with no ray florets but with many, large, bright purple disk florets (c), these surrounded by an involucre of many, overlapping, broad-based, greenish bracts with outward- or backward-pointing, long, sharp spiny tips (d); heads at ends of stems and branches usually bent to one side ("nodding" as in B and Plate 156A), those from leaf axils often nearly erect; **seeds** light brown, shiny, 4 mm (1/6 in.) long, egg-shaped with a small knob at the tip and a pappus (parachute) of short, unbranched (non-plumose), light beige hairs. Flowers from June to October.

Nodding thistle is common throughout southern Ontario in pastures, waste places, roadsides and around buildings, especially on coarse-textured soils.

Flowering plants are distinguished by their large, showy, bright purple flower heads (Plate 156A) surrounded by an involucre of broad-based bracts narrowed to long, sharp, outward- or backward-pointing spiny tips (d) and their heads nodding on long, non-winged stalks (b) at ends of stems or upright in leaf axils (compare with Plumeless thistle); non-flowering plants and first-year rosettes are distinguished by their deeply lobed, bright green to gray-green leaves, the lobes much twisted, wavy and spiny margined, and both upper and lower surfaces (apart from the spiny margins) always finely woolly-hairy and soft to the touch, in contrast to the harshly, almost prickly-hairy surfaces of Bull thistle. Plants which seem to be intermediate between Nodding thistle and Plumeless thistle may be hybrids between these two species.

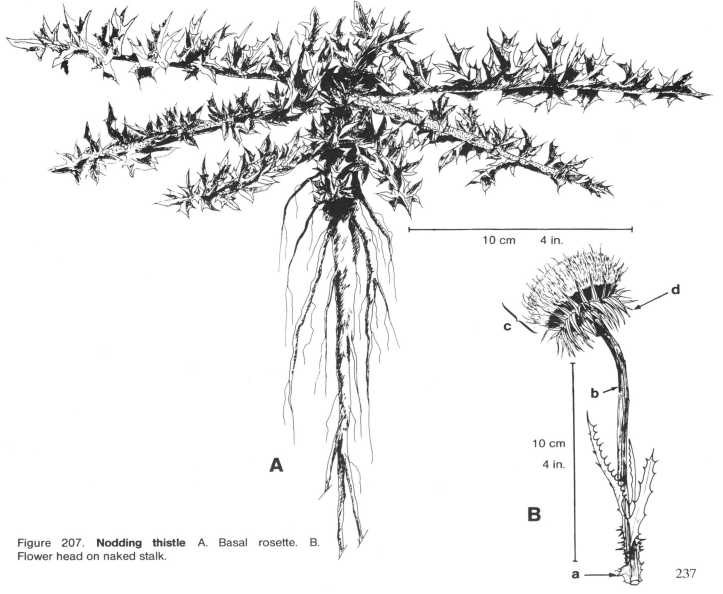

10 cm   4 in.

10 cm

4 in.

A

B

Figure 207. **Nodding thistle** A. Basal rosette. B. Flower head on naked stalk.

237

Plumeless thistle, *Carduus acanthoides* L., (Figure 208, Plate 152) [CRUAC, chardon épineux, Welted thistle] Very similar to Nodding thistle with its deeply lobed, spiny leaves but distinguished from it by usually having the lobes or clusters of lobes (b) separated from each other by distinct spaces (a) along the midrib of the leaf; the inner margins of these spaces usually with smaller and fewer spines than on the lobes; **flower heads** (c) smaller (usually less than 2.5 cm, 1 in. wide) and clustered or sometimes solitary but on shorter stalks which are spiny-winged right to the base of the head (d). The involucral bracts (e) surrounding its flower heads are narrower and more numerous than in Nodding thistle [Figure 207B (d)] and mostly point upward rather than outward or backward. Plumeless thistle occurs throughout southern Ontario in similar habitats to Nodding thistle and, where the two occasionally grow in the same locality, hybrids are often produced having characteristics intermediate between the two species.

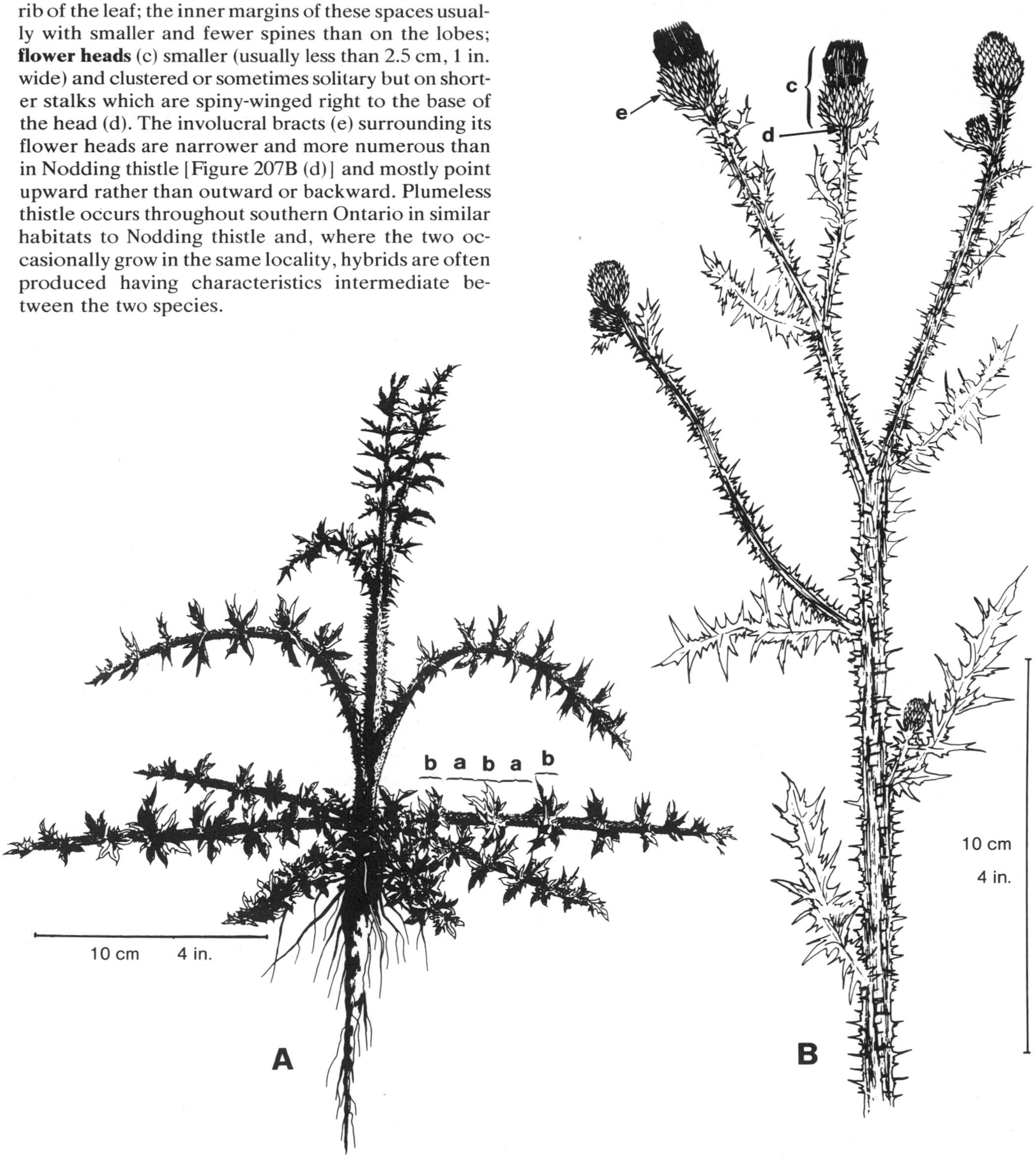

Figure 208. **Plumeless thistle** A. Rosette and lower stem leaves. B. Flowering branch with flower heads on spiny-winged stalks.

238

Canada thistle, *Cirsium arvense* (L.) Scop., (Figure 209, Plates 153, 156 C,D,E) [CIRAR, chardon des champs, Canadian thistle, Creeping thistle, Field thistle, chardon du Canada] Perennial, reproducing by seed and by **horizontal roots** (a) which produce new shoots, often forming dense patches. **Stems** erect, 30 - 150 cm (1 - 5 ft) high, usually branched, slender, smooth or occasionally with a few, narrow, spiny-margined leaf-like wings on the lower part; **leaves** more or less lobed and spiny, alternate (1 per node), elliptic to oblong in outline, stalkless and often clasping the stem; the wide variations in lobing, spininess, hairiness, texture and colour of leaves divide the species into 4 botanical varieties and are described in detail below; **flower heads** (see page 208) numerous, comparatively small, 5 - 15 mm (1/5 - 3/5 in.) wide and about twice as long, the involucral bracts (b) weakly spiny or almost smooth; ray florets absent but disk florets (c) prominent with purplish or sometimes white corollas; plants unisexual; although stamens and stigmas are sometimes present in the same flower, the flowers are functionally unisexual, all the flowers in 1 head and all the heads on 1 plant being either male or female; heads with male (pollen-producing) flowers somewhat shorter and narrower than heads with female (seed-producing) flowers; **seeds** light brown or straw-coloured, smooth, 2.5 - 4 mm (1/10 - 1/6 in.) long. Flowers from June to late autumn.

Four botanical varieties of Canada thistle occur in Ontario. They are distinguished by differences in leaf characteristics. Common names have not gained general acceptance for them but descriptive terms are applicable as follows:

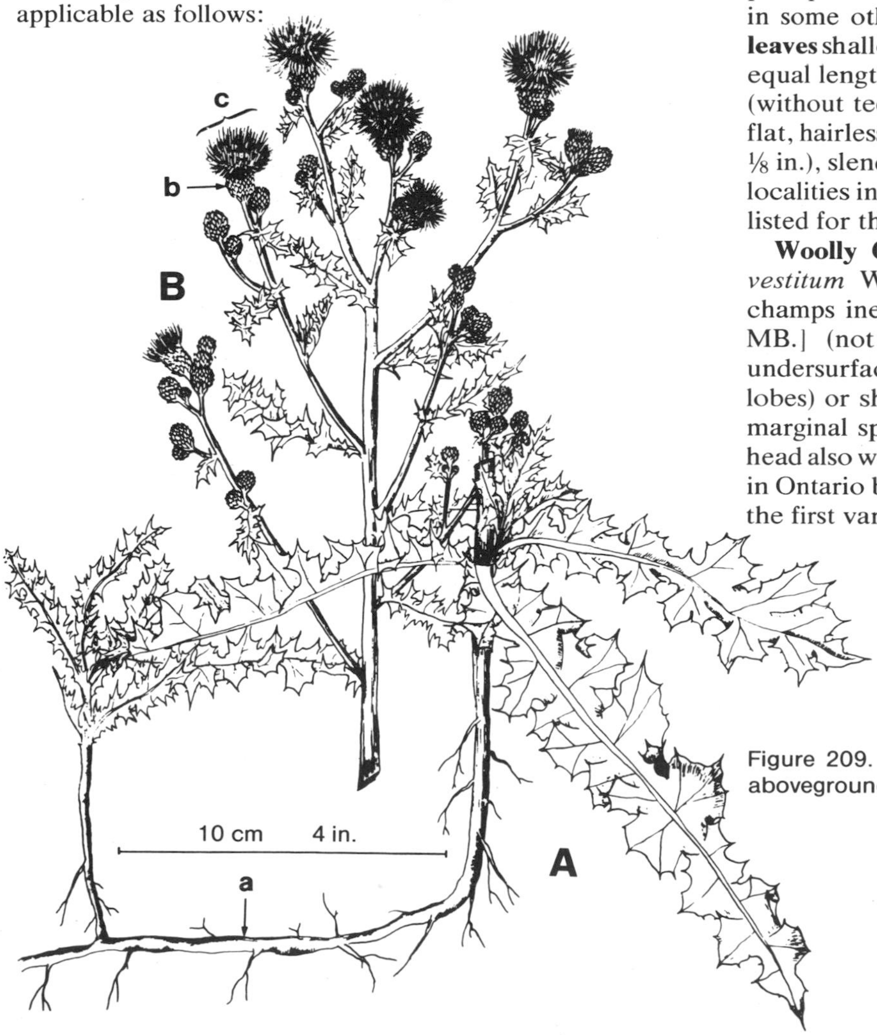

Spiny Canada thistle, *Cirsium arvense* (L.) Scop. var. *horridum* Wimm. & Grab., [CIRAH, chardon des champs à feuilles très épineuses, typical *C. arvense* var. *arvense* in some other publications] (Figure 209, Plate 156 C,D,E), **leaves** deeply and uniformly lobed along each side; the lobes pointed, twisted and wavy with many long, stiff, stout yellowish spines sticking out in all directions from their margins; the whole blade firm, stiff, mostly hairless and bright green to slightly yellowish-green. This is by far the most common variety, occurring throughout Ontario in grainfields, pastures, meadows, woodlands, waste places, roadsides, gardens and lawns in all soil textures and in saline (alkaline) soils as well as rich fertile soils. Plate 156 shows both colour forms of this variety, male (pollen-producing) (C) and female (seed-producing) (D) plants of the purple-flowered form and a male (E) of the white-flowered form.

Entire-leaved Canada thistle, *Cirsium arvense* L. var. *integrifolium* Wimm. & Grab., [CIRAI, chardon des champs à feuilles entières, *C. setosum* (Willd.) MB.] (not illustrated), all **leaves** entire (without teeth or lobes), thin and flat, or the upper ones entire and only the lower ones shallowly and uniformly lobed or wavy-margined, with only a few short (3 mm, 1/8 in.), slender marginal spines, hairless and green to rather dark green. Occurs in only a few localities in Ontario but able to grow in most habitats listed for the first variety.

Gentle Canada thistle, *Cirsium arvense* L. var. *arvense* [CIRAA, chardon des champs à feuilles peu épineuses, *C. arvense* L. var. *mite* Wimm. & Grab. in some other publications] (not illustrated), lower **leaves** shallowly to deeply lobed, the lobes often of unequal length and widely spaced; upper leaves entire (without teeth or lobes) or nearly so, all leaves thin, flat, hairless, green, and with only a few short (3 mm, 1/8 in.), slender marginal spines. Occurs in only a few localities in Ontario but able to grow in most habitats listed for the first variety.

Woolly Canada thistle, *Cirsium arvense* L. var. *vestitum* Wimm. & Grab., [CIRAV, chardon des champs inerme, *C. incanum* S. G. Gmel. Fisch. ex MB.] (not illustrated), **leaves** gray-woolly on the undersurface, green above, entire (without teeth or lobes) or shallowly lobed, flat and with a few weak marginal spines; **stems** and stalk below each flower head also white woolly. Occurs only in a few localities in Ontario but able to grow in most habitats listed for the first variety.

Figure 209. **Canada thistle** A. Horizontal root with 2 aboveground shoots. B. Flowering stem.

239

All four varieties of Canada thistle are distinguished from the biennial thistles in non-flowering stages by their perennial habit reproducing from spreading underground roots (a), by the absence of a distinct circular rosette of basal leaves, and by their mostly non-winged stems with generally slender stature, and from Bull thistle by the absence of prickles from the surface of the leaf blades (apart from spines along the margins); flowering stages are distinguished by their generally smaller flower heads, mostly less than 25 mm (1 in.) long and 15 mm (3/5 in.) wide, these unisexual, and the involucral bracts (b) surrounding each head either without spiny tips or with very short weak ones. They are distinguished from the Sow-thistles by the absence of white milky juice from stems and leaves.

Bull thistle, *Cirsium vulgare* (Savi) Tenore., (Figure 210, Plates 154, 156 B) [CIRVU, chardon vulgaire, Spear thistle, cirse vulgaire, pet-d'âne, piqueux] Biennial, reproducing only by seed. **Stems** erect, 30 - 150 cm (1 - 5 ft) high, rarely much taller, usually widely branched, short-hairy; middle and upper stems of large plants with narrow, very spiny leaf-like wings running lengthwise (a); on small plants the whole stem and its branches spiny-winged, the wing drying and disappearing as the stem gets thicker and woody (b); **leaves** in a large, flat basal rosette during the first year, each leaf deeply lobed, the lobes usually grouped in 2's or 3's together (c, D) along each side of the leaf with distinctly unlobed portions (d) between them, with long (about 1 cm, 2/5 in.), hard, sharp spines (e) from the tips of each lobe and smaller spines along the margins; under-surface light green, finely woolly-hairy and soft to the touch; upper surface dark green, with closely spaced, short, sharp prickles (f) and very prickly to the touch; stem leaves similar to rosette leaves but smaller upwards on the stem, alternate (1 per node); **flower heads** (see page 208) erect at tips of branches, large, 2.5 - 7.5 cm (1 - 3 in.) across, without ray florets but with long purplish disk florets (g) and surrounded by an involucre (h) of many, overlapping, very narrow, outward-pointing green bracts (Plate 156B), each tipped with a firm, yellowish spine (j); **seeds** about 4 mm (1/6 in.) long, grayish-brown with darker lines, shiny, the hair (pappus) at tip of seed long and branching feather-like (plumose) (C). Flowers from July to September.

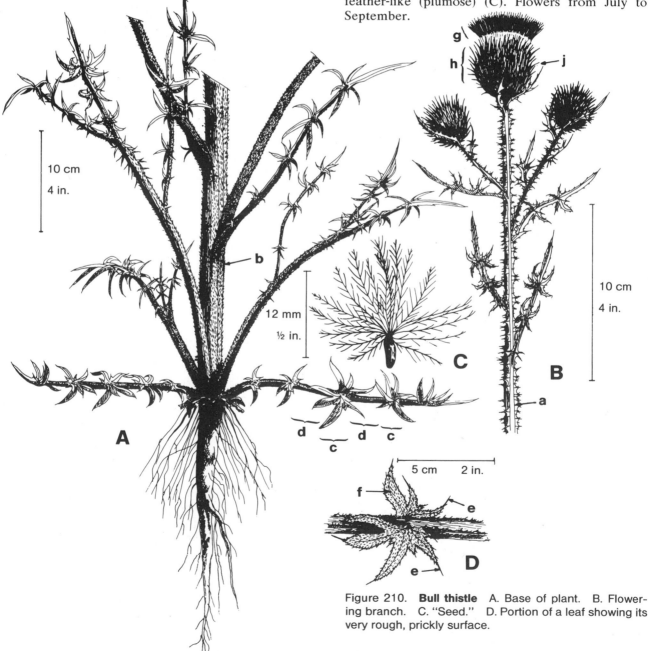

Figure 210. **Bull thistle** A. Base of plant. B. Flowering branch. C. "Seed." D. Portion of a leaf showing its very rough, prickly surface.

Bull thistle is common throughout Ontario in pastures, edges of woods, waste places, fence lines and roadsides; its rosettes are occasionally troublesome in lawns and gardens.

It is distinguished from all other thistles by the covering of short, sharp prickles (f) on the upper, dark green surface of the leaf blade, these prickles (apart from the obvious spines along the margins and tips of the lobes) make the surface very harsh to the touch. Its purple flower heads are larger than Canada thistle, its involucral bracts (h) surrounding the heads are more slender and usually more numerous than in Nodding thistle or Plumeless thistle and the hairs (pappus) on its seeds are feather-like (have plumes) rather than being straight and unbranched as in the latter two thistles.

Scotch thistle, *Onopordum acanthium* L., (Figure 211, Plate 155) [ONRAC, acanthe sauvage, Cotton thistle, White thistle] Biennial or sometimes annual, reproducing only by seed. **Stems** erect, tall, 1 - 2.4 m (3 - 8 ft) high, often much-branched, densely white woolly with broad, spiny, leaf-like wings (a); **leaves** of first-year rosette (A) large (to 60 cm, 24 in. long and 30 cm, 12 in. wide), lobed or coarsely toothed, densely white woolly (like a felt insole), margins wavy and spiny; stem leaves similar but smaller, alternate (1 per node), the margins of the leaf blades usually continuing down the stem as wings (a); **flower heads** (see page 208) at ends of branches and from leaf axils, large, 2.5 - 5 cm (1 - 2 in.) across, nearly spherical, surrounded by numerous, over-lapping, narrow, spine-tipped involucral bracts (b); ray florets absent; disk florets (c) numerous, purple, showy; **seeds** about 5 mm (1/5 in.) long, light brownish-gray to dark gray and wrinkled crosswise. Flowers from late June to September.

Scotch thistle occurs in scattered localities throughout southern Ontario in waste places, fence lines, and around old buildings, usually in gravelly soils where it has escaped from cultivation.

It is distinguished from all other thistles in Ontario by the very dense, white woolly covering on stems and leaves.

Globe thistle, *Echinops sphaerocephalus* L., (not illustrated) [ECPSP, boulette commune, échinope à tête raide] and **Milk thistle,** *Silybum marianum* (L.) Gaertn., (not illustrated) [SLYMA, chardon Marie, Blessed thistle, Lady's thistle, Marian thistle, chardon de Notre-Dame, silybe de Marie, silybus marial], were also introduced for cultivation as ornamentals but have frequently escaped to roadsides, fence lines and waste places. **Globe thistle,** a perennial without creeping roots, produces 1 to several tall leafy **stems** resembling Bull thistle, but its **leaves** are brighter green on the upper surface and whitish below, less spiny on the margins and harshly hairy but without prickles on the upper surface; with glandular (sticky) hair on leaves and upper stems; and its **flower heads** (see page 208) are globe-shaped or spherical with white to light blue to purplish-blue florets. **Milk thistle,** a winter annual or biennial, at first produces a large **rosette** with large, broad, spiny-lobed leaves, the upper surfaces of which are dark green and distinctively mottled with light

green to nearly white along the midrib and principal branching veins (hence "milk" in the English name); **stem leaves** similar to rosette leaves but smaller, the upper ones stalkless and strongly clasping the stem; **flower heads** (see page 208) purple, large, and surrounded by broad, almost leaf-like involucral bracts; these bracts usually having a broad or expanded middle portion with spiny margins, and ending in a long, stout spine; **seeds** large (7 mm, ¼ in. long), dark brown and tipped with a ring of light beige hairs about 15 mm (3/5 in.) long.

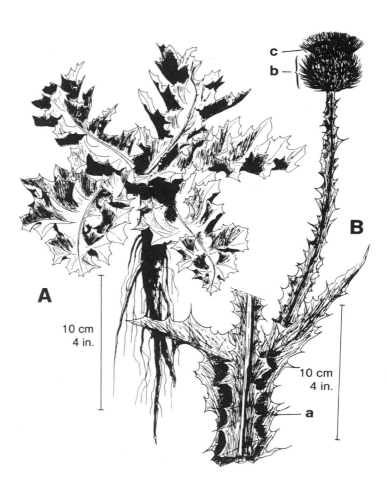

Figure 211. **Scotch thistle** A. Rosette of basal leaves. B. Branch with flower head.

241

Cornflower, *Centaurea cyanus* L., (Figure 212, Plate 157) [CENCY, centaurée bleue, Bachelor's button, Bluebottle, barbeau] Annual or winter annual, reproducing only by seed. **Stems** slender, up to 120 cm (47 in.) high, somewhat hairy, becoming white woolly near the flower heads; rosette and lower stem **leaves** lanceolate, up to 13 cm (4½ in.) long and 2 cm (4/5 in.) wide, often with a few shallow, slender teeth or with slender lobes; mid- and upper stem leaves narrow and linear, rarely as much as 1 cm (2/5 in.) wide, entire, hairy above and woolly below; **flower heads** (see page 208) solitary at the ends of branches, usually a bright, intense blue, occasionally pink, purple or white; florets all tubular (see Figure 177 C,D) with 5 pointed lobes (a); outer florets of each head much larger and longer than the inner florets and pointing outward like the yellow rays of a sunflower head; involucral bracts (b) yellowish-green; their margins membranous, finely toothed and varying from yellowish to light to dark brown; pappus at the tip of each **seed** consisting of fine hairs 2 - 3 mm (1/12 - ⅛ in.) long. Flowers from June to September.

Cornflower was introduced from Europe as an ornamental, escaped from cultivation and now occurs as an occasional weed in southern Ontario in fields of fall-sown crops, in waste places and along roadsides and railway tracks.

It is distinguished from Chicory (page 252) which also has blue flower heads by its narrow, linear upper leaves and its flower heads occurring only at the tips of branches, whereas Chicory has broader, usually toothed leaves, and its flower heads are on very short stalks along the main stem and branches.

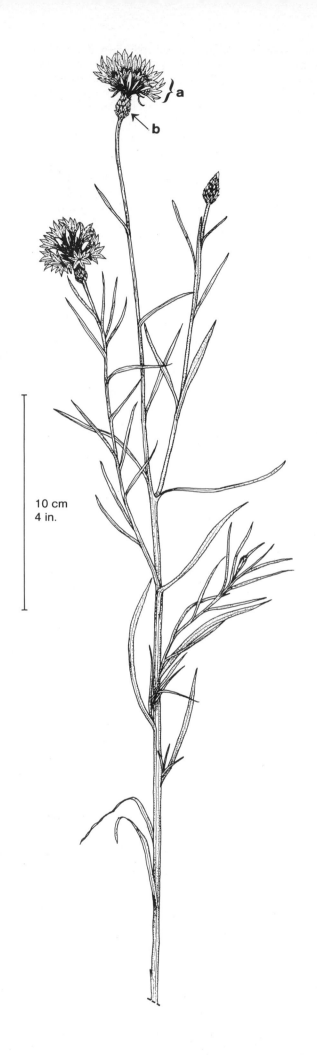

Figure 212. **Cornflower**

Spotted knapweed, *Centaurea maculosa* Lam., (Figure 213, Plate 158) [CENMA, centaurée maculée, centaurée tachetée] Biennial or short-lived perennial, reproducing only by seed. **Stems** erect, much-branched, 20 - 180 cm (8 - 72 in.) high, greenish or purplish striped; **leaves** in a basal rosette the first year, compound (pinnately divided) (A) with several simple (not lobed) or irregularly lobed leaflets (a) widely spaced along each side, the margins of each leaflet smooth or toothed; basal leaves long-stalked (b), with scattered, tiny, round, shining glands embedded in both upper and lower surfaces and and a few translucent dots through the blade; lower and middle stem leaves (B) similar to those of the rosette but smaller with shorter stalks, alternate (1 per node); upper leaves small, narrow, stalkless, simple (c) or with a few small lobes (d); **flower heads** (see page 208) small, erect on slender stiff branches, hard; ray florets absent; flower heads consisting only of many rosy, purplish disk florets; the corolla of each floret ending in 5 long slender lobes (e); the outer florets (e) longer than the central ones (f); the head surrounded by an involucre of small, somewhat dry and membranous bracts (g, C), each bract (C) ovate with a distinct brownish-black tip (h) ending in a fine fringe (j) like the teeth of a comb. Flowers from July to September.

Spotted knapweed occurs throughout Ontario but is most common in the southern part of the province, especially in Grey and Hastings Counties.

It is distinguished by its pinnately divided rosette and lower stem leaves, the leaves slightly woolly, with tiny shining glands in both surfaces visible to the naked eye as shiny specks and with a few translucent dots visible as pinpricks through the leaf blade when viewed against the light, and by its showy rosy-purple flower heads surrounded by involucral bracts (g, C) with dry and membranous brownish-black tips (h) fringed (j) like the teeth of a comb.

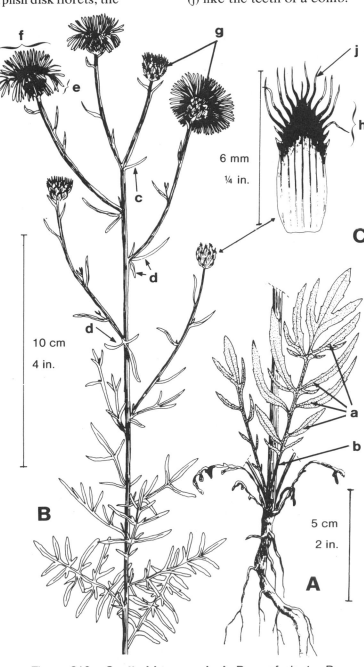

Figure 213. **Spotted knapweed** A. Base of plant. B. Stem with flower heads. C. 1 involucral bract.

243

Black knapweed, *Centaurea nigra* L., (Figure 214, Plate 159) [CENNI, centaurée noire] Perennial, reproducing only by seed. Similar to Spotted knapweed in general habit, but differing by having a coarser, more robust appearance, smooth (a) or undivided, irregularly toothed, somewhat rough-hairy **leaves** (b), and it involucral bracts (c, C) surrounding the flower heads having a narrow basal portion (d) and a broad, fringed, outer or tip portion (e), this outer portion and its comb-like fringes (f) dark brown to blackish (rarely light brown); the tips of its innermost bracts next to the florets sometimes just flared but not fringed; **florets** rosy-purple, compact, all about the same length only slightly protruding beyond the involucral bracts; rarely the outer row of florets (e) much longer and sterile, these plants possibly having hybrid parentage with Brown knapweed (see below); **seeds** light brown to light gray, 3 mm (⅛ in.) long, fringed at the top with a short pappus 0.5 - 1.0 mm (1/50 - 1/25 in.) long. Flowers from late June to October.

Black knapweed occurs throughout southern Ontario in pastures, meadows, fence lines, roadsides and waste places.

Hybrid black - brown knapweed, *Centaurea* x *pratensis* Thuill., (Figure 214B). Black knapweed hybridizes with the next species, Brown knapweed, resulting in plants with characteristics intermediate between the two. In its **flower heads,** the **outer row of florets** are usually long and sterile (e) (like Brown knapweed versus usually short and fertile in Black knapweed); its **involucral bracts** usually have brown to dark brown tips with comb-like fringes (as in C) (light brown and torn-papery in Brown knapweed), and its **seeds** have no pappus (like Brown knapweed, Black knapweed seed having a distinct pappus of hairs up to 1.0 mm (1/25 in.) long. Because these hybrids are fertile, they further hybridize with either parent as well as among themselves. As a result there may be extreme variability in this group — ranging from very nearly like Black knapweed to very nearly like Brown knapweed.

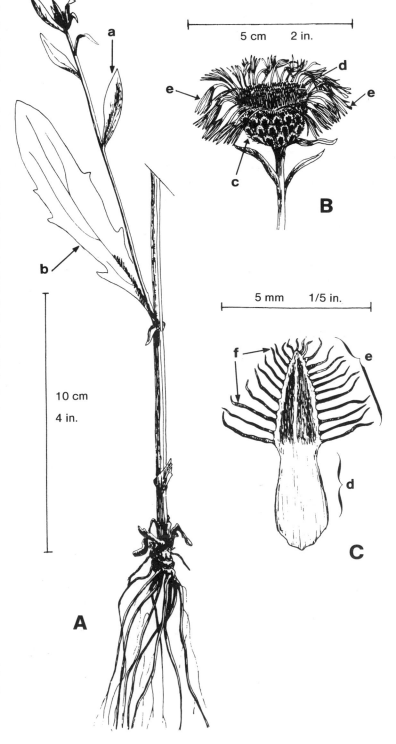

Figure 214. **Black knapweed** A. Lower part of plant. B. 1 flower head showing outer row of florets being longer than the inner ones, this suggestive of hybridization with Brown knapweed. C. 1 involucral bract.

244

Brown knapweed, *Centaurea jacea* L., (Figure 215) [CENJA, centaurée jacée, Common knapweed, Starthistle, jacée des prés] Perennial, reproducing only by seed. Similar to Spotted knapweed in habit and general appearance, but differing from it by having a coarser, more robust appearance, simple, undivided, but irregularly toothed, somewhat rough-hairy **leaves** (A, B, C), and by having the involucral bracts surrounding the flower head light brown, with the upper half of each bract (D) expanded or flared out and torn into irregular divisions rather than fringed like the teeth of a comb. Flowers from June to September.

Brown knapweed occurs chiefly in the western half of southern Ontario where it is sometimes very common in pastures, roadsides and waste places.

Russian knapweed, *Centaurea repens* L., (not illustrated) [CENRE, centaurée de Russie, centaurée toujours fleurie] Perennial, but differs from other perennial knapweeds by reproducing both by seed and from deeply penetrating, widely spreading, dark brown or black **roots** which can form extensive patches and be extremely difficult to eradicate once established. It is a finer, more slender plant than the other knapweeds, with narrow, undivided but shallowly and irregularly toothed **leaves**; **stems** and leaves covered with a white woolliness which peels off in strips as the stems get older; **flower heads** (see page 208) small (1 - 1.5 cm, 2/5 - 3/5 in. across), silvery-green before opening; ray florets absent; disk florets pinkish to light purplish; involucral bracts with a papery tip which is neither fringed nor irregularly divided. Flowers from July to September.

Russian knapweed occurs in cultivated fields and pastures in the central part of southern Ontario.

Figure 215. **Brown knapweed** A. Base of plant. B. Leaf and short branch at mid-stem. C. Leaves at top of stem. D. 1 involucral bract.

It is distinguished by its ability to reproduce from deeply penetrating and widely spreading roots, these with dark brown to black bark, its gray-green stems and undivided leaves, its small flower heads with silvery-green involucral bracts which are not fringed at the tip, and by the extremely persistent bitter taste of its stem and the inner parts of its roots.

Yellow devil hawkweed, *Hieracium floribundum* Wimm. & Grab., (Figure 216) [HIEFL, épervière à fleurs nombreuses, Yellow hawkweed, épervière à fleurs multiples] Perennial, reproducing by seed and by leafy stolons (runners) (a) and forming dense patches of rosette plants. **Leaves** in a basal rosette on a short, stout, upright, underground **rhizome**; leaves narrowly elliptic or wider towards the tip, 2.5 - 14 cm (1 - 5½ in.) long, gray-green, with long stiff hairs on both surfaces, especially along the underside of the midrib; horizontal leafy **stolons** (a) produced at about flowering time, usually rooting near the ends (b) and with leaves similar to but smaller than those of the main rosette; flowering **stems** (B) erect, 20 - 80 cm (8 - 32 in.) high, leafless or with 1 or 2 small leaves near the base, hairy with scattered, long, stiff, often blackish hairs; **flower heads** (see page 208) arranged in a loose, open, more or less flat-topped inflorescence, each head containing only strap-shaped ray florets (like Dandelion but much smaller), bright yellow, 7 - 8 mm (¼ - 1/3 in.) across when fully open and surrounded by an involucre of slender bracts (c) covered with short, blackish, usually gland-tipped hairs; all parts with white milky juice. Flowers from late June to August.

Figure 216. **Yellow devil hawkweed** A. Base of plant with 2 leafy stolons. B. Flowering stem.

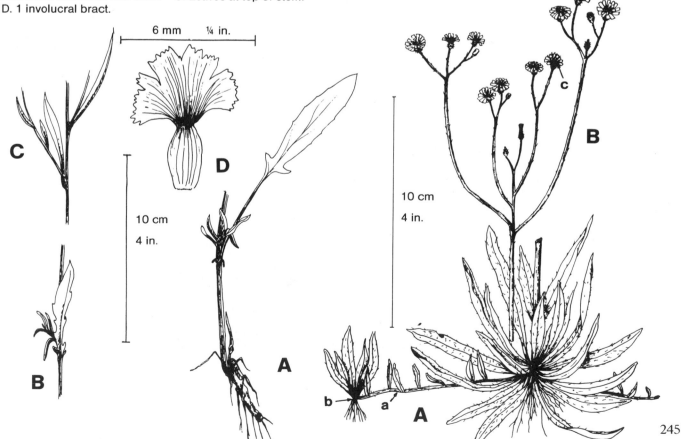

6 mm   ¼ in.

10 cm
4 in.

C

D

B

A

10 cm
4 in.

B

b   a   A

c

245

Yellow devil hawkweed occurs throughout Ontario, being most common in the south in pastures, meadows, waste areas and roadsides.

It is distinguished by its horizontal leafy stolons (a) produced at flowering time and rooting near the tip (b), its leaves with long hairs on the upper surface and along the midrib below, its yellow flower heads in a loose, more or less flat-topped inflorescence, and its involucral bracts covered by short, blackish, gland-tipped hairs.

King devil hawkweed, *Hieracium florentinum* All., (not illustrated) [HIEPO, épervière des Florentins, Yellow hawkweed, épervière florentine] Very similar to Yellow devil hawkweed, differing from it by having no horizontal leafy stolons (runners) but instead producing upright secondary **flowering stems** after the flower heads on the main stem have begun to open, and slightly larger **flower heads**, 10 - 11 mm (2/5 in.) across when fully open. It occurs mainly in southern Ontario in similar habitats and often mixed with Yellow devil hawkweed.

Yellow hawkweed, *Hieracium pratense* Tausch, (not illustrated) [HIECA, épervière des prés, épervière branchue] Resembling both Yellow devil hawkweed and King devil hawkweed but is distinguished by having the **flower heads** in a compact, flat-topped cluster, each head 10 - 11 mm (2/5 in.) across and appearing blackish due to a dense covering of black, gland-tipped hairs on the involucre; by having short bristly hair together with tiny branched hair requiring magnification to be seen on both upper and lower **leaf** surfaces; and occasionally producing short, horizontal, leafy **stolons**. Its distribution is similar to the two previous hawkweeds. Except for its yellow flower colour, it closely resembles Orange hawkweed (Figure 218, Plate 160).

Mouse-eared hawkweed, *Hieracium pilosella* L., (Figure 217) [HIEPI, épervière piloselle, piloselle, oreille de souris] Similar to Yellow devil hawkweed but shorter, forming dense masses of smaller **rosettes** 5 - 9 cm (2 - 3½ in.) across, and producing 1 to 3 (rarely more) leafy **stolons** (a) (runners); the shorter **leaves** broadly club-shaped, upper surfaces green and smooth except for long, slender, stiff hairs; undersurfaces softly woolly with slightly brownish matted hairs; stolon leaves similar but much smaller; **flower heads** (see page 208) yellow, generally larger than Yellow devil hawkweed (14 - 17 mm, about ⅝ in. long and 12 - 20 mm, ½ - 4/5 in. across) but borne singly or rarely 2 or 3 on erect, leafless, sticky-hairy, slender **stems**. Flowers from May to September.

Mouse-eared hawkweed occurs in southern Ontario in pastures, waste areas, roadsides and occasionally lawns, usually in poor, shallow soils in rocky or gravelly situations.

Orange hawkweed, *Hieracium aurantiacum* L., (Figure 218, Plate 160) [HIEAU, épervière orangée, Devil's-paintbrush, King-devil, bouquet rouge] Very similar to Yellow hawkweed (*Hieracium pratense*) in size, shape and hairiness of rosette **leaves**, in having short, leafy **stolons** (runners), and a compact inflorescence; but differing by having bright, showy, orange-red to deep dark reddish-orange **flower heads** (see page 208). Flowers from June to September.

Orange hawkweed occurs throughout Ontario in

246

pastures, meadows, edges of woods, roadsides and waste places in deep, rich soils as well as shallow, sandy or gravelly soils.

It is readily distinguished by its showy orange-red to dark reddish-orange flower heads (Plate 160B).

Narrow-leaved hawk's-beard, *Crepis tectorum* L. (Plate 161) [CVPTE, crépis des toits, yellow hawk's-beard] is frequently mistaken for one of the yellow-flowered hawkweeds. Although its bright yellow **flower heads** are similar in size and shape to those of Yellow devil hawkweed (Figure 216), and its inflorescence is also branched, Narrow-leaved hawk's-beard is distinguished by being an annual or winter annual with a deep taproot and a leafy **stem** 25 - 100 cm (10 - 40 in.) tall, its basal and lower **leaves** being 10 - 15 cm (4 - 6 in.) long and irregularly deeply lobed (suggestive of Dandelion or Perennial sow-thistle), its middle leaves more slender with fewer lobes, and its upper leaves very narrow and without lobes. Flowers from June to September.

Narrow-leaved hawk's-beard occurs in fields (usually fall-sown crops), pastures, waste places, roadsides and gardens at scattered localities throughout Ontario.

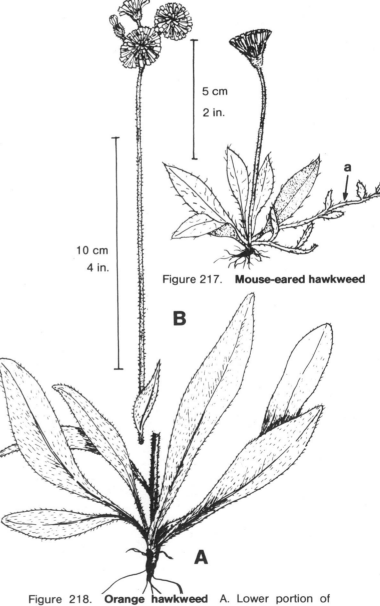

Figure 217. **Mouse-eared hawkweed**

Figure 218. **Orange hawkweed** A. Lower portion of plant. B. Flowering stem.

Perennial sow-thistle, *Sonchus arvensis* L., (Figure 219, Plate 162) [SONAR, laiteron des champs, Creeping sow-thistle, Field sow-thistle, Glandular-hairy perennial sow-thistle, crève-z-yeux, laiteron vivace] Perennial, reproducing by seed and from buds (a) on widely spreading, creamy white, brittle, underground **roots** (b). **Stems** erect, 60 - 150 cm (2 - 5 ft) high, smooth and hairless on the lower part but glandular-hairy towards the top and on branches, hollow; **leaves** of seedling plants (A) broadly club-shaped with irregularly toothed margins, the teeth ending in weak prickles (c), remnants of the cotyledons (seed leaves) (d) often visible; leaves of shoots from perennial roots (B) variable in shape, the lower ones shallowly to deeply lobed and irregularly toothed, reminiscent of Dandelion leaves but the teeth ending in small, weak prickles, with winged stalks (e); alternate (1 per node); middle and upper leaves similar but smaller with shorter stalks and clasping the stem with small, rounded basal lobes (f), or sometimes with larger basal lobes similar to those of Spiny annual sow-thistle as at (a) in Figure 220; uppermost leaves (g) small, narrow, without lobes and with only a few teeth; upper stems, branches and involucral bracts (h) surrounding the flower heads usually densely covered with dark hair (j); each hair with a tiny gland (k) at its tip (these hairs, when seen under magnification, resemble a tiny lollipop) (these glandular hairs do not occur in its sister variety, Smooth perennial sow-thistle); **flower heads** (see page 208) showy, bright yellow, 2.5 - 4 cm (1 - 1¾ in.) across; each head containing only strap-shaped ray florets (like Dandelion flower heads and similar to those of Smooth perennial sow-thistle); **seeds** brown with lengthwise ridges and finer cross ridges; whole plant with sticky white juice and a rather sour odour. Flowers from June to late autumn.

Perennial sow-thistle occurs throughout Ontario in cultivated fields, pastures, meadows, woodland, waste places, roadsides, gardens and occasionally in lawns.

Non-flowering plants are distinguished by their variously lobed leaves with weakly spiny teeth; by their soft, somewhat fleshy, bright green stems mostly arising directly from horizontal yellowish-white, fleshy, brittle, cord-like roots (b), these roots bearing many, small, whitish buds (a) able to grow into other new leafy stems; the whitish vertical underground portion (m) of each upright stem resembling a root, but usually not tapering downwards except in first-year plants (A) which started from seed. Flowering plants are distinguished by their showy, large, bright yellow flower heads and the covering of glandular hairs (j) on the involucre (h) and the upper stems and branches.

Smooth perennial sow-thistle, *Sonchus arvensis* L. var. *glabrescens* Guenth, Grab. & Wimm., (not illustrated) [SONAU, laiteron des champs glabre, Creeping sow-thistle, Field sow-thistle, Perennial sow-thistle, *Sonchus uliginosus* Bieb] Virtually identical to Perennial sow-thistle in seedling and juvenile stages, being distinguishable only after the flower heads (see page 208) begin to form and open. In Smooth perennial sow-thistle the stems and involucral bracts around the **flower heads** are smooth, completely lacking the dark

glandular hairs (see (j) and (k) in Figure 219 C) characteristic of Perennial sow-thistle. Smooth perennial sow-thistle occupies similar habitats to those of its sister variety. It is common only in extreme southwestern Ontario and in the northern and northwestern parts of the province, although it occurs sporadically elsewhere.

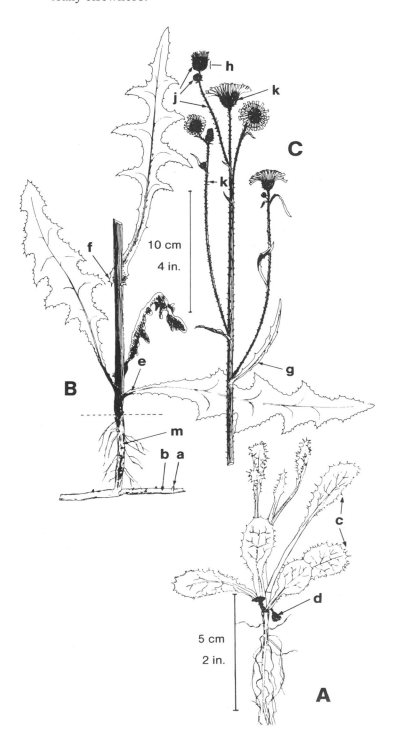

Figure 219. **Perennial sow-thistle** A. Young plant from seed. B. Base of plant from perennial root. C. Top of flowering stem.

247

Spiny annual sow-thistle, *Sonchus asper* (L.) Hill, (Figure 220, Plate 163) [SONAS, laiteron rude, Prickly annual sow-thistle, laiteron âpre, laiteron épineux] Annual, reproducing only by seed. Resembling Perennial sow-thistle in general appearance but distinguished from it by its annual **root** (tapering downwards from ground surface and not connected to a strong horizontal root that has other buds), lower and middle stem **leaves** (B) rather firm, clasping the stem with prominent rounded lobes (a); all margins with small, moderately spiny teeth; upper stems (b) and involucral bracts (c) of the **flower heads** (see page 208) smooth or sparsely glandular-hairy and the flower heads smaller. Before opening, the flower heads are short and cylindrical (d). When fully open (e) they are about 2 cm (4/5 in.) across and, after the yellow ray florets shrivel and fall, the heads become top-shaped (f) with a broad base and a narrow tip. Seeds (g) brown, 3 mm (⅛ in.) long, somewhat flat with several lengthwise ribs on each surface but without cross-wrinkles, each with a fluffy white pappus (h); whole plant with sticky white juice. Flowers from June to September.

Spiny annual sow-thistle occurs throughout Ontario in waste places, along fence lines, roadsides, around buildings and occasionally in gardens.

It is distinguished by the rounded, clasping basal lobes (a) on its rather firm leaves, the leaves lobed and generally tapering towards the tip, its tapering annual taproot, its small flower heads, and its seeds with lengthwise ribs but not cross-wrinkled.

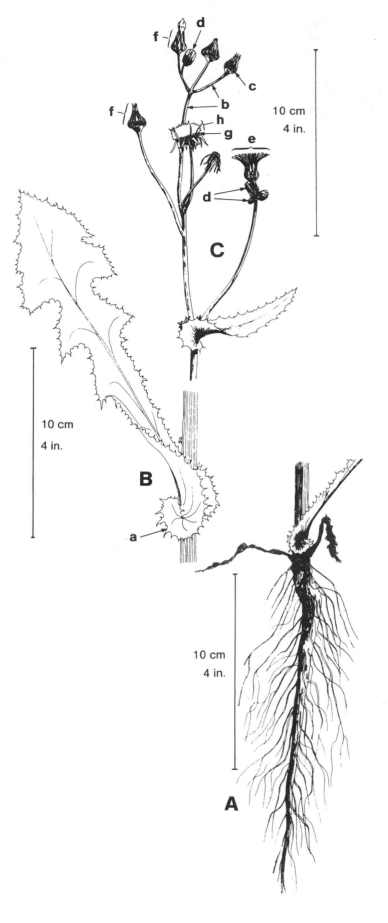

Figure 220. **Spiny annual sow-thistle**   A. Base of plant.
B. Leaf from lower or mid-stem.   C. Top of flowering stem.

248

Annual sow-thistle, *Sonchus oleraceus* L., (Figure 221, Plate 164) [SONOL, laiteron potager, Common annual sow-thistle, laiteron lisse, laiteron commun] Very similar to Spiny annual sow-thistle in general appearance but easily distinguished by having leaves which are deeply lobed with the terminal lobe being short, broad and rounded or triangular (a); the part of the leaf closer to the stem very narrow (b); the base of the leaf clasping the stem with 2 angular or pointed lobes (c); all margins with small teeth and soft weak spines; and seeds ridged lengthwise but each ridge with numerous small cross-wrinkles.

It occurs in habitats similar to those of Spiny annual sow-thistle.

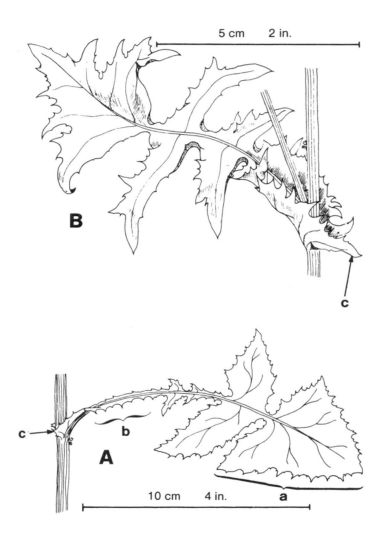

Figure 221. **Annual sow-thistle** A. Lower stem leaf. B. Upper leaf.

Prickly lettuce, *Lactuca scariola* L., (Figure 222, Plate 165) [LACSE, laitue scariole, Compass plant, Wild lettuce, laitue vireuse, scariole, *Lactuca serriola* L.] Winter annual, biennial, or sometimes annual, reproducing only by seed. **Stems** erect, 30 - 150 cm (1 - 5 ft) high, whitish-green, usually smooth with a few prickles on the lower part, rather finely branched at the top; **leaves** variable in size and shape, usually deeply lobed or nearly divided with backward-curving lobes (A, B) but sometimes with irregularly shaped lobes (C) or without lobes (D); the outer (convex) margin (a) of each lobe usually weakly spiny-toothed, the inner (concave) (b) margin usually without teeth or with much smaller teeth; leaves clasping the stem with basal lobes (c); underside of the midrib nearly always with a single row of stiff, sharp prickles (d) (hence "prickly" in the common name), these usually absent from the upper leaves (e) among the inflorescence and occasionally absent from the lower leaves of second growth after mowing; leaves alternate (1 per node), usually twisted near the stem so the leaf blade is oriented with the margins pointing vertically and the flat surfaces facing horizontally, leaf tips often (but not always) pointing north and south; **flower heads** (see page 208) small and very numerous on fine stalks in much-branched inflorescences; each head about 7 - 8 mm (¼ - 1/3 in.) long and about 3 mm (⅛ in.) across, with 5 to 12 yellow ray florets, the yellow colour often fading to bluish on drying; disk florets absent; **seeds** narrowly oval with a long beak tipped with a tuft of white hair (pappus); whole plant with sticky white juice. Flowers from June to late autumn.

Prickly lettuce occurs throughout Ontario in waste places, pastures, roadsides, cultivated fields, and occasionally in gardens.

It is distinguished from most other plants having milky juice and lobed or prickly-margined leaves by the single row of firm, sharp prickles (d) along the underside of the midribs of the stem leaves.

Tall blue lettuce, *Lactuca biennis* (Moench) Fern., (Figure 223) [LACBI, laitue bisannuelle, Biennial lettuce, Tall lettuce, laitue à épis] Biennial or annual, reproducing only by seed; similar to Prickly lettuce but usually taller (60 - 200 cm, 2 - 6½ ft high), stouter, with a coarser inflorescence and more irregularly lobed **leaves**; the leaves without a row of prickles on the underside of the midrib but either smooth or softly hairy along the midrib and the main veins; **flower heads** (see page 208) somewhat larger than in Prickly lettuce, 9 - 13 mm (1/3 - ½ in.) long and 4 - 8 mm (1/6 - 1/3 in.) across, with up to 17 ray (strap-shaped) florets which range from bluish to white or occasionally yellow; seed with a very short beak at the tip and ending in a tuft of light brown hair (pappus); whole plant with sticky white juice. Flowers from July to September.

Tall blue lettuce occurs in scattered localities in southern Ontario in open woods, meadows, old pastures and roadsides.

It is distinguished by its comparatively tall stature, its irregularly lobed leaves that do not have prickles along the underside of the midrib, its small, usually blue flowers and its seeds with a tuft of light brown hair.

Canada lettuce, *Lactuca canadensis* L., (not illustrated), [LACCA, laitue du Canada, Tall lettuce, laitue sauvage] Biennial or annual, reproducing only by seed; resembles Tall blue lettuce but is distinguished by its usually greater height (up to 250 cm, 8½ ft) its **leaves** usually slender with slender lobes and its **flower heads** always with yellow florets. It also occurs in open woods and meadows in southern Ontario.

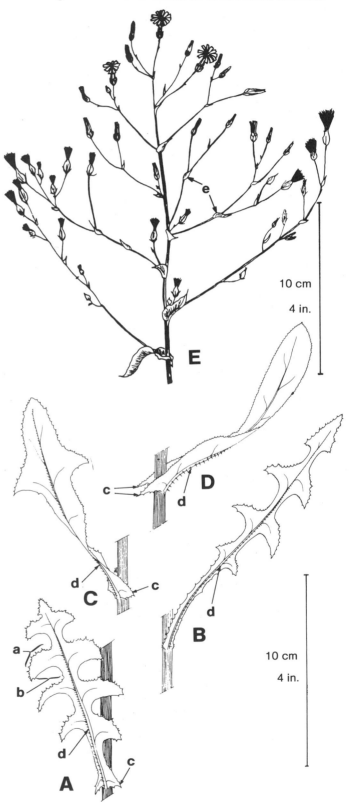

Figure 222. **Prickly lettuce** A-D. Variations in lobing of leaves on different plants. E. Top of flowering branch.

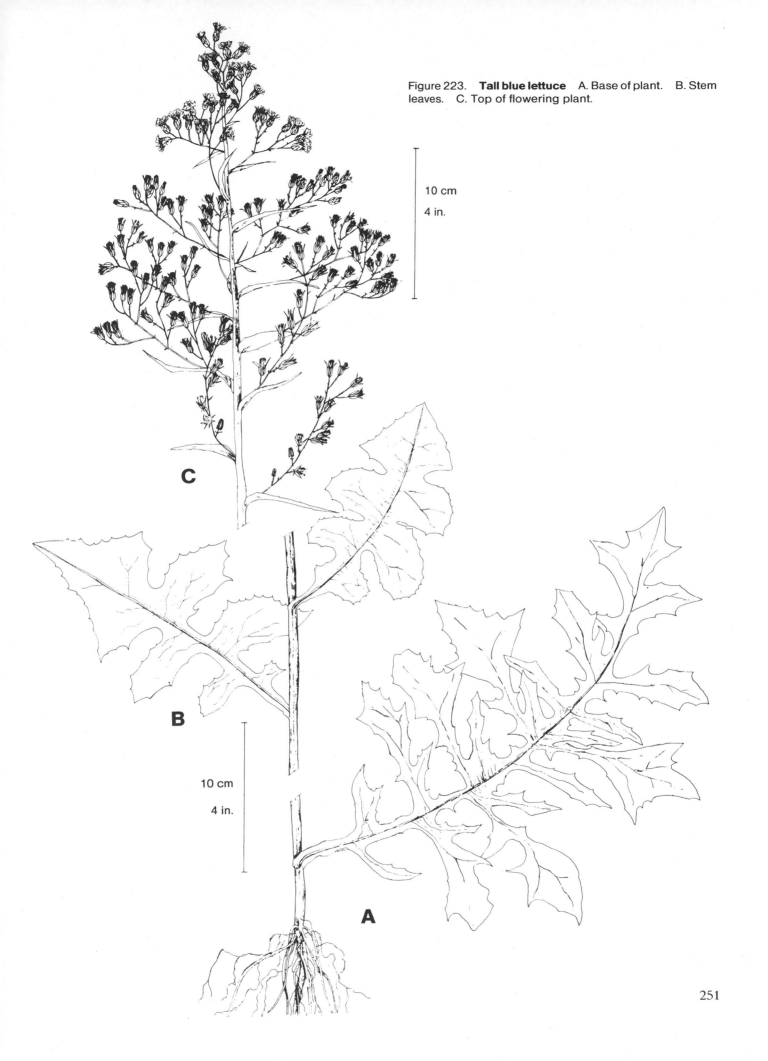

Figure 223.   **Tall blue lettuce**   A. Base of plant.   B. Stem leaves.   C. Top of flowering plant.

10 cm
4 in.

10 cm

4 in.

C

B

A

251

Chicory, *Cichorium intybus* L., (Figure 224, Plate 166) [CICIN, chicorée sauvage, Blue daisy, Blue sailors, Coffee-weed, Common chicory, Wild succory, chicorée] Biennial or usually perennial, reproducing only by seed. **Stems** erect, 30 - 150 cm (1 - 5 ft) high, usually with stiff spreading branches, hollow, rough-hairy especially on the lower part; first-year plants without a stem but forming a thick, vertical **taproot** (a) and a large **rosette** of leaves; leaves of the basal rosette large, coarse, resembling Dandelion leaves (as in Figure 225) but rough-hairy; **stem leaves** similar but smaller, alternate (1 per node), and bases of upper leaves clasping the stem; **flower heads** (see page 208) bright blue and very showy, stalkless or on short stalks in clusters along the branches, numerous; each head 3 - 4 cm (1¼ - 1¾ in.) across; only ray (strap-shaped) florets (b) present; these blue, occasionally pinkish or whitish; seeds short, angled, top-shaped but lacking a tuft of hair at the tip; sticky white juice usually present in stems and leaves. Flowers from July to late autumn.

Chicory occurs throughout Ontario in waste places, fence lines, roadsides and occasionally in gardens.

It is distinguished in rosette and non-flowering stages by its coarse, rough-hairy leaves superficially resembling Dandelion leaves, and when in flower, by its large, showy, blue flowers in stalkless clusters along the branches.

Dandelion, *Taraxacum officinale* Weber, (Figure 225, Plate 167) [TAROF, pissenlit, dent-de-lion, pissenlit officinal] Perennial, reproducing only by seed. **Leaves** in a basal rosette on a thick, deeply penetrating taproot (a), elongated, deeply and irregularly lobed along each side or sometimes just shallowly toothed, the amount and shape of lobing or toothing being extremely variable from one plant to another (A - F); **flower heads** (see page 208) showy, bright yellow, 3.2 - 5 cm (1¼ - 2 in.) across, borne singly on long, smooth, leafless, unbranched, hollow stalks (b) which arise from among the rosette leaves; only ray (strap-shaped) florets present; outer row of involucral bracts short and spreading or bent down; seed heads white, more or less spherical, 3.5 - 5 cm (1½ - 2 in.) across; seeds long, slender with a slender beak (c) tipped with a tuft of white hair (pappus or "parachute"); whole plant with sticky white juice. Flowers from early spring to late autumn.

Dandelion occurs throughout Ontario in virtually every kind of habitat, from openings in deep woods to cultivated fields, from rocky hillsides to fertile gardens, and lawns.

It is distinguished from other plants with milky juice and lobed or divided leaves in rosette stage by the soft texture and irregular lobing of leaves, the absence of prickles on margins or midribs, the smooth or softly hairy leaf surfaces, and a deeply penetrating taproot. Flowering plants are distinguished by their large yellow flower heads with only ray (strap-shaped) florets and borne singly on long, unbranched, leafless, hollow stalks which arise from among the rosette leaves, these followed by white, spherical seed heads up to 5 cm (2 in.) in diameter.

10 cm
4 in.

10 cm
4 in.

Figure 224. **Chicory** A. Base of second-year plant. B. Stem. C. Flowering branch.

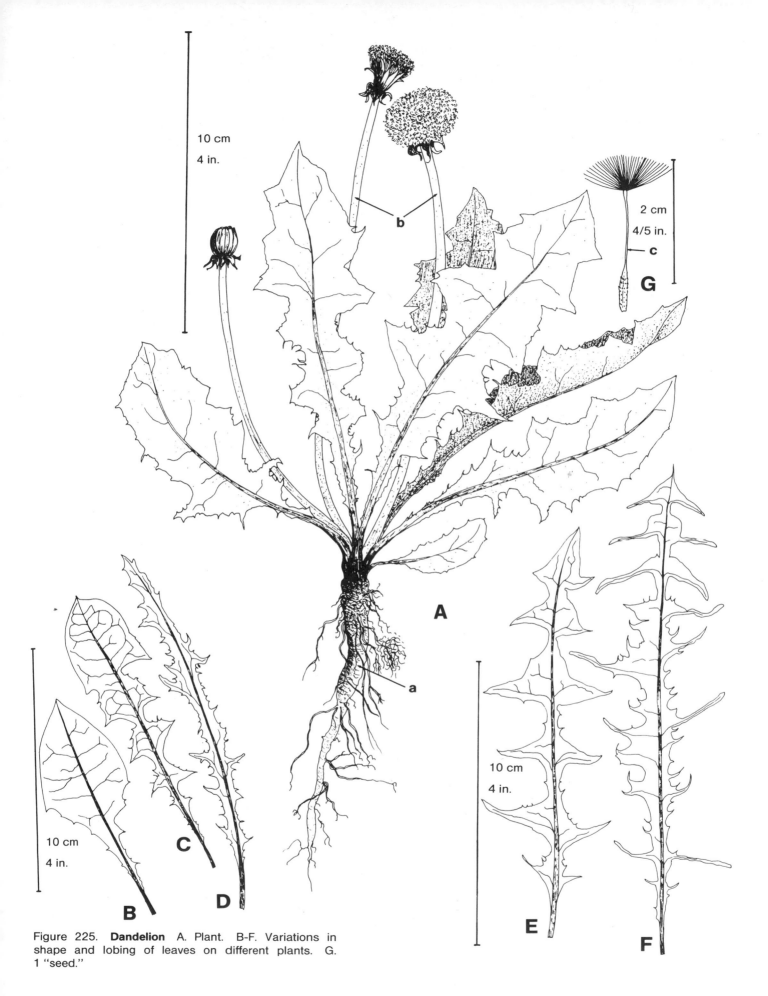

10 cm
4 in.

2 cm
4/5 in.

10 cm
4 in.

10 cm
4 in.

Figure 225. **Dandelion** A. Plant. B-F. Variations in shape and lobing of leaves on different plants. G. 1 "seed."

253

Fall hawkbit, *Leontodon autumnalis* L., (Figure 226)
[LEBAU, liondent d'automne, Fall dandelion, léon-
todon d'automne] Perennial, reproducing only by seed.
Similar in general appearance to Dandelion in having
basal **rosettes** of irregularly lobed leaves and bright
yellow **flower heads** (see page 208); but distinguished
by having a predominantly fibrous **root** system (a) with
a very short taproot (b) (usually only 1 - 2.5 cm, 2/5 -
1 in. long); its **leaves** shallowly to deeply lobed, the
lobes usually being slender, distinctly spaced, and with
rounded rather than sharp tips or points; its flower
heads (see page 208) usually smaller, up to 3.5 cm
(1½ in.) across, and on branched stalks with usually 2
or more heads per stalk, the stalks not smooth but
with many, scattered, small, scale leaves (c); its seed
heads only rounded above, rather than nearly spherical, 2.5 - 3.5 cm (1 - 1½ in.) across, its **seeds** slender but
without a beak and tipped with a tuft of light brownish,
feathery hair (pappus). All parts of the plant contain
white, milky juice. Flowers from June to October.

Fall hawkbit occurs in a few scattered localities in
southern Ontario in lawns, roadsides and waste places.

Its most important distinguishing features are its
usually 2 or more flower heads on each slender,
branched, scaly-leaved (c) stem, its predominantly
fibrous root system (a) (not a long taproot), its flower
heads and seed heads usually smaller than dandelion,
and its slender seeds without a beak but tipped with
light brownish, feathery hair.

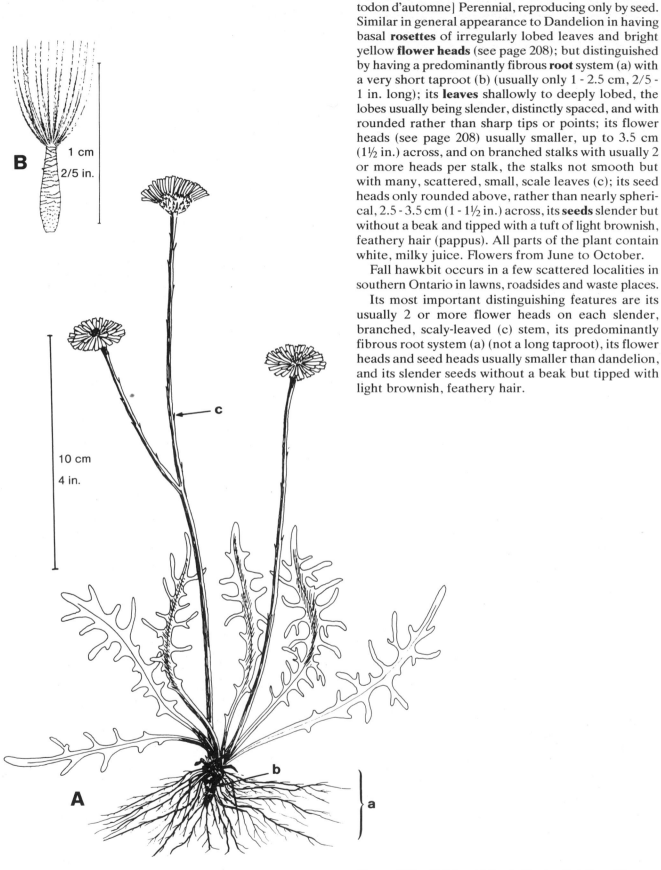

Figure 226. **Fall hawkbit** A. Plant. B. 1 "seed."

Goat's-beard, *Tragopogon dubius* Scop., (Figure 227, Plate 168) [TRODM, salsifis majeur, Western goat's-beard, Yellow goat's-beard, *Tragopogon major* Jacq.] Biennial, occasionally annual or short-lived perennial, reproducing only by seed. **Stems** 30 - 100 cm (12 - 40 in.) high, smooth, round, somewhat fleshy, from a deeply penetrating, thick **taproot**; stemless, juvenile annual plants and first-year biennials without stems resemble shoots of grass; **leaves** alternate (1 per node), long, linear, very grass-like but smooth and fleshy rather than firm or harsh; younger leaves somewhat downy-hairy; dry, brown, shriveled leaves (a) from the previous year's rosette frequently persisting around the base of leafy-stemmed and flowering plants; **flower heads** (see page 208) large, 4 - 6 cm (1¾ - 2¼ in.) across, showy, pale lemon-yellow, borne singly at ends of stems and branches (resembling Meadow goat's-beard, Plate 169); stalk (b) at the base (c) of the flower head very thick, hollow, tapering gradually downwards to normal stem thickness (d); involucral bracts (e) usually 10 or more, green, 2.5 - 4 cm (1 - 1¾ in.) long at flowering, elongating to about 7.5 cm (3 in.) or longer as the seeds mature; only ray (strap-shaped) florets (f) present, the outer ones opening first and the unopened inner florets somewhat resembling disk florets; flower heads opening and pointing towards the sun each morning, twisting slightly and following the sun until midday, and closing during the afternoon; mature seed head (D) a white, fluffy sphere, 7 - 10 cm (3 - 4 in.) in diameter; each **seed** including its slender beak about 3 cm (1¼ in.) long and tipped with a white, umbrella-like circle of feathery bristles (pappus) (g); whole plant, except the seed, with a white, milky juice. Flowers in June and July and occasionally continues until September.

Goat's-beard occurs throughout Ontario in pastures. meadows, roadsides and occasionally gardens.

Flowering plants are distinguished by their long, smooth, slender grass-like leaves, their lemon yellow flower heads surrounded by usually 10 or more, slender, tapering, green involucral bracts (e) which are longer than the yellow florets (f), their thick, hollow, gradually tapering stalks (b) below the flower heads, and their large, spherical seed heads. Non-flowering plants are distinguished by their erect, fleshy, smooth-textured, grass-like leaves with milky juice, the leaves usually long, gradually tapering, and not having crisped or wrinkled margins, and their long, tapering taproots.

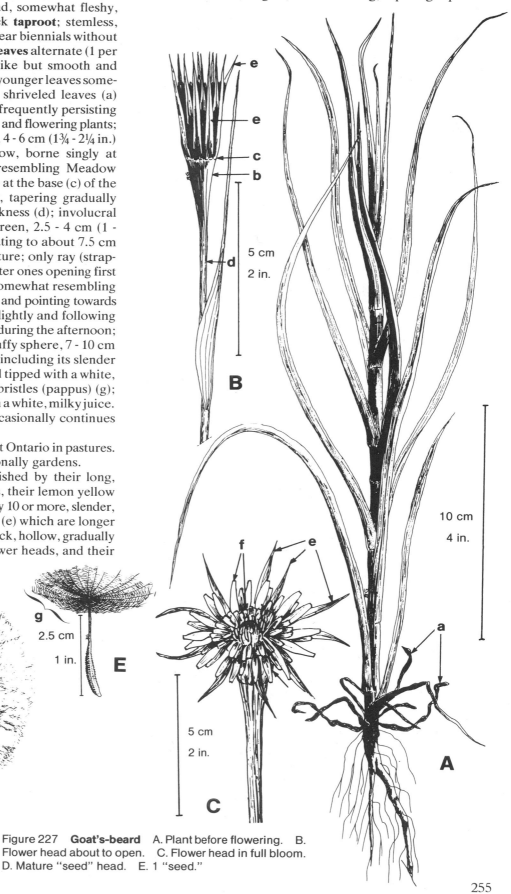

Figure 227 **Goat's-beard** A. Plant before flowering. B. Flower head about to open. C. Flower head in full bloom. D. Mature "seed" head. E. 1 "seed."

255

Meadow goat's-beard, *Tragopogon pratensis* L., (Figure 228 A-C, Plate 169) [TROPR, salsifis des prés, Johnny-go-to-bed-at-noon, Meadow salsify, Yellow goat's-beard, salsifis sauvage] Very similar to Goat's-beard in appearance and growth habit but differing from it by having **stem leaves** which taper more quickly into long, slender, curled tips (a) (Plate 169), and often have crisped or wrinkled margins; brighter yellow (canary yellow) **florets** (b) surrounded by usually only 8 green involucral bracts (c) which are about as long as or shorter than the florets; and the stalk (d) immediately below the flower head is abruptly narrowed to normal stem thickness, and is not hollow.

It occurs throughout Ontario in the same habitats as Goat's-beard.

Common salsify, *Tragopogon porrifolius* L., (Figure 228 D) [TROPS, salsifis cultivé, Garden salsify, Oyster-plant, Salsify, Vegetable-oyster, salsifis, salsifis à feuilles de poireau] Cultivated as a garden vegetable and occasionally escapes to roadsides and waste places; very similar to Goat's-beard in habit and appearance but is distinguished by having purple rather than yellow **florets**, and its **seed** tipped with brownish rather than white feathery bristles (pappus).

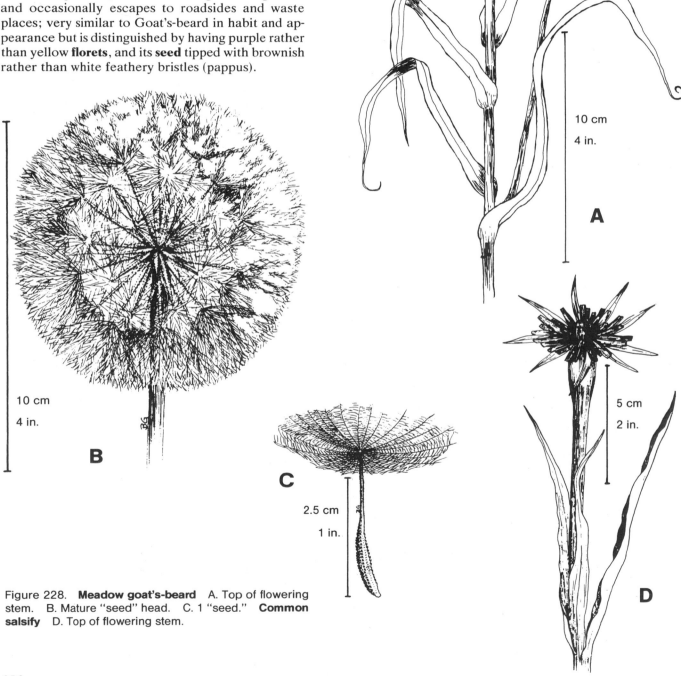

Figure 228. **Meadow goat's-beard** A. Top of flowering stem. B. Mature "seed" head. C. 1 "seed." **Common salsify** D. Top of flowering stem.

INDEX OF COMMON AND BOTANICAL NAMES

(Page numbers of illustrations are in bold face.)

266

269

272

INDEX OF BAYER CODE LETTERS

Plate 1 **Field horsetail** *fruiting stage* (p. 19)

Plate 2 **Field horsetail** *vegetative stage* (p. 19)

Plate 3 **Eastern bracken** *side view (scale units =*
10 cm, 4 in) (p. 20)

Plate 4 **Eastern bracken** *2 shoots viewed from above* (p. 20)

Plate 5 **Eulalia** (p. 28)

Plate 6 **Wild oats** (p. 29)

Plate 8   **Foxtail barley**   (p. 32)

Plate 7   **Quack grass** *A. plants in head*
B. leaf-base showing auricles   (p. 31)

Plate 9   **Silky bent grass** *A. infestation in winter wheat*
B. shattered seeds on soil surface under A   (p. 33)

Plate 11   **Smooth crab grass** *viewed from above*   (p. 36)

Plate 10   **Large crab grass** *viewed from the side*   (p. 36)

Plate 12   **Proso millet** *A. Plant with drooping panicle*
B. Hairy leaves and leaf sheaths
C. Variation in colour of seeds on different plants   (p. 37)

Plate 13 **Witch grass** (p. 38)

Plate 14 **Fall panicum** *A. zigzag stem with several panicles B. shattered seed on soil surface* (p. 39)

Plate 15 **Barnyard grass** *A. plants B. inflorescence with thick, dense branches* (p. 40)

Plate 16 **Green foxtail** *A. plants B. leaf-base with hairy ligule and ciliate margins of leaf sheath* (p. 40)

Plate 17 **Giant foxtail** *A. upper part of plant B. comparison of* **Giant foxtail** *head – left, with* **Green foxtail** *head – right* (p. 42)

Plate 18 **Bristly foxtail** (p. 42)

279

Plate 19 **Long-spined sandbur** (p. 44)

Plate 20 **Johnson grass** *A. infestation in field*
B. large whitish rhizomes produced after plants head out (p. 45)

Plate 21 **Yellow nut sedge** *A. infestation in field*
B. plant (p. 47)

Plate 22 **Wild garlic** *(left to right) base of mature plant,*
hard-shelled bulbs, young plants, germinated
bulblets, aerial bulblets, (top, right) kernels of
wheat (p. 49)

Plate 23 **Sheep sorrel** (p. 50)

Plate 24 **Curled dock** (p. 50)

Plate 25 **Prostrate knotweed** *A. plant on a dry lawn*
B. portion of stems showing ocrea (p. 53)

Plate 26 **Lady's-thumb** (p. 54)

Plate 27 **Pale smartweed** (p. 54)

Plate 28 **Green smartweed** (p. 54)

Plate 29 **Pennsylvania smartweed** (p. 54)

Plate 30 **Swamp smartweed** (p. 57)

Plate 31 **Wild buckwheat** (p. 58)

Plate 32 **Japanese knotweed** *A. plants   B. tips of young shoots in spring   C. flowering branch* (p. 59)

Plate 33 **Lamb's-quarters** (p. 60)

Plate 34 **Oak-leaved goosefoot** (p. 62)

Plate 35 **Russian thistle** (p. 64)

Plate 36 **Tumble pigweed** *A. bushy-branched plant   B. tips of branches with short, axillary spikes of flowers* (p. 66)

Plate 37 **Redroot pigweed** *A. young flowering plant with dull (non-shiny) leaves   B. thick inflorescence with short lateral branches* (p. 66)

Plate 38 **Green pigweed** *flowering plant with shiny leaves and slender inflorescence* (p. 68)

Plate 39 **Pokeweed** (p. 69)

Plate 40 **Purslane** (p. 70)

Plate 41 **Chickweed** (p. 73)

Plate 42 **Mouse-eared chickweed** (p. 75)

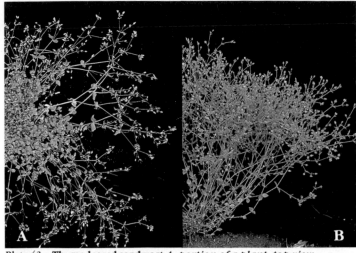

Plate 43 **Thyme-leaved sandwort** *A. portion of a plant, top view*
B. portion of a plant, side view (p. 75)

Plate 44 **White cockle** *A. male plant*
B. female plant (p. 77)

Plate 45 **Night-flowering catchfly** (p. 78)

Plate 46 **Bladder campion** (p. 79)

Plate 47 **Creeping buttercup** *left* (p. 84)
Tall buttercup *right* (p. 83)

Plate 48 **Common barberry** *A. spiny branches*
with clusters of red berries
B. flowering branch (p. 85)

Plate 49 **Wild mustard** *A. plants*
B. flowers and seedpods (p. 89)

Plate 50 **Dog mustard** *note seedpods in leaf*
axils (p. 90)

Plate 51 **Tumble mustard** *note very long slender seed-pods* (p. 93)

Plate 52 **Flixweed** (p. 96)

Plate 53 **Dame's-rocket** (p. 97)

Plate 54 **Wormseed mustard** *A. plant beginning to flower B. elongating inflorescences with seedpods* (p. 98)

Plate 55 **Yellow rocket** *A. plant beginning to flower B. plant with seedpods* (p. 102)

Plate 56 **Stinkweed** (p. 105)

Plate 57　**Field peppergrass**　(p. 106)

Plate 58　**Shepherd's-purse**　(p. 109)

Plate 59　**Small-seeded false flax**　(p. 110)

Plate 60　**Mossy stonecrop**　(p. 113)

Plate 61　**Rough cinquefoil**　(p. 114)

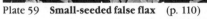

Plate 62　**Sulphur cinquefoil** *A. plant*
B. flowers and leaves　(p. 115)

Plate 63   **Yellow avens**   (p. 117)

Plate 64   **Black medick**   (p. 121)

Plate 65   **Common yellow wood-sorrel**   (p. 122)

Plate 66   **Tufted vetch**   (p. 125)

Plate 67   **Tuberous vetchling,** *note tubers, lower centre*   (p. 126)

Plate 68   **Prickly-ash**   (p. 127)

Plate 69   **Hairy-stemmed spurge**   (p. 130)

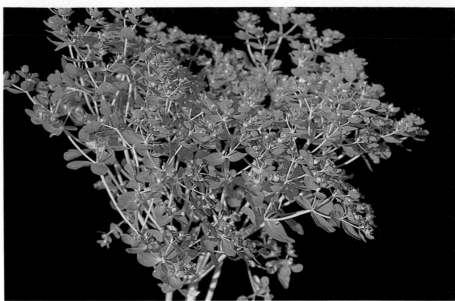

Plate 70   **Petty spurge** *inflorescence viewed from side*   (p. 133)

Plate 71   **Sun spurge** *viewed from above*   (p. 133)

Plate 72   **Cypress spurge**   (p. 134)

Plate 73   **Leafy spurge** *A. plant   B. portion of inflorescence showing cyathia between pairs of bracts*   (p. 135)

Plate 74   **Poison-ivy** *a typical patch showing sets of 3 leaflets hanging from upright petioles*   (p. 136)

Plate 75 **Poison-ivy** *A. clusters of flowers on an upright stem below the hanging leaflets   B. foliage turns to shades of orange and red in autumn*   (p. 136)

Plate 76 **Poison sumac**   (p. 138)

Plate 77 **European buckthorn** *A. flowering branch   B. branch with black berries*   (p. 139)

Plate 78 **Chokecherry** *variety with red berries*   (p. 139)

Plate 79 **Musk mallow**   (p. 140)

Plate 80 **Common mallow**   (p. 141)

Plate 81 **Velvetleaf** *A. plant beginning to flower B. flower and green seedpods* (p. 143)

Plate 82 **Flower-of-an-hour** (p. 144)

Plate 83 **St. John's-wort** *A. plant B. pairs of leaves showing transparent dots* (p. 145)

Plate 84 **Field violet,** *note 3-pointed open seedpod, lower centre* (p. 146)

Plate 85 **Purple loosestrife** *A. a typical strand B. flowering spikes* (p. 147)

Plate 86 **Yellow evening-primrose** (p. 148)

Plate 87 **Wild carrot** (p. 149)

Plate 88 **Goutweed** (p. 150)

Plate 89 **Poison hemlock** *A. plant before flowering B. inflorescence of several compound umbels* (p. 151)

Plate 90 **Water-parsnip** (p. 152)

Plate 91 **Spotted water-hemlock** *A. plants in a marshy area B. plants before flowering showing twice-compound leaves and horizontal thickened tuberous roots* (p. 155)

Plate 92 **Angelica** *flowers and young seeds in spherical compound umbels* (p. 155)

Plate 93 **Giant hogweed** *A. stand of mature 2-yr-old plants. Leafy canopy is about 1.5 m (5 ft) tall and seed-bearing stems about 3 m (10 ft) tall   B. a small plant beginning to flower   C. lower part of a stem and leaf petiole with a hunting knife for scale*   (p. 157)

Plate 94 **Spreading dogbane** *left – top of a flowering plant, right – maturing plant showing pencil-shaped seedpods*   (p. 160)

Plate 95 **Clasping-leaved dogbane** *showing deep perennial root from which 4 shoots emerged*   (p. 161)

Plate 96 **Common milkweed**   (p. 163)

Plate 97 **Dog-strangling vine** *A. plant B. pairs of leaves and pairs of spreading seedpods*   (p. 165)

Plate 98 **Field bindweed** *A. vine-like stems spreading over the ground. B. flowers turn pink with age*   (p. 166)

Plate 99   **Dodder** *twining around a host plant*
(p. 168)

Plate 100   **Blueweed**   (p. 170)

Plate 101   **Ground-ivy** *in a lawn*   (p. 175)

Plate 102   **Heal-all**   (p. 176)

Plate 103   **Henbit**   (p. 178)

Plate 104   **Motherwort**   (p. 179)

Plate 105   **Marsh hedge-nettle** *A. plant before flowering   B. 2 flowers in a whorl near the tip of a stem   C. coarse, brittle rhizomes*   (p. 180)

Plate 106   **Smooth ground-cherry**   (p. 182)

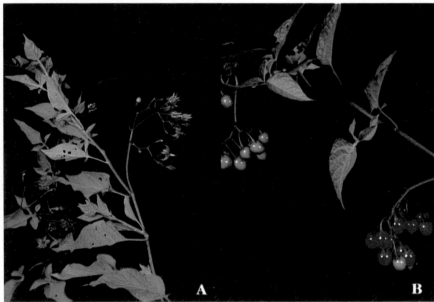

Plate 107   **Climbing nightshade** *A. flowering stem   B. stem with green and red berries*   (p. 183)

Plate 108   **Eastern black nightshade** *A. plant in flower B. cluster of black berries on a stalk from the side of a stem*   (p. 184)

Plate 109   **Horse-nettle**   (p. 186)

Plate 110   **Jimsonweed** *A. plant beginning to flower   B. portion of stem with spiny seedpods*   (p. 188)

Plate 111 **Common mullein** (p. 189)

Plate 112 **Toadflax** (p. 191)

Plate 113 **Dwarf snapdragon** *A. stand of plants in a strawberry field B. plant with flowers and seedpods* (p. 192)

Plate 114 **Thyme-leaved speedwell** *prostrate plant with upright flowering stems* (p. 193)

Plate 115 **Corn speedwell** *in a lawn* (p. 195)

Plate 116 **Narrow-leaved plantain** (p. 200)

Plate 117   **Smooth bedstraw** *A. mass of flowering stems   B. portion of a stem showing whorls of leaves and tiny 4-petalled flowers*   (p. 201)

Plate 118   **Cleavers** *showing backward- or downward-pointing hairs on stems and whorled leaves*   (p. 202)

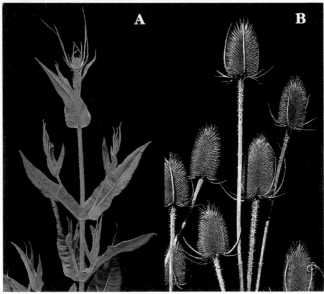

Plate 119   **Teasel** *A. plant before flowering   B. mature seed heads*   (p. 203)

Plate 120   **Wild cucumber**   (p. 204)

Plate 121   **Creeping bell flower** *A. mass of leaves covering the ground surface in early summer   B. several leaves and shoots from underground roots   C. spikes of flowers in late summer*   (p. 207)

Plate 122   **Black-eyed Susan**   (p. 209)

Plate 123　**Jerusalem artichoke** *A. top of flowering plant B. green shoots from sprouted tubers and young plants* (p. 210)

Plate 124　**Jerusalem artichoke** *A. dense stand of young plants in a cultivated field　B. tubers* (p. 210)

Plate 125　**Hairy galinsoga** *A. plant　B. flower heads* (p. 211)

Plate 126　**Tall beggarticks** (p. 212)

Plate 127　**Common ragweed** *A. plant beginning to flower　B. spikes of male flower heads ready to release pollen* (p. 213)

Plate 128　**Giant ragweed** *A. plant in flower B. young plant before flowering* (p. 215)

Plate 129   **Cocklebur** *A. clusters of burs in leaf axils   B. young plant*   (p. 216)

Plate 130   **Stinking mayweed**   (p. 217)

Plate 131   **Pineappleweed**   (p. 217)

Plate 132   **Scentless chamomile**   (p. 218)

Plate 133   **Yarrow**   (p. 218)

Plate 134   **Ox-eye daisy**   (p. 208, 219)

Plate 135 **Tansy** (p. 220)

Plate 136 **Biennial wormwood** (p. 223)

Plate 137 **Tansy ragwort** (p. 224)

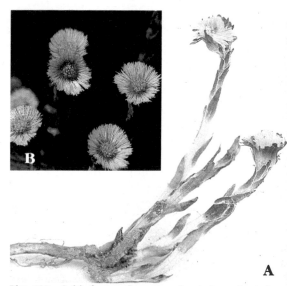

Plate 138 **Colt's-foot** *A. flowering shoots in early spring*
B. flower heads
C. flower heads in seed in late spring, with young leaves (p. 225)

Plate 139 **Colt's-foot** *vegetative (leafy) stage in summer and fall* (p. 225)

Plate 140 **Canada goldenrod** (p. 226)

Plate 141 **Annual fleabane** (p. 228)

Plate 142 **Rough fleabane** (p. 230)

Plate 143 **Philadelphia fleabane** (p. 230)

Plate 144 **Canada fleabane** *top of flowering plant* (p. 230)

Plate 145 **White snakeroot** (p. 234)

Plate 146 **Spotted Joe-Pye weed** *A. plant beginning to flower B. flower heads and seed heads* (p. 235)

Plate 147 **Boneset** (p. 235)

Plate 148 **Burdock** *first-year rosette* (p. 236)

Plate 149 **Burdock** *second-year plant beginning to flower* (p. 236)

Plate 150 **Nodding thistle** *dense stand of plants* (p. 237)

Plate 151 **Nodding thistle** *flower head, on a naked (non-winged) stalk* (p. 237)

Plate 152 **Plumeless thistle** *A. stand of plants B. flower head* (p. 238)

Plate 153 **Canada thistle** (p. 239)

Plate 154   **Bull thistle**   (p. 240)

Plate 155   **Scotch thistle**   (p. 241)

Plate 156   A. **Nodding thistle**   (p. 237)   B. **Bull thistle**   (p. 240)
            C. **Canada thistle** *(purple-flowered male plant)*   (p. 239)
            D. **Canada thistle** *(purple-flowered female plant)*   (p. 239)
            E. **Canada thistle** *(white-flowered male plant)*   (p. 239)

Plate 157   **Cornflower** *A. plant infesting alfalfa hay field*
            B. flower heads   (p. 242)

Plate 158   **Spotted knapweed**   (p. 243)

Plate 159   **Black knapweed**   (p. 244)

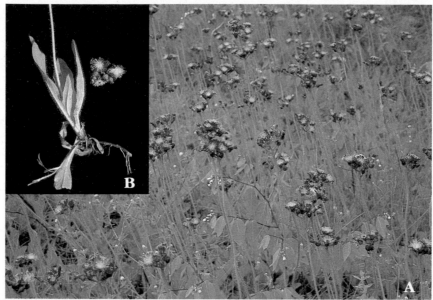

Plate 160 **Orange hawkweed** *A. plants in grassy roadside   B. base of a flowering plant with a leafy stolon and flower heads*   (p. 246)

Plate 161 **Narrow-leaved hawk's-beard**   (p. 246)

Plate 162 **Perennial sow-thistle** *A. group of flowering stem   B. one stem beginning to flower*   (p. 247)

Plate 163 **Spiny annual sow-thistle**   (p. 248)

Plate 164 **Annual sow-thistle**   (p. 249)

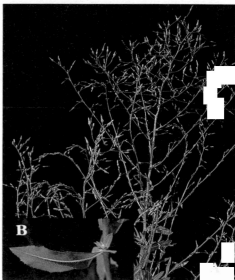

Plate 165 **Prickly lettuce** *A. top of flowering plant   B. underside of leaf showing row of prickles on the midrib* (p. 250)

Plate 166   **Chicory**   (p. 252)

Plate 167   **Dandelion**   (p. 252)

Plate 168   **Goat's-beard**   (p. 255)

Plate 169   **Meadow goat's-beard**   (p. 256)